Books by Janice Hardy

Foundations of Fiction
Plotting Your Novel: Ideas and Structure
Plotting Your Novel Workbook
Revising Your Novel: First Draft to Finished Draft Series
Book One: Fixing Your Character & Point-of-View Problems
Book Two: Fixing Your Plot & Story Structure Problems
Book Three: Fixing Your Setting & Description Problems

Skill Builders
Understanding Show, Don't Tell (And Really *Getting It)*
Understanding Conflict (And What It Really *Means)*

Novels
The Healing Wars Trilogy:
The Shifter
Blue Fire
Darkfall

As J.T. Hardy
Blood Ties

UNDERSTANDING
Conflict

(And What It *Really* Means)

Learn how to create compelling conflict in your fiction

Janice Hardy

Fiction University's Skill Builders Series

Contents

101 Ways to Create Conflict in Your Manuscript

127 Go Cause Trouble!

129 Thanks!

130 More from Janice Hardy

133 Acknowledgments

135 About the Author

Welcome to *Understanding Conflict (And What It Really Means)*

Like most writers, I've spent countless hours creating conflict in my novels. I've thrown exciting obstacles in my protagonists' paths, I've developed sinister antagonists to thwart my heroes, I've devised cruel ways to put my characters through mental anguish—and my beta readers have *still* told me, "This book needs more conflict."

Because despite what we "know" about conflict as writers, the concept isn't so cut and dry.

It's not just about the obstacles in the path, or the bad guy with the evil plan, or the mental anguish of the hero. It's not the plot or the character arc, even though we often talk about it like it is. It's a tapestry woven from multiple aspects of writing that work together to create a feeling that victory will *not* come easily to the characters, and it leaves readers dying to know what the protagonist is going to do about it. Conflict can be confusing because:

- *Conflict* is more than one single thing.
- *Conflict* changes depending on who you talk to.
- *Conflict* changes depending on how you use it.

Conflict is a pain in the butt that makes us want to bash our heads against the keyboard on a regular basis, and even makes us want to curl up and cry in the corner. I've been there myself, I know how frustrating it can be, and I've put this book together to help my fellow writers avoid some of that frustration and keyboard-bashing.

Creating conflict isn't that hard once you figure out what it means and how it applies to your novel. Realizing it isn't a one-size-fits-all means you'll be able to find the right conflict to suit your need, no matter what that need is. You'll learn how to parse feedback and how to diagnose your own manuscripts to spot trouble areas before they become problems.

What You'll Get From This Book

Understanding Conflict (And What It Really *Means)* is an in-depth study and analysis of what conflict means and how to use it in your writing. It will help you understand the different layers of conflict and how they work together to create the problems and goals in your story, as well as explore the elements of writing that affect conflict, such as stakes and character motivations. It will discuss the common problems that result from a lack of conflict, and offer suggestions and tips on how to strengthen conflict in your story.

By the end of this book, you'll have a solid understanding of what conflict is and have the ability to create strong and compelling conflicts in your own novel.

What Conflict Really Means

Ask any agent or editor to list the top three reasons manuscripts get rejected and you'll find "not enough conflict" on that list. Conflict is at the core of every story, and without conflict, there is no story. It's so vital, "conflict" and "story" are almost interchangeable when writers talk about it. It's common to ask, "What's your story about?" and have the author describe the conflict.

Which is part of the problem.

Since conflict covers such a wide range of storytelling, it isn't always clear what people *mean* when they say "conflict." This can cause a lot of frustration—especially for new writers. Does it mean the plot of the story? The character arc? Does conflict mean the characters have to argue? Does it mean a physical battle? Does it mean soul-crushing angst or a mustached villain plotting against the hero at every turn?

No. Conflict fuels the plot and character arc, but they're separate elements. You can have conflict without battles, without major angst, and without evil villains bent on world domination. Some of the best conflicts are those between characters who love each other deeply, but can't agree on what to do about a problem.

I think the biggest reason writers struggle with conflict is that it's not just one thing. Conflict is a one-two combo of a challenge faced and the struggle to overcome that challenge.

- The conflict of the plot (the physical challenges faced to resolve the problem)

- The conflict of the character (the mental challenges faced to resolve the problem)

These are the two sides of conflict and they appear in every story (and scene) in some fashion. Let's look at each of them a little closer.

The Conflict of the Plot

A plot is external. It's what the protagonist does to resolve the problem of the novel (the core conflict). The plot's conflicts are also external, consisting of the individual challenges the protagonist faces on a scene-by-scene basis. Resolving these conflicts creates the plot and leads the protagonist from page one to the final page of the novel. Think of it like the to-do list for the novel. Follow this list of challenges to resolve the plot.

The conflict of the plot *is what's making it physically hard* for the protagonist to do what she has to do.

For example:

▶ To sneak into the building, the protagonist must find a way to disable the security cameras and locks—the conflict (challenge) is the technology and security people preventing her from entering the building.

▶ To catch the love interest's eye, the protagonist must attend a party she hasn't been invited to—the conflict (challenge) is her attempt to get into that party when she's being excluded.

▶ To defeat the two-headed troll, the protagonist must find a way to use her physical fighting skills and wits to win over a much stronger foe—the conflict (challenge) is overcoming her physical limits to best a monster that could easily squash her like a bug.

Real conflict involves opposition to a goal and the challenges to overcome that opposition.

However, when people refer to the plot's conflict in a scene, it's often the *goal* they're talking about—which is why writers can sometimes think their scene has conflict when it really doesn't. They're referring to what the protagonist has to do, not the challenge *to achieve* that goal. You might have a goal of emptying the dishwasher, but unless that task presents a challenge to complete it, it's not a conflict.

For example:

▶ The protagonist must sneak into a building and steal the plans.

▶ The protagonist must ask her love interest out on a date.

▶ The protagonist must defeat the two-headed troll intent on eating her.

These are all goals that could easily move a plot forward, but these "conflicts" are just tasks to be completed—there's no challenge associated with achieving them. Without something in the way of completing these tasks, they're nothing more than simple obstacles. The conflict (in the story sense of the word) is what's *preventing* the protagonist from completing her goal. Otherwise, the protagonist can just waltz in and accomplish her task with little to no resistance. No resistance (no challenge) = no conflict.

Test Your Conflict: One trick to test if you have an obstacle or a conflict is to put the scene in an "if-then" statement.

For example:

▶ If she can disable the security, then she can break into the building (protagonist vs. security).

▶ If she can steal an invitation from the printer, then she can get into the party (protagonist vs. staff at the print shop).

▶ If she can move fast enough, then she can defeat the troll (protagonist vs. physical weakness).

You can quickly see what specifically has to be done to accomplish the task, and judge if there's a challenge or struggle associated with that task. For conflicts that are just obstacles, these "if-then" statements usually read a little differently.

For example:

▶ If she can get into the building, then she can steal the plans (notice nothing is stated that shows how "get into the building" will be a challenge).

▶ If she can get an invitation, then she can go to the party (notice this is basically how parties work, so there's nothing to suggest this is a challenge for the protagonist).

▶ If she can be tougher and stronger, then she can defeat the troll (notice this is close to the original, but can the protagonist really be "tougher and stronger" than a troll three times her size?).

The key here is to find the specific task that must be done to accomplish the goal. If the task is basically "do it" in some way, odds are there's no conflict. Let's look at some conflicts that aren't really conflicts:

For example:

▶ If she can disable the security, then she can break into the building (except she's an expert thief and the security is so old she could have cracked it when she was 10. In this case, "disabling the security" is a form of "do it." All she has to do is complete this task and she succeeds, yet this task isn't a challenge at all).

▶ If she can steal an invitation from the printer, then she can get into the party (except she works at the print shop and handled the invitation job, and all she has to do is slip one in her pocket. Again, no challenge to the task preventing her from her goal, so no conflict).

▶ If she can move fast enough, then she can defeat the troll (except she has special powers that give her supernatural speed and strength when she most needs it. "Moving fast" is how she completes this task, and it's not a challenge to do it).

No matter how impressive a potential problem seems, if there's no challenge in overcoming it, it's not a strong story conflict.

A word of warning here: It's up to each writer to decide if the conflict is a challenge or not. You can have what seems like a solid conflict on paper, but when the scene is written, the challenge isn't hard to accomplish at all and the conflict feels weak to your readers.

The Conflict of the Character

A character conflict is internal. It's the emotional struggle the protagonist faces to resolve her challenges. These conflicts make it harder for the protagonist to make decisions, because choosing what to do has emotional consequences, and often, the right choice is the one the protagonist doesn't *want* to make.

The conflict of the character *is what's making it emotionally hard* for the protagonist to do what she has to do.

For example:

▶ In order to steal the plans, the protagonist needs to use (and reveal) the thieving skills she's been trying to keep secret from her new boyfriend. (She can't get the plans and keep her secret, so she has to choose which is more important to her.)

▶ In order to get into the party, the protagonist must use the connections of the family who disowned her (She can't meet her love interest without revealing the truth about her scandalous past, so she has to choose if love is worth the risk.)

▶ In order to defeat the troll, the protagonist must fight it in the middle of town where it has limited mobility. (She can't beat the troll in the open, so she has to choose how many lives she's willing to risk to stop a greater threat.)

The conflict of the character is the emotional struggle the protagonist faces while deciding what to do about the external problem. Risk the secret. Reveal the past. Endanger the innocent. It makes the protagonist ask, "Is this goal worth the price I'll have to pay to get it?" Sometimes the answer is yes, sometimes it's no, and sometimes the protagonist tries her best to get the goal without paying the price, which rarely goes well for her.

However, when people refer to the character conflict in a scene, it's often the *character arc* they're actually talking about—which is why writers can feel all character conflict (internal conflict) needs to result in character growth, but it really doesn't. You can have internal conflict without a character arc. The protagonist can struggle over the right choice without changing as a person.

For example:

▶ In order to steal the plans, the protagonist will have to struggle against exposing her criminal past. (Yet exposing that past does nothing to make her a better person or cause growth, it's just a part of her the new boyfriend might not like, and he might break up with her over it.)

▶ In order to get into the party, the protagonist will have to struggle against relying on a family that disowned her. (Yet using the family does nothing to change the protagonist, and she's not going to reconcile with them because of this.)

▶ In order to defeat the troll, the protagonist will have to struggle against what she considers an acceptable loss of life to prevent wide-scale death. (Yet possibly sacrificing a few lives to stop a rampaging troll isn't going to make her quit adventuring altogether.)

All the challenges offer internal struggles to resolve, but they're not about changing the life of the protagonist in a fundamental way.

Conflict and the Character Arc

Quite often, when writers talk about the internal conflict they actually mean the character arc and how the protagonist grows into a better person, but the two are *not* the same thing.

A character arc is how the character changes by undergoing the experiences of the novel. Since change comes from an internal struggle to make the right choice, the character arc uses the internal conflicts of the novel to cause that change. Often this change is positive and the character grows, but it can also be a negative change, turning a good or happy person into a bad or unhappy one. It could even be a change in perspective or belief, with a character ending the novel exactly where she started, just with a different worldview after her experiences.

The internal conflict shows the emotional struggle the character undergoes to change. The external challenges force the protagonist to face those internal struggles. What she decides to do affects who she is as a person and teaches her an important lesson—even if that lesson takes multiple attempts to sink in and effect change (which is part of the plot).

Angst over choosing the right course of action is not a character arc, though it does show internal conflict. Repeatedly making mistakes based on personal flaws or beliefs that keep you from being happy until you learn not to make those mistakes and change your ways is a character arc. And this takes both internal and external conflict to achieve.

For example:

▶ The protagonist who needs to abandon her criminal ways to be happy will face situations where she must choose to go the straight and narrow. Those choices will be hard, testing her resolve and giving her every opportunity to fail.

▶ The protagonist who needs to overcome her fear of rejection to find love will be put in situations where she can be rejected, so she can learn how to deal with them. Those situations will have consequences for failure, which will make it harder for her to overcome this problem.

▶ The protagonist who needs to gain the confidence to face her destiny and embrace who she truly is will find herself in situations that require confidence to succeed. She'll need to trust herself and have faith in her abilities to overcome her problems, and if she doesn't, she *will* fail.

The character arc uses the conflicts of the story to change the character.

However...

Some stories—such as thrillers or police procedurals, or novels in a series—don't have character arcs. While the protagonist usually faces internal conflicts, there's no change or growth from the beginning to the end of the story. Lee Child's Jack Reacher is a good example here. Reacher doesn't change, and there is rarely an internal conflict over what he has to do. He's presented with an external plot problem and he goes out and solves it. Many mysteries follow this same format—the novel is about solving the puzzle, not how the protagonist changes while solving that puzzle.

Some stories have small character arcs, where there's a little change, but it's not the reason for the novel. Readers are happy to see the protagonist learn and grow some, but they didn't pick up the book to see a character's emotional transformation. They just want to see her learn enough to not make the same mistakes over and over again.

Here are some reasons why a story might not need a character arc:

The story is more about the plot and less about the character: If the point of the story is to solve the plot problem, and the readers' enjoyment comes from the puzzle and the intellectual exercise of the plot, they don't usually care if the protagonist grows over the course of the novel. It's about the adventure, puzzle, or problem.

The hero of nearly every adventure story is in it for the adventure, not the emotional growth. The classic police detective of the police procedural genre typically solves the case and goes back to his life. The disaster movie shows how ordinary people deal with disaster. We love *Die Hard's* John McClane because defeats the bad guys by being a good cop. Sherlock Holmes captures our attention because he's brilliant and we want to see how he solves the mystery. We wanted to see the soldiers in Kelly's Heroes get to that Nazi gold and escape as rich men.

The protagonist is the moral or ethical center of the story: Some stories use the protagonist as the moral rock the world is trying to break. The story isn't about the protagonist changing, but their being the catalyst to change the world. The growth comes from everyone else in the novel, while the protagonist does not change.

My favorite example here is Marvel's *Captain America: The Winter Soldier*.

Steve "Captain America" Rogers has no character arc in this movie. He's the steady, rock-solid World War II hero he always has been, only now he's in the twenty-first century and dealing with the changing morals and ethics of a new world. His role in this story is to be the moral center, the reminder for everyone else who has lost their way of what it really means to be "the good guy."

Steve knows what's happening around him is wrong, and he does what he can to stop it and make his friends realize the dark path they're heading down. He saves the world by *not* changing and forcing others to live up to his example.

If your protagonist is the one who represents what's right, and everyone else is wrong, then they probably don't need to change. If the entire point of the story is to have the hero be the example everyone else finally comes around to, thereby narrowly avoiding "disaster" (however that happens in your story), it's their job to stand fast. They must face the ethical choices and take the hard path, even if it costs them a lot personally. They bring about the change.

The story is part of a series with stand-alone books: Certain series in certain genres have protagonists who never change—which is why readers love them. James Bond is always James Bond, and he never undergoes any deep, meaningful soul searching to learn a powerful lesson. The protagonist might become better at what they do over the course of the series, but they don't change who they are every book.

On some level, you could even argue many romances fit this category. They're two people falling in love. In some romances, those people need to change to find love, but in others, they're overcoming whatever external issue is keeping them apart. They fall in love despite the obstacles in their way because of who they are and that never changes.

If you're not sure if your story is one of these, ask if it would still make sense if you read the books out of order. If each book is its own story and there isn't a stronger multi-book plot for the entire series, odds are you don't need a character arc. But if each book builds on the previous one and the series doesn't really make sense unless read in the right order, there's a decent chance you do.

While character arcs are fantastic to show the depth of a character and explore an emotional theme, not every novel needs one. If you write in a heavily plot-centric genre, you might not have a character arc, even though you'll probably have internal conflicts. Don't feel you have to shove an arc into your novel if it doesn't work for your type of story.

Putting It All Together

The plot conflict is all about the external action—what the protagonist does to overcome the challenges. The character conflict is all about the internal struggle—why it's hard for the protagonist to make a decision and act. The character arc explores how the conflicts create a change in the character.

Thinking about conflict in terms of what the *challenge* is helps clarify the struggle, problem, or issue the protagonist is up against in each scene.

In essence, conflict is all about making your characters struggle to solve problems. A *lot*. And you have multiple options for how to do that.

Common Misconceptions about Conflict

Conflict is one of the more misunderstood aspects of writing fiction, because as we just saw, it's not always clear what someone means when they say, "conflict." This has no doubt tripped up a lot of new writers (and even some experienced writers), and caused quite a few unproductive writing sessions. It's hard to create strong conflict in a novel if you're not sure what conflict is.

If a writer learned only one aspect or believes a misconception (such as, all internal conflict is a character arc), it's quite likely she won't use, develop, or discover the right conflict needed for the story.

Here are some common misconceptions about conflict:

Misconception #1: Conflict = Fighting

It's not uncommon for writers to throw battles they don't need into a story, cause animosity between characters for no reason, and have characters behave antagonistically just to cause trouble—all because someone told them they "needed more conflict." To these writers, conflict is an actual fight—anything from an argument to a full-scale battle.

Not only does this limit available plot options, it creates a boring story, because nothing ever happens in the book but people fighting. Even worse, repeated fights seldom have conflict, because there's no struggle to do anything aside from "win." Take out the fights, and nothing really changes but the time it takes to get to the novel's climax.

For example:

▶ The fantasy protagonist who has to fight her way into the evil wizard's lair, past an ever-increasing number of henchmen. (The fights are all delays that don't change the outcome of the story. Get rid of half the fights and she still arrives at the correct moment the same as if she'd faced those fights.)

▶ The romance protagonist who has argument after argument with her mother about getting married. (The arguments cover the same information and nothing is ever resolved, but it feels like there's a lot of conflict because these two characters are always at odds.)

▶ The mystery protagonist who encounters uncalled-for hostility in every single person she questions—even if they're just random witnesses. (The hostility is there to make things appear tougher on the protagonist, but doesn't move the plot or affect the character at all.)

Conflict isn't always violent, nor should it be.

Misconception #2: Conflict = Tension

This has probably caused more frustration than any other aspect of conflict, because these two are so closely linked they seem like the same thing—except they *aren't*. You *can* have conflict without tension, and tension without conflict. Struggling over which boy to go to prom with *is* a conflict, but if there's no sense of anticipation about that choice, there's no tension. Sexual tension between characters keeps readers interested, even though there's no conflict since both parties want the same thing. The tension comes from the anticipation of how they resolve that attraction.

Tension is the reader's need to know what happens next, and the sense that there's more going on than meets the eye. It's the anticipation of something about to happen. That's it.

Conflict *creates* tension by putting a character into a situation where the outcome is uncertain, and readers anticipate what will happen or what will be discovered.

For example:

- ▶ The fantasy protagonist sneaks through the dark, scary grave-yard and jumps at every sound, sure she's being followed. (Being nervous isn't a conflict since there's nothing opposing the protagonist, but anticipating what might be following her can create tension in the reader.)

- ▶ The romance protagonist banters with the love interest, but never acts on her attraction and leaves without doing anything. (Playful bantering isn't a conflict, but readers eagerly read on to see where that banter might go, creating tension.)

- ▶ The mystery protagonist eavesdrops on a suspect. (The potential for being discovered isn't a conflict, but the fear that she might be found can create tension, as can the anticipation of what she might overhear.)

While all of these examples can be filled with tension, there's no opposition, no struggle, and no choice to be made to resolve any of them. Eagerly waiting for the next summer blockbuster to come out has tension, but no conflict. Trying to decide if you'll go see the movie on opening night, even though your best friend can't go with you and you promised to see it with her, is conflict.

Conflict works *with* tension (as well as stakes, and a slew of other things) to put characters into situations that make readers want to know what happens next, and thus read the novel you worked so hard on to find out.

Misconception #3: Conflict = What's "in the Way"

This is a tricky misconception, because technically, it's true—but it's also false. The obstacles in the way of the protagonist's goal are the challenges that need to be faced, and usually, there is conflict associated with overcoming or circumventing those obstacles. But sometimes, those obstacles are just things in the way.

For example:

▶ The fantasy protagonist must navigate the desolate wasteland to reach someone with answers she needs. (While the wasteland *could* contain conflicts, if nothing has changed for her between entering the wasteland and leaving the wasteland, she faced no conflicts.)

▶ The romance protagonists always have "something come up" to keep them from kissing or getting together. (While this might work once, or even twice if done with skill, the "near miss" is a contrived obstacle that doesn't create actual conflict.)

▶ The mystery protagonist speaks with multiple witnesses and no one has any information to move the plot along. (While speaking to people of interest is a critical part of a mystery, if nothing is ever gleaned, suggested, or learned from those conversations, they were only a delaying tactic and did nothing to create or affect the conflict.)

What's "in the way" should cause a challenge of some type or it isn't truly a conflict. If the result of resolving the challenge is the same as if the protagonist hadn't encountered the challenge in the first place, it's just an obstacle. Sometimes a scene just needs an obstacle, and that's okay, but if the conflict in most scenes is something in the way, that's a red flag the overall story lacks conflict.

Conflict encompasses such a wide range that it's easy to misunderstand and misuse. Just remember it's how both sides (external and internal) work together to challenge the protagonist and you'll avoid a lot of the common conflict pitfalls.

Why Writers Struggle with Conflict

With the various aspects and multiple misconceptions about conflict, it's easy to see why writers face difficulties when creating conflict in their novels. Over the years, I've pinpointed the three most common reasons writers stumble over conflict:

Reason #1: Conflict Isn't a "One-Size-Fits-All" Issue

What works for one story might not work for another, and even within the same novel, you'll have different aspects of conflict depending on the needs of the scene.

Conflict is the push and pull of the character as she experiences the story. It's the combination of the external with the internal that rounds out the conflict and gives meaning to what the protagonist does. These two sides work in tandem to illustrate why the problem of the novel (the core conflict) is worth reading about. What has to be done, why it's hard, and why it matters.

Something might technically be a conflict (two sides in opposition), but it doesn't make a good *story* conflict, because a strong story conflict has to also create a situation that drives a plot and leads readers through that story. For example, a shootout between outlaws holed up in a cabin, while the sheriff's posse tries to apprehend them, has plenty of conflict, but two sides shooting at each other for hours isn't a very interesting story.

If the situation doesn't do anything to create a strong story, it won't feel like an actual conflict. This is tough, because what constitutes a "strong story" can vary by person. Readers have biases, likes, and dislikes, and that contributes to how they regard story conflict.

For example:

▶ Romance readers who enjoy reading about two people overcoming emotional issues to fall in love might think a thriller with no emotional arc for the protagonist has no conflict, and is just a series of obstacles to overcome to solve some random problem.

▶ Thriller readers who want to see tough puzzles solved to prevent a catastrophe might think romances lack conflict because nothing ever really happens and the ending is obvious from the start.

▶ Science fiction readers who prefer novels that revolve around exploring ethical questions and the meaning of the universe might think fantasy novels that make up the rules of the world avoid actual conflict by making everything fit too perfectly.

And they're all right, and all wrong.

You can ask five people how strong your novel's conflict is, and it's possible to get five different answers ranging from weak to strong. Expectations affect how a reader might view your book. This is why it's important to get feedback from people who read your genre (or to read widely if you don't have beta readers). A strong story conflict to a mystery reader might not be the same as a strong conflict to a middle grade fantasy reader.

Reason #2: It's Not Always Clear What People Mean When They Say "Conflict"

Even beyond genre, conflict means different things to different people. If two writers are coming at it from two directions, there will very likely be misunderstandings about what they're actually talking about. Getting feedback such as, "your novel lacks conflict" isn't helpful if the person giving that feedback is referring to a *different* type of conflict.

For example, if you're thinking of the core conflict, you might assume:

- The conflict is the major problem the novel needs to resolve
- The conflict is connected to all the other problems in the novel in some way
- The conflict is the plot force driving the novel (and the protagonist)

But if another writer is referring to the *internal* conflict, they might think:

- The conflict is the emotional struggle the protagonist is facing
- The conflict will affect the protagonist's choices in the novel
- The conflict will cause the protagonist to reflect on the issues facing her and what they mean

One conflict is external and requires external actions; the other is internal and requires more reflection and thought. Neither is plotted or written the same way, and trying to plot the internal conflict the same as the external conflict will lead to some troublesome scenes. You might look at such a comment, point directly to the core conflict of your novel, and disregard the advice (and then pull your hair out when you keep getting rejected).

Context is everything, and if you don't understand which *type* of conflict someone is referring to, it can lead to a lot of frustration and confusion. You might think your novel has all the conflict it needs, so any "needs more conflict" feedback you get just flat out doesn't make sense to you.

For example:

Say you're looking at feedback from your latest critique. Some comments scattered throughout the manuscript include:

- There wasn't enough conflict
- I was never sure what the novel's conflict was
- The protagonist's conflict felt weak

Did the critiquer mean:

"There wasn't enough conflict" because there was a problem with the core conflict driving the novel, or the individual scene challenges? Or maybe there was a lack of stakes, making that critiquer not care about the conflict that was there? Did the critiquer really mean they wanted more tension? Maybe they thought every challenge was too quickly resolved?

"I was never sure what the novel's conflict was" because there wasn't a solid goal for the protagonist to solve? Or maybe there were too many goals or problems and nothing stood out as being the main issue? Was it a lack of motivation making what the protagonist wanted unclear?

"The protagonist's conflict felt weak" because every challenge was solved without effort? Or maybe there was nothing internal causing the protagonist to struggle with choices? Maybe it was because the climax didn't matter to anyone in any significant way?

Unless the critiquer is clear about what the issue is, the writer might assume the wrong thing about the actual weakness of the story.

For example:

Let's say the writer believes in misconception #3 and thinks conflict is an obstacle in the way of the protagonist's goal. If so, then she might think:

"There wasn't enough conflict" means the critiquer felt the writer should put more obstacles in the way, and have more "stuff" that the protagonist must do to resolve a goal. But adding "stuff" only compounds the problem by adding tasks that have no meaning and do nothing to affect the story. No new information or insight is revealed by completing that task or overcoming that challenge—and often, no challenge is involved in completing this task. Climbing a ladder with ten rungs is no different from climbing a ladder with five rungs if it takes no extra effort to get to the top of the ladder.

"I was never sure what the novel's conflict was" means the critiquer felt the climax wasn't clear and exactly what the protagonist had to do wasn't obvious, so the writer needs to tell the reader exactly what was going on and what it all means. But this only leads to a climax that feels told and explanatory, and does nothing to fix the actual problem if the critiquer understood the challenge the protagonist faced, but thought it was too easy to resolve and didn't offer the protagonist an emotional challenge.

"The protagonist's conflict felt weak" means the critiquer felt the specific obstacles the protagonist faced in each scene weren't hard enough, so the writer goes over the top to create melodramatic challenges with multiple steps to overcome each obstacle. "Weak" is perceived as "needs to be more complicated," not "needs to be more emotionally difficult to decide what to do." Just making the obstacle harder or more complicated doesn't address the lack of *motivations* for the protagonist to face those challenges in the first place. The conflict was "weak" because there was no reason to face the challenge, not because the challenge was too easy.

Assuming the wrong type of conflict, or misunderstanding what the word "conflict" means to the critiquer, can cause a writer to change what doesn't need fixing and ignore what does. This can lead to a novel that keeps getting the same feedback, even though the writer feels she's addressed those concerns over and over again. And *that* can lead to a very frustrated and unhappy writer. When in doubt, *ask* your critiquer to clarify.

Special note for critiquers: All of this is just as important when critiquing someone's work as it is when getting critiqued. Remember to be as clear as possible what you mean and specify where something in a manuscript is lacking (or excelling). The clearer you are about any conflict issues, the easier it will be for the writer to address those issues.

Reason #3: Using the Wrong Conflict Makes It Harder to Write the Novel

Use the wrong conflict and things don't quite mesh in a novel. This is most often seen when trying to plot using the internal conflict of the character arc. For example, an internal conflict might work wonderfully to support the character arc, but internal conflicts don't create plot—

they just make it emotionally *harder* to overcome those external challenges. What the character physically does to resolve that internal conflict is the plot.

Let's explore this further using one of the examples:

Say you have a novel about a woman with a criminal past who gets out of prison and wants to go the straight and narrow and get her life back together. That's a character arc—to get what she needs (her life back together) she has to change her ways. Many writers would say this book is about "a woman who gets her life back together after she's released from prison." And they're right—but many of those same writers would have trouble creating a plot to support this story.

The reason? There's no conflict in that description of the book.

"Getting her life back together" doesn't show a plot, because nothing in this statement provides an external goal to pursue. There's also no conflict—nothing is preventing her from getting her life back together. Without those details, the goal isn't specific enough to know what external challenges she might face as she tries to get her life back together.

However, "getting her life back together" *is* a solid character arc to explore. It's what she *does* to put her life back together that will create the plot, and what's preventing her from putting her life back together will create the conflicts (both internal and external).

Without knowing the details of those two things, you can't write this book. If you try, you'll most likely end up with fifty to one hundred pages that show the protagonist getting out of jail, returning to normal life, and interacting with the people she left behind, plus a lot of backstory that explains how she ended up in prison in the first place and why she wants to change.

And then it'll probably stall, because there's no conflict to drive the plot forward and give the protagonist something to do once the setup is over. If you're reading this book, odds are this has happened to you at least once. If you have a manuscript that's stalled before page one hundred, it might be a good idea to examine your conflict to make sure there's a conflict or challenge for your protagonist to face and overcome to move the plot forward.

Trying to plot with a character arc can create a lot of frustration for writers, because the focus is on the internal struggle to change, not the external action, so the specific tasks (the goals) aren't as defined as they need to be. It's like trying to bake a cake without putting it into the oven. The external heat is what turns the ingredients into dessert.

To figure out what those two details are and find the conflicts of this story we'd ask:

1. What constitutes "getting her life back together"

2. What's preventing her from doing that?

Let's say she wants to return to school to be a counselor so she'll be able to use her own mistakes to help others avoid her fate. Maybe she met a counselor in prison who made a difference for her, and she wants to follow in her footsteps. Her goal: return to school and get her degree.

Now the book is about a woman who wants to go back to school after her release from prison. But notice there's still no conflict. She has a solid goal, and we can see how this plot is likely to unfold (how she goes back to school), but we need to be more specific about what challenges she might encounter in pursuit of this goal.

What are some possible conflicts she could face in trying to return to school? The first problems that pop into my head are:

- Money to pay tuition and support herself

- Admission to the school she wants

- Past associates who want her to go back to crime

These are potential obstacles she might face, but they're still not conflicts, because there's nothing preventing her from doing these things yet. Let's choose the money issue as her goal, because money and crime have the strongest potential for conflict. Let's also play with past associates who might lure her back to her old life. These cover both external and internal conflicts. How might we turn these obstacles into tough challenges?

She'll need money to pay tuition, so that means a job that pays enough to cover all her bills and school, financial aid, or a scholarship. This is the honest, non-criminal way to achieve her goal of going to school.

But maybe no one will hire an ex-con, or she can only get part-time jobs that pay under minimum wage. If she can't get a decent job, she can't support herself, and she can't pay for school. Without a job and with her criminal record, she's a bad risk and no bank will give her financial aid. She barely graduated from high school, so she's not eligible for any scholarships. Getting the cash for school is no longer easy.

But it's still *possible* if she's willing to work multiple jobs and take one class a semester. It'll take her longer, but if she's patient, she'll get there (and be a pretty boring book).

That's where the past associates come in. They're a tempting carrot to create a little internal conflict to draw her back into the life she wants to leave behind.

What if these associates ask her to help rob a rich guy rumored to keep a lot of cash around the house? It goes against her need to go legit, but *does* fulfill her desire to pay for tuition. Her internal conflict is between taking the easy path of crime to get what she wants, or the harder path of legality to get what she wants.

Now there's conflict that challenges both her external need to pay for tuition, and her internal need to not steal anymore. She can't have both, so which does she choose?

Since she wants to stay away from crime, of course she says no—it's common to show the protagonist trying and failing at the start of the character arc. She does her best, but her job search won't go well, and any job she does get will not last. Her past will haunt her and create more trouble for her, keeping her from her goal of school and her need to get her life in order.

But the harder it gets to be good, the easier it is to decide she can handle "one more job" and get out. Which of course goes badly, gets her into more trouble, and pushes her even farther from her goals. It won't be until she accepts the harder path that things will start to turn her way—but only if she works for it and grows as a person.

At its most basic, conflict (internal or external) is the challenge to over-come whatever is preventing the protagonist from doing what needs to be done—physically, emotionally, or mentally—to resolve a problem and move forward.

To truly understand conflict and how to use it, we need to first under-stand the other writing elements that affect it.

Things That Affect Conflict

Since conflict is deeply connected to so many aspects of a novel, it's impossible to talk about it without understanding what affects it and what helps create that conflict. This is why it's easy to mistake one type for another, and get confused about what people mean when they refer to conflict. For example, readers "not caring about what happens" could indicate a lack of stakes, while claiming "nothing happens" could be due to a lack of goals or motivations, or a general sense of *"meh"* could be the result of low to missing tension—but each reader might say, "There's no conflict," because the issue is in how those aspects *affect* the conflict, not the conflict itself.

In this section I've used real-world examples from movies and TV shows to further examine the topics discussed. If you haven't seen these movies or shows and feel the examples might confuse you more than help you, it's okay to skip them. They're optional for those who want to dig a little deeper, or who want an example they can study on their own time at their leisure.

Let's dive in.

The Genre: What Readers Expect from the Conflict

Your novel's genre influences what types of conflicts will be at the core of that novel, and what types of conflicts the reader expects. This can drive you crazy when you're trying to figure out how to use conflict in your writing.

For example:

- If everyone keeps telling you, "all novels need a strong character arc," you might think you need to shove an emotional journey subplot into your police procedural (when what you have is just fine for that genre).

- If you heed advice from thriller writers, you might force an action-packed plot into your literary novel (which ruins your quiet character journey about redemption).

In essence, the genre determines what challenges the protagonist will struggle with over the course of the novel. Thrillers explore how the protagonist struggles to outsmart a worthy foe and make hard choices about people's lives. Mysteries revolve around the struggle to be smarter than the criminal—focusing on the procedures and challenges required to solve a crime or puzzle. Literary novels show the character's journey and the emotional struggles that change the protagonist, while romances explore the reasons two people are kept apart and the challenges they face to be together.

Different genres have different expectations, and readers typically want to see a certain type of conflict central to those genres.

For example:

- A happily-ever-after romance isn't likely to have a core conflict that revolves around stopping a madman from blowing up the town hall.

- A thriller probably won't have a core conflict that revolves around the two main characters overcoming their personal hangups and falling in love.

- A literary novel usually doesn't have a core conflict that revolves around stopping a serial killer.

One caveat here: With novels that mix genres, there is wiggle room for the type of conflict. For example, romantic suspense readers expect a thrill mixed in with their courtship dance. Almost every novel regardless of genre has some type of "mystery" to solve. When you mix genres, each genre's conflict expectations will also potentially affect the novel.

While all novels have both internal and external conflicts, the genre also influences how *strong* they will be in that novel. Plot-driven novels typically have conflicts that are more external and plot based, so the challenges frequently revolve around external issues. Character-driven novels typically explore internal conflicts that lead to character growth, so the challenges will be over internal issues and support a character arc more. Plenty of novels have both, using the external conflicts to bring about the internal growth of the characters, so the challenges will be over external factors that *cause* that internal struggle.

Keep in mind what type of conflicts are common in your genre and how they challenge your protagonist.

The Antagonist: The Person or Thing Driving the Conflict

Since so many stories are about one person trying to prevent another person from acting, the antagonist is the embodiment of the conflict. The villain, the bad guy, the one trying to muck up the entire plan and create chaos. We can't talk about conflict without asking, "Who's the antagonist?"

Because we so closely associate the antagonist with a person, it's easy to forget that the real question is, "Who *or what* is the antagonist?" It's not always a person, even if a person represents the conflict of the story.

For example:

- ▶ In *The Lottery*, the antagonist is the society that stones people to death (Person vs. Society).

- ▶ In *Jaws*, the antagonist is a shark (Person vs. Nature).

- ▶ In *The Matrix*, the antagonist is the technology enslaving mankind (Person vs. Society/Technology).

The people in these stories are affected by the antagonist, such as the mayor in *Jaws* effectively "siding" with the shark to keep the beaches open, opposing Sheriff Brody's goal of closing the beaches to protect the people. The conflict is, "shark wants to be a shark," and that causes trouble for Brody and the town—but the *people* were actively opposing Brody's desire to close the beaches. The conflict came from the choice of, "Do I risk my job by opposing the mayor and closing the beaches, thus losing the town millions in revenue, or do I protect visitors from possibly being eaten by a shark?" An external conflict with an internal struggle.

The shark created the challenge Brody had to face, and the conflict had ripple effects throughout the story (as good conflicts do). How the other characters in the story dealt with that conflict put Brody in tougher and tougher situations and forced him to make harder and harder choices.

In essence, the antagonist is the person or thing responsible for the challenges in the first place. What the other characters do about that creates the conflict (and plot) of the novel.

What *Mama* Can Teach Us about Antagonists

Once in a while, a story comes along that blows me away. It might be a novel, a movie, a game, or a TV show, but how it's written or structured illustrates an aspect of storytelling that expands my writer's mind.

The film, *Mama*, by Andrés and Barbara Muschietti is one such story. How it handles antagonists is a thing of beauty we can all learn from.

The premise is this: Two young girls abandoned in the woods are rescued by a tormented spirit who decides to raise them as her own. When the girls are found five years later, things get...complicated.

Although classified as horror, this film is more psychological suspense in the "peek-through- your-fingers-while-on-the-edge-of-your-seat" way. It will utterly creep you out, but also make you laugh so hard you can't breathe. And it makes you care—deeply—due to the incredible conflicts it creates among these characters.

There's no true "bad guy" in this film. Everyone has an agenda, but each character also has the best interests of the children at heart. They're all antagonists to Mama's goal of keeping the children, even though she's technically the antagonist of the film.

Here's what's so good about *Mama*:

It provides an antagonist you sympathize with, even though everything says you probably shouldn't.

Mama is a tortured spirit, but she saves small children (one and three years old) and cares for them when they would have otherwise died. But she also has a homicidal side that's not especially kid-friendly. We know all this, we see how deadly she can be, but we still wish they could all just live happily ever after. We *care* about Mama's goal, even when she's freaking us out by her creepiness.

How this affects the conflict: Antagonists with relatable goals can make readers care more deeply about what's going on in the story. The antagonist whose goal makes sense makes the conflict that much more interesting for readers, because they see both sides of it.

It offers incredibly well-rounded conflict not based on good vs. evil.

This is where so much of the genius of the film springs from. The conflicts are real, human, and based on complex (yet simple) emotions. Who *can't* understand the love and devotion of a mother for her children? Who can't understand the loyalty those children would feel for their mother? But that becomes something much more complicated when you add in the spirit aspect and an uncle who also loves his nieces and wants them to be safe and happy. And then there's his girlfriend, who never wanted to be a mom, but is now struggling with two extremely weird and damaged kids. Even the psychologist who wants to take them away for their own good has the children's best interests at heart. Every character has a conflict that's both relatable and understandable, but no one is "evil." Not even Mama.

How this affects the conflict: Sometimes the best conflicts come from people trying to help, not hurt. "What's preventing the protagonist from getting what she wants" can be helpful as easily as hurtful. A situation with no right answer can be a fertile field for conflict.

It has layered characters who feel like real people.

Every character in this movie could have easily turned into a cliché, but they didn't, because they were real and layered people. The girlfriend is a perfect example. Her boyfriend (the girls' uncle) has been searching for his nieces for five years, and she fully supports that even as he's going broke. Many stories would have made this a source of conflict between them with arguing and antagonism.

When the uncle finds the girls, and they're feral, she sticks by him and keeps supporting him. It's clear this isn't what she signed up for, but it's the right thing to do because she loves him, and these girls need help and support. This character could have become the whiny, bitchy girlfriend, but instead she became a rich person struggling to do the right thing under extraordinary circumstances.

How this affects the conflict: You can develop well-crafted conflicts by creating real people with layered, complex emotions and desires and giving them a challenge to overcome. One-dimensional characters will act one dimensionally, and thus become predictable. But rich, layered characters bring more options and interest to the story.

You never know what to expect, because it defies expectations.

Unpredictability is often difficult because there are only so many logical things that can happen in a scene. With *Mama*, you're never sure where the story is going to go, because Mama has such a strong and compelling story arc herself. She *could* win, because you care about what happens to her. Her conflict, even though she is technically the "bad guy," is compelling, and part of you *wants* her to keep the children.

It plays off viewer expectations in a masterful way. You think "evil spirit," but Mama defies that by her love for these children. She acts in ways you don't expect spirits to act, and the children she's saved treat her as Mama, and not an evil spirit. Those relationships change everything.

Mix in the varied emotions, and you're laughing at things that are scary, gasping at things that are sweet, and crawling out of your skin when things are completely normal. It turns what you know and how you feel upside down.

How this affects the conflict: Look for the unexpected in your conflicts and don't fall back on clichés or stereotypes, or even classic tropes. The more you surprise your readers, the more you draw them into the story because they'll be dying to know what happens next.

It has masterful pacing and manipulation of tension.

By the end of the movie, you feel as if you've run a marathon. It puts you through the emotional wringer, but you enjoy every nervous step, because you never know what the payoff will be. Sometimes it's a scare, but just as often it's something funny or flat out adorable.

Scenes creep by when you need to feel every step, but they rush when the intent is to make you gasp. And sometimes, one comes immediately after the other, so before long, the slower scenes are almost more tense than the ones that take your breath away. You *know* something's about to happen and have no idea what it will be or how it will make you feel.

How this affects the conflict: Every scene is created to evoke emotion from viewers and make them care about the outcome of these conflicts. The writers and director vary that emotion in a wonderful rise and fall of feelings and anticipation that draws you in and holds you there. You care, so you're invested in how these conflicts turn out.

It provides an ending that's perfect for the story, even if it's not the ending viewers probably wanted.

With a story like *Mama*, happily ever after would have felt wrong, but so would something dark and depressing. Because you want so many different things for these characters by the end of the film, it's hard to know what a "win" would be. The writers handled it perfectly. You want to cry (and might, I did a little), but you know in your heart that it *had* to go that way.

It might not end the way you want it to, but that's okay. It has the right ending for the story arcs presented. It's a rare story that can *not* give viewers/readers what they want and still satisfy them.

How this affects the conflict: What's right for the characters can also be right for the readers if you set it up correctly. A strong resolution to a well-crafted story arc can be much more satisfying an ending than a "right" or "happy" ending if there's no basis for it.

Mama proves that antagonists don't have to be evil or cause problems to create a successful conflict. Even when every character in the story wants the same thing, conflict can develop through not knowing what the right thing to do *is*. Antagonist doesn't mean villain, and not every "bad guy" is all bad.

The Goals and Motivations: The Reasons for the Conflict

The protagonist's goal is the reason a conflict exists in the first place— she wants it, and someone or something is keeping her from it (that opposing force). The protagonist's motivation for that goal (why she wants it) is what makes readers care about the outcome.

This is the basis for the classic GMC (Goals-Motivation-Conflict) trinity of storytelling. The goal is created by the motivation (what the protagonist wants and why), which *leads* to the conflict (what's preventing the protagonist from getting it). A lack of GMC is why random conflict feels contrived and uninteresting.

For example (and bear with me, because this is going to get a little silly):

Evil wizard: **"Haha! I shall enslave this town and force everyone to work** in the mines."

Protagonist: "Okay." Then she moves away.

If the protagonist has no desire or need to stop the antagonist, she won't try. If she won't try, there is nothing in conflict. Forcing her to stay and fight feels shallow without a solid reason behind that decision.

Evil wizard: "Haha! I shall enslave this town and force everyone to work in the mines."

Protagonist: "No you won't, I shall stop you."

Evil wizard: "Why?"

Protagonist: "Uh, 'cause slavery is bad?"

Now our protagonist has a goal, but her reason for risking her life is weak (aside from the fact that it's always a good idea to stop evil wizards from enslaving lands). There's a conflict, but with nothing behind the goal but some lip service, the protagonist can pack up and leave as soon as things get rough. She has no solid motivation to take on the evil wizard. So let's *give* her a reason.

Evil wizard: "Haha! I shall enslave this town and force everyone to work in the mines."

Protagonist: "No you won't, I shall stop you."

Evil wizard: "Why?"

Protagonist: "My family has lived in this town for generations! I know these people and care about their lives, and I will defend them to my last breath. I shall not see those lives ripped from them for your petty gain."

Evil wizard: "Yeah, okay, this sounds like too much work. I'll try the town next door."

Wait...what? See, goals and motivations *aren't* just for the good guys. Without a strong motivation to act, even the bad guys can walk away from the conflict when things get tough. And if they don't, readers might wonder why this guy is fighting so hard for absolutely no reason. Even if the conflict involves two sides fighting over a town filled with people, neither side actually cares or has any reason to fight. Let's give our bad guy his own motives and see what happens.

Evil wizard: "Haha! I shall enslave this town and force everyone to work in the mines, because a bigger, eviler wizard is trying to steal my territory and I need resources to fight him off."

Protagonist: "No you won't! I shall stop you to save the people that I love and preserve their way of life."

Evil wizard: "Then we shall fight to the last soul!"

Townsfolk: "Excuse me? We'll be happy to work the mines for a fair wage if that means keeping that other evil dude off our doorstep."

Evil wizard: "You will? Because that would seriously free up my minions to fend off the other wizard instead of standing guard over you guys."

Protagonist: "But he's an evil wizard!"

Townsfolk: "Have you *seen* the job market out there? This will be a *huge* boost to our local economy."

And now we see why "life and death" stakes don't always work to create a strong conflict. If the problem can be easily resolved, there's still no conflict. Unless the evil wizard is determined to cause pain and suffering (and he'd need a good reason to do so, otherwise his actions will feel contrived), a non-violent way to resolve his problem is a far more likely approach.

Regardless of genre, we see this type of conflict all the time in fiction. One side is acting to be "evil" and the other side is fighting against it. But when we dig down a little and ask why, there's no good answer. Evil is being evil for evil's sake, and good is being good for good's sake. The conflict is manufactured and based on superficial elements.

One caveat here: There *are* stories, such as fairy tales and horror, where evil *is* just evil. The difference is in the antagonist. Monsters can be evil because they aren't people. Just like in *Jaws*, a shark eating people is just being a shark. It doesn't need motivation, though "I'm hungry" *is* a perfectly acceptable reason for eating people from the shark's perspective. But *people* being monstrous typically need reasons or their actions feel shallow at best, contrived at worst.

This holds true for the thriller (crazed madman wants to blow up a landmark because he's crazy), the mystery (killer murders lots of people in complicated ways just because), the romance (couple fight and don't like each other because of a misunderstanding that would be resolved in two minutes if they spoke to each other about it), the fantasy (antagonist decides to summon demons to destroy the world, just so the hero has a reason to do something), or any other novel that relies on someone being bad and someone being good and both characters trying to stop each other without cause.

Strong conflicts come from strong goals and stronger motivations. Let's see what happens with our town when we toss in some personal issues behind the protagonist's motivation.

Evil wizard: "Haha! I shall offer this town a decent wage to mine the resources I need, because a bigger, eviler wizard is trying to steal my territory and I need help fighting him off. In return, I will protect this town as long as it's beneficial to me."

Protagonist: "No you won't! I shall not allow you to take advantage of these people!"

Townsfolk: "Sounds like a good deal to me."

Protagonist: "But I'm your hero! It's my job to protect you from evil. That's why you love me, and I need that validation or my life is meaningless. I have nothing else."

Townsfolk: "Your personal hangups are not our concern. We told you to learn a real skill, not all that sword swinging and inspirational speaking. This deal protects the town better than one gal with a shiny stick."

Evil wizard: "We have an agreement then?"

Townsfolk: "We do. I'll send you a contract by the end of the day."

Protagonist (muttering): "I'll show them! I'll sabotage their efforts so they're open to attack, and then fight off that other, *eviler* wizard to prove that I am *indeed* the hero this town deserves, and then they will love me again!"

Evil wizard: "Is this gal for real?"

Townsfolk (sighing): "Afraid so. We keep trying to get her help, but her parents were killed by an evil wizard and now she won't stop putting herself in harm's way."

Evil wizard: "Her interference is seriously going to complicate things."

Townsfolk: "I know. We'll deal with that when we have to. Her parents died saving the town, so we kinda owe them."

As ridiculous as this example has gotten, aren't you much more interested in how this last problem turns out? We have a town struggling to survive not only an attack from an evil wizard, but job loss and economic hardship. We have a wizard struggling to protect his own territory, who might lose it because some would-be hero with emotional baggage will get in the way of his plans. We have a local gal struggling to live up to her parents' memory, who doesn't realize she's her own worst enemy here and is creating the reasons why no one in the town loves her.

In other words, we have conflict backed by goals and motivations.

If the only reason the protagonist wants to oppose the antagonist (and vice versa) is because she's the good guy and he's the bad guy, then you're missing an opportunity to create real conflict by adding a strong goal and a personal motivation to strive for that goal and cause that conflict.

Let's look next at a real-world example.

Optional: What *Scandal* Can Teach Us about Goals and Motivations

The first season of the TV show *Scandal* has some of the best plotting and tension I've ever seen, because it has a firm hold on its characters' goals and motivations. *All* the characters have strong goals backed by solid motivations, so you always feel that anything can happen at any moment and you're dying to know what happens next.

It's just seven episodes, so it unfolds more like a long movie than a series. This makes it easy to watch and study how the writers and creators of this show handled the many conflicts the characters struggle with.

Scandal centers around Olivia Pope (Kerry Washington), a political fixer who ran the president's election campaign and is now helping others fix their problems (usually scandals, hence the name). She and her staff call themselves Gladiators, and typically fight for "the good guys," or at least help those who haven't done what they're being accused of. But in the political realm of Washington, DC, it's often hard to know who the good guys actually are (which is a good example of how an environment full of inherent conflict can be used to strengthen a story).

The first season's main story arc is worthy of any great political mystery or thriller. It focuses on a woman claiming to be the president's mistress, and the White House coming to Olivia to help fix the ensuing scandal. This is tough for Olivia because A) she doesn't want to work for the White House anymore and B) she had an affair with President Grant during the campaign and they are the loves of each others' lives. She doesn't believe he had the affair and takes the case to prove that. This is a great example of how the internal conflict can affect the external goals. Working with the president tempts her to rekindle the affair, which is what she's trying to protect him from.

It's not long before the story twists and turns and dives. You never know where it's going or what's going to happen next and you're glued to the screen to find out. The tension is fabulous and the pacing fantastic. You *need* to find out what's *really* going on—and that's the beauty of the multiple layers of conflict in this show. Everyone faces challenges and struggles to choose the right way to handle those challenges, but there is no "right way" that's good for all involved. This is the element worth capturing in your own novel.

Here are a few of the things *Scandal* does so well to create conflict through goals and motivations:

Everyone has secrets.

Every character has a past and things to hide, so they're personally motivated to protect these secrets, even at the expense of the story goal. Some secrets are small, more embarrassing than dangerous, while others could bring down regimes.

How this affects the conflict: Characters with things to hide will act in ways to keep those secrets hidden. These characters can be obstacles to your protagonist's goal without actually being villains, because it's not about the protagonist—it's about keeping *their* secret. Sure, the best friend *wants* to help the hero save his mother, but that requires revealing that he spent six years working as muscle for the local drug dealer. He'd be ruined if anyone found out, so he doesn't share his contacts or admit that he recognizes the man in the photo connected to Mom's kidnapping.

Secrets don't need to be this dangerous to be effective, though. Avoiding things that skirt too close to something embarrassing can also cause trouble if it distracts the protagonist and works as a red herring. Why is Jane lying? Is she in on the evil plan? What is she avoiding?

Viewers (readers) don't know what they *think* they know.

This is my favorite aspect of the show. You think you know the truth about a character or a situation, and as you uncover delicious facts and details and you're sure you have it all figured out—*wham!* You get one more piece of the puzzle and everything you thought you knew has changed—because you never knew the *true* goal or why someone wanted it. A character you were sure was a victim turns out to be the villain. A fact you knew was true turns out to be a lie. Characters you'd never trust turn out to be the people who can save the day.

How this affects the conflict: A character's goal and motivations can be used to trick readers, lie to them, and lead them down the wrong path (in a good way). Hiding the *real* goal can help create conflict in the story, because odds are the protagonist won't know that real goal either. She'll act based on what she thinks is true when someone is hiding things from her. A character with a secret motive might also try to prevent the protagonist from acting, and those reasons could be misunderstood in delicious conflict-creating ways. Just don't tip it *too* far—it can become a problem if the author purposefully hides information a character would have known or figured out *just* to trick readers or force a conflict that wouldn't naturally occur.

The characters lie.

Olivia Pope has her team of investigators verify *everything* they learn, because they know that no one—especially powerful people in trouble—tells the whole truth. People lie, even if it's not malicious in nature. These lies cause trouble (conflicts) because if Olivia doesn't have the whole picture, she can't help her clients. When she doesn't understand the real goals and motivations behind the choices and decisions, she acts on bad information—which leads to wonderful disasters.

How this affects the conflict: Lies can delay actions or revelations, influence decisions and behaviors, or change the path the protagonist takes (leading directly to more conflict). White lies told to spare someone's feelings could turn out to be horrible mistakes that cause tremendous trouble. Unraveling lies could be the challenge to solving a problem. Not every character has to be a liar (that would get tedious), but people usually don't volunteer exactly the information someone needs when they need it, and their reasons for it vary wildly.

Characters work at cross purposes.

Olivia frequently clashes with Cyrus Beene, the White House Chief of Staff. They both want to help the president, but she does what *she* thinks is best, and *he* does what he thinks is best (classic conflict situation). These plans often flat out contradict each other. Even when they're both trying to accomplish the same task, they can make things worse by not talking to each other first.

How this affects the conflict: Characters can be wrapped up in their own lives and problems and just not think to tell anyone what they're doing. They might have the same end goal in mind, but have different ideas on how to get there and act without sharing that information with other characters. Sidekicks might try to help and inadvertently change how the plot unfolds. Actions by other characters might affect the plans of the protagonist. Good intentions can turn into the very obstacle preventing the protagonist from acting or succeeding.

Answers lead to more questions.

Scandal's pacing of reveals is beautifully done. You get an answer, and it's great, but it leads to more questions and you're eager for the next piece of the puzzle. Every bit of information is rationed out so there's always something you *need* to know. *Scandal* also mixes up the size of the reveals, so sometimes they're small details you were curious about, and other times they're major plot-changing twists.

How this affects the conflict: Readers might notice a character has an agenda (a goal) that's not in the protagonist's best interests. They'll be intrigued and want to know why. They might wonder why one character is trying so hard to avoid another character—and wonder what happened between them. Readers might wonder if a character is telling the truth or not—and wonder if that character is really on the protagonist's side. It's all about tiny breadcrumbs leading the reader to the payoff. But be careful—if you give too much away too fast, there's nothing for readers to crave.

Season one of *Scandal* is a fun and educational way to see how to weave goals and motivations into your story to create strong conflicts that keep readers hooked.

The Stakes: The Reason the Conflict Matters

Stakes are the consequences facing the protagonist if she fails to overcome her challenges. They're the "or else" in a threat, the "I didn't see that coming" in a plan, and the "worst that can happen" in a risk. The more the consequences affect the protagonist personally, the higher the stakes will feel to readers. In most cases, the more personal the stakes, the stronger the conflict, because there's more to lose.

Without stakes, the conflict is just "something in the way."

Stakes are often misunderstood, especially since people like me advise you to make them as high as possible (which is good advice, but "high stakes" isn't what everyone thinks it is). High stakes aren't stakes in which the world is ending and there's a total disaster on the way. They have nothing to do with the size of the consequence or the number of people who might suffer from it. High stakes are stakes that affect the protagonist in a profound and meaningful way that matters to readers.

For example:

- Big, end-of-the-world stakes are exciting and huge and wonderful, but they happen to *everyone* in that world, not just the protagonist, so why care about one person over millions?

- Small, my-life-is-going-to-change stakes are personal and wonderful, and they often happen just to the protagonist, so it's easier to relate to the risk and care about the character and her problem.

From a purely structural standpoint, personal goals + personal stakes = personal action, and that's what plot is all about: the individual conflicts that illustrate the protagonist's struggle to win. If the risk is personal, the character's motivations are much clearer and it's easier to determine what she'll do and why, because the stakes will be clearer, too.

Let's look at a typical high-stakes story idea: A man learns an asteroid will hit Earth in six months and prepares himself for the end of the world.

Is there a conflict here?

Some will say yes, others no. I would say no, because there's nothing the man can do about the problem, and there's nothing here that shows why "preparing himself" is going to be difficult (aside from the obvious "we're all going to die" thing). So while it seems like the highest stakes of all, there's really no conflict. Nothing about this setup shows anything keeping the man from preparing.

What about this: A terminally ill man learns he has six months to live and sets out to find the son he abandoned.

Is there a conflict here?

I still say no-ish, because there's also nothing here that shows how this is going to be difficult. This is what he has to do, but what's preventing him from doing it?

However, an abandoned son has *inherent* conflict of its own, so we can guess where *potential* conflict might lie, even though that's not clearly stated—which is where trouble can lie with conflict if you're not clear about it. Not everyone will assume the same thing you do, and what's worse, if you're not clear about the conflict in your mind, you might not make it clear in the novel. Sure, we can assume just finding the son could be a challenge if the father doesn't have access to more than Google. Plus, odds are the son isn't going to welcome his father with open arms and forgive him for taking off. But none of this is *stated* in the story description, so we can't be sure the writer plans to do any of those things. The writer might not even know at this point (which is why some novels hit a wall in the first fifty pages).

But what if we clarify that goal for the father in how we *state* our conflict?

A terminally ill man learns he has six months to live and sets out to reconcile with the son he abandoned.

One word change, but "reconcile" is a clear goal with conflict, and it's much harder than simply "finding" the son with a vague assumption that also means reconciling. Now we see the *specific* goal the conflict will come from—he wants to fix his relationship with his son before he dies and the son probably won't want that. How resistant to reconciliation the son is will determine how strong this conflict is, and how much the father will have to struggle to resolve it.

Not every story is going to require deep, soul-wrenching, personal stakes, but it doesn't hurt to consider what the protagonist is risking versus the average person. Even in an action-focused thriller with lots of people at risk, there's usually one character who has more to lose than anyone else.

Stakes make readers care about the conflict in the scene. The more compelling your stakes, the more compelled readers will be to see how your protagonist will resolve the conflict she's facing.

Let's examine a story that *should* have worked, but didn't, due to a lack of stakes.

Optional: What *Burnt* Can Teach Us about Stakes

The movie *Burnt* is technically well done. It has an amazing cast, great actors and acting, good production values, strong writing, solid bones in the plot—everything a good story ought to have to be successful. What it lacks are *stakes*.

In *Burnt*, Adam Jones (Bradley Cooper) is a chef who destroyed his career with drugs and diva behavior. He sobers up and returns to London to redeem himself by opening up a top restaurant and gaining three Michelin stars. Classic redemption story of the Person vs. Self conflict type, with a strong potential character arc to boot—can he change his ways enough to be successful and get his stars, or will he crash and burn again?

Adam has all the makings of a wonderful character with past problems hurting his future—a talented chef with a rough past who threw it all away and is desperate to regain what he lost. He burned bridges and ruined relationships, and pretty much did everything he could to ensure he'd never work as a chef again. The struggle for redemption is right there, rife with a ton of inherent conflict.

Except...

None of his troubled past matters. Nothing he once did has any ramifications on what he wants to do now. There's no antagonist. No one is standing in his way of getting his stars. The only obstacle he faces is that he has to randomly wait for the Michelin people to show up and judge him.

The *potential* for high-stakes conflict is there:

- The sous chef he wants to hire doesn't want to work for him.

- He needs a past colleague he betrayed to work with him again.

- He has no money to start his restaurant and his reputation makes him a bad risk.

- He must deal with the personal failings as a human being that ruined him the first time.

Great problems to overcome, right? But *nothing* is actually a problem. These are all just tasks he completes with little to no effort.

- He speaks to the restaurant owners and the sous chef gets fired so she can work for him. And she does. And stays, even though he treats her like dirt—but getting her fired *could* have been a strong source of additional conflict, or a challenge that took effort and personal change on his part to achieve.

- The colleague comes to work for him when he asks, with "no hard feelings" about the betrayal (more on this later).

- His old boss vouches for him, and as long as Adam takes a drug test every week and goes to a therapist, the old boss will financially back the restaurant. There's a hint of stakes here, but there's no conflict to Adam getting the money. He asks, he receives.

- Adam's being a horrible human being is overlooked by everyone because "he's so talented" so the thing that caused his downfall isn't a problem anymore, and he doesn't have to grow to succeed.

What Adam wants, Adam gets, no problems whatsoever. He doesn't have to struggle to overcome anything at all. His "flaws" don't hurt him even though they should. He's actually *admired* for being a royal jerk and treating everyone around him badly.

There's a hint of potential conflict at the end of act two when the Michelin reviewers (who dine in secret) come to the restaurant, and the colleague sabotages Adam, just like Adam did to him. Adam has a huge meltdown; he thinks he's going to get a bad review and lose his chance at that three-star rating, and he goes on a bender. Classic Dark Moment. Even though there's been no conflict yet, it looks like things will turn against Adam and he'll have to struggle to finally win.

Except...

There are still no stakes. Adam's meltdown should have been the end of him, the rock bottom he might not be able to climb back from that would force that internal growth he needs. Adam is supposed to take a drug test every week and talk to the therapist to get his money and keep his restaurant open. It's made very clear that if he screws up, he's out.

And he screws up big time.

Yet *nothing happens* because of it.

He doesn't get tested. He doesn't get into any trouble for falling off the wagon. His therapist never even finds out. The only stated stakes in the movie were fake, as no one ever held Adam accountable for anything he did or did not do. Had that whole aspect not been in the movie at all, it would not have changed anything.

In fact, it turns out that the diners he *thought* were Michelin people were just regular diners. The colleague that sabotaged him didn't do Adam any harm at all (another fake stake), and he's able to get rid of the threat before it can hurt him. So there he is, hungover and feeling crappy, when the real Michelin people show up and he has to serve them.

Which he does and gets his star. Easy peasy.

His only obstacle is that he's hungover after his rough night of drugs and alcohol. Gee, it's a good thing he has an entire staff of highly trained chefs to make the meal under his guidance.

If there's nothing to win or lose, then what happens doesn't matter, and there is no conflict. Even when the story *has* stakes, also make sure the consequences are real and occur if the protagonist fails.

It's always a shame when a story with everything going for it falls flat, especially when a few minor tweaks would have made all the difference. If *Burnt* had embraced the potential conflicts and stakes it had in the story, it would have been a terrific movie. But at least we can all benefit from its mistakes.

A conflict is only as strong as its stakes, so make sure your stakes are personal and dire, and that they come due when the protagonist messes up.

The Tension: The Reason Readers Keep Reading about the Conflict

Tension is a critical aspect of conflict, because if there's no sense of something about to happen, odds are the outcome of what's happening isn't in question. No question = low to no conflict.

Though we often associate tension with characters in danger, it's really just the reader's *anticipation* of something: waiting for the killer to strike, hoping for that first kiss between beloved characters, wondering when a life-changing bit of information will finally be revealed—these are all things that pique readers' interest and keep them reading.

For example:

- ▶ Will the protagonist set off the alarm and alert the security team?
- ▶ Will the protagonist stumble over her invitation to dinner?
- ▶ Will the protagonist uncover the two-headed troll's weak spot?

It's not uncommon for people to say, "There's no conflict" when they really mean, "There's no tension." There's no sense of something about to happen, because there's no fear that the outcome *won't* unfold exactly as expected. Nothing in the scene is going to change that, so there's no sense of conflict.

Except...

Sometimes the conflict itself is just fine, but the outcome is too obvious because the path is so clear. "Press the button or die" isn't a hard choice to make. Everyone is going to press the button. "Press the button to pick which of these two innocent people to kill" is a harder choice, and creates more tension. People will have different reasons for choosing who dies, but it's still probably not a choice that will *really* hook a reader. "Press the button to pick which of your children will die" is an impossible choice loaded with tension. How can a parent possibly pick a child to die?

But tension doesn't have to be life or death to be compelling. Every joke you've ever heard has used tension to capture your attention until the punchline. Movie trailers tease you with details about a movie until you can't wait to see it. Holiday decorations remind you every day about the upcoming date and all the fun (or dread for some) associated with it.

Conflict relies on tension to make readers want to know what happens. Tension relies on conflict to offer enough choices and possible outcomes to make the resolution uncertain. Together, they make readers eager to see how a scene turns out.

Optional: What *Downton Abbey* Can Teach Us about Tension

Even if you don't watch TV, odds are you've heard someone somewhere mention *Downton Abbey*. One of the things that really impressed me about it was the sense of tension. It's a fantastic example of how tension can work without explosions or a hero hanging off the edge off a cliff just by making viewers want to know how the lives of the characters unfold.

Let's examine how *Downtown Abbey* uses tension to strengthen its conflicts.

The story starts with a challenge.

Right away, something has happened and there's a direct consequence to the main characters because of it. In this case, the *Titanic* has sunk and the two main heirs to the lord of the manor have died. No heir = major problem, and the only way for the characters to keep their home and wealth is to marry the eldest daughter to the next heir in line to inherit the estate (clear core conflict with a strong story question—will they marry off the daughter and save the estate?).

How this affects the conflict: A problem with high stakes makes readers curious, and the more unpredictable the outcome, the more tension readers will feel. It clearly matters to the characters in a "life and death" way without actually having someone's life in danger. But their lives will forever be altered for the worse by what has happened. The only way to fix it is to do something the characters would rather not do (more conflict, going against their beliefs). It also leaves questions about the outcome. What will the new heir be like? Will the eldest daughter catch his eye? Will they be able to arrange a marriage or will they be tossed out on their ears if he decides to move into the manor and keep everything for himself? What will they do if that happens?

Starting each scene with a challenge gives the protagonist a problem (and conflict) that has to be solved, and potential outcomes for readers to anticipate (tension).

Things do not go well.

What the characters hope will happen, doesn't. In fact, the opposite occurs. The heir is not at all what the family expected, and he and the daughter do not get along. Not only is the family at risk, but so are the honor and traditions of the estate, which is like a family member to them.

How this affects the conflict: The challenge to overcome is clearly stated and the path to resolve it is laid out, along with the stakes if they fail. It's very clear where the story is going, so it's easy to anticipate possible issues that might occur—both good and bad. The daughter has to win over the heir or the family loses everything. Since the heir doesn't understand what being lord of Downton Abbey means, he's not acting in a predictable way, so tensions are high. Anything might happen and none of it looks good.

Don't give your protagonist a break. Let things *not* go her way, either through her own actions, or the actions of others, and you'll keep tensions high.

Things get complicated.

Once the main storyline is set up, the subplots kick in. The show isn't just about the noble family, but the staff who live and work there as well, since their lives are also affected by what's going on in the main conflict. Every character has goals, hopes, and challenges of their own, and a conflict with at least one other person. Nothing really story-driving, but when combined with everything else going on, there's always *something* that could blow up at any moment. There's tension because there are people who all want different things, and those things could create trouble at any moment. Often, the smaller issues threaten to boil over at the worst possible times for the larger plot, so even these small conflicts can have big effects.

How this affects the conflict: It helps take the pressure off the main story, holds the viewers' attention, and gives viewers even more things to worry and wonder about. These are the subplots and supporting characters of a story, and better still, their actions have consequences and influences on what the main characters are doing. Petty grievances lead to bigger-than-intended problems.

Don't forget to give a few of your secondary and supporting characters problems of their own to deal with (look for characters with problems that also affect the core conflict or protagonist in some way). You don't want to create subplots that require their own book to resolve, but let the other characters have lives of their own that influence what happens around them—they're not just there to prop up the protagonist. Small issues can affect the protagonist and core conflict, and create tension because what the protagonist might need from another character could go against what that character wants. Or what a smaller character does could adversely affect the protagonist.

People make mistakes at the worst possible times.

Tension works when the reader feels that anything might happen at any time and it'll likely be bad. *Downton Abbey* excels at tension-building, because the characters make mistakes—sometimes huge mistakes that threaten everything they want, but also honest mistakes, petty mistakes, and evil, deliberate "mistakes" that are anything but.

How this affects the conflict: It helps keep things unpredictable, and keeps the stakes escalating. It also shows that any character is capable of throwing a wrench into the protagonist's plans, so just because something *looks* like it'll turn out as expected, there's always the chance that someone will make a mistake that changes things.

Let characters act in ways that affect your protagonist when she least needs the distraction or problem. Supporting characters can even help you set up a bad situation that the protagonist can't get into on her own (or create a plot situation that would otherwise feel implausible). Let your protagonist make mistakes, too. Nobody is perfect and people do the right thing for the wrong reasons (or the wrong thing for the right reason) all the time. They even do the stupid thing for the selfish reason.

Not everybody is nice.

Two words for the fans: O'Brien and Thomas. These are two characters you love to hate, but things in the Abbey would go way too smoothly if they weren't there. Yet despite their horribleness, these characters are not really antagonists—they aren't standing in the way of any main characters' goals, just causing general discord that affects everyone in unpredictable ways (they're practically environmental conflicts). O'Brien and Thomas are petty, selfish, and mean-spirited, and they don't care who they hurt to get what they want. They're the stones that cause ripples in the pond that affect everything.

How this affects the conflict: Without a traditional villain antagonist (the antagonist here is a nice guy who just doesn't want what they want), there's no one in the show to root against. These characters take on the role of "characters we hate" so the other characters can shine a bit more. They can also be counted on to make things worse or cause trouble when the plot needs it, and you believe it because they're mean people. Because their actions are deliberate, the consequences have so much more tension and impact than an accident or something contrived for plot reasons.

A nasty character with an agenda can add tension, as readers wonder how far this person will go. They can be unpredictable, vengeful, and petty—and anything can happen with a person like that.

It's all personal.

Every character in this show has something to win or lose, so when things happen, someone is affected by it—usually multiple people in various ways. Nothing happens just to happen.

How this affects the conflict: The sense that even the smallest event can drastically alter someone's life is powerful. It makes readers pay close attention to what's going on, because they know it'll matter somehow, even if it's not clear when it first occurs.

Don't have things happen unless they matter to someone. Even if the problem just affects a small character who interacts with the protagonist only a few times, let that problem have an impact in some way. Let your world and story change the lives of your characters so readers will watch and wonder what each thing will do.

The unexpected, out-of-your-control happens.

For the Abbey, it's World War I. Just when they think things are working out—BAM! The world explodes. It's a nice reminder that sometimes, events larger than the people of the story will occur, and those events can change lives in ways no one ever saw coming.

How this affects the conflict: Sometimes you need outside forces to shake up a story or send it in a direction the characters themselves can't. Plots in the Abbey had played themselves out as far as they could, and forcing new challenges would have felt contrived. Adding a war changes everything; suddenly the petty problems become less vital, and the important problems become more so. This is a particularly helpful device for a series.

Sometimes things *always* going wrong for the protagonist gets tedious and loses impact on the reader. In some cases, you might have to make your protagonist act like a total idiot for her to make a mistake or cause a problem. There's nothing you can do to make things worse or muck up the works, but you still need things to go wrong. An outside event could be the right answer to that.

Even on a smaller level, things can happen in the world or a character's life that are outside her control and have serious effects. It doesn't have to be WWI-level drama to make it work. Something a character couldn't possibly see coming works just as well.

Downton Abbey is a wonderful study of tension and how small things can be just as gripping as huge action events—often more so because they're so personal.

The Environment: The Reason the Conflict Is Harder

The environment is often filled with potential conflict for the protagonist. It might tap into personal fears, such as heights, the dark, or dogs. It might offer physical challenges, such as chasms or dangerous weather. It could even put moral or ethical problems in the way, such as the protagonist risking losing an entire town if she stops to help innocent bystanders during a natural disaster.

For example:

▶ The protagonist who must escape capture will have a harder time doing that in the fields of Ohio than on the crowded streets of New York City.

▶ The protagonist who wants to make a good first impression on her date would have a much tougher time if the sky opened up on the way to that date, and she had to decide between arriving on time and getting drenched.

▶ The protagonist who must use a magic ability to defeat a monster that's rampaging through town will find it much harder if magic is outlawed in that realm.

Unless it's a Person vs. Nature story (where the conflict is all *about* surviving whatever nature throws at the protagonist), the environment can bring additional pressure on the protagonist to make her challenges more difficult. It can intensify internal conflicts or fears, or add an interesting layer to external conflicts that need more depth.

For example:

▶ The protagonist trying to go the straight and narrow might have finally gotten a job at an outdoor event—which gets canceled due to bad weather. Now, she has no way to get the money she needs to pay her rent. Does she resort to crime or does she look for another option?

▶ The protagonist trying to overcome her fear of rejection might find herself on a date doing something she's terrible at, such as miniature golf. Now she's self-conscious about everything she does and feels exposed—the environment makes her uncomfortable, which in turn makes her act in ways that will likely get her rejected.

▶ The protagonist trying to build up her confidence might have to fight a troll in a city filled with innocents, where one wrong move could result in dozens of people dying—so she second-guesses everything she does and doesn't fight at her full ability, too scared to do what needs to be done, and the troll gets away and hurts someone.

Think about the setting and where your protagonist fits in that environment. While you don't want to whip up a tornado just for the drama of it, a story set in Kansas or Oklahoma during tornado season might benefit from some bad weather at the worst possible time.

Optional: What *Sanctum* Can Teach Us about Environmental Conflict

The movie *Sanctum* is a master class in how the setting can affect both the conflict and the tension of a story. Cave diving is an incredibly dangerous activity—so *many* things can go wrong and kill you on a cave dive—and to survive, you might have to make horrific choices. *Sanctum* didn't pull any punches here, and used the environment to make the conflicts the characters faced as challenging as possible.

Here's how they did it:

They created a setting ripe with hazards

Cave diving can be deadly. It's secluded, there's no easy way out, and if something goes wrong you're on your own. In Sanctum, a hurricane traps the characters in a cave, and rising waters force them to find another way out. People are scared, hurt, and tired, which makes them prone to mistakes and bad judgment calls.

How this affects the conflict: If the only way to move forward is to go through more danger, you leave your protagonist little choice but to risk it. If cutting off the escape route isn't feasible, try making one way riskier than the other. The path the protagonist *wants* to take won't work, so she has to go the way she *doesn't* want to go.

Look at your scenes. What kind of environment is your protagonist in? Is she in a place where if something goes wrong she can easily escape or deal with it? This works for emotional escapes too, such as, the protagonist not wanting to face an emotional issue but being in a place where she can't get away from facing it. If you cut off the escape route, the protagonist must deal with the conflict during the worst possible time.

The characters make dumb mistakes

When you ignore the cave diving expert who tells you how to survive the terrible situation you're in, don't be surprised when you die. In an unforgiving environment, one mistake can kill you (which can also be used in our stories). *Sanctum* lets the protagonists get themselves into trouble.

How this affects the conflict: If the protagonist doesn't have all the skills or information needed to get out of trouble, problems *will* develop.

What mistakes might the protagonist make that could cause a catastrophe? A physical mistake that affects a plan? An emotional mistake where she acts without thinking or in a way contrary to what's smart? Perhaps she makes a mental mistake and misreads a situation or vital clue?

The characters *have* to make really awful choices (the good kind)

My favorite aspect of this movie was the truly horrible choices the protagonist had to make to keep as many of his people alive as possible. When something goes wrong in a cave deep underwater, you might have to choose between letting one person die or having many people die. Sometimes, you can't save everyone no matter what you do. If the choices your protagonist has to face are horrible choices, the reader will agonize right along with her.

How this affects the conflict: Not every situation needs to be life or death, but there are plenty of opportunities to choose one person over the other. Make that choice have consequences that add to the problems (potential or real) piling up. Such choices can strongly affect the internal conflict. Is there a line your protagonist refuses to cross? Something she swore she'd never do? How close can the environmental forces push her to that line or that action?

Being in a situation where there is no right answer, and every choice sucks and ends badly for someone, is tense.

Putting characters in an environment rife with potential trouble makes everything they do matter more. One mistake, one slip up and disaster could come crashing down on their heads.

The Different Levels of Conflict

Now that we understand the general problems writers run into with conflict and how it works with its fellow literary elements, let's further explore the different layers of conflict and how they work to build a novel.

What's nice about the layers of conflict is that they work together to create a strong story, so when you understand how to use them, it is easier to develop your novel. The external conflicts create the physical challenges and external obstacles of the plot and the situations that must be resolved to win (however that works in your novel). The internal conflicts provide the internal struggles to make the right choices. They might also create the character arc that shows how the character changes by undergoing the experiences in the novel. The environmental conflict ties the whole team together by giving the plot and the characters a challenging place to work out their differences.

The dictionary definition of conflict nicely illustrates the different forms conflict can take, so let's run through that first:

1. To come into collision or disagreement; be contradictory, at variance, or in opposition; clash.

"Things in opposition" sums up the concept fairly well. The protagonist wants something/believes something/is trying to achieve something, and the antagonist opposes her in some way that requires effort in order to overcome.

For example:

- ▶ Two politicians both want to be president. (They strive to persuade voters to vote for them.)

- ▶ Two scientists try to prove opposing theories. (Each works to prove his idea is the correct one.)

- ▶ A child wants to go to summer camp and Mom says no. (They struggle over freedom vs. parental control.)

At the core, two sides with different ideas about the right thing to do each try to get their way. They're not necessarily enemies (though they could be), just in opposition to each other's goals—only one can succeed.

2. To fight or contend; do battle.

Conflict can, of course, be the physical—a battle to determine the victor. This side versus that side. But the fight doesn't have to be physical. It can be a metaphorical "war."

For example:

- ▶ War between two villages over water rights in the desert. (They do battle to claim ownership.)

- ▶ Federal agents raid a drug kingpin's compound. (They do battle to deny or maintain freedom.)

- ▶ Two lifelong enemies both want to marry the same person. (They do battle to win love.)

The "fighting" type of conflict typically contains a lot of animosity—this isn't a disagreement, it's a battle. The challenge is to overcome or escape the opponent.

3. A fight, battle, or struggle, especially a prolonged struggle; strife.

Sometimes the conflict isn't something that can be decided in one fight, but is, instead, an ongoing problem the protagonist is struggling with or against.

For example:

- ▶ A rebel works to overthrow a tyrannical leader. (She struggles to change things for the better.)

- ▶ A girl battles a terminal illness. (She struggles to survive.)

- ▶ A woman fights to get worker's rights for the employees. (She struggles to improve working conditions.)

The "long struggle" type of conflict typically isn't resolved by winning once, but by repeated victories to change the status quo.

4. Controversy; quarrel: conflicts between parties.

These types of conflict have two sides that disagree, usually over a belief or sense of what's right vs. wrong. You'll often find moral or philosophical issues debated here, and each side struggles to have their way.

For example:

- ▶ A gay male student wants to run for prom queen. (He struggles to change minds.)

- ▶ A husband doesn't want his wife to work. (He struggles to maintain the status quo.)

- ▶ Doctors disagree whether a patient should be treated with an experimental drug. (They struggle over the correct course of treatment.)

This conflict is about convincing the other side that the protagonist is right (or that the other side is wrong), or defying the side the protagonist disagrees with.

5. Discord of action, feeling, or effect; antagonism or opposition, as of interests or principles.

This is more the traditional villain type conflict—the bad guy is actively trying to stop the good guy from winning (or the good guy is trying to stop the bad guy from being bad). The two sides are actively trying to stop each other from succeeding.

For example:

- ▶ A police officer tries to prevent a serial killer from killing again. (She works to stop a murderer.)

- ▶ A local farm boy tries to stop an evil overlord from enslaving the land. (He works to prevent tyranny.)

- ▶ A woman tries to escape from her abusive husband. (She struggles to escape an abuser.)

The conflict here is typically more adversarial, with two sides that can't successfully coexist working to defeat one another.

6. A striking together; collision.

These types of conflicts are often things that can't be avoided, but also aren't personal. Events prevent the protagonist from succeeding, but they aren't being done specifically to that person, it's just bad timing. Natural disasters and forces of nature are good examples here, though any "wrong place, wrong time" situations can also apply.

For example:

- ▶ A girl is the lone survivor of a plane crash in the middle of the ocean. (She struggles to survive.)

- ▶ A man searches for his missing son during a blizzard. (He struggles to find a loved one.)

- ▶ A woman goes to the bank just before it's robbed and she's taken hostage. (She struggles to remain safe.)

Collision conflicts are often unexpected and unavoidable, because they involve forces outside the character's control. The challenge is to endure or survive.

7. Incompatibility or interference, as of one idea, desire, event, or activity with another.

In this type of conflict, the protagonist is often portrayed as her own worst enemy. She wants to live, act, or behave in a certain way, and others in her life are interfering with that and trying to get her to change her ways. It could also cover conflicts between people who have different views on how to accomplish a task, or conflicts people who interfere with each other's goals.

For example:

▶ A party girl refuses to acknowledge her self-destructive behavior. (She actively ignores a painful truth.)

▶ An obsessed workaholic won't let anyone help him. (He strives to maintain control.)

▶ An estranged married couple refuses to compromise. (They fight to have their way.)

Whatever the problem is, the protagonist is making it harder on herself than it needs to be through her actions or refusal to act. The challenge is in doing what she doesn't want to do.

As you can see, conflict encompasses a wide scope of problems and situations, and can be as varied and interesting as you want to make it. But no matter what type of conflict a character faces, it presents a *challenge* in how to resolve the conflict. That challenge leads to a choice on the best course of action, and that choice forces the character to act. And that's good, since those challenges, choices, and actions create the plot (the combination of internal and external conflicts). Without conflicts, the protagonist would have no problems at all (and there'd be no story).

Let's further explore the different aspects of conflict and discuss how writers use them in their stories.

The Core Conflict: The Heart of the Novel

The core conflict is the main problem at the center of a novel. It's what the book is about and the whole reason your characters are putting up with all the terrible things you do to them. If you removed this conflict, you would have no story. This is the conflict (problem) that creates the plot.

In essence, it's what the protagonist needs to do over the course of the novel. Resolving this conflict is the reason the book exists.

Conflicts fall into one of four general categories: Person vs. Person, Person vs. Self, Person vs. Society, and Person vs. Nature (more on these next).

For example:

- A Person vs. Person conflict is typically more plot-focused as two sides struggle over a single goal (the gallant knight trying to stop the evil wizard from enslaving the land, or the FBI agent trying to prevent a madman from blowing up the Super Bowl).

- A Person vs. Self conflict is typically more character-focused as a person struggles over a damaging behavior or belief (the addict trying to get clean, or the consummate bachelor trying to find real love).

- A Person vs. Society conflict typically uses both the plot and character arc as one side struggles to change the society (the girl who believes all women should be able to read, or the man who believes reliance on artificial intelligence will be the death of the human race).

- A Person vs. Nature conflict also typically uses both the plot and character arc as one side struggles to survive against nature (the man trying to save a town from a volcano, or the woman trying to survive abandonment in the desert).

The core conflict is also the conflict the antagonist will be connected to. The core conflict is caused by the antagonist in some way, either deliberately, accidentally, or as a consequence or response to an action.

For example:

- ▶ The murder mystery antagonist causes the novel's conflict by killing the victim (Person vs. Person).

- ▶ The literary fiction antagonist causes the novel's conflict by refusing to seek help for depression (Person vs. Self)

▶ The fantasy antagonist causes the novel's conflict by forcing children to fight to the death in a battle arena (Person vs. Society).

▶ The thriller antagonist causes the novel's conflict by being a volcano that erupts in Los Angeles (Person vs. Nature).

The core conflict typically appears in the novel in one of two ways: A) The protagonist is living her life when something happens to put her into conflict with something else and she can't walk away from the problem; or B) The protagonist acts to obtain a goal and the antagonist prevents her from obtaining that goal. Sometimes there's a blend of the two, with the protagonist acting in a benign way that has unforeseen consequences leading to conflict.

For example:

▶ The protagonist wants to go to school, but only the rich can be educated in her world. (The protagonist causes this by wanting an education in a world she knows won't let her go to school, and the antagonist blocks that goal.)

▶ The protagonist is kidnapped by his ex-wife, and he needs to figure out a way to escape her before she kills him. (The antagonist causes this by abducting the protagonist.)

▶ The protagonist wants to go out with the cute new girl in algebra class, but her brother won't let him near her. (The protagonist triggers the problem, but it's the antagonist who escalates it into a conflict.)

Every novel has one main problem the protagonist is struggling against. The conflict drives the protagonist to act, and it's why the antagonist is acting against her. Whatever that core conflict is determines how you plot (and write) your novel.

Here are the classic story conflict types and how they define the basic conflict structure.

Person vs. Person

This is the most common type of conflict—the classic character against another character, people vs. people, even if those people are non-human. The person standing in the way of your protagonist is another person.

For example:

- ▶ A wizard wants to kill the hero and enslave the world.

- ▶ A scientist needs to find the cure and stop the madman with the virus.

- ▶ An orphan girl needs to save her sister from bad men.

These conflicts are useful for stories that revolve around competing goals, the need to stop something from happening (or cause something to happen), or the need to triumph over another person or group (to name a few).

Key Aspects of a Person vs. Person Conflict

- ■ The conflict is people up against each other.

- ■ Each side wants to prevent the other from getting the goal.

- ■ The antagonist creates the challenges and problems the protagonist needs to overcome, either directly or indirectly.

What makes a problem a Person vs. Person conflict is that the other person has motives to work against the protagonist. For example, the shark in *Jaws* is "in opposition" against Sheriff Brody, but there's no motivation or goal for the shark—it's just a shark doing what sharks do. That's what shifts it into a Person vs. Nature conflict.

A great example of a Person vs. Person conflict is the classic mystery or thriller novel. A crime has been committed (or is going to be committed), and the protagonist is tasked with catching the criminal. James Patterson's Alex Cross must catch the killer and solve the crime, pitting his wits and skills against the murderer's. Lee Child's Jack Reacher must find the criminals and stop them from executing their sinister plan. Both protagonists want to catch and stop the antagonist, and the antagonist will act in ways to escape capture and complete his goal.

Person vs. Person conflicts are usually straightforward (as in, what has to be done), and the problems in the novel arise from the obstacles the antagonist puts in the protagonist's path. There are plenty of twists and turns and interesting things happening between the discovery of the problem and the resolution, but "getting or stopping the bad guy" is usually the goal of the novel—even if the bad guy isn't all that bad.

For example:

► The head of a rival sorority house wants to close the protagonist's sorority. (The challenge is to stop the rival from getting her way and getting the house closed.)

► The manager of a local manufacturing plant doesn't want to implement the procedures the new boss wants. (The challenge is to convince the manager that the new procedures will help him and the company.)

► The mother of the love interest doesn't think the protagonist is good enough for her son. (The challenge is to prove to the mother that the protagonist is worthy of her son.)

The trouble with Person vs. Person conflicts is that their deceptively simple structure means it's far too easy to have the conflict be nothing more than a series of obstacles to overcome. Antagonists act in ways that work in the protagonist's favor, and there's no actual struggle to succeed. As basic as they seem, they can be difficult to do well.

In a Person vs. Person conflict, the antagonist can make or break the story. He's the one creating the situation the protagonist will have to resolve. The harder he makes it, the more she'll have to work to resolve it. But an antagonist who doesn't *really* try to stop the protagonist weakens every victory the protagonist has.

Such antagonists can easily become cardboard clichés, because the focus is on what makes them bad and what they do to hinder your protagonist. They're plot devices to cause the protagonist trouble, not fully developed characters who create challenges by their actions.

The easiest way to avoid this pitfall is to develop your antagonist the same as you would your protagonist, even if the antagonist isn't a point-of-view character. Give him both good and bad traits and a history that shaped him to be what he is in the story. Most important, give him sensible motivations for opposing the protagonist. Let the reader think, "Well, gee, if I were him, I'd probably do that, too."

If you're writing from the antagonist's point of view, making him a real person with real goals also makes it a lot easier to develop strong conflicts, because it isn't about what he's doing to the protagonist—it's about what goal he's trying to achieve and what obstacles are in his way—and those goals just happen to affect the protagonist. Create strong conflicts by making the antagonist more than a plot device that forces your protagonist to do what you need her to do. Make him a character who stirs up trouble trying to get what *he* wants.

Person vs. Self

These conflicts are popular in novels with strong character journeys where the character is at odds with herself and struggling with internal challenges. These conflicts are typically deeply personal and follow a strong character arc, and the protagonist grows from the experience. The person standing in the way of your protagonist is herself, and only through change can she succeed.

For example:

- ▶ Overcoming an addiction problem.

- ▶ Facing her fear of commitment so she can find happiness.

- ▶ Realizing her overblown ego is sabotaging her career and keeping her alone.

Person vs. Self conflicts are good for emotional journeys and stories about personal change. The protagonist's challenge is within. If your protagonist is her own worst enemy, odds are you have a Person vs. Self conflict.

Key Aspects of a Person vs. Self Conflict

- The struggle is internal, but the conflict is externally driven.

- The conflict affects a belief or behavior that needs to change.

- The character cannot obtain the external goal until the internal change occurs.

These stories are a little tougher to write, because the antagonist isn't a person, but a thing to overcome, such as depression, or a self-destructive streak. Technically, there's no "person" plotting against your protagonist—it's a personal belief or behavior holding her back.

But like in any good plot, even if your protagonist is dealing with something internally difficult, she'll still have an external force to reckon with and a goal to work toward. She isn't sitting in a room trying to will herself not to be depressed/grief-stricken/addicted.

Which can make this type of conflict confusing, because while a Person vs. Self conflict drives the *external* plot (the problems come from what the protagonist does), the challenge is about overcoming an *internal* problem (the protagonist's reasons for those actions in the first place).

For example:

- ▶ A Person vs. Self conflict with a protagonist in trouble for stealing from her family to buy drugs is really about her addiction to drugs, not the fact that she stole. The stealing is just how the addiction problem is illustrated. But dealing with that theft is how the addiction problem will be resolved.

- ▶ A Person vs. Self conflict with a protagonist who cheated on her boyfriend so he'd break up with her is really about her fear of commitment and how that's sabotaging her happiness. The cheating is just the external symptom of her internal problem forcing her to examine her life and her behavior.

- ▶ A Person vs. Self conflict with a suicidal protagonist who goes on a dangerous and reckless adventure is really about dealing with the depression, not the adventure itself. Repeatedly putting herself in danger is how she realizes she has a problem and provides insights on how to heal.

The external problem is what the protagonist has to face *because of* that internal conflict. Basically, in a Person vs. Self conflict, the internal conflict is the reason there's an external problem that needs solving, and solving that problem becomes the plot.

That's why a Person vs. Self conflict typically has representatives of the protagonist's problem that work as antagonists. The problem might be the addiction, but *people* are involved somehow in dealing with that addiction. Think of it as a symbolic antagonist.

For example:

▶ The addicted protagonist might have a best friend who drags her out to the club scene every night.

▶ The protagonist who fears commitment might have an unhappy sister in a miserable marriage who constantly tells her, "Never get married."

▶ The arrogant protagonist might have a husband who feeds her ego and tells her she's doing the right thing for her career, even when she's failing.

Let's return to our protagonist with the addiction problem. Say she isn't trying to seek help. She doesn't think she has a problem, she just enjoys cutting loose at the bar to reduce stress. She's still going to have a goal of some type driving the plot, even if that's to get everyone off her back and leave her alone. She will act externally in ways to achieve that goal.

The novel's plot (and core conflict) isn't about "a woman who gets over her addiction." This is her character arc—her inner journey. The problem she's created *because of* that addition, and the actions she takes *because of* that problem, is the plot. If she's not doing anything but being addicted while people try to help until she gets better, you have a premise but no plot yet—because *there is no conflict.*

But the internal conflict is what turns this from a situation into a story. She needs to get over her addiction to get what she truly wants (whatever that is), and by facing the external plot challenges (the conflicts), she'll be forced to make decisions and realize personal truths about herself. These decisions and truths will force her to change her ways and get sober (the internal struggle).

In our story, this woman is on a self-destructive path and needs to get over her addiction. But her party-hearty husband keeps pulling her back into the life. She doesn't think they *have* a problem, it's just fun and games—until something happens that forces her to see how this is bad and she can't keep doing this (the inciting event). Maybe it's an accident, or a death, or a humiliating situation that she can't avoid, but she realizes she needs help. Her behavior is ruining her life.

Problem is, if she quits the life, she also quits the husband, who doesn't want to sober up. But she knows she's not strong enough to stay with him and *not* drink, and he refuses to stop the partying. Now there's external conflict to support that internal struggle, because her choice to sober up has consequences. The plot is about a woman who must escape a marriage that threatens her sobriety. "Leave the husband and get sober" is the goal driving the external plot. "Stop drinking or keep her husband" is the choice driving the internal conflict. "Find the strength to walk away from the addiction ruining your life" is the character arc. Until she stops drinking and finds the strength to get sober, she can't walk away from her marriage. It's all interconnected.

The actual conflict (the Person vs. Self) is getting sober when it will cost her her marriage. That's what's driving the story. But the plot needs an external goal and symbolic antagonist, so the husband becomes the person who represents what the woman is struggling against within herself. Walking away from *him* symbolizes walking away from her need to drink. If the husband left her tomorrow, she'd *still* have a drinking problem. Her issues would not be solved (which is why he's *not* the real antagonist, just a symbol of what she's fighting), even if they might be easier to deal with without him.

The plot of this tale would be her facing situations that will force her to choose which path she'll take—stay with the husband and keep partying, or walk away and get sober. She'll likely have other people or things trying to keep her from her goal of sobriety. Maybe it's her mother who puts pressure on her to stay married and work it out, unaware of the problem. Maybe it's friends who like the husband and don't see the destructive behavior. Maybe it's the bartender who knows what she's going through and thinks her drinking is her way of dealing with a bad marriage.

Let's shift a little and look at a Person vs. Self conflict with a goal that isn't quite as clear as "stop drinking."

Say your protagonist is battling a mental illness. She *knows* she's depressed and *wants* to overcome her depression, so getting healthy is the goal. But what does "getting healthy" entail? What tangible goal can she work toward that also includes the stakes and rising tension that every good story needs? Perhaps she wants to go to her daughter's wedding, or see the Eiffel Tower. She wants to get better because...why? What *specifically* needs to happen to achieve that goal? Just like the symbolic antagonist, what goal represents her "getting healthy."

The depression itself is the conflict, but it's still not doing anything to directly oppose the protagonist. It's a cause of personal problems for sure, but there should also be challenges to overcome that aren't just her illness. *Something she's doing* is in the way of her getting better. Maybe getting healthy means getting treatment, reconciling with estranged loved ones, proving she can hold down a job—to heal, the protagonist will have things to *do*. Therapy. Medication. Lifestyle change. Something.

Thus, the plot of a Person vs. Self conflict comes from *what the protagonist does to both cause and solve her internal problem.*

There's a choice the protagonist has to make, a realization she has to have, sacrifices she has to accept—goals and stakes are all about choices and sacrifices, hence you have plot. The story question driving the novel isn't "Will she get well?" but "Will she figure out and work through the problem so she *can* get well?" It's a subtle difference, but it's the difference between watching someone go through a rough patch and rooting for someone struggling with a problem and wanting them to win. That goal matters, because it's the internal struggle that needs to be resolved.

A Person vs. Self conflict focuses on the things the protagonist needs to do externally to overcome the problem they have internally. The behavior, beliefs, or attitude is the challenge in the way to victory.

Person vs. Society

In this conflict, the protagonist has a problem with something that is status quo in her world. It's not any one person who is causing trouble, it's how things are being done. Everyone is standing in the protagonist's way, but not everyone is at fault.

For example:

▶ A man tries to change an unfair law.

▶ A girl rebels against a tyrannical society that forces kids to fight to the death.

▶ A woman questions why she can't go to school like her brother.

These conflicts revolve around how societal rules or norms affect the protagonist. They're usually unfair and put the protagonist in a desperate or untenable position. Either she has no recourse but to fight back to survive, or she's so angry she strikes back in defiance. If your protagonist is battling something unfair or unjust about the world she lives in, odds are you have a Person vs. Society conflict.

Key Aspects of a Person vs. Society Conflict

■ The protagonist has a different opinion about how society should be.

■ The protagonist suffers for having that opinion.

■ The protagonist fights to change the aspect of society that is making her suffer.

Just like in a Person vs. Self conflict, "society" will have representatives of the problem the protagonist struggles directly against. Some of them will be innocent people just doing their jobs or living their lives (this is the way society is after all), while others will be those creating or responsible for maintaining the society.

There may or may not be a character arc, though it's not uncommon to have the reason the protagonist wants to change the world be connected to an internal belief, such as a need to be free or a desire to survive. Often, the internal conflict is less impactful on the plot than the external conflict (there's a lot of wiggle room here, so don't worry if your story doesn't have a strong character arc—it might not need one).

Although "society" is often portrayed as a large, evil empire, it can also be a smaller group, such as the culture surrounding an office or school. A society can be any group with rules and ways to enforce those rules.

For example, let's say the society is the wilds of high school. There are cliques, social castes, authority figures, outcasts—all the same elements of any other society regardless of its size. This society functions by its own set of rules and cultural norms, and stepping outside those norms results in punishment. The protagonist is a teen girl on the outskirts of popularity who is tired of how the upper-class elite control the school. She decides one day to oppose the most popular girl is school.

Except...

No one wakes up and says, "I think I'll risk everything and try to change the world today." Something happens that makes the status quo unacceptable, and *causes* the protagonist to want to shake things up. Or, she might not start out wanting to change the society, but find a way just to survive it. Whatever the trigger is, it will most likely be deeply personal and a strong enough catalyst to make the protagonist risk her place in that society to try to change it.

Say the protagonist is an average student, and her teachers grade on a curve. In a normal class this wouldn't affect her much, but in this school, the popular kids all get special treatment and automatic As. So on a grading curve that gives the popular kids the As, the actual A students wind up with Bs and Cs, while average students like the protagonist get Cs and Ds. Bad grades hurt her future and can prevent her from going to college or getting a good job after graduation.

Naturally, the protagonist is pissed at how unfair this is.

Then come the plot challenges. Typically, these challenges will be examples of the system and why it's bad—how it hurts the protagonist, the detrimental effect it has on the people she cares about, etc. There will be examples of society trying to reassert control, and you'll most likely have characters filling the roles of society here, with people the protagonist can fight.

Before long the protagonist will find the one person or thing that is the biggest symbol of the society she's trying to overcome, and the personal issues she's trying to resolve. Quite often, destroying, stopping, or altering this person or thing is what brings about the needed change.

By the end, the protagonist has either instigated a change (for good or bad), or has lost to the system. How far to either side this goes depends on the story. The protagonist might blow society out of the water or she might do just enough to start society on a path toward change, even if she fails. Or she might die in utter failure, stoned to death by her neighbors.

A great example of a Person vs. Society conflict is the movie *In Time*. It's a world where people have been genetically altered to stop aging at 25, with a one-year-advance on their lives after that. To continue living, they need to accumulate more time. Working pays them wages in actual time (as in minutes get added to their lives). The rich live for centuries, the poor struggle with just days (or less) left. The protagonist is a poor man named Will who is living hour to hour so to speak.

Will's beef is with the society he lives in. He just wants to live. He isn't trying to bring down a specific person; it's the system he hates. And the system doesn't care one whit about him. The culture and ideals of the world he lives in make it impossible for him to survive let alone be happy. His mother dies in his arms before he can give her more minutes, and he decides to fight the system, and thus fight the society he lives in. The rules of that society are the obstacles and challenges he has to overcome.

In Will's case, the symbolic antagonist is a timekeeper (a cop) who's just doing his job and trying to keep the system running. Even he has no personal stake in Will's problem, but he represents what's wrong and is the person getting in Will's way and helping to drive the plot and provide stakes.

Eventually things get personal, and Will does find a bigger symbol to focus on: a man with enough time to live forever who controls the time banks and the system itself. Bring him down, change the system.

This is a key element to a Person vs. Society conflict—changing the status quo. Whether or not it happens doesn't matter; it's the fight to do so that provides the goals and narrative drive.

A Person vs. Society conflict focuses on the problems the society is creating for the protagonist, and often explores what has to be done to change that society into a world the protagonist wants to live in.

Person vs. Nature

This conflict puts the protagonist up against nature, and that's what's keeping her from her goal. The challenge is against a force of nature that cannot be beaten, but must be endured or survived. There is no person standing in your protagonist's way, only nature Herself.

For example:

- ▶ A guy is trapped in a blizzard and has to survive.

- ▶ A city manager fights an unexpected volcano erupting in downtown.

- ▶ A crew battles a killer storm on the open sea.

Person vs. Nature conflicts differ from the others because often there is no villain to defeat or overcome. Nature conflicts force the protagonist to use her wits, intelligence, and creativity to survive or lessen the severity of the problem.

Key Aspects of a Person vs. Nature Conflict

- ■ The protagonist fights a natural phenomenon, animal, or creature.

- ■ The challenge is to survive the conflict, or prevent the severity of the conflict, not necessarily stop it.

- ■ Facing nature taps into something personal about the characters.

In a Person vs. Nature conflict, someone is often responsible for triggering the natural disaster inadvertently, such as in *The Core*, or putting themselves at risk as in *The Perfect Storm*. Mother Nature is the problem and she doesn't care who or what she's going to destroy. It can be a volcano or hurricane, or something smaller and less aggressive, such as a boy trying to reach the top of Mount Everest (as in Roland Smith's *Peak*).

The easiest example of this is a traditional disaster movie such as *Volcano*. Unbeknownst to the people in the sleepy little town of Los Angeles, an active volcano is about to rise in the La Brea Tar Pits. The protagonist, Mike Roark, is the city's director of city management and it's his job to handle all city-related crises. What begins as a routine earthquake turns into a major event that puts the entire city at risk. To save lives, Mike and his thrown-together-by-chance geologist partner, Dr. Amy Barnes, have to deal with the volcano and the repercussions of its sudden emergence.

If the conflict is large scale, you'll often see several of the lives that will be affected by it. Even if the story is more personal, a one-on-one tale, you often "meet" other people through memories or flashbacks, because these are the people the protagonist is trying to save or get back to. It isn't just about the protagonist and nature; you also see examples of how this is affecting everyone else, usually using the lives of the characters you meet in the first and even second acts. Yes, a volcano is raining lava and ash all over LA, but it's also setting fire to people's homes, sending lava down subway tubes, and putting other folks in danger at the same time.

In *Volcano*, we meet: the lead guy of the city works crew who later sacrifices himself to save a subway driver; the ER doc who's married to the rich developer who indirectly plays a key role in the climax; the geologist's partner, who's funny and whose story doesn't end well; Mike's second in command, who jokes about stealing his job the whole time—until it gets serious and Mike's life is in danger. And for that extra special touch, Mike's teenage daughter just happens to be visiting this week, so he has the added stress of protecting his child.

What makes these personal stories work so well with the conflict is that they intertwine beautifully and show how Nature is going to affect everyone around her. Even if at first you don't know why you're following a particular character, the roles all fit together by the end to help form the solution to dealing with the volcano.

Just like a storm, Person vs. Nature conflicts tend to start out soft and build. It's probably the most obvious example of the traditional goal-problem-disaster structure. The protagonist acts to stop the disaster, fails, things get worse and he has to try something else. This keeps happening until his back is to the wall, lives are at stake, and he has to do something crazy to win. And then you hit him with a major "oh, no!" moment.

In *Volcano*, Mike has a background in handling floods, so he tries flood control measures to dam the flow of lava. This fails. But then Amy realizes the lava is flowing right into neighborhoods and families, so they try collapsing the street to send the lava into the storm canals. This also fails. And then they realize the lava is headed right for the over-packed hospital they've been sending victims to all day (and where that nice ER doc happens to work). Mike decides to bring down the half-built high-rise across the street as a dam and divert the lava away from the hospital. But just as they start detonating the charges, Mike sees his daughter in the blast zone, looking for a lost little boy.

In Person vs. Nature conflicts, things keep getting worse, wearing the protagonist down and sapping all his physical and emotional strength. In order for him to win (survive), you first need to rob him of as much as possible (without getting melodramatic of course).

Surviving the event is almost always at the center of a Person vs. Nature story (even if the protagonist doesn't survive). Survival can be literal, as in a disaster movie, or it can be thematic as in *The Old Man and the Sea*. The old man *could* simply cut the marlin free and head home, but bringing that fish home and not giving in is the whole point. It's all about the protagonist digging deep and finding the strength he didn't know he had to overcome the challenge in front of him.

This is what makes these types of conflicts so compelling. It's not about being smarter than the bad guy, or outmaneuvering the villain; it's about finding the strength within yourself to overcome the threat/event/situation you find yourself in. It's personal perseverance. It's the ultimate underdog story in a way. The "nature" is going to run its course, but how the protagonist handles it is what really matters.

A Person vs. Nature conflict focuses on the struggle to survive or out-last an aspect of Nature, and the lives Nature touches as she passes through.

Whatever conflict you use, the key thing to remember is that no matter who or what is in your protagonist's way, they/it create the challenges that make it harder for the protagonist to resolve the problem. Take out that antagonist and your protagonist can just waltz in and win with no struggle. No evil wizard, no one to fight. No drug problem, nothing to overcome. No unfair law, no reason to protest. No blizzard, nothing to survive.

No core conflict, no story.

External Conflicts: What's Driving the Plot

External conflicts are challenges the protagonist has to physically over-come to resolve the core conflict problem (and all the smaller problems along the way). They're the actions she takes to fix the problems pre-venting her from getting her goal. They're what make up most of the action in the plot, since this is what the protagonist does from scene to scene.

In essence, external conflicts are the physical challenges the protago-nist needs to overcome to resolve a problem.

For example:

▶ Protagonist wants to find her missing sister, but someone has stolen the security tapes covering the parking lot she was last seen in.

▶ Protagonist wants to impress her date on their trail ride, but she has no idea how to ride a horse.

▶ Protagonist wants to surprise his girlfriend with breakfast in bed, but he has to get her kids out of the house first.

External conflicts are based on how the protagonist uses her intelli-gence, skills, and resources (or lack thereof) to overcome an external challenge. The key thing to remember with external conflicts is that resolving them takes action—the protagonist does something. While she might take a moment (or longer) to come up with a plan to overcome the challenge, it's what she *does* that resolves it.

Generally speaking, the scene will unfold like this: The protagonist will be trying to achieve a goal when she's presented with a challenge (she's trying to do something in a scene and something stops her). She'll either react on instinct and try to overcome that challenge, or take time to decide what to do (how much time is up to the writer). The difficulty of the challenge, the level and type of conflict, and the competence of the protagonist determine how that challenge is resolved. What happens at the end of the challenge leads to the next goal of the plot and the next challenge.

This is essentially plotting in conceptual form. Pursue a goal, face a challenge, outsmart or overpower it, proceed to the next challenge with a new goal.

Of course, while most external challenges just require skill, strength, or intelligence to overcome, others will be much harder to resolve due to personal issues. This is where the internal conflicts kick in, so let's look at those next.

Internal Conflicts: Making the Protagonist's Life Harder

Internal conflicts are the emotional, ethical, or mental struggles a character faces while trying to decide what to do about an external problem. The challenge isn't a physical thing in the way, but a struggle within the protagonist to make the right choice.

In essence, it's the mental and emotional debate the protagonist needs to have in order to resolve an external problem.

For example:

▶ Protagonist wants to save her missing sister, but doing so will reveal a secret she can't afford to have known.

▶ Protagonist wants to be loved, but her refusal to compromise keeps her alone.

▶ Protagonist wants to romance his girlfriend, but he doesn't want to risk making her kids mad and their not liking him.

An external task that's easy to complete can be made difficult by adding an emotional roadblock. What needs to be done is clear, but the protagonist doesn't want to resolve it that way for personal reasons. Either the right choice has consequences she doesn't want to suffer, or there is no good choice—whatever she does has serious ramifications.

Internal conflicts are based on who the protagonist is and what has happened to her in her life, and this past makes it harder for her to make decisions and resolve her external challenges. They typically come from the morals and ethics of the character, and more often than not, choosing one side negates the other and the protagonist can't have it both ways.

Common places for internal conflict:

A contradiction to the belief system: What a character thinks is true affects behavior. If the right choice contradicts what the protagonist "knows" is true, she probably won't choose it. At the very least, she'll struggle and do some serious soul searching to resolve that conflict and make that choice. For example, a woman who has been badly mistreated by men her entire life will very likely believe that all men are bad people not to be trusted. So if she has to make a decision based on trusting a man, there's a good chance she'll have trouble making it.

An act against morality and ethics: How a character believes other people should be treated will also affect how she makes a decision. For example, if she believes killing is wrong, any choice that requires killing someone (or even killing an animal) will be met with fierce resistance. The character's morality is rooted in her personal rules and laws of acceptable behavior. But if killing is the only way to save someone she loves, or prevent something terrible from happening, she might be tempted. Doing a bad thing for a greater good can be a persuasive argument.

A crisis of conscience: Sometimes a character wants to do things she knows is wrong. For example, it might be a minor transgression, such as lying to a friend to get out of going somewhere when she's tired and wants to stay home, or a major breach of ethics, such as stealing from her employer because he cheated her out of a promised bonus. What she wants to do goes against what she knows is right, and she's doing her best to rationalize why it's okay to do it anyway.

When fear sways better judgment: Even the best person can act badly out of fear. If a character is focused on survival or avoiding a terrible fate, she might make bad decisions or go against her morality. For example, a character might stay quiet about a belief and not stand up for someone being mistreated out of fear she'll be attacked in turn. Or, she might lie or agree to something she knows is wrong to keep something of value to her (such as a job).

Embarrassment or shame: Shame is a powerful emotion. People can ignore their ethics and personal beliefs if it means saving themselves from a terrible secret being revealed. (Think back to middle school or high school.) They'll act to avoid standing out or looking foolish, which can keep them from doing the right thing at the right time to prevent a problem. Someone who witnessed a crime while doing something embarrassing isn't likely to tell anyone for fear their own transgression will be exposed.

Internal conflicts are great opportunities to put the protagonist in the hot seat and force her to decide who she is and what she stands for. How far is she willing to go to help a friend? What will she risk? What does she value? Her struggles while making a decision shows readers who she really is as a person.

Environmental Conflicts: The World Really *Is* Out to Get You

Conflict also exists in the world *around* the characters which has nothing to do with them personally—it's just the inherent conflict of the world. The setting can be rife with problems that prevent your protagonist from solving her challenges and even add to her internal conflicts.

Getting food when you live in a big city is different from getting food if you're lost in the woods with no gear or survival training. Dealing with a backstabbing co-worker during a team-building ride in a hot air balloon is more problematic when you're terrified of heights.

In essence, environmental conflicts are the issues and situations that make it harder to solve the problems and face the challenges (internal and external conflicts) of the novel.

For example:

▶ Protagonist gets evicted from her boarding room and has no place to stay, but staying out in the open after dark will likely get her assaulted, captured, or even killed. (The world itself is dangerous and those dangers have to be dealt with before the protagonist can fix her story problems.)

▶ Protagonist goes home to visit family, because her sister is getting married, and she knows everyone will hound her about her love life. (The protagonist's life is a constant reminder of her problem and won't let her walk away from it.)

▶ Protagonist lives in a small town where everyone knows everyone, so the killer hears about her every move. (The setting and people in it add another layer of difficulty to an existing problem.)

Let's say you have a scene where you want your protagonist to feel uncomfortable because she's confronting a coworker who just stabbed her in the back at work over a promotion.

Where would you set it?

The most obvious choice is at work, since that's where she interacts with this person. She'd likely do it somewhere familiar to her, because she'll want a position of strength for this confrontation. But that means she'll be in familiar and safe territory, which will probably keep her calm and lessen her apprehension of this meeting. Being calm and feeling safe will not add conflict to this scene, so the setting is doing nothing to help it.

Let's move this meeting to a location that puts the protagonist at a disadvantage, so the stakes go up and the tensions are raised. Instead of work, let's choose a place that makes her uncomfortable and let the setting reflect the emotions we want both the character and the reader to feel.

For example, if she wants to confront the coworker in private, let's force her to confront her coworker in a public place where anyone might overhear. If she's a recovering alcoholic, we'll send her into a bar where drinks are flowing heavily. If she dislikes kids, we'll make her attend a birthday party for twenty ten-year-olds. Whatever triggers her discomfort is a potential setting, because it will add another layer of difficulty to her objective.

If we use the environment to push the emotions of the protagonist to new heights, we'll make her goals harder to accomplish, which adds conflict and raises tensions, since it's far more likely something will go wrong.

Sometimes, the world really is out to get you, and just getting through the day is a huge challenge. Take advantage of what your environment can do to layer in emotions, create conflict, and make a character really work to resolve her challenges.

Together They Are Stronger

Employing layers of conflict also helps with plotting, because you'll have multiple options for creating unpredictable outcomes (and provide your characters challenges) in every scene in your story. Unpredictability keeps readers guessing and turning the pages.

Common Reasons for Weak or No Conflict

Conflict issues most often come down to a lack of goals, motivations, or stakes. Frequently, you'll see several of these at once, since weak conflict in one area can affect the entire novel. With a weak conflict, the protagonist and other characters drift through the plot doing what they're told, but they don't truly care what happens. They're acting because the author tells them to.

This is why you can have an action-packed novel and still get rejected due to a "lack of conflict." It's also why you can have an emotional, soul-searching saga that puts your readers to sleep because "nothing happens." Action and emotion aren't enough if the conflicts aren't backing them up. They're just "stuff in the way" obstacles.

By now you should have a solid handle on the various types of conflict and how those conflicts work with, and are affected by, other writing aspects (such as goals and stakes). Let's look at the most common problems writers run into when creating (or failing to create) conflict.

The Conflict Doesn't Drive the Plot

Resolving a conflict is what a plot is all about, so a problem with the goal is one of the more common reasons for conflict troubles. Goal issues include:

There Are No Goals

Since conflict is the challenge preventing the protagonist from getting what she wants, wanting something is pretty critical. No goal = no
conflict. If the protagonist isn't trying to achieve or obtain something,
there's no reason to throw challenges in her way. If you do anyway, you
usually wind up with a novel about someone who wanders around aim-
lessly until something makes her stop and solve a random problem.

For example:

- ▶ A random person asks the protagonist for help stealing a rare
  coin and she agrees (even though there's no reason for her to
  help and she doesn't actually want the coin).

- ▶ The protagonist's plane is hijacked and she sits quietly the entire
  flight, but is then taken hostage by the hijackers and dragged all
  over the city from one danger to the next as police chase them
  (plenty of conflict for the police and hijackers, but the protagonist is just along for the ride and does nothing).

- ▶ The protagonist has lucky encounter after lucky encounter that
  lead to her getting a big reward at the end (even though she never wanted that reward and did nothing to earn it).

Characters "swept up in danger" or "swept away by events" *can* work
to get the protagonist *into* trouble and start the story (they make good
inciting events), but after that, the protagonist needs goals to work toward and challenges to overcome or there will be no conflict.

If you can't pinpoint the main goal—the one thing that has to be resolved or the book won't work (remember the core conflict?)—odds are
that's why the novel feels like it has no conflict.

If you do have a solid core conflict goal, then look at what's preventing
the protagonist from obtaining this goal. Who or what is the antagonist? Who is logically in opposition and creating the challenges the
protagonist must face and struggle with to resolve the goal? If you see
no antagonist, add that opposition.

If the main goal is working and you have the right antagonist, then the problem might lie with how your plot resolves your core conflict. Look at each scene and determine if it has a goal and if those goals are working to lead the protagonist to the climax of the novel (the resolution of that main goal). Look for ways to make the protagonist more active in solving problems and wanting to solve those problems.

Let's look at another common goal issue in a weak conflict:

There's Only One Major Goal

Sometimes the problem isn't a lack of goals, it's that every single goal in the novel is the same one, and the path to getting that goal is too clear. It's obvious where the plot is going and what's going to happen to get there, and nothing in the protagonist's way feels like a real problem.

For example:

▶ The protagonist must stop a biological outbreak before it escapes the lab, and the goals are a series of situations with her trying to prevent the virus from getting loose in some fashion (so the conflict is just her delaying when the virus gets free until she finds the right way to stop it, but nothing that would create any expectation that something else is going to happen before the end of the novel).

▶ The protagonist needs to dry out in rehab, and the goal of every scene is her fighting against the people trying to help her until she gives in (so there's no sense of her learning or overcoming anything, she just stops fighting when the book is over).

▶ The protagonist is trying to find an object and every goal is another lead to where that object might be, but it's never there (so nothing the protagonist does has any actual effect on the plot until the final clue that leads her to the object).

The problem with "one-problem novels" is that every scene is basically the same scene with different details. It feels like there's plenty of conflict as each scene will have a goal, a challenge, and stakes, but when you look closer, not a single challenge advances the story or plot. The only possible outcomes are "yes" and "no." Yes, the protagonist gets the goal, or no, the protagonist does not get the goal.

Since the protagonist can't get that "yes" until the climax, every goal ends with "no" and basically starts over. Nothing that happens matters, because only the last goal advances the plot, and even then, it's usually not a real conflict because it doesn't matter if the protagonist fails— that's been proven over and over again throughout the novel. If failing the last ten times didn't matter, the final try won't either.

However, if each failure teaches a lesson, and the protagonist is learning from those failures, then the loss means something. It's not just a pointless roadblock, but a challenge that results in furthering the character arc or emotional journey. A good example here is every sports underdog story, such as *Rocky* or *The Mighty Ducks*. These teaching moments are what separate a "one-problem story" from a compelling story arc.

Mysteries are another good example. Yes, there is one main problem— catch the killer—but not every scene involves the protagonist against the killer and the killer getting away. The goals are varied in the pursuit of the killer, so there are various problems to overcome before the killer is caught.

Conflicts with a "one problem" issue often have a lot of exciting scenes that seem as if they're moving the plot, but nothing changes from the protagonist's experiencing them. If you took out random scenes in the novel, losing those scenes wouldn't affect the outcome of the plot. Since the goals don't cause anything to change, cutting several of them doesn't affect much of the overall story.

Randomly reorganizing the scenes is another way to test your goals— would it change the story much if the scenes unfolded in a different order? Sometimes we want to keep these scenes because they contain information we think is relevant to the plot—sometimes it is, other times it isn't. Cutting the scene would lose that important information, but that's all that would be lost because the scene does nothing to drive the plot. Odds are that information could easily be added elsewhere.

And then there are the novels that try to do *too* much.

There Are Too Many Goals

These novels have multiple protagonists, multiple problems, multiple conflicts to resolve, and every character pursues a different goal. There are so many goals and conflicts that nothing stands out as the core conflict or what the novel is about.

For example:

▶ Protagonist A wants to save her father from the mines, protagonist B wants to avoid getting sent to the mines, protagonist C wants to keep his job running the mines, protagonist D needs the mines to maintain her wealth and power, and protagonist E wants to shut down the mines to stop an environmental disaster that will kill everyone. (Sure, everything revolves around the mines in some way, but exactly what is this book about? And what do any of these goals have to do with each other aside from being loosely connected to the mines?)

▶ Protagonist A wants to meet someone and fall in love, protagonist B wants to get a promotion so he can afford to get a boat and see the world, protagonist C wants to find a way to manage four kids by himself, and protagonist D wants to leave her abusive husband once and for all. (While these are all potential conflicts, what exactly is this novel about? How are these goals leading toward a single larger conflict that connects them?)

▶ The protagonist wants to find out the truth about her mother, but she also wants to get into the King's Guard, and then there's her dream of competing in the Regional Jousting Games. But before she can do any of that, she has to help this cute guy she met at the inn find the Amulet of Viznet, otherwise his entire village will be eaten by dragons. And she'll also have to figure out how to defeat the dragons, while falling for the cute guy, who has a dark secret that might have something to do with her mother. (Any one of these could fill a novel, but throwing them all into a single story pulls the protagonist in too many directions, so it's not clear what actually matters here.)

Strong, clear goals lead to strong, clear conflicts, so think about what your protagonist wants in every scene of the novel, and how that smaller goal contributes to the larger core conflict.

The Readers Don't Care about the Conflict

No matter how strong the conflict is, if readers don't care about it, it won't make them want to read the story. Most often this is due to a lack of stakes, or a lack of choices about what happens. Stakes issues include:

There Are No Stakes

For readers to care about a character's problem, there needs to be a consequence that makes resolving that conflict critical—the stakes. "There's not enough conflict" often translates into, "It doesn't matter if these people win or not." Nothing happens if they fail.

For example:

- ▶ If the protagonist doesn't pass the test, she'll have to take it again at a later date. (So why worry about her failing the first one?)

- ▶ If the protagonist doesn't break into the suspect's home, she'll have to find the evidence somewhere else. (If she can get the evidence elsewhere, why does she have to risk breaking into this house?)

- ▶ If the protagonist makes a total fool of herself at the company picnic, she'll get laughed at on Monday. (Which won't be fun, but there's nothing here that shows why that would be particularly bad for this person.)

Stakes tell readers how important the protagonist's goal is, which makes them worry about overcoming the challenge to get that goal. The stronger the conflict, the higher the stakes should be. Failing should matter and cost the protagonist something she'd rather not lose.

For example:

▸ If the protagonist's ability is exposed, she'll be used as a weapon against her own people.

▸ If the protagonist remains inflexible, she'll spend her life alone and miserable.

▸ If the protagonist doesn't risk her family's security, a killer will go free and escape to kill again.

Problem is, sometimes you can have what feels like high stakes and readers *still* don't care. This often equates to the dreaded, "It was well written, but it just didn't grab me," type feedback. It sounds crazy, but this is often due to the stakes being too *high*, giving the conflict nothing to build toward. The most common offender here is death.

Death is a lousy stake. How many protagonists actually die by the end of the novel? Almost none, and readers know this, so threatening the hero with death isn't as dire at it ought to be. Same with killing large numbers of faceless people. Right this second, people all over the world are facing conflicts that could cost them their lives. Do you care? Probably not. Faceless people don't affect us the same way as people we know. Yes, we care in a humanitarian way, but it doesn't keep us from living our lives, and it won't make us care about a bunch of story people we don't know.

Writer: My hero must stop the evil wizard before he destroys the land and kills everyone!

Reader: So? Why should I care?

And the reader is right—why should anyone care about this? There's no conflict, just a bad guy being bad and a good guy trying to stop him because one is good and one is evil.

However...put something personal at risk that the protagonist cares about, and make it clear that those consequences can and will happen if the hero fails, and suddenly readers are more interested.

Writer: My hero is forced to choose which friend she must sacrifice to stop an evil wizard from destroying the land.

Reader: Oooh, tell me more.

Stopping the evil wizard from destroying a land readers have never seen isn't nearly as compelling as watching the protagonist struggle to decide which of her friends she must send on a suicide mission to stop that wizard.

Now let's look at a situation that's pretty far from life or death and hardly a story-driving conflict:

Say little Joey is home with the babysitter, who wants him to finish his dinner before bed. The babysitter demands he eat his broccoli. He refuses; she insists. There's no *compelling* conflict here, even though there is a conflict over the consumption of broccoli. It doesn't *really* matter if Joey eats his broccoli. Nothing will happen to him or the babysitter if he doesn't. The babysitter saying, "Eat your vegetables," doesn't get much of a response. "Eat your vegetables or else" is a little better, because the "or else" could be something bad. The conflict (consumption of vegetables), forces the child to make a choice (say yes or refuse), and the "or else" is the consequence for that decision. How much readers care about this conflict depends on those consequences.

Right now, nobody cares about this conflict.

But what if Joey is highly allergic to broccoli? He tells the babysitter this fact, but she doesn't believe him. Joey knows if he eats that broccoli, he's going to wind up in the hospital sick as can be. And after countless refusals, the babysitter is not above holding Joey down and shoving that broccoli down his throat. She's a lot bigger than poor little Joey, so the chances of Joey avoiding his broccoli are slim. There are even stakes for the babysitter, because putting a kid in the hospital will really cut into her babysitting gigs.

Curious what happens now? Probably, because the stakes are higher. Joey eating his vegetables has *real* consequences to both sides. The conflict matters.

Stakes don't have to be huge. They just have to be interesting enough for readers to want to see how the conflict turns out.

Even when the stakes *are* high, if the outcome of the conflict is obvious, readers might not care about it.

There Are No Choices

Choices drive every single conflict in a novel. The protagonist wants something (the goal), something is in the way (the conflict), and she must make a choice about what to do (to get what she wants). The opposition might be direct or indirect, but it's the challenge faced and the choices made to achieve that goal that make the conflict (and the novel) work.

If the choice is obvious and no one would ever choose the other options, it's not really a choice, and any conflict in making that choice goes right out the window.

For example:

▶ Protagonist has to choose between going on an adventure that could change her life or staying home watching TV all weekend.

▶ Protagonist has to decide between helping the bad guys break into the boss's office or refusing and having them kill her child.

▶ Protagonist has to decide if he should date the wonderful physical therapist he met at the gym or the delightful attorney he met at the dog park.

Making a decision is one of the most important things your characters will ever do. Readers turn the page to see what happens next, and decisions are all about the "next." As long as they *care* about that choice.

"Should I have the eggs or the cereal?" is a choice, but no one is going to stay up late to see how *that* turns out. Because the other half of choosing is the fear that you're making the wrong choice (the struggle side of internal conflict).

Now, here's where it gets tricky.

The characters will have their own concerns, but what makes their choices matter is how *readers* feel about it. If readers care about the outcome of a choice, that choice matters to them even if it doesn't matter to the character (who might not realize the importance of the choice yet). If readers don't care, no matter how important that choice is to the character, it won't matter to readers.

If a choice is a core conflict choice, then it should have major consequences. If the entire book is *about* that choice (such as a romance or character-driven novel), there has to be high stakes for making it. If the choice isn't that important to the overall story, then it can have lesser consequences—but honestly, if the outcome doesn't matter, why have it in the book in the first place? The choices don't have to all be bad options, but they should have a consequence that matters to readers and characters.

Let's look at a very common choice in fiction—choosing between two romantic options. If the choice is, say, between two men, and there are no consequences aside from hurting one man's feelings, the stakes aren't high enough to carry a whole novel—because it isn't a choice readers are likely to care about. Sure, readers will have a preference between these two men, but unless more is going on in the novel, they can just flip to the back and see who wins.

As a core conflict, a choice between two good things with no consequences for making that choice is probably not going to hold a reader's interest. But as a subplot, or in conjunction with an internal conflict, it *can* be an effective choice and provide higher stakes—but only if it also has the potential to cause trouble for your protagonist. And this is key.

Let's go back to those two men...If hurting one of them was all the consequence the protagonist had to worry about, so what? Harsh as that sounds, whoever "loses" will likely just go on with his life and find a much better gal than the one who dumped him. As for the woman, nothing bad is going to happen to her for breaking his heart. It's probably not going to hurt her in the long run, even if she does feel bad about it for a while.

If, however, the man was so upset he killed himself, that's a pretty serious consequence to her actions that she'll have to carry around the rest of her life (if a clichéd one). If he decided to make the protagonist's life miserable in revenge, that would cause her trouble. If the man she dumped was her new boss's brother, she might be in a world of hurt at that new job.

The consequence doesn't even have to be this overt, and might have subtle ramifications for the protagonist. It can cause emotional troubles—it can make her so guilt-ridden it keeps her up nights and causes a ripple effect. It might make her realize the callousness of her actions and trigger a change to be more compassionate toward people. She might choose not to make a choice and get herself into real trouble by continuing to date both men.

Whatever the choice, it should have the power to affect your protagonist in some way (usually adversely), even if that problem is down the road a bit. If there's nothing to gain by overcoming a challenge, there's no point in winning or seeing who wins and how. Just look at all the fans who leave a sporting event before the end when it's clear who's going to win. The conflict is no longer important because the outcome is obvious.

There's No Point to the Conflict

Sometimes a conflict occurs because the writer feels the scene needs "more conflict." But random conflicts usually feel, well, *random*. Just making the situation harder seldom makes it a more compelling problem, and it can even verge on melodrama if you take it too far.

For example:

- ▶ The protagonist is running from the hitman when a car comes out of nowhere and crashes into her (and it's just some poor drunk who shouldn't be behind the wheel).

- ▶ The protagonist is late for a huge meeting that could earn her the needed promotion when the bank she's in gets robbed (and this has nothing to do with the story).

- ▶ The protagonist gets into a big fight with her spouse over something irrelevant to the plot, and the argument is resolved before they go to bed (and it had zero effect on the plot or story).

This is why antagonists with plans and goals of their own lead to much stronger conflicts, even if readers never see inside their heads. Their plan is grounded in strong motivations and goals just like the protagonist's, so when the protagonist is trying to solve one problem, the antagonist is chugging along on his own causing trouble there or somewhere else. When "random" things happen, there's a reason.

Everything Is Too Easy to Overcome

Failure to care can also happen when it's too easy to overcome a challenge. The problem might look insurmountable, but the protagonist completes the task without any trouble at all. Sometimes these not-challenges are especially problematic, because they *look* as though they have everything a strong conflict needs. The only thing missing is the actual conflict part. Make the conflict a *real* challenge and it'll work just fine.

For example:

▶ The protagonist must face a labyrinth of traps to escape the evil wizard's dungeon— but she figures out the solution to each and every trap on the first try and gets away without a scratch.

▶ The protagonist terrified of public speaking must give a presentation to an auditorium of co-workers at the last minute—but once she starts talking the words flow right out and she nails it.

▶ The protagonist must find the cure to a deadly virus—and all it takes is one long night in the lab to find it.

No matter what stands between the protagonist and her goal, she overcomes it with little to no effort. Sure, she wins, but she doesn't earn the victory, so readers feel unsatisfied with the conflict.

Special note about easy wins: Sometimes an easy victory is just that, but other times the victory can make the entire scene (or novel) feel contrived. We'll talk more about that next.

When readers want to see how the protagonist overcomes a challenge, they care about the outcome of that conflict.

The Conflicts Are Contrived

Contrived plots not only stretch plausibility, they also hurt an author's credibility with readers. Readers trust us to tell them a solid tale, and they lose that faith if we cheat by forcing events to unfold that allow our protagonists to win with no effort.

Some argue that every story is contrived, because as writers, we manipulate what happens to tell our tale. On one hand this is true, but it's *how* we manipulate that determines how contrived a story reads. For example, if we show our protagonist coming home from her karate class in the first few pages, it's no surprise to readers when she's able to fight off an attacker later. But if we mention she's a black belt *after* the attack has been thwarted—or worse, comment that, "It was a good thing she'd just earned that black belt" *during* the attack, then the scene will likely feel contrived. The vital skill wasn't in the story until it was needed.

That's the key difference between plots that feel contrived and ones that feel plausible. Coincidences happen, and it's not uncommon to have one or two occur in a story to make the whole thing work, but they typically work best when the coincidence is what brings people together or triggers the novel's conflict, not the force behind getting the protagonist out of it.

General rule of thumb: If the contrivance hurts the protagonist, it's usually okay. Contrivances that help the protagonist usually feel forced or overly convenient.

Let's look at some of the more common situations that could mean a contrived plot:

The Protagonist Is Incredibly Lucky

The incredibly lucky protagonist is probably the most common way we force our plots to unfold the way we want them to. Whatever needs to happen for the plot to move forward does, even if the protagonist doesn't do anything but show up. These situations can feel perfectly fine to us as writers, because the information and forward movement is what needs to happen for the scene to work—the problem is that the protagonist did nothing to earn it, so there's no conflict. And since a key piece of information often drops in the protagonist's lap out of the blue, there's no goal either, and probably no stakes.

Lucky breaks include:

Always being in the right place to overhear vital information: You can get away with one of these in a book, but more than that stretches credibility—especially if there's no reason for the protagonist to be where she hears the information.

Taking a wrong turn or getting lost puts the protagonist where she needs to be: These are particularly tricky, because they commonly come after a harrowing escape or chase scene that feels exciting, so it does seem like the protagonist "did something" to get there. But all she really did was happen across the right place by sheer luck, not because she worked to get there.

Random people give the protagonist what she needs with no effort on her part: This is one of the more common contrivances in a novel, because the protagonist is technically working toward her goal—it's just that everyone she speaks to gives her what she needs without her having to do anything but show up. For example, she's at a dead-end in her investigation and stops at a random diner for lunch, but while talking to the waiter, he just "happens to know" exactly the information she was trying to discover all day.

A problem is solved out of the blue right when the protagonist needs it: The most common example here is the person with money trouble who receives an inheritance right when she needs it, but any unexpected "rescue" can be a problem. The protagonist finds herself in a situation that will take a lot of effort to get out of, but someone or something appears and either solves it, or makes it trivial to obtain success.

Bad guys constantly make mistakes that aid the protagonist: The poor, unlucky villain who never catches a break falls into this category. The reason the protagonist wins is because the antagonist messes up; it's not due to any effort on the protagonist's part. What's worse is that often the only way the protagonist *can* win is if the bad guys fail, so it's not really a win. Had the protagonist not been there, the same outcome would have occurred.

If luck always breaks *for* the protagonist (even bad luck), then you might have a contrived conflict on your hands.

There Are No Motivations to Act

In a contrived conflict, characters rarely have a plausible reason to do what they're doing. If a scene requires everyone to act antagonistically toward one another, they will. If a scene requires them to be suspicious, they are. If a scene requires them to run off into the desert on a hunch, off they go. So you wind up with scenes that leave readers asking, "Why in the world are these people doing this?"

For example:

▶ The protagonist believes every word from someone she has zero reason to trust and a list of reasons not to trust (except the plot says *this* time she can, because this needs to happen for the story to move forward).

▶ The protagonist completely changes her opinion about something with no reasons to explain why (except that she must feel that way for the scene to work).

▶ The protagonist is prophesied to stop the antagonist, so the antagonist sends his minions to kill her—even though the protagonist has no clue who the antagonist is and has no reason to stop him *until* he attacks her first and forces her to fight back (which causes the conflict the antagonist wanted to avoid, creating the situation and fulfilling the prophecy).

Whatever the scene is, the situation is twisted so events turn out how the writer wants them to, even if there's nothing in the story that would logically lead to that situation or outcome. The scene might contain all the right pieces to create conflict, but without plausible motivations for the challenge, the conflict feels like a huge coincidence at best, a contrived plot at worst.

Contrived motivations include:

Characters who act "on a whim" or have and do the exact thing needed to move the plot forward: Anytime you use the words "suddenly," "on a whim," or "on a hunch," stop and make sure there's a logical reason for the character to be doing whatever she's doing. Actions triggered by following logical clues and plausible segues are great and lead the protagonist where she needs to go, but be wary when the only reason she acts is due to a wild hunch based on nothing.

Characters who have "sudden suspicions" about someone they have no reason to suspect—and they're right: While very similar to the "whim" issue, this one is created when a character has trusted or believed another for a large portion of the book, and then out of the blue, the protagonist gets suspicious. The character has done nothing to make anyone suspicious, though the protagonist thinks, "They've been acting weird lately," and acts against them in some way—most commonly by following them, searching their belongings, or preparing for an "inevitable betrayal" they had no reason to think was coming. Naturally, these sudden suspicions always turn out to be correct.

A test for plausible character motivations is to simply ask, "Why shouldn't my protagonist just walk away?" If the only answer is, "Because then there's no one to stop the bad guy," odds are there's no reason for the protagonist to act other than that the plot requires it. When you think about it, the whole point of the book is to stop that bad guy (however that appears in your story), but it's the *why* that makes readers want to see how *this* character resolves *this* conflict. The protagonist should have a reason for not walking away and letting someone else deal with the problem.

Things Feel Too Convenient

While coincidences *do* occur in real life, when there are too many of them in a novel it steals all the credibility from the story. The conflicts are there only because the antagonist needs to oppose the protagonist at that moment, and whatever it takes to get those characters into that situation is what happens—even if there's zero groundwork laid to do it.

For example:

▶ A character decides on a whim to search through the company's personnel files and then finds the person they needed to find to move the plot forward.

▶ A character treats the protagonist with undue hostility for no reason and they're the person actively keeping her from the goal.

▶ The protagonist is stuck with a ticking bomb, but somehow has not only the right tools, but the right knowledge to disarm it—even though nothing was ever mentioned before that she had these skills.

Readers are willing to suspend disbelief for a few small coincidences—that's just the nature of novels, especially to set up the premise—but when the critical elements of the plot hinge on characters acting in ways they never would (or never have so far), readers can feel the author pulling the strings and forcing the characters into predetermined roles, which prevents the story from unfolding organically.

Some common coincidences include:

An unmentioned-before-it-was-needed detail provides the reason for something to happen: Like the karate example from above, we backfill the necessary reason so the plot works the way we want it to. Often, these slip in because we realize we need a reason for X to happen when we're writing it, so we create a reason on the fly without ever laying the groundwork. Luckily, these contrivances are easy to fix—just slip in the information before it's needed.

People running into each other when there's no reason for them to do so: Sometimes we need to have two people randomly bump into each other at the right times. When the groundwork has been laid to show that it's plausible for this to happen, it feels like a natural coincidence and readers read right past it. But when there's no way these two people would ever be at this location, let alone at the same time, it's going to stretch credibility. But be extra careful here—it's easy to *create* a contrivance while trying to establish a reason for them to meet in this way.

The conflict should be a result of the protagonist's goal and the choices she made to achieve that goal. If the protagonist chose to ignore A to deal with B and now A is coming back to bite her in the butt, it'll feel plausible to the plot. Or maybe she tried to fix X and that made B happen. But if B happened out of the blue, or due to a *lot* of carefully orchestrated coincidences, it'll feel contrived to readers.

Coincidences *do* happen, and plots *are* all about getting the characters to do what we want them to, but the beauty of a good novel is that it doesn't feel like we're behind it pulling the strings.

In a novel, we have to manipulate events a *little* to tell the story we want to tell. The trick is to nudge the characters and events just enough to direct the story without forcing the story, or drawing the reader's attention to what we're doing.

The Conflict Is *Just* a Delay Tactic

An obstacle course has plenty of obstacles to get in the way, but do you really want to watch someone running it for hours upon hours? I doubt it. After the runner's skill is established, there's nothing to hold your attention or make you care. You know how every obstacle will be overcome, and even if you don't, you know it'll be circumvented and the runner will reach the ending.

Obstacles do not equal conflict.

I've read (and written if I'm being honest) plenty of scenes where the "big problem" was to get past an obstacle in the way. It might be getting around a bad guy, or scaling a giant wall, or solving a puzzle, but the goal of the scene was to overcome the obstacle in the protagonist's path. Technically, "something in the way" is conflict, but it's not a challenge that requires a choice or has any stakes, so it does nothing more than delay the protagonist from getting to the next problem.

In novels with weak to no conflict, that next problem is just *another* delay tactic, leading to another pointless task until the novel ends at the climax. Sure, there are plenty of "exciting things" happening so it feels as though the novel has a lot going on, but the pace is slow because readers aren't invested in the outcome of those tasks and they don't *care*. They *know* the problem doesn't change anything. Overcoming that obstacle will reveal no new information nor change anything that happens next.

For example, a fallen tree across the road isn't a conflict, though it is an "obstacle in the way." However, a guy in the road with a gun *feels* like it ought to be a strong conflict. The driver wants to pass, the gunman wants to stop her—but it's not a conflict readers are likely to care about if it doesn't do all the things a strong conflict *also* needs to do. It's just a random guy who appears for no reason other than to delay the time it takes for the protagonist to get past this obstacle.

Obstacles *can* work if the whole point of the obstacle is to delay the protagonist so she misses something critical that *does* have larger ramifications. The delay actually causes problems for the protagonist. Had she not been stuck handling that problem, she would have been on time to do whatever she needed to do (but you need to be careful with this, or too many of the novel's conflicts don't actually mean anything to the story).

This is why "stuff in the way" doesn't hold a reader's interest, even though it technically might seem as though there's conflict in that scene. It's the challenge to choose the *right* path that turns a "something in the way" obstacle into a conflict that needs a resolution.

Ways to Create Conflict in Your Manuscript

Even though the many layers and different aspects of conflict can be confusing, they do have one great advantage for writers—they provide us multiple options for adding or strengthening the conflict in our novels. We're not limited to one type that every plot needs to adhere to, or one set character arc that always unfolds the same way. We get to mix and match and develop conflicts however they work best with our stories.

Here are ten different ideas for creating conflict.

Think Like a Villain

Conflict is the challenge, struggle, and opposition facing the protagonist, so thinking like the bad guy puts us in the right mindset to be that opposition.

Writers typically spend more time thinking about what the protagonist will do and how she'll get out of trouble and less about how she gets into that trouble in the first place. There's nothing wrong with that, it's just good plotting, but *not* considering the antagonist's side can lead to scenes that go directly to the planned outcome and skip opportunities for conflict.

For example, when I was working on a scene for my second novel, *Blue Fire*, I found myself with a scene I knew wasn't strong, even though it should have been. My protagonist, Nya, had to break into and out of a prison and fight a bunch of bad guys. I knew when I started the scene that she got away, but it needed to be a tough fight. The problem: Since I knew she'd escape, I had her acting to achieve *that* goal, and the scene unfolded as if escaping was an inevitable conclusion. So instead of it being a tough fight, it felt too easy. I knew something was wrong. Then it hit me...

The conflict wasn't about how Nya *escaped*, it was about how the bad guys tried to *stop* her from escaping. The conflict was in the challenge she faced trying to achieve her goal.

Once I flipped sides and looked at the scene through the bad guy's perspective, it all fell into place. These poor guards were just doing their jobs and this girl was busting into their prison to free some of their prisoners. This was bad for them. What would they do to stop her? What contingencies did they already have in place to handle potential prison breaks?

After imagining the same conflict from the guards' perspective it was much easier to create the challenges Nya had to face and overcome to rescue her friends. Just to be clear, I didn't actually *write* the scene from their perspective, I only thought about what they'd do to stop her and then had her encounter those things.

Let's go through this step-by-step with a different example:

Bob, Jane, and Sally are all survivors on the run during a zombie apocalypse. They're trapped in a Denny's, with zombies all around them. They need to get out before they're the ones on the lunch menu.

Traditionally, we'd examine the scene and look for potential obstacles to cause trouble (conflict).

Let's imagine zombies are covering all the exits. They're bashing themselves against the doors and windows and the glass is going to break any time now. Maybe Sally and Jane have differing opinions on what to do and are arguing, making it hard to focus or get everyone to work together.

What's our conflict? The trio wants to escape, the zombies want to prevent them from leaving. The challenge for Bob and the gang is to get past the zombies without anyone getting hurt or eaten.

What are the challenges to the goal of escaping? The zombies. Bob and the gang are low on ammo. The kitchen is on fire. Jane is injured.

With these problems the scene will most likely play out like this: Zombies try to get in, Bob deals with each problem as it occurs. He runs out of ammo, searches for other lethal items, maybe even uses the fire to kill enough zombies to escape. Since we know Bob is going to escape, the scene is more a matter of, "How is Bob going to use these pieces to get out of there?" Because of that, there's no real tension that he *isn't* going to get out of there. The scene is going to unfold as expected, because the zombies are more obstacle than challenge. The conflict is fairly weak.

Right now, the zombies are pretty mindless in this story, so they're more monster than villain. To strengthen this conflict, let's turn them into real bad guys (because that's where the fun is). What if these particular zombies are not the kind Bob has been encountering all along? Maybe these particular zombies came across a secret government safe house and ate some test subjects for a new brain enhancing serum, so now they're *smart* zombies.

These zombies aren't going to just whack their heads on the door until it breaks. They'll have a plan. This will certainly change how Bob acts, but even so, it'll still be along the lines of what Bob has to do to get out, and when we plot this, we'll most likely think about things that Bob can do to achieve that ultimate goal of getting away.

Now flip it.

Think about it from the smart zombies' perspective. What will these zombies do to get into that Denny's so they can eat Bob and the others? Shove dumpsters against the windows to prevent escape? Create a situation where the only possible exit is into a trap they've set? Sacrifice the regular zombies to send the fire deeper into the restaurant and force Bob out? What if these zombies *set* the fire in the first place? If you were a zombie, what would you do to get to these people?

Suddenly it's not just about Bob getting away. It's about Bob having to overcome challenges that aren't so easy to guess the outcome. Failing here is a real possibility, so the tension is jacked high and the conflict feels stronger. Readers don't know what will happen next because anything could. And Bob is going to get a huge shock when zombies aren't acting like he's used to seeing. He'll have to make tougher decisions, because what he's always done won't work anymore. This will add a lot of uncertainty to the scene and raise the tension.

It's the same situation, but this time, we're not plotting for the win we're plotting for the *loss*, and making Bob earn his win by figuring out how to overcome the challenges and making the right choices to succeed. And by thinking like the bad guy for a bit, we're not picking the easy way out. We're creating tough situations that will require some fancy footwork by the protagonist to overcome.

Create stronger conflicts by getting inside the heads of those bad guys and thinking about what they'd do to get what *they* want. You might find yourself saying, "There's no way my protagonist can get out of that," but do it anyway and make her work for it. Because the harder *you* have to think, the harder your *protagonist* has to think, and the more challenging that conflict will be to overcome.

Work Against the Protagonist

Sometimes the protagonist is following along with the plot and doing what she needs to do, and even though things are problematic, there's no sense that there's *really* anything in the way trying to stop her. Sure, it's hard, but she just needs to fight through it to the next step of the plot—classic "stuff in the way" obstacles that aren't true conflicts.

When the protagonist is just mowing down obstacles in the way, add conflict by making her do what she *doesn't* want to do.

Ask the protagonist to go against a personal belief: Create a situation where the "right" answer or course of action clearly, absolutely goes against everything the protagonist knows is right and true.

Make the protagonist face a choice she doesn't want to make: Sometimes we have to make decisions we don't like, especially when we know they'll come back to bite us later. Will the protagonist be strong enough to make that choice?

Force the protagonist to make a bad choice: This is one of my favorites, since mistakes are great fodder for plot. The protagonist can act, and that action can cause more trouble than she was trying to prevent in the first place. This works even better if she makes the wrong choice because she's trying to avoid violating a personal belief.

Make the protagonist face an *impossible* choice: Some choices have no good outcomes and the protagonist must choose the lesser of two evils. Maybe the only way to save the child is to let the mother die? No matter what the options are, no matter what the protagonist decides, something horrible will happen—but not deciding is even *worse*.

Let the protagonist fail: This one can be dangerous, so be wary of putting your characters in situations that stop the story, but sometimes failing is an unexpected and compelling path to take. It's not just a setback, it's real failure with real consequences. If those consequences play off an internal conflict or past bad choice, so much the better.

Force the protagonist to do something she'll regret: This works well if what she does early on affects the plot later—a choice she makes trying to avoid a consequence that directly leads to a far worse problem or situation. Maybe she sees this regret coming and has no choice but to do it anyway. Maybe she has no clue what problems she's about to bring down on herself. Or better still, *she* doesn't, but the *reader* does.

Force the protagonist to address an issue she's been avoiding: This is a great conflict for characters who need to learn a lesson and grow. Characters don't always want to face their demons, but they have no choice if you shove those demons in their faces—and the fallout can be devastating.

Don't forget about the other characters who might be working against the protagonist as well. If everyone is on the same page and working as one, you could be missing out on potential areas for conflict.

Let someone actively prevent the protagonist from getting or doing what she wants: Give people reasons not to help your protagonist, such as a clerk who won't tell her what she needs to know, or a guard she can't sneak past. Maybe a minion of the antagonist has a full-on plan of his own to stop her.

Let someone disagree with the protagonist: Even if two people want the same thing, they might have different ideas on how to get it. Give supporting characters other ideas about what the protagonist is doing. Maybe they flat out think she's wrong, or maybe they agree but think she's going about it the wrong way and want to keep her from making a mistake. Even good intentions can create trouble if the person hearing the advice doesn't like it.

Give other characters agendas that interfere with the protagonist's plan: If two guys are after the same girl, one might try to sabotage the other. Or maybe a secondary character thinks she's protecting the protagonist by making sure she fails.

Let characters keep things from the protagonist: Secrets can add a lot of conflict, especially if keeping that secret affects the protagonist or her plans. Even a minor secret that does little more than embarrass a character if she reveals it could affect how that character acts or what she does to support (or not support) the protagonist.

Shift your thinking from, "How do I get my protagonist to the climax?" to, "How can I keep my protagonist from the climax?" and you'll spot all kinds of delightful opportunities to create compelling conflicts in your scenes.

Extra tip: For a lukewarm scene try writing it with the *opposite* outcome instead and see how it works. Sometimes what we *don't* plan is exactly what the scene needs.

Let the Protagonist Want What She Can't Have

A fun way to create internal conflict with external challenges is to let the protagonist want something that's not good for her.

I call it the Halloween Candy Principle.

Every year, millions of kids go trick or treating and bring home buckets of candy. What they want is to eat it in huge quantities. What's best for them is to eat a few pieces at a time. The conflict is, "I want to eat a pound of candy, but it will make me sick." And thus, vast sums of kids do what they want and get sick every year. Those who learn not to eat too much the first day get to enjoy the candy for months. Those who don't, get sick a few times and the candy is taken away.

If this was a scene it would look like this:

The goal: To eat lots of candy.

The stakes: Gut-wrenching pain and nausea, loss of treasured candy.

The conflict: Risk pain to eat candy.

Each kid has to face the hard choice of satisfying that urge to gorge or prevent sickness and candy loss.

Great story conflict can come from the protagonist doing what she knows is going to have unpleasant consequences because she *wants* to do it. It's the choice to act in spite of the risks that makes it interesting.

Let your protagonist want things that are bad for her (even if that "bad" thing ultimately gets her what's good for her in the end).

Look at the conflict in your current manuscript:

State the goal: What does your protagonist want?

Your protagonist will want many things throughout the course of the novel. Some of them will be small goals to drive a scene, others will be the larger core conflict goals that are the reason the book exists. No matter what the scope of that problem is, the structure is the same—protagonist has a goal and works to resolve that goal, overcoming the challenges preventing her from achieving her goal along the way.

State the stakes: What happens to your protagonist personally if she doesn't get that want?

Look for a consequence akin to getting sick from candy (only on a scale to match your story). It's personal, it's a direct result of what the protagonist does, and it's something she doesn't want to have happen to her because it's horrible, or it might cause worse problems (like losing the candy).

State the conflict: What does your protagonist want that is "bad" for her?

"Bad" is subjective. It's "bad" because it will cause pain before it brings happiness (or as in our candy example, it will cause brief happiness before pain and thus risk ongoing happiness). If the want was truly bad for the protagonist, odds are it wouldn't be the point of the novel. But to get that ultimate want (be it to escape a situation, prevent an injustice, find love, or be happy) there will be hard choices to make and prices to pay. If it was easy and cost nothing, it wouldn't be a story-worthy problem.

If your protagonist doesn't want *anything* that's bad for her, that's a red flag that you have low or missing conflict in the scene. Characters need to face tough choices and make sacrifices by the end of the novel. The conflict comes from the struggle to get what they want, even though it's hard (if they ration the candy they can enjoy it for months).

Look for the story equivalent of Halloween candy in your scenes and let your characters make the hard choice to eat or not to eat.

Put the Protagonist's Needs and Wants at Odds

When the conflict is focused on getting the external goal only, then what is thrown in the protagonist's path is just a delay tactic, no matter how amazing the path to get there is. We might enjoy seeing those obstacles overcome, but without the protagonist facing tough challenges that require tougher choices, there's no *actual* personal conflict.

While this can work in a movie (*Raiders of the Lost Ark* is probably the best-known example here), it tends to feel shallow in a novel. Action is quite compelling visually, but it has less impact when described. The emotional side is typically more compelling in written form (maybe that's why love letters are so effective).

Let's look at an example:

In my novel, *The Shifter*, my protagonist Nya wants to find (and later save) her sister, Tali. That's her goal and what she wants. But what she *needs* is freedom—the literal "not be oppressed by the occupying army" type, as well as the "free to be who I really am" type. In most aspects of her life she's trapped, and that's the theme of the novel.

So naturally, the conflict in finding Tali is Nya having to do the one thing that is guaranteed to make every bad guy in the land want to kidnap her and trap her forever.

What she *wants* (to save her sister) conflicts with what she *needs* (to be free). Having one means she loses the other, and she's not willing to give up on her sister. But to win, she has to embrace who she is and use it to save Tali (and herself). Until she becomes who she truly is, she'll never be free (her character arc). To become who she truly is, she has to risk that freedom.

Of course, she doesn't realize this at the start of the series, as needs can be unconscious goals. She knows she wants to be free of what's trapping her, but she has no idea what will actually make her free. She has to undergo the trials of the plot to figure that out, which also creates her character arc.

Needs can be (and often are) unclear for protagonists at the start of a story. What they think will make them happy (the want) isn't what will actually make them happy (the need), but they have no clue what they really need until they get the want and find it lacking.

Most of the smaller scene-driving challenges in the novel are due to the conflict of want versus need. Nya gets caught stealing and wants to escape, and she uses her special pain-shifting ability to do it—which draws attention to her and risks her freedom. She gets plenty of opportunities to be the person she wants to be, but they all come with a price she doesn't want to pay. Sometimes she refuses, sometimes she compromises, and sometimes she pays it, knowing what it will mean later, but also knowing that *not* paying it is the worst option.

This "you can have what you want, but it'll cost you" concept creates personal conflict that makes readers care about the characters and the outcomes of their actions and choices. It creates the story-driving conflict the plot is trying to illustrate. Yes, Nya can save her sister, but she'll have to become the most-wanted girl in two nations to do it. But Nya won't leave family behind so she'll make the sacrifices, even though she fights how much is taken from her every step of the way. Stripping her of her armor and protection (her anonymity) is what eventually reveals the real her, and when that's all she has left, she has no choice but to embrace it.

Which is what readers have been waiting for all along (because Nya can kick some serious butt when she cuts loose).

Look at your current project and ask:

What does your protagonist want? This is the core conflict problem she needs to resolve in the novel. It's what the book's plot is about. Why does she *think* this will make her happy? Will it—why or why not?

What does your protagonist need? This is the character arc. This is what *will* make her happy and allow her to be the person she really wants to be. Is it an unconscious or conscious need?

How do those two things conflict with each other? This is where the actual challenges will lie and where you'll draw much of the conflict from. The other problems in the book are just examples that illustrate this core conflict. The protagonist can't have both goals (need and want), and having one creates a problem with the other.

How does one force her to make sacrifices to have the other? If the protagonist can have both the want and the need without paying a high price, it's not a conflict. What are the downsides to having (and losing) the want versus having (and losing) the need?

If you don't see a clear or strong conflict, brainstorm ways you might add that conflict. Or, look deeper at what your story is *really* about. It's possible you have an inkling of what the protagonist's need is, but you never articulated it. You have a gut feeling you can't quite put into words, but it's guided you so far.

Once you find (or clarify) it, look at your story again. Odds are you'll see scenes that will be much stronger if you add an aspect of that newfound conflict to them. On plot-heavy novels, you might even see the exact character arc you need to make that story sing.

Ask What the *Other* Characters Want

It seems simple, but what often saps the conflict from a scene is that non-point-of-view characters know what the protagonist wants (because the author does) so they just go along with it or don't try all that hard to stop it. Friends of the protagonist are on her side and support whatever she's doing and how she's doing it. Everyone is always on the same page because that's where the plot is going, so even when the bad guys are trying to stop the protagonist, it doesn't always feel like their hearts are in it (like we talked about in "Think Like a Villain").

To create conflict, consider who in the scene might not want what the protagonist wants.

Let's say you're writing a scene with three people at a restaurant—Kate, the protagonist; Robert, the husband; and Brenda, the waitress. Kate and Robert have been having trouble getting along lately and things are strained between them. They're having dinner at the restaurant where Robert proposed years ago. Kate wants to ask Robert to start going to marriage counseling, and by the end of the scene, he'll agree and move the plot forward.

The scene will likely play out with some conflict, as Kate is nervous about asking and Robert will be hesitant and not want to do it right away. This is a scene that will show how these two don't always agree, but maybe there's still hope. It's easy to see how a scene like this could end exactly as Kate wants it to—she gets her way and they go to counseling. The author knows this is where the plot is going and this scene is just a way to get there.

There's also a good chance that this scene won't have a compelling conflict making readers eager to see what happens. Going to counseling is a predictable conclusion (since it's Kate's goal) so they expect it to end that way. They might even be looking ahead already to see what happens once the unhappy couple *gets* to the counselor's office.

But...

What if we forget what Kate wants for a minute and ask what *Robert* wants. And don't just give him a weak goal that helps Kate get her way— give him a real goal that fits who he is and also opposes what Kate wants.

Let's say Robert doesn't want counseling; he wants a divorce.

This is the opposite of what Kate wants, and it gives Robert motivation to oppose Kate's goal. Maybe he's met someone else, or he doesn't like who Kate has become, or he's just tired of trying to be the man she thinks he is all the time. Whatever his reasons, make them personal to him and separate from what Kate wants.

With this conflict the scene takes on a new dynamic, because as we write it, we know exactly why Robert is balking and what he might say to reject Kate's idea. He'll hem and haw, try to talk her out of it, and finally have to either give in and tell her he wants a divorce, or cave in and do what she wants even though it's not what *he* wants. It might even enrich the plot because now the outcome isn't so certain. Even if he agrees to counseling, readers know there's more going on here because of what was revealed (or suggested) in this improved scene.

But let's not forget Brenda, the waitress. What does *she* want?

Brenda wants to get out of work early because she has a final exam the next day she's barely studied for.

This is a minor moment in the big picture of the plot, and honestly, no one will care what Brenda-the-walk-on-character wants. She's a nobody, but she's in the scene and you *can* use her to raise tensions and add conflict by thinking about what she wants and having her act accordingly.

For example:

▶ She might rush them to order, sparking Robert's annoying impatient side that Kate wishes he'd work on.

▶ She might bring Kate's well-done steak out too soon and cause her to send it back, something that always drives Robert crazy.

▶ She might be distracted and let them sit instead of checking back on them, giving them time to remember the night they got engaged and reconsider where they go from here.

▶ She might show up during personal moments of the conversation and make Kate and Robert uncomfortable and back off from being honest about what they want.

Sure, she's a small character, but she has the *ability to put pressure on an already tense situation* and make it harder to overcome the challenges Kate and Robert face.

Knowing what every character in a scene wants doesn't mean you have to explain or reveal that goal to the reader, though. It's a little trick to remind *you* that people act independently of each other, and that applies to novels as well as life. Giving each character something to strive for can add a layer of interest to a scene, and turn a predictable conflict into a compelling one.

Make Characters Make Tough Choices

Choices are big in fiction. Every protagonist faces countless choices in a novel, and the ones that really make her struggle are the ones the reader is going to remember. But as we're plotting our stories, are we remembering to make those choices *tough*?

To put that conflict back in, present challenges that will force the protagonist to make tough choices. You could:

Add internal struggles: Internal conflict is often where the fun stuff happens. Maybe everything about your protagonist wants her to go one way, but she kinda *has* to go the other way to get what she wants. Is she willing to sacrifice something to get her goal? Can you make it harder on the protagonist to know what the right thing to do is? Give the protagonist a choice in how she overcomes the conflict, and make those choices difficult and push her to her limits or out of her comfort zone.

Make the choices hard: A difficult choice is one that has consequences no matter what's chosen. It also allows readers to consider what *they* might do in the same situation, helping them to connect to the character better.

Be careful not to mistake a hard choice with one that only looks hard, but really isn't. If the "right" choice is clear, even though that choice is something that will be hard to do (or hard to deal with), it isn't really a choice. It's just something hard the protagonist has to do.

Make the outcome difficult to predict: No matter how tough the choice, if readers can see it coming it won't keep them all that engaged (unless it's something they've dreaded coming and see it barreling down on them). Make sure there's some mystery to which way the story will go, and there's not a direct line from what the protagonist wants to what she needs to do to get it.

Write yourself into a corner: Although it can be scary, sometimes the best thing we can do is write ourselves into a corner (where even *we* don't know how the protagonist will get out of the problem). It forces us to think outside the plot and focus on what would be best for the scene based on what's happening in that scene.

If your protagonist *is* facing tough choices and the conflict still feels weak, it might not be the choice itself that's the problem, but the stakes in making that choice.

Tough Choices Need Strong Stakes

A choice is only as hard as the consequence for failing to make the right choice, so consider the stakes the protagonist is risking.

For example, readers are more likely to care about a father trying not to let his four-year-old daughter down on her birthday than a police officer who's trying to save the city from a terrorist. Seeing the tears in the child's eyes, knowing how much she wants her daddy to be there, watching the father struggle to make it—all of these things are personal and relatable and tug at a reader's heartstrings. But millions of people dying and a guy trying to stop it because it's his job doesn't affect us the same emotionally (though it might pique reader interest from an intellectual perspective—which is why genre matters to conflict).

What the protagonist and other characters have at stake determines how well the conflict works. Let's explore the various levels of stakes and how they affect the conflict:

Low Stakes: Low stakes are situations where there is a consequence, but it doesn't change the life of the protagonist all that much. Making a choice doesn't affect the story in any major way, and the end result will be the same regardless of which choice the protagonist makes at that moment.

Common low stakes include situations where a consequence is possible, but when that consequence happens it's not a big deal and nothing actually changes. It also includes decisions where either choice works for the protagonist (it doesn't matter what she does, it still gets her where she wants to go), or decisions where there really *is* only one option—such as one choice leads to certain death, the other to victory. Yes, there are choices to be made with low stakes, and those choices may actually move the plot forward a little, but they're not making readers worry about the outcome so the conflict is weak.

For example:

▶ A young girl is spying on her brother, but getting caught just gets her yelled at and nothing comes of it.

▶ A detailed plan to break into the antagonist's lair unfolds without a single problem.

▶ A choice between two potential romantic partners—and either could make the protagonist happy.

Medium Stakes: Medium stakes occur in situations where the consequence will change the life of the protagonist, but not in any long-lasting way. The stakes have an effect on the bigger story, and will probably make things a bit tougher, but failing isn't going to change the protagonist that dramatically in the long term. These stakes are often fun and a little exciting as they can make the individual scenes more interesting. It's not about worrying if the protagonist will win, but how this choice is going to make things worse down the road.

Common medium stakes include situations where readers care about the outcome, and that outcome will cause a change in how the protagonist moves forward from this point. Making a mistake has larger ramifications and the protagonist can usually see what the risks are and must decide if they're worth it or not. They also include choices where the protagonist knowingly makes things tougher for the sake of achieving something that matters more, such as risking capture to rescue a friend.

For example:

- A young girl is spying on her brother, who plans to rob the local gas station with his friends. Getting caught could cause her personal problems *with* her sibling, but revealing what she knows could create even bigger problems *for* her sibling.

- A detailed plan to break into the antagonist's lair requires the characters to separate, and odds are high that not everyone will make it out alive.

- A choice between two potential romantic partners—one can provide the protagonist with the financial and emotional stability she needs, and the other can offer her the passion and excitement she craves.

High Stakes: High-stakes situations have consequences that will severely change the protagonist's life. The decisions made have far-reaching consequences and failing here will change who that protagonist is.

Common high stakes include situations where failing will shake the protagonist to her core and cause long-lasting personal damage (either physical, mental, or emotional). They also include choices where the protagonist must make a sacrifice about something she cares deeply about, such as choosing to walk away from someone she loves because it's the only way to save his life. It's about how that choice and the consequences of that choice will irrevocably change the protagonist forever.

For example:

- A young girl agrees to help her brother rob a gas station with his friends, but plans to stop him before he can do the job.

- Breaking into the antagonist's lair to save the best friend requires the protagonist to give up the one item she's spent all novel trying to obtain.

- A choice between two potential romantic partners—either can make the protagonist happy, but choosing one means abandoning a lifelong dream, and choosing the other means leaving a family behind. Or the third choice—walking away from both people.

Anything Can Be High or Low Stakes

What makes something high or low stakes is how it affects the protagonist on an emotional level. The smallest, most mundane event can be devastating to the right person in the right circumstance, while the largest, most horrendous event can be just another day at the office to someone commonly facing that threat.

If the stakes matter to the protagonist *and* the reader, the outcome of the choice will also matter.

Let Characters Screw Up Their Decisions

As people, we want to make the right choices, so it's only natural that those are the choices that first come to us as we write. But doing the right thing doesn't always cause wonderful conflict (though when it does it's writing gold). Characters shouldn't act like people who have had three weeks to consider their options just because the author took that long to write the scene. A decision made in the heat of the moment isn't the same as one made with weeks to consider.

Here are some fun ways you can have your characters make the wrong choice next time they're faced with an all-important decision:

Let them be impulsive: This is a helpful flaw for characters who need to learn patience, or who don't always consider how their actions affect others. Snap judgments, quick decisions, charging full-speed ahead without thinking beyond the now. If you need to get your protagonist in over her head fast, consider this mistake.

Let them make a decision under pressure: When you think about it, you should always force your characters to do this, because a ticking clock is a reliable way to raise stakes and increase tensions in a story. Small pressures build to big explosions, so if you need your characters to blow their tops, try looking for small ways to eat at them leading up to that explosion.

Let them over-analyze something: If characters are so busy trying to figure out the right thing to do, they might totally miss the opportunity to act at all. Lost chances a character can regret later make wonderful seeds to plant early on in a story, and can cause huge emotional trauma during that Dark Moment of the Soul at the end of act two. Overanalyzing can also work to sneak in possible dangers and outcomes, helping to raise tensions and keep things unpredictable since so many bad things might occur.

Let them assume they know it all: Perfect for the protagonist who needs to learn a valuable lesson about working with others. Let her be convinced she's right and doesn't need advice from anyone else. The fall here when reality strikes will be devastating and all the more satisfying.

Let them not consider all the options: Choices made without the benefit of a solid foundation of knowledge can lead to a myriad of delightful screw ups. Maybe there's no time for research, or there's something the protagonist just doesn't want to think about (denial, much?). Missing key information can send a character into a mess of their own making.

Let them not ask advice: Who needs a long-winded story from some old geezer about how he did it when he was younger? Times change, and what worked then surely won't work now. This is a flaw for the protagonist who doesn't respect tradition or the counsel of others. The more people she pisses off, the fewer there will be when she needs them at the climax.

Don't let them make alternative plans: Who needs Plan B? An overconfident protagonist might never see the need for backup plans, because everything is going to go just like she expects. So when things start falling to pieces, she's very likely incapable of wise action to correct her mistake. This causes events to snowball, getting her into more and more delicious trouble.

Making smart choices is vital in the real world, but making conflict-creating bad choices is a must for the fictional world. While you don't want your characters to be stupid (unless it's by design), try adding a few bad decision-making moments to your characters and enjoy the fun.

Cause Trouble Without Making Trouble

Smaller, quieter conflicts can add challenges to a scene without turning it into a big, melodramatic mess. They're especially good for character-driven novels where the focus is more internal than external, but they also work well for internal goals and character arcs in a plot-driven novel.

Anything that gets in the way of what the protagonist wants to do is a potential conflict to develop. These quiet moments also give you a chance to examine multiple sides of an issue without it coming across as preaching or infodumping. Two characters having an honest debate can share a lot of information in a natural way that fits the story and flows seamlessly into the narrative.

The key to non-violent trouble is people with different wants. You want to take a nap after a long day, your kids want to play Monopoly with you. What you want is in conflict with what they want. But this isn't going to turn into a battle, and there's no bad guy here. Just two sides who both want something different.

Here are some ways to create problems without putting your protagonist's life in danger:

Make her balk: She who hesitates is lost. Not acting at the right moment can cause all kinds of trouble. And then there's that lovely guilt and second guessing you can play with later.

Blow her mind: Discovering something shocking that changes the protagonist's worldview can send her into a tailspin. Having her world turned upside down can affect her judgment, her belief system, or her very self-image. When everything is off kilter, anything can happen.

Let her be wrong: We all make mistakes. A flawed protagonist who screws up and has to fix it is a great plot tool. The protagonist might need to win in the end, but until then, she can mess up a lot.

Let her be right: Have you ever lied to someone and they called your bluff? The protagonist can call a bluff, too, and then cause worse trouble than if she'd just let it go. Embarrassing someone she'll later need help from will cause trouble for sure.

Let characters disagree: Disagreements make folks dig in their heels even if they're not ready to break out the heavy weapons. For example, Mom sends her daughter back upstairs to change out of a too-sexy outfit, even though the daughter *really* wants to wear it. Your boss makes the protagonist work over the weekend when she has other plans. These aren't life-shattering issues, but if the mother and daughter already have a strained relationship, this simple conflict could ignite that larger fuse. And if your protagonist is already in hot water over working too hard, another missed weekend could end in divorce.

Let her try to avoid hurt feelings: Some conflicts stem from love or friendship. For example, the protagonist wants to go to a party, but her best friend wasn't invited. If she goes, she'll hurt her friend's feelings. Hurting someone's feelings is a great conflict that might have huge repercussions later on when the character *needs* that friend to be there. They're also a wonderful way to mirror a larger emotional issue or show a character's growth (or the need to grow). Since these are personal, the stakes are naturally higher even if the conflict is mundane. No one wants to hurt someone they care about.

Let things get competitive: Rivalries and friendly competition can cause conflicts, especially if they start out friendly then turn more serious. Even a playful one-upmanship rivalry can make readers curious to see what happens between those characters. Who will get the upper hand this time? Will there ever be a moment when that upper hand matters? They're even handy to show a skill the character might need later on without shoving it in the reader's face.

Find the humor in the conflict: Some conflicts can be all about the funny, like Mom trying to put a diaper on a toddler who's running around laughing. Their goals are in opposition (Mom wants a diapered baby, baby wants to be naked and free) but there's nothing adversarial here. While funny conflicts probably won't work all the time (there's often little to no stakes in this type) they can add enjoyable levity and work well with more serious moments. A light scene right after a dark scene can be the calm breather readers need before everything breaks loose. It can give your character something to do if the scene is mostly dialogue and feels static. A funny conflict that distracts your protagonist might allow her to miss something she'll need later. Or the funny conflict might just be a way to share some aspect of your protagonist and make readers like and care about her—very useful for opening scenes.

A little goes a long way, so don't feel you have to add a ton of challenges to every single scene. If it takes seventeen steps to get a glass of milk from the fridge, you might be piling on the conflicts a little thick—just sprinkle them in where they'd have the most impact.

Non-violent conflict is wondering what decisions the characters will make or how they'll react to something profound. It's not the literary equivalent of special effects; it's about wondering what a character will do.

Add Small Problems to Your Plot

When you're creating your characters and their lives, don't forget to add in the little things that can cause them trouble, even if it's not earth-shattering trouble. Think about the bad days you've had, where nothing went right, and how that escalated into you snapping and yelling at someone who didn't deserve it. Or caused you to do something you wouldn't have ordinarily done had you not already been stressed by stupid little things.

In other words, pile on the problems.

For example, in *The Shifter*, finding food and work is a small problem my protagonist has to deal with every day. It's not a major event in the book, but it does cause her extra trouble, and it does start her down the path that becomes the major conflict of the story. It's also something that can add a layer of difficulty to everything she does. Life is hard for her, even the simple everyday things. A hard life makes everything more difficult.

Places to look for conflict:

World building: What inherent problems occur in this character's world?

Work: What problem issues can come up on the job?

Family: Are there any family issues that can throw a wrench in the protagonist's plan?

Friends: Can a friend come to them for help at a bad time?

Health: Is there a medical issue that can cause recurring trouble?

Sometimes in our stories, we need our characters to act in ways contrary to what the average person would do. Take a chance, make a bad choice, be reckless or mean. A bad day can go a long way toward shoving someone in the right (meaning wrong) direction.

Add pressure prior to a big turning point: Small conflicts can put the protagonist in the wrong mindset during a major turning point. Find those moments that need extra conflict and go back a few scenes (or even chapters). Look for places where the protagonist's day/goal/problem would be made a little bit worse by one more thing going wrong.

Strengthen slow scenes by adding additional problems: Slow scenes can benefit from added small problems, so check any spots that drag and look for ways to make things a little more difficult. These could be good spots to add those pressure points.

Add conflict with the emotions: Emotional situations or turning points can be made more powerful by a small issue or conflict that underlines or further illustrates that emotion—or is completely contrary to it. What might happen if the protagonist had to fake being happy when she wanted to curl up and cry?

Be wary of tossing in a small issue just to add a small issue, though. Empty problems will read like "stuff in the way" and make the book feel full of random obstacles without a real plot or story.

When you add a small problem, make sure it creates the right pressure to cause conflict in the scene. It might:

- Put stress on an existing problem

- Add a ticking clock

- Push an emotional button

- Take advantage of a character flaw and bring it to light

- Undermine the character so they're in bad shape for the next problem

- Raise the stakes

- Provide an opportunity for the protagonist to fail

- Provide an opportunity for the protagonist to learn a skill they'll need later

Things happen in our lives all the time, so it makes sense to let our characters experience that same chaos and uncertainty that will make everything they do a little more challenging.

Take Advantage of the Environment

We all know *what* happens in a story is important, but as we saw earlier, *where* it happens can have a profound effect on the characters and how they resolve their conflicts as well. If your setting doesn't add something to the story, you're wasting a great opportunity to deepen your novel or layer in more conflicts.

A solid example of how setting can affect the conflict of a novel is the movie *District 9*. In the movie, a ship full of aliens are space-wrecked on Earth and have spent the past twenty years living in a controlled area called *District 9*. Naturally, the aliens and the humans have difficulty living and playing well together and conflict ensues.

One of the things I found most interesting about this movie was the choice of setting. The alien ship could have settled over any city, but the writers chose Johannesburg, South Africa. I think that the events depicted in the film would not have happened the same way had this been set in, say, Los Angeles, Chicago, or London. The setting brought a cultural history to the problem that made it very believable for things to have happened as they did. Since South Africa has a history with racial strife and apartheid, attitudes toward the aliens were strongly affected by that past. In this case, it wasn't an issue of race, but of species. What happened in the movie fits very well with the history of the setting.

Setting also played a big role in *The Shifter*. Many of the problems Nya faces are directly related to the fact that her city is under enemy occupation. Her attitude about nearly everything is colored by this fact and her experiences with this. Were I to move the setting, the book would lose many of its more interesting aspects. The layers of conflict and meaning wouldn't be there anymore, and those layers are critical to the story.

Here are some ways to use the environment to create or deepen the conflict:

Choose the worst setting for the protagonist to face her challenge: Walking through a clean room isn't hard, but walking through a room strewn with broken glass or ten thousand LEGO bricks is a lot more problematic. What about your setting might affect the conflicts in your novel?

Use the setting to push the protagonist out of her comfort zone: Fighting for your life in the dark when you're afraid of the dark makes it even harder to keep your cool. The setting can make the protagonist physically or emotionally uncomfortable, which can make her less capable of handling the challenge at hand.

Let the setting give the antagonist the advantage: It's much easier to gain the upper hand when you're familiar with the terrain. Setting a scene in a location that works for the antagonist adds another layer of difficulty to the task.

Use the setting to put the protagonist at a disadvantage: Even small disadvantages can add up and put the right pressures on a character. Narrow hallways can limit a large or agile protagonist. Cold might cause trouble for the protagonist who isn't dressed appropriately for the weather. Having to defend yourself while wearing high heels at a party can even be a problem (though it could turn out to be the solution if you use the heels as a weapon).

Let the location enhance the thematic elements of the conflict: If your characters are worried about how they're going to pay the rent and how their latest get-rich scheme failed, letting them discuss this as they're walking through a poor neighborhood gives you opportunities to show the poverty-stricken world and reinforce what they have to lose if they can't come up with the money.

Let the location illustrate a character's state of mind: If they're happy, a park or beach might help reflect that. Or you could even use something traditionally dark and gloomy to contrast against their happiness (and vice versa). Someone who is scared might see dangers all around them and give you an opportunity to show the lurking troubles inherent in their world. You can also use that setting to reinforce the emotion you want the reader to feel.

Deepen your conflicts by putting your protagonist into an unlikely or difficult environment. Where we are definitely influences how we feel and what we do.

Go Cause Trouble!

Congratulations! You made it.

Many writers have struggled with creating compelling conflicts in their novels, and I hope this in-depth analysis has given you new insights into how to create conflict in your stories. Often, all it takes is a small push or a slight tweak to an existing situation to bring out the conflict and deepen the scene. Take the tools and the lessons learned here and find the hidden gems scattered throughout your novel.

If you've found this book helpful, please share with friends or leave reviews on your favorite sites.

Most of all, best of luck and good writing!

Janice Hardy
August 2017

Thanks!

Thank you for reading *Understanding Conflict (And What It Really Means)*, the second book in my Skill Builders series. I hope you found it useful!

- Reviews help other readers find books. I appreciate all reviews, whether positive or negative.

- If you enjoyed this book, look for the other book in my Skill Builders series, *Understanding Show, Don't Tell (And Really Getting It)*, available in paperback and e-book.

- Books in my Foundations of Fiction series include *Plotting Your Novel: Ideas and Structure* and the *Plotting Your Novel Workbook* and my Revising Your Novel series: *Fixing Your Character & Point-of-View Problems*, *Fixing Your Plot & Story Structure Problems*, and *Fixing Your Setting & Description Problems*, available in paperback and e-book.

- I even write fantasy adventures for teens and adults. My teen novels include The Healing Wars trilogy: *The Shifter, Blue Fire,* and *Darkfall* from Balzer+Bray/HarperCollins, available in paperback, e-book, and audio book formats. As J.T. Hardy, I write fantasy novels for adults, available in paperback and e-book formats.

- **Would you like more writing tips and advice?** Visit my writing site, Fiction University at Fiction-University.com, or follow me on Twitter at @Janice_Hardy.

- **Want to stay updated on future books, workshop, or events?** Subscribe to my newsletter. As a thank you, you'll receive my book, *25 Ways to Strengthen Your Writing Right Now*.

More from Janice Hardy

Award-winning author Janice Hardy (and founder of the popular writing site, Fiction University) takes you inside the writing process to show you how to craft compelling fiction: In her Foundations of Fiction series, she guides you through plotting, developing, and revising a novel. In her Skill Builders series, she uses in-depth analysis and easy-to-understand examples to examine the most common craft questions writers struggle with.

Understanding Show, Don't Tell (And Really *Getting It)* looks at one of the most frustrating aspects of writing—showing, and not telling. Learn what *show, don't tell* means, how to spot told prose in your writing, and when telling is the *right* thing to do. The book also explores aspects of writing that aren't technically telling, but are connected to told prose and can make prose feel told, such as infodumps, description, and backstory.

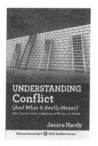

Understanding Conflict (And What It Really *Means)* looks at how to develop and create conflict in your fiction, and discusses the misconceptions about conflict that confuse and frustrate so many writers. The book also helps you understand what conflict really is, discusses the various aspects of conflict, and reveals why common advice on creating conflict doesn't always work.

Plotting Your Novel: Ideas and Structure shows you how to find and develop stories from that first spark of inspiration to the complete novel. It walks you through how to develop the right characters, find your setting, create your plot, as well as teach you how to identify where your novel fits in the market, and if your idea has what it takes to be a series. Ten self-guided workshops help you craft a solid plot. Each workshop builds upon the other to flesh out your idea as much or as little as you need to start writing, and contains guidance for plotters, pantsers, and everyone in between.

Plotting Your Novel Workbook is the companion guide to *Plotting Your Novel: Ideas and Structure* for those who like a hardcopy approach with easy-to-use worksheets. Its larger workbook format is perfect for writers who enjoy brainstorming on paper and developing their novels in an organized and guided format. No more searching for ideas jotted down on bits of paper. No more losing notes just when you need them most. With more than 100 exercises for the novel-planning process, you can keep all your thoughts in one handy place.

Fixing Your Character & Point-of-View Problems takes you step-by-step through revising character and character-related issues, such as two-dimensional characters, inconsistent points of view, excessive backstory, stale dialogue, didactic internalization, and lack of voice. She'll show you how to analyze your draft, spot any problems or weak areas, and fix those problems. Five self-guided workshops show you how to craft compelling characters, solid points of view, and strong character voices readers will love.

Fixing Your Plot & Story Structure Problems guides you through plot and story structure-related issues, such as wandering plots; a lack of scene structure; no goals, conflicts, or stakes; low tension; no hooks; and slow pacing. She'll show you how to analyze your draft, spot any problems or weak areas, and fix those problems. Five self-guided workshops show you how to craft gripping plots and novels that are impossible to put down.

Fixing Your Setting & Description Problems focuses on setting and description-related issues, such as weak world building, heavy infodumping, told prose, awkward stage direction, inconsistent tone and mood, and overwritten descriptions. She'll show you how to analyze your draft, spot any problems or weak areas, and fix those problems. Five self-guided workshops show you how to craft immersive settings and worlds that draw readers into your story and keep them there.

Acknowledgments

As always, this book would not be here without the help and support of some amazing people.

Huge hugs and thanks to everyone who helped me wrangle this book into shape. My critique partners, Ann and Bonnie; my beta readers, Connie, Joan, Lisa, Peggy, and Trisha; my awesome proofreader, Dori. So many pairs of sharp eyes caught the things I missed, and your inquisitive minds asked some fantastic questions that made this a better book. You guys are the best.

Thank you all.

About the Author

Janice Hardy is the founder of Fiction University, a site dedicated to helping writers improve their craft. She writes both fiction and nonfiction.

Her nonfiction books include the Skill Builders series: *Understanding Show, Don't Tell (And Really Getting It)* and *Understanding Conflict (And What It Really Means)*, and the Foundations of Fiction series: *Plotting Your Novel: Ideas and Structure*, a self-guided workshop for planning or revising a novel; its companion guide, *Plotting Your Novel Workbook*; and the *Revising Your Novel: First Draft to Finished Draft* series.

She's also the author of the teen fantasy trilogy The Healing Wars, including *The Shifter*, *Blue Fire*, and *Darkfall*, from Balzer+Bray/Harper Collins. *The Shifter* was chosen by the Georgia Center for the Book for its 2014 list of "Ten Books All Young Georgians Should Read." It was also shortlisted for the Waterstones Children's Book Prize (2011) and The Truman Award (2011).

Janice lives in Central Florida with her husband, one yard zombie, two cats, and a very nervous freshwater eel.

Visit her author's site at janicehardy.com for more information, or visit fiction-university.com to learn more about writing.

Follow her at @Janice_Hardy for writing links.

Printed in Great Britain
by Amazon

The Fortune Teller's Factotum

Nick Sweeney

Hear Our Voice LLC

Part 2 Chapter 8 was published under the title A Man with a Lot of Explaining to
Do in Commuter Lit magazine, November 2020.

To Jacqueline, who was with this book from the beginning

Part 1: Ashley

Lights from cop cars strobed the vitrines of the St Maz mall, and the backed-up traffic in lots and on ramps of the multi-story looked like little toy cars. One young woman was glad not to be trapped in one but knew if she wanted to get home she could not just stand on the road.

Ashley Hyde heard the word *explosion* hissed urgently into phones. She smelled fire and oil – what, and rubber? Maybe, but dust for sure, and under the surface a hint of something sweet but hideous. Ten minutes before in the depths of the St Maz College ladies' restroom, she had sensed rather than heard a crump of released air – nothing to do with restroom business.

"Explosion." A kid materialized to utter the word – well, a young man Ashley had seen around at college. He rode the bus too, she thought. "Hey yeah – sure *thing*." He sounded agitated, as if she'd disputed it. "I *knew*."

Ashley noted that he could have passed for a twelve-year-old. She said, "I guess you always know an explosion, right?"

"Totally." Out with his phone to snap the stalled and frustrated shoppers of St Maz, the lights – that traffic. "Terrorists."

"Seriously?" Terror, in St Maz? Ashley had often wanted to blow the place up. "Could be, huh?"

"Oh, *hey* yeah. A foregone sure thing."

Ashley never worried about terrorists. About walking past a careless moment in a meth lab? Sure. Unlikely though, in gleaming, fake St Maz. Getting through her pre-med science classes to empower her to clear the hell out of town and claim the place Columbia had grudgingly allotted her – now *that* was a worry. When the dust settled on her grades and on her footprints and she was living a real life in a real place among real people who didn't pose questions whose answers they already knew, *then* she'd worry about stray explosions.

"You got a car?" the kid asked.

There was that very vexing thing in her mind. Ashley could have said, "A guy wrecked my car to shake me down for the insurance." She'd have relived greedy eyes on her, and others, flashing unhelpful pity. "And my well-meaning parent and his plain old mean partner think it's... *appropriate* for me to ride the bus meanwhile because I crashed a car the month before... another car – a *different* car... and that time kind of *was* my fault... It's complicated." The temptation to continue, "You see me on the bus, little boy – so *you* tell *me* if I have a car, huh?" Maybe she'd got it wrong though, and this wasn't that kid from her college who caught the bus, was some other kid, out where explosions happen and scared, summoning up nerve and verve to talk to young women who towered over him. She just said, "No."

"Hey, wouldn't do you no good, anyhow." *This* kid gestured at the cars, part of the motionless background, the discontent at the stasis discernible in the voices and the occasional rumble of a vehicle in a low gear. "So, like, where do you live?"

"Falkender." Ashley conjured up her town's windows and doors, eyes and ears, pointed fingers and pointless questions.

"Cool." The kid made an impressed face he dropped almost at once. "Wait – what?" He nodded toward a vehicle lumbering onto the sidewalk. It crawled in their direction. He snorted out a laugh. "Like to see how far *he* thinks he's going to get."

A deep gray Lexus SUV boss car with blacked-out windows; its lights flashed. People peered, but Ashley knew those lights were aimed at her.

"Guy's a psycho." The kid adopted gruffness and guffawed. "Hey, psycho," he called. He raised his phone and trapped that car in its camera. Maybe he picked up some sign from the car's language that made him ask, with a touch of comedy, "Friend of yours?"

People rubbernecked, disapproving, or amused. Some saw it as a valiant move, albeit doomed, and offered sarcastic applause. But with roadblocks ahead and gridlock all around and the smell of an explosion in the air, any diversion would do. People wavered in the hope of fun starting. Their officious faces full-on, a couple of rotund, uniformed security guards kept their distance.

The car's nearside window hummed down to reveal Ashley's neighbor, Martin Ferrie. Compact man in his sixties, eyes a startling blue, teeth unsettlingly white, skin scarred minutely, salt-and-pepper buzz-cut hair an even length all over, like a GI Joe boys' doll. Ex-military, Ashley knew; sometimes when she saw him up close, she wondered whether he'd been blown apart in some skirmish and restored in a lab.

Martin Ferrie said, "Going your way."

"Oh, you are?" Ashley pointed to the still life around them. She opened the passenger door anyhow and got in. "You think so?"

"Say what?" said the kid at Ashley's elbow.

"Psycho?" Martin Ferrie kept the window down. "Was that *psycho* you said?"

"Not at all." The kid looked stung and lost a further year: an indignant child. "And anyhow – what, you can *lip read*, or what?"

"Yeah, I can." Ashley's neighbor checked that the kid had nothing more to say, then hissed the window up. It hid Ashley's lopsided smile from the kid and a tiny wave, fingers next to her ear.

"Friend of yours?"

"No." Ashley felt guilty about the denial, but he *was* just some kid, comic because he was so serious, charming because he was charmless. She'd never see him become a man; she'd be out of there long before that.

"*Psycho.*" Martin Ferrie shook his head.

"Mr. Ferrie, it *is* a bit weird, though? I mean, just where are we *going* from here? The roads are totally closed."

"See what we can do, huh?"

Martin Ferrie walkie-talkied the security guards to facilitate the maneuver of the car into what looked to Ashley like a paneled wall on the side of the mall. It tipped up like a garage door to reveal a ramp into a part of the mall's innards, storing police, fire and security vehicles and equipment. Ashley saw a mystery of tunnels; an amusement park ride from a scary movie.

She said, "Hey, amazing."

The easiest thing in the world, Martin Ferrie conveyed with a gesture that nevertheless appreciated her amazement. They were guided through the tunnels and onto a hoist to a mezzanine and through more humming doors, waved through by more guards.

On the other side, more men in uniform: cops. After a nervous double-take, hands on the butts of their pistols, they waved the car on, not fast or far. Martin Ferrie stopped, leaned out, and addressed a grizzled plain-clothes man. They made disconnected greetings; onetime colleagues, not friends exactly.

"Little accident?" Almost laughed out. The question almost got a laugh in return.

"Sure. Looks like they never *meant* for this to happen. At least not at such an inconvenient moment."

"*Jihadis?*"

"Well." The cop noted Ashley there and said softly, "Not from the look of... what we got left."

The conversation supplied answers to questions Ashley might have asked. She gazed out: a diorama of smashed vitrines and displays concertinaed, goods on the sidewalk, paper all over, and vehicles that looked as if they had simply been parked wrong rather than scattered with violence. It converged on the wreck of a big blue car.

Ashley's semi-idle look was transformed into a shock of recognition. Something fluttered in her chest, paused, and pumped to life again as a deep breath. Did the car belong to a friend? Impossible. She had no friends. This had to be her imagination: it was a parody of the Ford that had written off her second car, her gleaming but boring tin can Nissan. She was wondering how to ask who had been in the Ford – a combination of three tattooed losers in their thirties, maybe? And had it been registered to one Harold Shester, voluntary baldhead in a sweatshirt, Bermuda shorts, and beat-up training shoes that looked like pigs' faces? He had rustled up witnesses to say that Ashley ignored a stoplight and appeared, daydreaming, in front of him just in time for the impact that crumpled her front passenger side. Lucky she had no friends, then, huh? And lucky too that she had just dropped a co-worker home, what with the passenger door, seat, wheel arch, window, and glove box reduced to airbag and junk, leaving her almost comically unhurt. One whisper about Ashley Hyde in Falkender was that she was a survivor, but her cars weren't.

Even her spectacular two crashes had never reduced a car to the condition of the blue Ford: bent chassis, ballooned-out remains of a trunk, the skeleton of an engine framed by scraps of hood. There was a smell of burned paint and oil and, no denying it, smoked meat.

"If it's not *jihadis*," Martin Ferrie said, "you've got to put that out there quick."

"I'll leave that to the PR people." The cop's humorous tone didn't hide his annoyance at the superfluous advice. "We ran the plate. Not a Muslim name but, you know, all kinds of people are Muslims these days."

"Sure. But–I mean–hey, you found a *plate* out of that?"

"Guy name of Harry Shester. Ring a bell?"

Martin Ferrie had lost interest. He shook his head.

Had Ashley misheard? She looked from one man to the other.

"Some felony record, but nothing like this."

"Listen." Martin Ferrie reached a hand out. The men shook, spoke over each other for a second. "I appreciate the exit here. You take care."

To Ashley: "Blowing up the *mall*, huh?"

Still stunned at the revelation of the driver's name, she said only, "Jesus."

Her neighbor made a *go-figure* gesture. Signaled through barriers, he steered past the outrage. Ashley surveyed the stuff from the stores that had been blown out of shattered windows: fancy notebooks, greeting cards, pastel napkins, envelopes, shiny or folksy gift wrap, wedding confetti making like snow, plus hundreds of pages of the local newspapers.

Her eyes were drawn to a billboard and the giant features of a woman. In fact, it was the TV face of Janet Snyder, Ashley's stepmother, underlined by the legend *Morning Without Maxine: Can You Bear It?*

A link of sausages swinging gently from the light at the top of the billboard had to be the only non-paper article dislodged by the explosion. But there was no butcher store in the mall – all that stinky flesh and brown blood in the St Maz mall? Definitely not. The sight had almost escaped her gaze when she realized Harold Shester's entrails were hanging from a billboard light so then... it followed that his corner would no longer be defended by his car insurer and... she'd have no case to answer anymore. Jests from her dad and jibes from her stepmother would still come but would be easier to deflect. As

Martin Ferrie accelerated onto the highway, Ashley sank into her seat, unsure of what to make of this end to her college day.

2

Martin Ferrie lived diagonally opposite Ashley, his bungalow taking up a street corner. A man out on his front lot much of the time, visible, maintaining its foliage. Or on his porch when the sun was gentle on that side, or in refuge from it when it flooded his back yard.

Ashley spied him motionless at his windows sometimes. Next time she looked? Gone, and she'd wonder if she'd imagined him. She sometimes heard the whine of his garage door in the middle of the night and noted him in motion, incoming or outgoing. Ashley passed a lot of her nights with only the slightest hold on sleep, alive to the sounds of the dark and the changes in the light. She wondered if Martin Ferrie was an insomniac too.

Out of St Maz the evening of the explosion, Martin Ferrie muttered something about the approach through Firemont being snarled up. Ashley was glad; Firemont and its housing projects depressed her. But dirty old Barnton was not much better, nor Aliceville, grim despite the fancy name. No escape from her childhood feeling that the five towns held mischievous spirits that let her travel only so far up those roads between them till they compelled her to travel back down them again.

A stoplight in Aliceville and Ashley looking at the site of the crash engineered by Harold Shester. She nearly said this to her neighbor but instead asked, "Did you see that back there—on the billboard?"

"Sure." Wise eyes, she thought, noting and remembering everything. "*Morning with Maxine*." Martin Ferrie gave Ashley a sideways glance and confessed, "I don't catch the show so much."

Ashley's turn for a sideways glance. Could he seriously have missed the exploded man's livid, dripping entrails? She said neutrally, "Morning *Without* Maxine."

"She's done with the show?"

"*I* wish." Ashley almost curbed her impatience. "She's going on vacation. But listen though, Mr. Ferrie?"

"What?"

"What happened back there?"

"Apart from the obvious?"

She said, "Well... yeah?" Pictured Harold Shester after he totaled her car five weeks before, living, breathing, seething, finger in her face, eyes darting, cop car lights in them. A confusion of rubberneckers and people talking at her. On the periphery of her vision, the agitated baldhead's injured friend sprawled in the road holding his own bald head and groaning. Finally, a minion working for her dad prised her away from her second car crash in a month and drove her to the hospital in Barnton for a health check and an embarrassment no doctor could cure.

"Some crazy thing." Martin Ferrie sounded unsurprised. Served in the Gulf, Ashley recalled. Central America, too, she had the idea. Vietnam, for sure. He had surely seen crazier things. "I don't know. Some bad hat, up to some crazy business."

Ashley was on the point of signaling her connection to Harold Shester. Then she wanted it to herself for a little longer, the marvel and wonder and, if she was honest, something else. The benefit? It was deep in her mind still, not quite visible though she knew it was there.

A moment of distraction drew her attention to something on her hand: three tiny pieces of pastel. Plastic confetti? The question begged to be asked, but she settled for an impatient noise. Because the world really needed more plastic crap and stupid weddings. Debris from the explosion would be in the air for weeks, she guessed. An emphatic flick got rid of a piece. Sweat kept the others clinging to her hand. She wiped them onto her other hand, tutted, and drew a note of non-verbal sympathy from Martin Ferrie, who reached in the glove box and passed her a Kleenex.

"You don't have your car yet." Martin Ferrie knew she had no car. Comment with a barb: *your folks are loaded, and you don't have a car.*

With no question, Ashley chose no response. Who wrote off two cars in the space of a month? Only Ashley Hyde. She understood why her dad was wary of getting her another. And as her stepmom kept pointing out, it *kind of* didn't matter whose fault it was. She was *kind of* right. And also, *kind of* a bitch. Understanding didn't ease the sting. In that scenario, Harold Shester now being mostly vapor was *kind of* irrelevant.

And anyhow something in Ashley had prompted her to rise to the challenge of completing her college year without a car. Ruled by bus schedules, she liked what it did for her duty to time, and an hour stalled in traffic was more profitably spent in bus-seat studying rather than in stop-start gas and brake control.

"Dark nights." Martin Ferrie tossed his head toward trees and fields, the broken structures and abandoned vehicles that blended into them and barbwire fences that divided them, the pylons that punctuated them. "Dark places. You *need* your car." He almost whispered, "America, contrary to what we want to hear, is a bad place in the dark."

"Sure." Ashley didn't point out the summer evening surrounding them.

The five towns edged toward one another without merging. They were separated by woodland whose green had turned black and bisected by gray rivers and yellowed clearings frosted with debris. There were vast fields where crows killed time alongside cows, all sensing the rumor of a big cat, a descendant of a zoo escaper, savaging livestock and pets and eating children, burying the bones. The fields were interrupted by industrial leftovers, a hospital closed down by diseases, and ruinous government buildings whose purpose had never been clear. The required complement of gas stations and truckers' stops, auto mechanics and used car lots, strip malls and lone clapboard stores added color and clamor. There were modern factory sites too, leisure centers, and movie complexes. A ridiculous living history farm museum had been knocked up on the fields of a torn-up lunar park, though it was as dead as anything around it. Ashley, with her part-time job there, knew that particularly well.

The landscape hid its stories of the men who rose out of it to snatch the inattentive, the curious, the drunk, the carefree, the careless and the carless. The amused candor on those men's faces hid the power to draw you into the darkness and bury you in it. They'd reduce you to a grainy photo on the side of a milk carton or a re-enactment in a crime show for spooking viewers but also entertaining them. They'd footnote you to a scrawl on a hand-done poster rotting on a tree, the word *missing* the only prominent part of it and yet the only part nobody needed to read. How come the carton-printers and poster-distributors and documentary-makers didn't know that the disappeared were gone for good? They were out in the toxic woods Ashley glimpsed from Martin Ferrie's car, tendrils and tree roots fixing their bones in place forever.

That image was burned into a shelf in Ashley's head. It took form in the real world in the basement of the Hyde house: a thousand *missing* posters, give or take. And on them, to accompany that powerful and yet impotent word? The face of Ashley's mom Sally Hyde. She vanished when Ashley was nine. Ashley wondered every day about her, to no purpose other than a fear that one day she might stop wondering. Then it'd be like Sally Hyde had disappeared twice over.

"Want a loan of a car?" A genuine offer from Martin Ferrie. Not for the first time. Could she accept it? Sure, but she didn't need a fortune teller to predict a world of trouble from that at home.

"Loan me a chauffeur, too?" Ashley sort of laughed. She got a sort of laugh in return, though something in the raising of Martin Ferrie's brow and downturned smile told her that her request was under consideration.

Sally Hyde's first-born: bone tired, glad she wasn't on the bus nor stranded in a mall waiting for cops to do their endless thing. The sounds and smells of the evening, its lights and sights, the echoes of words like *explosion* and *terrorism*, fell away. She slumped almost contentedly, the dying but eternal brightness of the sunlight sweeping in when the angle allowed it to illuminate a face that wore something like a smile, startling her when she saw it in the wing mirror.

3

The calm face Ashley saw in Martin Ferrie's wing mirror was fantasy. Her actual face grimaced from many shiny surfaces: eyes creased, nostrils distended, teeth bared, braced to stop a wail tearing out.

She was long-limbed, with just a hint of curves. Her hair was collar-length in an indefinite shade of brown. Her head was slightly larger than perfect proportion allowed. Had she ever needed to describe herself–to a blind person, for example–she thought of that troubled face first.

She wanted her old face back. Any other was a mask to help her through the complicated days of her life at age twenty, in which all eyes in Falkender swiveled when she passed. The gazes lingered long enough to let her know their owners were onto her spectacular way with cars, with a resumé of Martin Ferrie's implied critique. *Your folks may be millionaires*, the eyes said, *but you still take the bus along with the poor fat crazy people.*

The other hand they played? A reminder that she had been dumped out of the only romance of her adult life by local heart-throb Michael Stambolisky.

Ashley had toughed out jealousy as a kid. Adults had always been behind it; kids didn't care if you came from a cheesy TV dynasty.

The week they hit sixteen a day apart, Ashley's best friend Chloe Gustavson said, "We're young and good looking–oh *yeah*. And smart." Chloe was summing up the reasons for the hating. Were those attributes true? Of Chloe, sure. Ashley awarded herself... seven out of ten for looks. And only she knew that she'd studied her nut off to convince the world that she was smart. Her worrying herself super-thin over her grades had been glossed over in a *laissez-faire* attitude toward teen-girl anorexia.

Chloe glossed over *rich*, but they were by any standards. She forgot too to cite the relationships abandoned noisily when Ashley's TV producer dad Adam Hyde got together with Janet Snyder, eighties pop girl and presenter of a tragically bad breakfast show.

"So, what's not to hate?" Chloe struck a note of bravado. "Do we *need* them? We got each other."

True, back then. They hung onto the illusion of remaining close after school, but the chemistry changed. It was in the lingering spirit of meet-my-bestie that Ashley introduced Chloe to Michael Stambolisky at a mansion party near Elizabethtown. An unremarkable moment of formality, one would think, but Ashley had at once felt like an outsider, dazzled by the beam crossing from Michael's face to Chloe's and back.

The first inkling Ashley got that they were not staying over at the party was Michael shoving her coat and bag at her. She was used to his habit of making last-minute changes to arrangements set in stone. Whatever the reason, they were leaving in Ashley's little Peugeot.

And this paragon? Heir to a family fortune courtesy of the importation of food from the east of Europe, nostalgic stodge for American Slavs. Michael Stambolisky had retro movie star looks, okay, and was a convincing talker of the talk, true, plus sported the *mien* of a man going places. She had idly watched him speed round the five towns in his Porsche until one day it screeched to a stop near her. For four months Ashley had spent every spare moment, plus moments she didn't have to spare, with a man with endless time and money who didn't understand people with schedules and commitments. The confident look on his face? That of a player. He dared everybody to knock that look off his face. It hit Ashley that even she was included in the sweep of his challenging gaze, despite the distracted assurances of his love. Or, at least, his... *respect* for her.

By the night of that party, Ashley realized that things with Michael had been skewed for some time. In her world politeness was lip-service and perfunctory, okay, but still present. She noticed that Michael never said *please* or *thank you* when out dining, shopping–wherever–and that when she said them, he looked at her as if she'd farted. At a fancy Philly restaurant one time, a waiter helped Michael out of his overcoat, took it and his wet umbrella in one hand, and with the other pulled a chair out for him, told him welcome, and handed him a menu. Sure, the waiter was pushing his agenda a little, but it was *absurd* that Michael didn't acknowledge *any* of these attentions. Generous with money in general, he stiffed waiters or cab drivers on a tip if they were anything other than obsequious. And in Baltimore one time Michael told a panhandler to eat his dog if he was hungry. *What?*

Michael Stambolisky held strong opinions about the TV shows Ashley's dad worked on. Sure: a mess of ugly lady makeovers, patronizing chefs, performing pets, unhelpful self-help books and diets that didn't work on fat people, they were contemptible. It was cool for Michael to say so once or twice, but then he should have put a sock in it. Ashley did not diss Michael's dad for buying pickled food cheap in Europe and selling it dear in the US. Nor for dressing, talking, and swearing like a Miami gangster in a seventies movie.

Just before that mansion party, an intimation of the final straw had arisen when Michael asked Ashley to check a text alert on his phone–he was shaving, and they were awaiting confirmation of a dinner reservation. She did so but also spotted a text from one of his friends reading *Caution: congealed entrance*. There had been something evasive in Michael's laughter when she read it out. Ashley quizzed him at pain-in-the-butt length. She learned that Michael's friends texted the three words to one another after they'd hit home with some girl–some foolish girl, Ashley guessed, some gullible girl, some girl, she saw, just like her. She had been perturbed by his frat boy friends for a while, groomed and good-looking, good at *every*thing but devoid of manners and heart. "I won't ask the question that's occurring to me," she told Michael. Unnecessary; the look on his face said that she needed to lighten up and get over the fact that he'd sent his friends the same three words the night she let him take her all the way.

Ashley would always feel that a part of her had been lost to stupidity in those few months. Michael Stambolisky dazzled a light in her face and disorientated her. Did he get her to forget Columbia? Almost, and with it the refuge she'd found in science, its adventures that blocked out the chaos around her.

After the party, she and Michael reached Falkender in silence. Ashley hunched at the wheel, brooding on that smile between bestie and boyfriend. She opened her window and breathed in the nip of a late frost. On an icy corner on the edge of Falkender she lost control of the steering and then the brakes, bounced the car off three parked vehicles then into a mailbox on a concrete post. The fissure in the car's front was deep enough to hold it on an axis as the back wheels worked a semi-circle into a lawn.

The cars were repaired and pampered. Not hers–beyond redemption. The sidewalk was cleaned of rubber streaks, the mailbox replaced, and the lawn landscaped. Gardeners, builders, and mechanics gathered to give that corner the makeover of its life. The only people not involved in the incident were cops.

Nearly home the evening of the St Maz explosion, Ashley's newfound face changed when she spied that corner. That mailbox gleamed and put all the others to shame.

So Ashley lost Michael Stambolisky and Chloe Gustavson, a passing obsession, and the bond of a childhood–and a car, her first–but at least she was still on course for Columbia, thanks to her college tutor Jessica Ensley. The college induction meeting: Mrs. Ensley remembered Ashley from a stint as a trainee teacher at Firemont Junior School. The provenance offered? "You were the kid who read." True. Ashley had been big on reading. About to feel touched at being remembered, Ashley realized it was a warning: the Jessicator, as Mrs. Ensley was sometimes called, would remember everything.

Ashley's course featured an eye-watering workload. Her interlude with Michael led Mrs. Ensley to telegraph both sympathy and censure to wonder: what happened to the scholarly young woman who started fall semester all bright-eyed? She knew of Ashley's romance, of course, but what else? All the books Ashley had not read, the classes she'd cut, obvious to the Jessicator's all-seeing eye. She knew too about Ashley's unceremonious dumping. Ashley abandoned her lame lies about being unable to settle and indulged in some shame-faced grade-groping. The promise she made led her to three hours of homework a night. Her course seemed as if it had been written in a foreign language. She mastered it each night only to discover that it had changed by the time she took her place in class next day, her peers looking at her as if she were an intruder.

"You're studying hard?" Martin Ferrie was reading her mind, was he? "I don't see you around so much."

"Sure *thing* I'm studying hard."

Nosy old Martin Ferrie knew she didn't go anyplace in Falkender anymore. The work she needed to do that very evening made her mood drop a click south. Men exploded, intestines ended up on billboards, insurance claims were destined to whiz back and forth between dull bureaucrats, but no matter what happened Ashley Hyde would be reading, writing aides-memoires and typing up prompts, building the trail in her head that would lead her to the Ivy League. She gave Martin Ferrie a snappy version of this.

He stopped in front of her house. Their voices were loud in the street as she thanked him for the ride. The evening was bright after the gloom from the SUV's tinted windows and felt warm after the car's air con. Ashley, aware of curtains twitched and blinds lifted, eyes on her back, kept her head down as she walked up her path.

4

Ashley's dad wasn't home. She could always tell. Her stepmom Janet Snyder's presence or absence was rarely apparent, as she spent most of her time at home up the stairs in
a suite of rooms out of bounds to Ashley and her sister.

And Ashley's mom was not home. Sally Hyde would never
be home. Ashley rarely failed to remember that whenever she
entered the house, stood in the hallway and heard its sounds
and silences.

TV, squawking in the lounge. Ashley's sister Donna lay on
her back on the five-yard-long sofa, phone at her ear. She let
out a laugh. Nothing girlish in it, and it could have come from
some uncouth boy.

It made Ashley think for a moment of the young man at the
St Maz mall.

Donna Hyde grew up as one of those kids whose head
bobbed from side-to-side as she walked, and whose heels
clashed sometimes and felled her. She'd be shocked, but only a
little, picking herself up and carrying on. Her smile hid secrets,
and she often looked as if she were addressing a room full
of imaginary friends; that was exactly what she was doing.
Nobody noticed Donna in transition to her sixteenth year,
with a kind of cool that was a notch too detached, slipping
only occasionally to reveal the ungainly child she'd grown out
of.

Ashley stared, perplexed. No getting away from it but, while
Ashley was hanging on with fingertips to Michael Stam-

bolisky's fast-moving late-night world of parties and gigs and bars, cars, booze, drugs... sometimes... Donna had been left to the mercies of her own devices. It seemed to Ashley that they had not done her much good. Their dad's hot-and-cold approach to child guidance had suited Ashley so well that she never thought of its drawbacks; either liberal to the point of careless, or unsustainably Draconian. By the age of eleven Ashley had developed an instinct about exactly what she could get away with. She'd also developed enough self-discipline to make accurate judgments of the consequences. Donna never could. When Ashley took notice of her again, Donna owned a steely-eyed gaze and an unhealthy pallor, limbs too thin to be elegant, lifeless hair, and smiles studied and calculating. She looked to Ashley like one of the underage junkies she'd spied from Michael's car one time when they got lost in Philadelphia's West Kensington area. Ashley had no clue how she could restore her sister to be the kid she'd known.

Ashley could bid pre-adolescent Donna, "Make me giggle," which got Donna doing the voices of actors from the old movies their dad watched, the names lost to them. They replayed dialogues in the most exaggerated way they could. They had no clue why that was funny, just knew it was. What else? Other comic faces and voices and mysterious rituals she and Donna mastered or failed to master, but gloriously. And Donna's laughter, sparkly, ringing. She missed it.

She listened and worked out who Donna was talking to. She moved and blocked the light from her sister's face. Donna looked up and caught Ashley's eye. Not a beat of her conversation was missed.

Ashley made a hesitant wave and turned back to the hallway. She stepped into the library, opened her bag and dumped her books onto the table. Ashley caught her laptop before it hit the surface. She went upstairs to her bathroom and washed her face and hands.

No smile for the mirror. There would be no... diluting her luck by grinning like some fool. She got it straight in her head again: Harold Shester's insurance company would not be pursuing its bogus claim for compensation on behalf of his blue guts, and at the moment only she knew that. Ashley's dad's insurance agent, Mr. Carr–the coincidence in the name was pure nails-down-a-blackboard to Ashley–could now do whatever such men did, and restore what was left of her good name.

Back downstairs Donna, free of her phone, said, "Hey, Shannon told me there was, like, an explosion in Smaz?" She wielded the remote in search of news channels.

"There was, too." Ashley's voice was upbeat, her expression... composed. Inside her face, she ground her teeth. Shannon Seeley was the bad news that turned up when you took your eye off your sister and kept it on some guy who did not deserve you. Shannon, with her sidekick James Dufrayne, was a top *dawg* at Falkender High. Clever, maybe–well, no, for *sure*: they were both equipped with a default intelligence that would take them a long way. They were also equipped with parents who paid for school resources, built scout huts, hired stadiums for local sports days, gave fat checks to charities and threw Fourth of July parties for entire streets. Ashley suspected a determination by Shannon and James to lead Donna into dark places where they would abandon her. They made her fear for Donna's scrawny body and shrinking soul.

"Really?" Donna flicked around the news. "I thought maybe she was lying."

When Donna made the classic no-no move with vampires and invited them into the house, James and Shannon conducted conversations with Ashley in earshot, the way small children and people in sitcoms did, clever but not clever. *Hey, they saw that guy around town–what was his *name*, the *guy*, the one with the red *Porsche*, Funny-Foreign-Name guy–yeah, that was him. And who was that he was *with*? Did Ashley rise to the bait? Tempting. They smirked and avoided eye contact. And Donna? Looking from one to the other of them, gauche enough to expect a punchline.

Chloe Gustavson was welcome to the passenger seat of Michael's Porsche and its wonky upholstery, a spring out of line by a very annoying quarter inch. And if it stabbed her back the way she had stabbed Ashley's? Fitting. She could also have the smell–oily, stale coconut?–that came through its dash after an hour's driving. Chloe would inherit the lechy looks from Michael's dad and his cronies and the tedious high fives and bogus dude talk from Michael's friends. And maybe she would care for the early morning stinky-breath sex Michael liked so much. Chloe could have it all. Michael was welcome to his blonde beauty of a prize.

"I guess Shannon wouldn't lie to you."

Donna didn't pick up on Ashley's tone.

"Well." Ashley conjured the scene in St Maz again, heard those repeated words, saw the faces, strobed, worried. "There really was an explosion."

"At the mall?"

A line of anxiety in Donna's expression. She was thinking of the clothes and accessories and fancy goods stores, the food courts, pink beauty parlors. And *not* thinking of her sister out of the college behind the mall, maimed by blast and fire or vaporized. Did Ashley care about that? Of course, but she said only, "Yeah."

"Weird." Donna surfed channels and stopped on the report. That squad car light show: cameras cut between the wreckage of the car, the broken windows, and the scattering of paper goods. A voice-over stated the obvious. Storekeepers were interviewed, all saying a variation of the words *oh my* good*ness*. The dead man, as yet unidentified, was not a terrorist, viewers were assured.

"Wait–what? He blew himself up by *accident*?" Donna said. "How do you even *do* that?"

Not a rhetorical question, not from Donna. Ashley flopped on the other end of the sofa, kicked off her shoes and brought her legs up. Two sisters: head-to-head, not quite touching, as they had lain the day their dad bought that ridiculously lengthy sofa and aimed their voices at the ceiling.

Ashley said, "Easiest thing in the world."

"What is?"

"Blow yourself up."

"*Seriously*?"

Some margin for error with chemicals, but only up to a point. Stupid people passed it–careless people too, arrogant people, and it made no difference most of the time. Except when they were dealing with explosives. Ashley said, "Explosives are volatile."

Donna tensed as she considered the word–excited by it, Ashley could tell–and said, "What does that even *mean*?"

"It means they're not stable. They go *boom* if you don't look after them properly."

"An exploding man." Donna laughed.

Donna sometimes found laughter on the edge of cruelty. That worried Ashley a little. Why would you laugh at an exploding man? But somehow, the way Donna said the words did indeed prompt a laugh. She and her sister communicated joyfully in this way for a minute. Ashley said, "All men explode if you don't look after them properly," and they giggled again.

A presence in the room: wondering at the noise, the cat put her nose around the kitchen door. A flash of her unknowable eyes for Ashley alone. She interpreted Ashley's stare as mild hostility. Correctly. She was a sleek black beast that Janet recruited to her show to raise the profile of animal shelters. A double-Z-list celebrity panel came up with six ridiculous names for her and trusted the viewers with the final decision–daytime TV viewers, trusted. Ashley sometimes marveled at the few words. Their choice? *Araby*. Nobody knew what that meant. One of Janet's minions found out that it was a poetic name for Arabia. That was already a poetic name for those ugly Middle-Eastern states full of oil and grit and camels. Easy on the ear, a popular choice, save for those who made the odd call to the TV station like how our brave boys were fighting those murderous *tersts* over there, and how come they didn't give the cat a good old American name? Ashley pictured them in darkened, camouflage-netted rooms: survivalists, eyes glued to daytime TV as they cleaned their carbines and planned for the apocalypse. Araby raised her nose, and, briefly, her tail, and stared back at Ashley. She lost interest and turned toward the TV. Maybe she knew the people beyond the glow in its rectangle loved her.

Ashley was not ready to let Donna in on what she knew of the exploding man. She and Donna talked disconnectedly, one barely listening to what the other was saying until a word triggered a verbal double-take. An exploding man made little difference to the discussions of sisters on the verge of adulthood–did Ashley know how long it took to get an appointment with a school counselor now to get, like, a morning out of school for even a proper reason? "Like what?" Ashley wondered, remembering that Donna was on some truancy report system. Donna was also in trouble for sassing a visiting speaker with the words, "You have some of my full attention," a thing Ashley had heard Shannon Seeley say. "Oh, a *thing*," Donna waved it away. "He just exploded, though? Wow."

Yeah. A man had left nothing behind him but the blue wreckage of his car and his blue-tinged intestines, and it was remarkable–really, it was–but Ashley still didn't want to talk about it. She let Donna prattle about something involving one of the princesses from school and a shopping trip to New York, a moment's distraction ending in a lost suitcase full of shoes worth forty grand, oh and that reminded Donna: she couldn't find her sunglasses, spent, like, an *hour* looking for them... well, ten minutes anyhow, and their dad was going to kill her because they were a hundred and ninety dollars and the second pair she'd lost in, like, six months. And it was sunny out now and she *needed* them. Ashley was pricked by suspicion: was Donna referring to the loss of Ashley's two cars? But Donna didn't *do* oblique.

So, did Ashley know their dad and Janet had extended the European trip they were going to take? "How long by?" Ashley wondered. Donna didn't know: they added an extra city or two, in... Austria? Ashley teased her sister with the question, "Berlin?" Could be, Donna thought.

Their dad once promised Ashley they would do an extensive tour of Europe one day; he pronounced the names of all those cities like he was tasting them, pointed to them in atlases, and, later, on CD-ROMs. Those spiky names, the... *gravitas* in them, intrigued Ashley. The trip of their lives, Adam Hyde promised. But that job of his never afforded him the time–only the money. And sure, okay, he took his girls to Disneyland, right, and, yes; they had wanted to go, all right, so could not complain. Hollywood too, the west coast, summers by beaches with D-listers' brats from a bewildering number of liaisons. Bar Harbour as well, Martha's Vineyard, once, and Colorado, skiing with more TV and movie brats and people taking to the slopes with the bright clothes of the pastime and the bright eyes and shrill voices of prehab and rehab. But not to Europe, to all that history, all those people still living where civilization rose and burned itself down to ruins and rose again. No, he was wasting the Grand European Tour on Janet. Was Ashley as angry as she seemed to be? No: it was pretense. She no longer cared. She wanted her dad to be happy. If that was from the money, the cars, the gadgets, and from dropping the names of the worthless people he collected from his working life, then that was fine. "So now it's like... three *weeks* they'll be away," the sisters agreed, seemingly unbothered by the absence of the parent and his paramour.

So anyhow, did Ashley know there was a fortune teller in Barnton? A dramatic change of subject. Ashley wondered how it had arisen. Donna asked, "What do they do?"

"Eh?" The question was basic, even for Donna–they had seen plenty of fortune tellers time and again in those old movies, after all. "Well, they... tell you what'll happen in the future."

"Really? How, though?"

"I don't know."

The fortune teller was not in Barnton. She was in Aliceville. Francie, a girl with whom Ashley worked, had talked about the fortune teller, prompted by the sight of an article in a local rag headed *Madame Tudora Predicted Wedding Bells for Me*. This quoted a dim, shapely heiress to a porcelain fortune–a bathroom stuff empire stretching invisibly through pipes under the land. Francie claimed that Madame T was spookily accurate though, no–in true slacker style–she hadn't *actually* gone herself. She knew somebody who knew somebody who did, though. Ashley didn't continue the discussion by telling Francie she had already called the fortune teller and, in the depths of her dumped-days doldrums, made an appointment. A few weeks on, she had forgotten it. She only felt slightly ashamed as she listened to Donna describe a conversation with girls at school almost identical to the one with Francie. She told Donna, "I guess they make stuff up."

For a short time, Ashley had wondered if the mysterious madame would have been able to tell her when her misery would end. Really, she could have told any fortune teller how that would only happen when she quit Falkender for Columbia in the fall and escaped into the life she saw in the crystal ball that glowed in her skull, and, sometimes, shone its light out through her eyes.

5

Ashley's stepmom Janet Snyder had once screeched out forgettable eighties pop-girl anthems. She sported an exaggerated punk hairdo, wore the same high-fashion-urchin rags and clumpy boots as Madonna but a month later, and made her Detroit accent into showbiz parody. Her alter-ego Maxine Wasserman was no upgrade, just an older version of the same annoying thing: the same baby face, squinty eyes and tiny mouth that once graced the covers of record albums and magazines. Her show Morning With Maxine went out to all the major towns in the state. Janet was supposed to have two distinct personalities, surely? To nobody's good, Ashley thought, Janet had been subsumed into Maxine, a public woman even in her own home.

Janet came into Ashley's and Donna's lives when they were at so-called difficult ages. Both girls had made it clear that Janet would not be their mother. When the penny dropped, it signaled that Janet was too self-absorbed to care.

On the evening of the St Maz explosion, the sisters didn't hear Janet pad down the stairs. She appeared abruptly before them, barefoot, a phone in each hand. Her strawy hair was messily tied with a scarf. She was in black velour, a tracksuit-cum-nightwear affair, children's clothing for adults, Ashley thought, part of a daily metamorphosis: Janet turning into one of her viewers, pajama-clad gazers from the other side of the screen. She looked at neither Ashley nor Donna, but offered a kind of soldierly greeting as a half-constructed salute, not quite a wave. Awkward? Slightly, as if they were guests in her house. In some ways, that was true.

"There was an explosion in Smaz," Ashley said. Donna joined in with the entire story, embodied in an utterance about the exploding man. Except, Ashley thought, in a mixture of awe and girlish glee, it was *not* the whole story.

"I *know* it." Janet sounded hyped. "Show'll be full of it tomorrow."

No. A voice was loud in Ashley's head. *You don't* know *it. You've just* heard *of it. It's* me *who* knows *it.* At least it was something for Janet to *put* on her stupid show; they never went *out* anyplace, but daytime TV viewers had to be made aware of the dangers out there. The voice entertained Ashley by turning into a catcall.

It was unheard by the cat. Her mistress's voice drew Araby out of the kitchen; leisurely padded paces to Janet. She disguised herself in Janet's plush pants legs.

Noise and movement outside, a cab, Adam Hyde. Ashley pictured his Chrysler PT sitting darkly in the garage. She remembered that he would be away soon. She'd miss him, she realized. She'd track his key down and take a joyride in the Chrysler, she also realized.

"You heard?" Adam Hyde was last home, yet disappointed not to be the one to bring the news fresh. His features had once been Saturnine but were by then sinking and pudgy and, as a result, benign. His graying hair was a little too long. He was in expensive, unimaginative clothes in muted colors.

"Tricky times." He shook his head. "Huh?"

Janet had news hounds on the incident. She waited tongue-on-lip for calls back, eager to give her show a sharper edge than could be supplied by disgruntled storekeepers and spooked shoppers. The hounds howled; Ashley heard Janet railroading her show's counselors into volunteering to stand by with earnest faces, employing her habitual use of the words *excuse me* like a weapon. The crazies who would phone the show to call for all TNT-wielding foreigners to be interned or deported or shot, or all three, would supply light relief as usual, but still had to be catered for with an answer; one was requested, its few trite words much discussed and approved for rehearsal.

Ashley waited for any of her family to remember that she attended St Maz College and finished class around the time of the explosion. Would they? Would they hell. She hovered on the verge of an anger that made her hands unsteady. She would aim a barb at them the next day, say, "Well, none of you even *asked* me." A triumph, she knew already, but, she sensed, a bitter one.

Sally Hyde's maternal instinct would have prompted her to drive to St Maz and plow through the crowds in search of her daughter. Wouldn't it? *Yes.* Ashley looked at Janet, cat clutched to her chest, and at Donna, seemingly taking part in the conversation but intent on the transmission of texts.

Looked at her dad too, still bemoaning the trickiness of the times. She wanted to say to him, "I'm not your kid." She imagined her mom whispering the words into her ear, urging her to say them. "If I was your kid, you'd have come and *rescued* me from the St Maz explosion." Ashley got the sure impression that Sally was saying, "I know my *kid*," into her ear from the ether. "I know my own *kid*." She savored the moment, but soon it was gone, just like Sally Hyde. She had left her features in Ashley's face–not so much in Donna's–and joined what local history scholar Edmond Demonte, Ashley's boss at her part-time job, had dubbed 'the theoretical Americans'. Sally Hyde didn't have the dignity of the dead: no existence outside the pile of posters in the basement. If her mom died in an accident or after a wasting illness, Ashley would have gotten the platitudes offered to other orphans and half-orphans: a *good* woman, *so* missed. The people she was thinking of wore not only their hearts on their sleeves on such occasions; they wore hearts, lungs, spleens, livers and intestines. Sally Hyde was one of those people who had gone out one day into America never to come back. No hymns, no speeches, no chanting ministers, no cars, no caterers, no sad fashion parades in always-fashionable black. Silence had taken the place of them all.

The story was clear: a few days after Ashley's ninth birthday, Sally Hyde drove to Philly on a shopping trip. And yet her car had been sighted parked in Bethesda, and she had been spotted in a diner in Scranton with a woman, though at the same time a guy reported her wandering down a street in Chestnut Mill, while a kid saw her in a phone booth in some other place Ashley could no longer remember. At the same time, it was *not* clear at all. Sally had disappeared into a fog of impressions familiar in missing person cases, out of which no sure-fire truth could be gleaned.

All traces of her had been consigned to a place for putting things nobody wanted but which couldn't be thrown away. No matter what Ashley did nor what news she had, good or bad, a shadow fell over it when she remembered that Sally Hyde would never share it. As if she were standing in the same spot at different times of the day, sometimes the shadow was long and sometimes short, but it was always there.

In the big front room they were talking, but there was nothing to talk about, not really. There would not be unless Ashley intervened. Adam was in and out of the drinks cabinet asserting that you could drink a gin and tonic any time of day once the weather started getting balmy. And did the girls know that was balmy with an 'l' and not an 'r'? Janet rolled her eyes at that, did a kitchen to-and-fro tracking down ingredients for a sandwich, fielding calls, and weaving in and out of the conversation. She eschewed gin for a tumbler of white wine. Donna looked up from her phone occasionally to nod or shake her head to make it look as if she were taking part.

Ashley watched as Janet took calls and gulps of wine and kept track of various tasks by snapping out interrogatives. Adam waved an empty glass by way of apology for interrupting the conversation, such as it was, to get a refill. On his way, he put a hand on the back of Janet's neck and squeezed it gently.

Ashley would like to have done that, only... not so gently.

Ashley never forgot that when she came into their lives, Janet Snyder had prevailed upon Adam to get rid of all traces of Sally-*healthier* for them all, she argued. Scorched earth: everything gone-photos, letters, postcards, diaries, clothes, and other keepsakes. At nine years old, Ashley was too young to care about the ephemera of her mom's time on earth, too... *unformed* to protect her mom's memory. That had been her dad's job. He had failed. It had taken years for Ashley to understand why Janet wanted to eradicate the memory of Sally Hyde: it was a bee in Janet's bonnet that became a *project*, Ashley finally realized. Janet got an idea, got teams of people on it for however long it took, then it was done. It was the way showbiz worked. Nobody in Janet's world or her dad's cared about leaving anything behind. Everything was throwaway, geared toward a show on the day, then forgotten in the rush to do the next day's show.

Sally Hyde's existence had been reduced to the single photo of her that had survived; that was the one on the poster that described her in large, black letters as *missing*. Ashley's copy of it was behind glass in a wooden frame over her bed. Donna's had also been over her bed; the frame had gotten broken, so Donna had the drawing pinned to the wall. That act had seemed like vandalism to Ashley. One day the previous December, Ashley had been passing Donna's room and noticed the photo gone. She called her sister's name, got no answer. She was on the verge of upset to think that Donna had thrown the photo out. Ashley forgot sometimes that Donna was five when Sally disappeared and had not formed a bond with her. She reminded herself of this, but it didn't help. What *did* help was her realization that the photo had simply fallen; Donna was too lazy to pull the bed out and look for it. So Ashley had done so. She found the photo. She also found an eighth of weed wrapped in plastic film, three condoms, and eighty-something dollars in a banking coin bag.

Ashley had finally believed Donna's scornful riposte that if she'd been dealing, she'd have made more than eighty-odd lousy dollars. No, Donna had been putting money aside to buy some more weed... and it didn't *matter* who from... and no, she didn't use it *that* often... and *no*, she wasn't using anything else.

"And *any*how." A demonstrative sniff from Donna, with a searching look.

"What?"

"You tell *me*."

Ashley didn't need to tell her; Donna obviously knew about Ashley's occasional use of cocaine during her time with Michael Stambolisky. Her defense would be that she knew what she was doing, of course, but that was a shameful defense. More to the point, it was unusable. She flushed a little.

"But *any*how."

"*What?*"

Who was Ashley–she wasn't Donna's *mom*.

"No." Ashley waved the photo at Donna. "*This* is our mom," she said. "Put it back where it belongs." She left Donna without asking about the condoms. At least they were sensible things to have.

The night of the explosion at the St Maz mall, Ashley had to stop her hands from shaking. Had to stop... *dwelling* on this... *poison*. She threw her voice into a lilt and addressed her dad with the words, "You're going to... Vienna, right?"

Adam said, "Sure *thing*, we're going to Vienna."

"I *told* her that?" Donna, glued to her phone.

She said Berlin, Ashley remembered, but didn't say.

Janet leaned out of her call into the real world to say, "*Don't* talk to me about this trip." Ashley resisted saying something very like, *I'm going to talk to* you *about as little possible, as usual.*

A hiss from the cat. Reading Ashley's mind? The sound elicited Janet's calming hand on the beast's head, fingers between her ears. Adam Hyde acknowledged Janet's comment by shielding his mouth and stage-whispering, "She's *loving* it all, really. Vienna, though, hey?"

Ashley lost track of her dad's mental map. He said they had to go to so-and-so-town because it had the whatsit museum with such-and-such an *object*. But then if you were going there, you might as well take in the town of what's-it-called, which had a little-known but exquisite chapel and a gallery too with so-and-so's greatest work... and restoration of the town hall clock.

"You're going to see a *clock*, Dad?" Ashley cackled. Donna contributed a snigger.

"God." Janet waved from the middle of her call "This *clock*." She managed to make it sound as bad as e-coli.

And the opera house in whereverville? Tiny but to die for, and even had its own ghost? Had Adam mentioned that? Ashley thought so.

She lost interest in towns and museums, even in clocks. She lost interest in Vienna. Right then Ashley Hyde would have settled for going anyplace as long as she was at the wheel of a car. She was going to be vindicated–well, kind of. At any rate, Harold Shester's insurance agent no longer had a client to testify that Ashley had driven recklessly. And her agent, Mr. Carr, would not have to keep making his veiled suggestions that Mr. Shester, all due respect and all, was pulling a scam, being well aware that *his* client came from a wealthy background. Mr. Carr would of course be informed in due course that the claim would not be pursued by Harold Shester's earthly remains. Ha!

"Ha!" Janet startled Ashley with the seeming echo. Janet gave the air a punch. "Got a *name*." She repeated it and wrote it down. The exploding man was going to be *Harry* to the media as well as his questionable baldhead pals in mourning. Janet set the hounds on *Harry's* family, friends and sketchy acquaintances as she wandered into the kitchen and one-handedly manipulated herself another sandwich and half-pint of

Chardonnay. "*Anybody*." Her voice was now the usual evening sandpaper rasp of anybody who talked all day long. "Dangle shekels," she ordered. "Shoppers, strollers, idlers. Wheel them all out."

Adam Hyde was full of his clocks, museums and towns, a tiny Leonardo painting on a palace wall in Poland, a little-known opera by Mozart. He knew the names of Mozart's circle better than he knew the name of Harold Shester, Ashley realized. He believed in leaving the details to the people he paid to deal with such things. Ashley pretended to listen to her dad–he was already a parody of an American overseas–and looked out the window.

6

Across the street: Martin Ferrie at his window. As ever, Ashley found it weird, even though she was doing the same. His *stillness* was odd though, like he'd put a lookalike scarecrow there. Too far to share eye contact, but if she could see him, then he could see her. She waved one time, but he did not stir; she inferred disapproval from the lack of response, as if she'd broken the unrecorded rules of some game.

A wave of something like claustrophobia descended on her, even though the room she stood in was the size of a tennis court. Maybe it wasn't good to keep secrets; maybe she ought to reveal her connection to the exploding man. A lowlife fooling with explosives for who-knew-what reasons, but he was a man just the same. It was suddenly shocking and saddening.

But she had–what?–three hours of college work to get through? Well, she would do two. At least. And the time was racing on.

Her dad was urging her opinion on some... *thing*. She turned and gave some suitable answer.

When she turned back to the window, Martin Ferrie was gone. Across the road, closer, a Japanese car in a shade of green reminiscent of plastic leaves. It belonged to Donna's friend James Dufrayne. Ashley stepped back, out of sight.

A giggle from Donna's phone–a ringtone dedicated to James, or maybe Shannon Seeley. Donna headed for the hallway. Ashley kept up a pretense of listening to her dad but was all ears for Donna. A face occurred to her to put on and hide behind in plain sight: preoccupation with a recollection, the need to make a note. She moved toward the hallway. She did not have to hear much from Donna's side of the conversation to work out that her friends were trying to persuade her out of the house. It was ten minutes to Donna's school-night curfew of nine o'clock. Adam was not amenable to discussing it, since Donna had been in hot water at school all year over her attendance, grades and behavior. James and Shannon knew that.

"They're *all* here," she heard Donna say. "I *can't*." They were forcing her to repeat the same words: rubbing her nose in it. *Friends* didn't do that. She was trying to tough it out but sounded abject. Outside, loud revs; the tease continued.

Ashley strode back to the window. She didn't care if James saw her this time. She dared him to acknowledge her. He revved the engine again.

Donna was unraveling a tale to her dad about urgently needing to go see Daisy Lampleter, who lived a few blocks away, about some... schoolwork–a *thing*, a *project* thing they had to do for next day? "Oh *yeah*?" Adam kept saying in an increasingly comic voice. And how that was Daisy on the phone? And how she needed Donna's help with something... with this *thing*? He *knew* Daisy, right? "Sure thing. I *remember* her," Adam said. That should have alerted Donna that he knew she hadn't hung out with nerdy, studious Daisy for at least a year. Donna said she wouldn't be gone long–like an *hour*, tops? Adam brought the conversation to an end with a burst of low laughter that finally made Donna's escape bid peter out. "You're sweet," he told her.

"Wait–what?" Donna frowned. "I can *go*?"

"Anybody's sweet when they think they're kidding you. It's like her." Adam indicated the cat. "Wails that she's hungry when she's just been fed. *So* sweet."

"I can go?" Donna just about clung to the ghost of a smile. "Or what?"

"Sorry, honey." The humor left Adam's face.

"Dad, listen," Donna said. "I'm not kidding you. I... *need* to go see Daisy."

"You're not going anyplace this time of night." Adam pointed to the clock. "*Daisy* should have called you earlier." Adam moved his shoulders and made a them's-the-rules-and-you-know-it face.

Ashley kept her eye on the car. She was tempted to pull back the drape with a flourish to reveal the scene, but that would have been a *little* too theatrical. She got a sense of Donna's rage from the silence behind her, broken only by Janet doing the occasional *uh-huh* into her phone. James revved again, gently this time. The car moved off.

Ashley turned her back on the window. "Well," she said brightly.

Adam smiled distractedly. Donna scowled at Ashley. She gathered her homework, her phone, a bag, pens.

"*Plans*," Ashley prompted. "*Europe* and all. It'll be a big old... *trip*, huh?"

"A *jaunt*," Adam corrected. "That's totally the word for it. Right, Donna?"

Donna's features were taut. She said, "Whatever."

Ashley was hungry, though too lazy to make food. She was tired. She was not going to make her revelation about the exploding man and her privileged view of his last scene – now *that* was theatrical – so the conversation was over for her. And anyhow she needed to go do some work – an hour then, if it was not to be two.

Donna glared at her. Ashley was used to it. Donna strode toward the hallway. Her dad called after her, "If you're heading up, say goodnight."

"What*ever*." Donna didn't look over her shoulder.

"It's *polite*."

Donna thumped up the stairs.

Adam Hyde turned melancholy eyes toward Ashley. He made a troubled smile and showed a palm. Ashley returned the smile. Silence. Janet was off the phone. She jotted a note, threw her pen down and sat back on the armchair, stretching. Janet was trying to catch Adam's eye, Ashley could see, so it would suit them all if she left. "I got to work awhile," she said. Adam sent her an approving nod, stepped forward and pecked her on the cheek.

She stopped off at the kitchen. She filled the coffee machine's reservoir and pushed in a sachet of decaff. While she waited for it to do its stuff, she scattered a plate with a few items of food that had some passing appeal. In truth she'd gone past hunger.

Amid the debris on the worktop, she caught sight of a dark object that was out of place: Donna's fancy sunglasses. She held them up to the light, admired them for a few seconds. Then she pedalled the garbage can open, chucked the glasses in, and shoved them down the side with the food waste.

7

The good thing about Ashley barely keeping up with college work was that there was no time to get bored with it. She had two months to stick it out. Her fear of failure was behind all she did: a dread that there would be no Ivy League for her. On the contrary, the rusted shades of another fall in Falkender then another year subject to sideways gazers and whisperers.

The morning her parent and stepmom set off for Europe, she was in the basement. She often rose early and worked there because there were no distractions, just her brain and books, a pen and a notebook. She perched on a stool to work on a shelf of wood covering deep boxes of racked and rarely used household tools. Unlike in her study or the library, in the basement she was unaware of what was going on in the rest of the house. It was cool there in the summer and warm in the winter from the hot-water pipes.

Sally Hyde watched her from the rows of posters Ashley fixed on the wall one day when she was twelve. Janet ordered the help, Mrs. Meydel, to take them down. Ashley put them up again, and this time painted layers of clear varnish over all forty-nine of them. A morning's obsessive work. They trapped that portrait of Ashley's mom inside a white frame with that stark word *missing* at the top and under the photo, the details of Sally's last movements and a police contact number. Ashley didn't know what to do with the four hundred or so posters gathering dust on a nearby shelf, knowing only that she didn't want them thrown out.

She let herself be caught in Sally's gaze. No kindness in those eyes, Ashley had come to admit, just spaced-out distraction. Sally had done a lot of cocaine in the seventies. And the eighties. Adam should... *not* have told her that. Part of Sally's brain had been subsumed into some glowing hyper state somewhere, Ashley thought: a parallel universe made of the missing parts of people's drug-fried brains, Sally Hyde one of its denizens.

Ashley had been up since five, engrossed in biological case studies, fueled by prescription speed purloined from Janet's bedside cabinet. Gradually the noises from upstairs spilled down through the plaster and woodwork to distract her: the arrival of Mrs. Meydel, the fuss involved in getting Donna out to school, the packing of last-minute luggage, and the small detail of a TV mobile unit setting up in the living room, through which Janet conveyed her goodbyes to her public. One more repeated braying of the question *Can you bear a morning without Maxine* got Ashley snapping her files shut and sharing a look with Sally Hyde. She could almost imagine her mom saying, "Heaven forbid her *public* should get up, go out, get some air, take a walk, huh?"

"A *year* without Maxine," Ashley said. "That would suit me."

She was answered with the words, "You not going up to say goodbye?"

Mrs. Meydel made Ashley jump with her question. The Hydes' help had been Janet's dresser back in her pop kid days. She had the general habit, and talent, of silence. Sometimes if Ashley was engrossed in a book or the TV she'd sense a presence, a minute change in the light, and watchful Mrs. Meydel would be there, thin-lipped, bright-eyed. She was Janet's creature entirely, and Ashley had never trusted her.

THE FORTUNE TELLER'S FACTOTUM

Mrs. Meydel's unsaid remark about Ashley talking to herself remained in her face. Ashley waited for it in words, then gave up and said, "They're leaving now?"

"On the point of it. The TV people all but packed up, any rate. Here." She held up clothes, starchy and pristine, on a hanger. "Where do you want these?"

"There will do fine." Ashley pointed to a hook banged into a wooden strut.

The hanger was draped with an off-white long-sleeved calico blouse, a long dark cotton skirt, a starched white apron, a woollen shawl in a brown shade of gray, and a mob cap. They formed Ashley's disguise for her part-time job at the Ancestor Farm Living Museum out on the highway on the old Allentown Road. She was background, meaning that she sat in the scullery till visitors ventured in. Then she would mime the tasks an eighteenth-century scullery maid would have to do. Some keen but naïve newcomer to the museum's admin had floated the idea that whoever was placed in the scullery could cook food from the period–a locally-produced Amish cookbook had been suggested as a plausible though bogus source–and that the scullery could become a real-life cafeteria. Ashley's two cents' worth went a long way: firstly, she was at salad-burning level of cooking and secondly, no minimum-wager was going to be cooking anything. Thirdly, if they needed more, the museum's visitors were pathologically cheapskate, makers and bringers of sandwiches, and of supermarket-brand drinks and family-size potato chip offers, rainy day parking lot picnickers. The idea had petered out to leave it as the perfect job for a non-cooking, non-people-pleasing student with a backlog of work to catch up on. At Ancestor Farm Ashley mostly studied, in yet another oasis with few distractions.

She watched Mrs. Meydel's face as she hung the clothes, careful to the point of supercilious. Mrs. Meydel did not approve of Ashley doing a job, especially a minimum-wage one, when there was all that money up the stairs. Most of the people Ashley knew failed to understand it. She thought Mrs. Meydel might, as she was from a world of crones and cleaners, gofers and clearer-uppers, but if anything, she was even more snooty about it than Ashley's erstwhile friends. Ashley donated her wage to a charity. She had mooted working as a volunteer and not accepting it, but her boss, Edmond Demonte, had told her it would have been difficult to swing it with the books, and figured, correctly she supposed, that she would lose interest if she were a volunteer.

"So, the *job* today." The expressionless face and the innocuous remark served only to underline Mrs. Meydel's disapproval.

Ashley didn't address it, said only, "Better go say goodbye." She closed her book, and followed Mrs. Meydel up the steps.

8

E quipment and cables strewed the driveway, but Janet's
team were expert outside broadcasters and soon had it
packed into a truck. Janet was out amid the bustle, making sure
of this and that, hugging that one and this one and dispensing
mwah mwah kisses. In the hallway, Ashley counted eight suit-
cases.

Adam Hyde was in the kitchen, looking helpless. He seemed
happy to be distracted.

Ashley was set on ribbing him about the insane amount of
luggage, but something in him stopped her. She was left with
silence. She had been looking forward to having the place to
herself... and Donna, she supposed... but now she was not so
sure. It was not like she and her dad paid *that* much attention
to each other–she sometimes went days without seeing him.
But it was one thing to not see him, a different one to know
that he was not someplace nearby.

There had been a palpable anxiety dug into his face the night
before to accompany his wish, not quite a request, that Ashley
keep an eye on Donna. The sense of it lingered in Ashley's
mind rather than anything he said. She reminded him that
Donna was a big girl and could look after herself; cue a snort
from Janet and a deepening furrow in Adam's brow. Ashley
and Donna were his kiddies at such moments, Ashley guessed.
He would not say that, though the stupid TV shows he put
on were full of people who would, drawing approval, tears,
standing ovations, all for furthering the sentimental myth of

the American family. The thought of them twisted an icy fist into Ashley's kidneys. Adam Hyde would be away, but he had bequeathed daytime America the platitudes of his work.

There was no way Ashley could stop Donna doing whatever she wanted – even if she cared. She did not. She and Donna were going to do whatever they were going to do. She knew what that was going to be in her case... partly... but in Donna's? Even Donna herself never knew she was doing a thing until she was in the middle of it.

She swept the trouble in these thoughts aside and asked her dad, "All set?"

"Sure thing." He did not sound sure. He sounded nervous as he recited the bright spots of the itinerary and the connections, and dropped names. He said how they were going to start off in some washed-up junky crooner's pile in London then fly over to spend a few days in some movie director's *chateau*–"Like a *castle*, Ash?"–in France. His eyes wavered, and he licked his lips and stared at Ashley, begging some response.

She nearly managed it, laughed dutifully at least, though she could have just been clearing her throat.

Two minions came into the hallway, nodded to Ashley and started transporting the luggage outside.

"Well." Adam watched the bags go. "So I mean, you... you'll be okay here, huh?"

"Sure, Dad."

"You and Donna."

"Yeah."

Adam looked troubled by the claim. He said, as if just for the form of it, "And no parties–remember?"

"*Ha ha*, Dad." Ashley was not laughing, just saying the words. It was a private joke between her and her dad, its origins in an old movie she had forgotten.

"I know what goes down." Adam wagged a finger. "I was young once. At least, I think I was."

This prompted Ashley into a genuine laugh. Her dad spent most of the weekends of his adult life going to parties–bigger, better ones than he was ever invited to in his geeky youth. And Ashley had been so spoilt for parties during her time with Michael that she became sick of them. She had no time to party, anyhow. She was done with it till she got to Columbia. Then she would party again–oh *yes*–and party hard, but with her peers. When did the idea of that become so important to her? She was not sure, but it had.

She promised, "No parties, Dad."

Mrs. Meydel was nearby to cast a look to warn Ashley that she would keep an eye on the place anyhow and–for sure–there really *would* be no parties. Or was she trying to remind Ashley that she knew she had no friends to invite to a party? Probably both. Short-assed *bitch*.

She thought about the time ahead. Nothing wonderful was about to happen when her dad and Janet were away. And if it did... there was nobody to share it with. But if it *did*? No, nobody. Ashley did not have to read the word *missing* on those stupid posters, nor did she need Mrs. Meydel's glances; *every*body was missing from her life.

Adam Hyde made no move from the mirror. It looked to Ashley like he no longer wanted to go. She said, "You take care over there, Dad, huh?"

"Sure thing." Adam hesitated, as if unsure over whether he ought to say his next words. "But the explosions happen here, huh?"

Ashley had nearly forgotten about Harold Shester and the mystery he left behind: the exciting headlines and the spiels of news anchors, the puzzled cops, the open verdict, along with the wreckage of himself and his cheap car. She deflected her dad's comment with a joyless little smile. She was not *quite* ready to forgive either him or Janet for being so focused on the news aspect of the St Maz explosion–like Morning With Maxine was watched for its Pulitzer-winning news coverage–that neither of them even asked if she was there that evening. And yes, her telling them the next day that she had, and that she had known the identity of the exploding man all along, had seemed like a hollow little victory. Better than none at all, though.

"Yeah. *Boom*." Ashley was dismissing the subject, and Adam knew it. "But they'll start blowing up Europe by mistake now, huh?" American soldiers were all around the world, Ashley knew, keeping it safe for American tourists or at least popping their heads over the parapet to draw the bad guys' fire, flipping a finger at them, mooning. It was ninety-nine percent certain that the bad guys did not catch Morning With Maxine, so Janet was probably safe. "So, you take care."

Janet, faultlessly made up, came in for her jacket and hand luggage. She hugged and mwahed Mrs. Meydel then stood, waiting. She looked at Ashley and the question occurred to her: "No college today?"

"Work today," Ashley said.

Janet's lip curled at the mention of the word. She exchanged a brief glance with Mrs. Meydel. "Oh, okay," was all she said. She tossed her head at Adam and said, "Mister, an entire continent's waiting."

Ashley had nothing more to say. She never did when Janet was there because she never wanted to address them both with words meant only for her dad. Janet's presence sucked the life out of Ashley's words, out of her sentiments and her expressions. She made her wishes and kissed her dad and stood at the door with Mrs. Meydel as the travelers got into the car, and waved.

As the car disappeared down the drive, Ashley caught the somewhat lost expression on her dad's face. He was gone. It hit Ashley all over again; on planes, on trains, on buses... well, maybe not buses, but at the mercy of crazy European car drivers. Ashley feared for her dad's safety and sanity over there. Europe was amorphous and terrifying, suddenly–it was the old world, full of superstition, monsters, darkness. Janet had toured the world during her singing career, though she admitted she saw little of it aside from hotel rooms and concert halls. Adam had made the odd trip with work but had been chaperoned the whole time. He was helpless away from his books, his computer; away from people to help him, prompt him, steer him. Ashley recalled stray snatches of conversation from which she understood that they were engaging minions over there who would arrange transport, restaurants, sightseeing, safety and the alteration of reality to accommodate people who were no longer sure what it was. She relaxed.

Mrs. Meydel's smile vanished along with the car. Ashley supposed her own did too. Mrs. Meydel stood aside for her, held the door open, and shut it behind them. She walked in with a businesslike bustle to start her routine of clearing up the breakfast stuff, and then getting on with the cleaning, laundering, and ironing. Both Ashley and Mrs. Meydel made non-committal noises of farewell.

As Mrs. Meydel stacked the crockery in the dishwasher, Ashley went up to her bathroom and showered. She dressed and gathered all she would need to bring in to work. She took the steps down through the house to the basement and brought everything together: her books, notepads, laptop, her phone, her work clothes, rolled up on their hanger and forced into her bag.

As she finished her packing, she felt a slight thrill of alarm, the feeling that she was being watched. She looked over at the steps, expecting to see Mrs. Meydel again. Then she heard her upstairs, a broom knocking on furniture. It was not Mrs. Meydel; Ashley had been caught in the gaze of Sally Hyde, mother, coke fiend, depressive, absentee, theoretical American. The strange thought occurred: was Ashley also going to disappear when her dad was away–was Donna? As if her dad being there or not had anything to do with it. But he took his eyes off Sally Hyde and let her disappear, didn't he? She had a flash of anger that bit into her, and of that all-encompassing darkness her neighbor Martin Ferrie had invoked. She had not been able to imagine it in the sun of a summer evening. She shut her eyes and had a vision of shapes moving in and out of the dark trees and over blistered clearings, dead river beds full of gravel and rags, rusted metal and dead dogs. She caught a glimpse of a face: Sally Hyde, wearing that unchanging expression, vulnerable and yet full of power, compromised and yet unwilling to compromise, to admit anybody to her world. She looked again, and it was Donna, getting into a man's car at the side of the road near the trees. Donna's head turned and the face became Ashley's own, on the verge of a scream. She shook all the faces out of her head.

She felt watched still and, despite the evidence of her ears, turned to the steps again. Still not Mrs. Meydel, but the cat, a few steps from the top. A crisis at the kennels, Ashley remembered, some kind of animal disease, Janet freaking out at the idea of a state-wide outbreak. Donna had unthinkingly volunteered both her own and Ashley's services in looking after the little beast. Ashley was not very bothered; both she and Donna knew that Mrs. Meydel would do the cat care.

The cat followed Ashley with her eyes. Ashley said, "You're just a cat. That's all," she told her. "Don't think you're not."

The cat smirked.

"*Araby.*"

The cat swished her tail.

"That's not even a real *name*," Ashley said. "You don't fool anybody left in this house right now, not at all. I'd stop smirking if I were as fresh out of friends as you." She turned to check that she had remembered to grab some fruit to take in to work with her. She turned back to the cat to tell her, "I really would," but Araby was gone. Ashley stood and watched a beam of sunlight make its way in through the ground-level windows to light up those hopeless portraits of Sally Hyde, grabbed her stuff and left to catch the bus for Ancestor Farm.

9

Ashley had plenty to get on with, so it wasn't like she and Donna were going to do anything as lame as throwing the party their dad had warned against. But then Mrs. Meydel's daughter gave birth to a very premature baby: exit Janet's spy in the house to Portland Maine to become a part-time carer and full-time grandmother for a week at least. Donna caught Ashley at a moment of doubt that became weakness, and then the party was on.

Donna's fleeting friends only came by in their fancy cars, it seemed when Donna could *not* join them. Ashley was glad they were staying away, but there was something about Donna that was so hangdog that Ashley got an urge to make her happy. A year before, she would have pulled Donna to her and given her a hug. She might also have prompted her into a laugh and some banter, maybe an exchange from a lost movie. That would never happen again; it was a piece of their relationship gone.

A few days before the party, Ashley and Donna sat at the computer, allowing quantity to overrule quality while blowing the home delivery allowance on the cheapest beer and spirits they could find. Ashley's optimism had disappeared by then. A premonition: their party would end in disaster. By then Donna had invited everybody she knew and, Ashley suspected, some people she didn't know. Ashley was already trying to distance herself from it, even if only in her mind. If she could have gone out to escape it, she might have, but she didn't trust Donna or her friends to draw the line at the boundaries of the stupidity possible at teen parties.

She mulled over thoughts of inviting people from college. There was a group of students who adopted silk ties and wingtip shoes, shirts with French cuffs–Ashley was unsure why they should be desirable, unsure even what they *were*–pinafore dresses and button-strapped Maryjane shoes. They discussed moody French movies and also French novels, in translation, arranged artfully in their bags. They liked European bike racing, *they claimed,* and threw its names and terminology around. One of them even wore a beret once. They brought espressos and croissants into the refectory before morning classes, from the expensive continental bakery in the St Maz mall. When Bobby Dusenberg had to go to class and leave the golden crumbs on the table and the sludgy bubbles in coffee cups, he would declare, "*On y va,*" and light up the faces of Mona Bradley, Darren Jacks, Toria Pallister and the others. They fought to answer first, "*Qui mal y pense,*" and glowed with their continental cleverness.

Since Ashley's resumption of college, it was obvious that handsome, intellectual Bobby had taken a shine to her. He was too cool to really have the hots for anybody, she suspected. He presented her with his embossed visiting card.

Such a move cut no ice with Mona and Toria, it was plain, and Darren seemed resistant to admitting more girls into the clique. The hallos Ashley had gotten from them had not become quite warm enough to cross the distance and waft her over to their table with the option to pick a croissant out of the bag or listen to the reading out of the mystifying cycling results. Ashley knew one thing Bobby did not: she had no time either to make out or even hang out, with anybody, no matter how handsome, intellectual, smart, no matter how good at French or how bad.

All the same, she got as far as feeding Bobby's number into her phone when she saw a scene of the French-cuffed wing-tipped Maryjaned croissant-munchers at a party full of drunken kids and her reputation gone past the S-bend and all the way down the can. The four years between her and Donna made a difference; Donna and her crowd were children, more or less. Ashley was indifferent to the idea of her own popularity in a town she had washed her hands of, but even so didn't want to be remembered for inviting people to Falkender's worst-ever night out since Stonewall Jackson's rednecks trashed it in the eighteen sixties.

"You're not asking anybody at *all*?" Donna's scorn forced a rethink on Ashley. Finally, she asked neighborhood friends she had not hung out with for a year or more. She grew up alongside some of them, sharing the feminine silliness of childhood and adolescence. In case they remembered it as vividly as she did, or better, she resented them, these bad-hair-day ghosts. In the car culture in which they all lived, she rarely passed them on the streets but saw them in stores and restaurants, avoided them at the doctor's, at the pool, ignored them at stoplights with the weather inconveniently good and car windows inconveniently down. Ashley felt embarrassed for all of them whenever they were forced into pausing and saying hi, cornered into conversational doodles, saying, "Oh, *goodness*, look at the time, got to get going." What she meant was, "Get out of my face and stop reminding me of the person I was, and that time I shared a secret with you, when we both knew I made it up just to seem interesting. And forget those terrible clothes I wore. And I'll never convince you it wasn't me who stole your expensive mascara that time, because we both know I did. So just... *cease*. Disappear."

One of them, Maura Anderson, said with silences that Ashley had blanked her since graduation. So what was going on? "Did you get dumped, or what?" Maura double-bluffed the question into a joke, giving Ashley a turn at silence. Instead of getting mad, she heard herself laugh, almost, and say, "I... just thought it was time we stopped drifting apart and all."

Variations of this became her song sheet for the others. She called Sue Shah, whose recklessness had gotten her and Ashley caught shoplifting when they were eleven and subsequently not arrested, of course, but lectured and grounded anyhow. She called Matt Gadden, who christened her Nacho Breath after she kissed him at a kids' party after eating a bag of the horrible things, an e-number rush addling her head with a deadly duo of desire and confidence. She called Shoshannah Ross, whose expensive mascara she had indeed once stolen. She could hear Shoshannah's accusation about it in her monotonous voice, all those years on. She called Dru Kallista, who was Greek, and ranted, enraged, at her mom's old-country Greek habits in cooking, dress and keeping up appearances. Ashley called a few other one-time friends, recalled the humorless intensity that children brought to such bonds. She had virtually the same memories, and the same conversation, with them all.

But not with Chloe Gustavson. A month before, it would have pained her not to be calling Chloe. Now it no longer mattered. The feeling both pleased her and made her uncomfortable.

She put the phone down and lay on the long sofa. She gave in to a wish to be away from there in the darkness coming down, taking her chances out there in the bad and dangerous places, among the missing.

10

Not one lame party, for a time, but two. Ashley's was her catch-up-with-people-she-no-longer-liked effort. Matt Gadden had a sulky emo girl in tow. Her affectation of boredom didn't hide the fact that she *was* actually bored. She kept her phone in her hand all the time in case a magic bleep alerted her to a better night out. Shoshannah Ross brought a geeky guy a few years older than anybody there. She told everybody that he was a guy she worked with, and not–*you* know... the father of her future brood. She was wearing too much mascara. At school, Shoshannah had been one of a set of pushy girls who were borderline princesses. Ashley liked her without knowing why and *had* missed her a little. Dru Kallista was accompanied by cousins. Dru had often had an honor guard of cousins, Ashley remembered: olive-skinned girls, beauties but with frizzy hair and, like Dru, comically hairy arms and, again like Dru, in clothes that were expensive but for a more formal kind of party, that had taken place thirty years before. Maura Anderson was alone, mouth full of braces and occasionally spitty talk of friends and relatives Ashley barely remembered. As Maura seem uninclined to talk to anybody else, Ashley spent more time with her than she might have.

No need for guilt; they had all played their part in drifting. They were all trying, in different ways, to change their lives and change the people in their lives, to make new marks of their own.

Ashley had drifted into drinking alcohol with Michael Stambolisky, but had not touched a drop since. She did not miss it. She held onto the same glass of white wine for an hour. She sipped it once, found it warm and sour, and tipped it.

The other party in the room was Donna's. It reminded Ashley of the beginning of some story she couldn't exactly remember: adults away, a bunch of kids left to their own devices, and, if not intent on doing irreversible damage, then not averse to it if it happened. Ashley kept one eye on Donna's friends. It was like two generations in there: Ashley's friends talked while Donna's squealed; Ashley's ate the cheap party food but Donna's disdained it and just drank; Ashley turned the music down, and Donna cranked it up.

Donna's pal James Dufrayne walked in carrying a twenty-four pack of fancy German beer and a bag clinking with wine and spirits. Ashley registered the gestation of some smartass remark. A finger pointed at his face, she told him, "Don't open your mouth, or you can turn round right now and leave." He made a few comic *but-buts* then saw she meant business. "And the booze goes in the kitchen," she told him. "Or it goes out the door with you." He looked about to challenge that but meekly handed it over, detached a can and went to find Donna and Shannon Seeley.

Ashley should not have listened. Then she would have missed him greeting them with the words, "I didn't know *she* was going to be here."

A couple of hours and a lot of drinks later–Ashley's hour-long glass had by then turned into several–the party was like any old house party, loud and crass. Donna and her pals were shrieking away, and the music pumped. Kids sucked at bottles, made out half-heartedly on couches, danced insanely one minute, and were coma-like the next. Some looked distinctly stoned. Ashley sniffed in corners and checked upstairs regularly, but found no evidence that her smoking ban had been breached inside the house. At one point some startlingly drunk kid kept putting on the same ancient Linkin Park track, till another broke the CD and disdainfully handed over the money for it. That was the closest the party got to a fight; it wasn't even interesting enough for that.

She was glad she had not invited Bobby Dusenberg and Mona Bradley and their Frenchified friends. The croissant set would have referred to the party as *denim*; at college, the word sparked a devoted laugh from them, signifying anything deemed mundane, something not necessarily bad, just *ordinary*, the kind of thing their hip dads would do.

For a time, Ashley watched as if from outside. She wanted it to be over. She asked a couple of shitfaced teens to go someplace else if they wanted to do whatever it was they were doing, and they looked at her like she was their aunt. She took a bottle of vodka away from an ugly twelve-year-old. He tried to mutter something defiant at her, but was visibly shocked to find himself wordless in the realization that his brain had turned to mashed potatoes.

She checked upstairs to see if anybody had gone into her dad's and Janet's rooms. She checked the bathrooms to see whether the medicine cabinets had been ransacked for downers, a favorite at parties–she had done that herself a time or two. All seemed okay, except for that face of hers under the scary overhead light. She came back each time, watched James and Shannon, batted their looks back. She warned Donna to keep an eye on all her guests.

"Guests?" Donna was puzzled by the word.

"Your friends."

"For what?" Donna wondered. "Man, it's a party. Lighten up."

Maybe Ashley was just tipsy enough for the advice. She danced a little and drank a little more. Things went blurred, and time passed beyond her reach and detailed understanding. Next thing she was alone in the kitchen and there were shouts and cars in the street as the last of the invaders headed home.

II

Ashley had a memory of sleeping in an armchair fully dressed, but all the same she woke in her bed on Sunday afternoon. Her clothes made a trail to the door. She had been sick on her pillow, but not enough to wake her. No more than a bilious cough.

Her thoughts locked on at once to the certainty that she no longer belonged among her old friends. Her party face the night before: a rictus of pretense from a grudging host, and the mean-spirited feeling that she ought to be at better parties with better people.

Donna, when finally roused, was gray and subdued. It had ended up as Donna's party, Ashley thought, so it was down to Donna to suffer the hangover and clean up the mess while Ashley crept quietly back to her life.

Nobody had done anything to require calling interior decorators out. She and Donna filled garbage sacks, loaded the dishwasher and scrubbed at stains. They were at this for an hour before it became apparent that Araby was not there. The sensation of a mild panic scratched at the nape of Ashley's neck.

Ashley thought of those pet pictures on missing posters, those people's pictures on milk cartons. They were fuzzy and ill-defined and comically out of date and all the same because they shared the same characteristic: they were never coming back. The thought that the cat had joined them threw a chill over Ashley. Araby being a celebrity cat, it would have been like losing Brad Pitt.

Araby would not last a second outside the house. She had never seen a dog. Any of the people she met fawned over her. Cars were fabulous carriages that ferried her to studios, not marauding creators of roadkill. Ashley's first thought was that some... *moron* at the party had let the cat out. She went and searched the front drive and backyards, but saw no sign of her.

"Ash." The sound was long and drawn out, childish, almost: Donna, with the voice she adopted when avoiding responsibility. Ashley followed the sound up the staircase. Donna was pointing at a kind of Ottoman thing on the mid-stairs landing. A delinquent at the party had barfed in it. Some good news in this: Araby lay glassy-eyed in the mess. "Jesus, Ashley," were the only words Donna got out before she joined the phantom puker and made her own contribution. Avoiding the floor out of instinct, she managed to get most of it into the Ottoman to give Araby a comprehensive refill. Donna crouched next to the thing and went into a brief trance.

Ashley swore, pulled her tee-shirt off, and used it to pick up the cat. Araby struggled, ears twitching. Ashley caught the violence of the moment in her, the deep-seated rage of a proud animal rendered helpless. Araby twisted onto her back on the palms of Ashley's hands, rear legs spasming rhythmically as if she were riding a bike. It was an astonishing performance. When righted, her claws drew blood from Ashley's forearm and the back of her hand, and more cursing.

Ashley carried her up a flight to the nearest bathroom–hers and Donna's–to place her in the shower. She held onto Araby's fancy jeweled collar with one hand, and with the other sprayed her with the shower nozzle, an outrage that elicited hisses and yowls. As soon as Araby was clean, Ashley wiped her with a towel and left her looking pristine but bewildered.

She went down the stairs to find that Donna too, looked slightly bewildered. She snapped out of her catatonia, at last, to point to Ashley's stomach, bra, and boxers all covered in puke. "You've got…" she almost advised.

Ashley thanked her. She helped Donna to her feet and steered her up to the bathroom. They stood by the shower stall door and looked at Araby, who was blinking strangely, slowly and deliberately. She worked up to a violent shudder, shook some water off herself, then was still again.

Ashley remembered a trip out of town one day in Michael Stambolisky's car and a rabbit that sat at the edge of the highway all addled and refused to move. "That disease they get?" Michael had said. Ashley told him it was myxomotosis. "Whatever," he sort of agreed. "Kindest thing? Turn back and run him over." Now Araby seemed to have that same troubled air, that same distance-seeking stare.

"I got to call the vet," Ashley decided. "And I guess I'm going to have to take her there."

"Uh, right. Hey." Donna looked from Ashley to Araby, and said, "She's hardly going to die, though."

"You don't think?"

Donna bent to peer at Araby. Ashley noted her sister looked fixed on the immortal memories route herself but was more worried about a headline in the local news, something like *Celebrity Cat Dies in Drunken Teen Rave.* She imagined searching questions being asked. Of her mainly, as on any occasion when both she and Donna were in potential trouble, Donna reverted to the guise of a thumb-sucking innocent. "Yeah," Donna decided. "She might die, too."

Ashley found a vet's number, a place in Barnton. She listened to a relentless ringtone, then a message assuring her they valued her and her little companion and would be with both of them just as soon as they could. Donna, carelessly washed and hair stringy wet, signaled urgently from the stairs. Ashley kept the phone in one ear and offered her sister the other.

Donna said, "You could take her to Mr. Ferrie."

Ashley shook her head in inquiry at the mention of their neighbor.

"Mr. Ferrie?" Donna said. "The guy who lives over at–"

"I know where he *lives*," Ashley told her. "Why would I want to take the cat to him?"

"He's a vet?"

"Mr. Ferrie is a..." Ashley had once asked Martin Ferrie what his job was. He said, deadpan, that it involved ensuring that minimum-wage joes came up with a maximum-wage service, but that he was happily too clapped-out for a real job. "He's a *security* consultant," she recalled. "Or something like... Hey, you dork."

"What?"

"He's a Viet*nam* vet."

"So? Whatever."

"*Jesus.*"

"Jesus your*self.*" Donna flopped on the couch. Ashley resumed the rigmarole of the call. When she got a receptionist, she explained about the cat being sick. She did not mention the party, nor any exposure to crazed teens. The receptionist said she had better bring her in. "Does she have a plan?" she asked Ashley.

"Wait–what?" Ashley asked back. "A *plan*?"

"A *medical* plan?"

"Uh, she's a *cat*?"

That brought out the inner Ashley: high and mighty and scornful and, for a second, shrill. But it hit her that Araby surely *did* have a plan at some vet's, someplace. She was the second celebrity in the household, and it was inconceivable that she was not insured by the studio where Janet did her devil's work. She was about to tell the receptionist that she was right and would find out the details and contact the insurer's designated vet. Then she froze. It would be a stupid thing to do if she wanted Araby's funny little turn to remain a secret, not to mention the party at which it had taken place.

"No? Okay." The receptionist cheerfully recited a scary list of definite, probable and possible charges. "Bring her in."

"I'll have to," Ashley thought she ought to make known. "She doesn't have her own car, either."

As usual, Araby would have to be chauffeured. That would be the good part. Ashley felt herself lighten up almost at once. She showered and dressed, her feet feeling light, then stowed Araby in her small basket under her blanket. Ashley was barred from using her dad's car when he was away but she had taken the precaution to ask what if it was an emergency? Her dad hooted at that and enquired, reasonably enough, "Like what?" The question had fizzled out. Adam Hyde had left the key and, he said, had made a note of the mileage. He had not; he was too scatty and, in any case, not controlling enough to do that.

Was this an emergency? What was, if this wasn't? *Potentially dead celebrity cat loved by millions* had to be. Dealing with it would avert the grief-fest that Janet's viewers would indulge in whenever anybody they did not know died, as long as they were from the never-never land the other side of that screen.

Ashley had already been for a cruise in the Chrysler. She had driven to no place at all really, through the five towns and along the freeways and through the dark spaces and back, to no purpose at all. She had to keep this from Donna though, in case her sister had one of her little blurting-out moments.

"Donna." Ashley prodded Donna's shoulder, made her turn a mumble into a groan. "I'm heading to Barnton with the cat. That means–Donna, are you listening?"

"Kind of."

It didn't look like it. Ashley prodded Donna again, and said, "That means you get to finish off cleaning the place up."

"I feel sick," Donna whined. "I got a headache."

"Sure you do." Now it was Donna who looked to Ashley like that roadside rabbit from another life. "Take some codeine and sleep it off a while. But then you got to clean up some more."

Donna tried to nod. Ashley poked her tongue out at her. She was about to point around the room: all kinds of obvious things to be done. They had no mother though, and Ashley was not going to substitute for one. She forgot it. She left Donna to it and walked out into the afternoon, her dad's car key clutched in one hand and in the other Araby, basket and blanket and all, wedged into Janet's Dolce and Gabbana bag.

12

It was liberating to be behind the wheel of Adam Hyde's Chrysler. As he hardly ever used it, it was in prime condition. Ashley enjoyed the route to the vet's in the ghostly Sunday deserted center of Barnton. She was almost cheerful as she parked and locked the car.

A perplexed pause on the steps of the vet's; neither a movement nor a sound from the bag. Ashley was about to put it on the ground and peek in but then worried that Araby, under the weather or not, would be up and out of it and away.

Ashley had never been to a vet. The people in the waiting room looked frankly at her, almost nodding in greeting. They glanced at one another–did any of them recognize her? She thought they were wondering. They went back into their little worlds; she was not one of them.

She gave her name at the desk to a receptionist whose elegance was spoilt by waxy skin patched with powder, who bade her take a seat. She did so and risked a look into the bag. Araby didn't look up. Ashley wiggled a finger gently behind the cat's ears. Araby mewled, widened her eyes, and poked her tongue out. Ashley thought her charge looked spaced out.

The posters told their share of missing pet stories. There was other info on the walls: puppy training, feline grooming, and personal training for the aspiring show cat, plus seminars for empathizing with caged rodents. Ashley thought any of those would stress out any animal. There was also a pet funeral service, plus bereavement counseling.

The dogs in the waiting room were visible. Two were wrapped in identical pastel blankets with embroidered edges and clutched in the arms of a pair of middle-aged women dressed up for a trailer park night out. They cooed at the tiny hounds, not much bigger than rats, as if they were babies. The cats present were in carrying cages, one of them a scaled-down two-wheeler horsebox. A geeky kid had a little cage containing a bird. It was covered, but its hiccupping and hopping with fear in the presence of all those bird-chasers was audible, and, thought Ashley, terrible. No snakes though, thankfully, nor any toughs sitting there with spur-damaged cockerels. There was an ostrich farm out on the Philly highway; a sick one *would* have been interesting. A group of Peruvian musicians in charge of an ailing llama could also have been a welcome distraction.

Ashley repulsed attempts to talk to her by pointing at her bag and putting a finger to her lips. She did some mental arithmetic to work out how much of the emergency fund she would have to hammer out of her dad's credit card. It was an upfront fifty-dollar charge just for the receptionist to show teeth in a hallo. There would be charges for medication. And maybe they would have to keep Araby in–did vets even do that? She guessed so.

At that point, she remembered later, there was nothing to get troubled about. There was no party, and Araby just got sick, as animals sometimes did. They–she–dealt with it, and that was that.

Pets and their owners were summoned, went in, and came out. The cat could have died in that time, but Ashley fretted more about whether she had fed enough money into the parking meter. She was just about to get up and go check when her name was chirped. She approached the desk.

"And?" the receptionist asked.

"And... what?"

"What is your pet's name?" The girl smiled the words out sweetly.

Ashley was about to tell her when she saw those cat-murder headlines again. People obsessed with their own animals, she reckoned, surely got obsessed with other people's. If anybody looked upon Araby as a celebrity, it was the people around her. She said the first word that came into her head, one from the news, which was, "Fatwa."

"Fat-wa." The receptionist's smile grayed out as she frowned over the word and wrote it down. Ashley heard a whispered echo behind her. Then she relaxed. Pet-owners, she recalled, did their charges the discourtesy of giving them the most ridiculous names.

"Would you like to come in with him?" the receptionist was asking.

"Her," Ashley said. "No."

"Owners like to." Ashley sensed the receptionist's disapproval and that of the people around her. "We have facilities."

"For... what?"

"For..." The receptionist had to think about it. "For... uh, the, uh, observation of the care of your pet."

What were they, Ashley wondered–a chair? X-ray spex? She was almost certain that vets hated owners breathing over them when they were trying to work. She said, "She's not exactly mine." Irrelevant, but it made the receptionist abandon her line of persuasion. Ashley was also tempted to add that she would be back for Araby in six months if they didn't auction them off, like at the dry cleaners. She hefted the bag up.

The receptionist took it with an air of further disapproval. She said, "You don't have a cage?"

"She's not *savage*." In fact, the little monster could be. Ashley immediately wanted to rub at the scratch-marks Araby had left on her. She would have liked to keep her in a cage the whole time.

"I, uh... *No.* I mean, for traveling?"

"No." Ashley refrained from saying that Araby had the run of the back of a car driven by one of Maxine Wasserman's lackeys at least once a week. The cat would have engaged an animal rights lawyer at the mere mention of a cage.

The receptionist made a hold-on-there gesture, reached under the counter with her free hand, and handed Ashley a brochure. She said, "We stock a wide range of pet conveyancers for sale. Please feel free to browse." Ashley promised she would.

She deposited the brochure in the trash then went out to check the meter. She had maybe ten minutes left, so went back in and sat near the door. She half-listened to the muted conversations. It seemed to her that the owners enjoyed this sojourn in the vets among like-minded people. They were animal gaolers, she thought, had to know deep down that their captives suffered from the call of the wild–they were like the Tyrannosaurus Rex in *Jurassic Park*; they didn't want to be fed, wanted to get out there and hunt. That was probably most of whatever was wrong with them.

Every time Ashley looked around, the owners seemed to be looking at her. Her wait took on the dimensions of a burden. All her thoughts oppressed her, of parties, messed-up houses, messed-up kids and parking meters with gaping mouths and of exploding men, teeth and entrails flying. Harold Shester called her name: startled, she heard it again but it was only a nurse at the counter, saying, "Got to keep her in, I'm afraid."

"You do?" Although Ashley had been joking to herself about this, the reality of it stung. "Really? Why – what's up with her?"

"I don't know exactly." The woman put on a little smile that said something like *I'm just a nurse* or *I can't be bothered to explain*.

"Well, can I talk with the vet?" Ashley felt anxious for Araby. To be honest she also sensed retribution: beyond the door to the practice, back along those roads, back home and out in TV Land.

"Yeah." The nurse gave the word a few syllables. "But it won't be for some time. It's Sunday?" She waved toward the people waiting. Ashley understood that she meant it was like the emergency room in any hospital on a weekend night of alcohol and fights and road accidents. She found herself nodding. The nurse passed her back to the receptionist, who took a hundred and fifty dollars off her for the examination and, she explained, against medication and accommodation. 'A basket,' Ashley thought. She had to fill out another form, and then she was out of there.

13

W as Ashley worried about the cat? Yes... *but*, she reasoned, out in the air, not *so* worried. Araby was in the care of people who knew their stuff. She walked to the car and felt liberated all over again. She opened the door and slid behind the wheel. She forgot the cat and drove.

The evening was coming down. The roads were empty. Ashley cruised into the hills just to see the towns all lit up and looking fine, better than they ever did when she was in them.

She drove down into St Maz anyhow for a glop stop, a milkshake in a burger bar. She tried to think who she would have liked to share her ride with. Nobody came to mind. Only a short time before, she might have wished she could share it with Michael Stambolisky, or Chloe Gustavson. But now? She marveled that she had ever seen anything in either of them. Sharing with nobody was better than sharing with people who despised her enough to betray her. The gloom stopped short and she was content to sit and ingest a million calories in her shake and to half-watch the people around her as they sat with kids and chattered.

A voice said loudly, "I love this pattern so much it makes me cry." Ashley half-turned and saw a chubby, pretty woman with a deliberately sixties hairdo, all Alice band and flicked-up ends, She was holding up her kid's yellow plaid blanket. Her friends joshed her till they saw that she was really crying and got up out of their seats and did a group hug around her, pledged support and love. She looked back at them, blinking, her sixties make-up melting. It seemed to Ashley like the woman did not know her friends at all at that moment; it was like she was waking from a dream in which she had been abducted by aliens. The scene creeped Ashley out.

She pictured home and its disarray. She did not regret her abandonment of it as soon as Araby's distress had made itself clear–and as soon, of course, as Ashley had realized that she would be able to go out in the car. She was sure that Donna would not have done a stroke to tidy up.

The faces of those friends of Donna's invaded her head and bugged her. At the party she noticed that they never handed one another stuff but threw it, never picked stuff up but grabbed it, never put things down but clattered them. Nor did they eat, just crammed food into their mouths; did not talk, instead yelled. They never laughed for themselves, she had noted, but only to let everybody else know they were laughing. Some of them had been in and out of the house since they were in short pants. Others she remembered vaguely from school. At the party they were bigger, louder, more hurried and more garbled. Ashley had been perturbed at the crash-test dummy nothingness in their faces once they had gotten a few drinks on board. Their eyes only sprang to life when they were the center of attention, glazing over again once the focus drifted. She remembered some moment or other, something catching her eye or ear and her thinking how there was an... *offhand* cruelty in the throwaway things they said. What could you do with kids like that? Kids like that, everybody hated them. And yet they loved that and hated one another too and even, deep down, hated themselves. They'd come to realize it only in courthouses and Juvenile Hall or facing psychologists across desks. There was no place to go with kids like that except to fear and shun them. She did *not* want Donna to turn into one.

Ashley's good feeling fizzled out. She got up and left. She drove past the smug houses and lawns of the burbs and through the run-down centers of the towns. She looked out at it all and thought of the ill feelings festering behind the lit-up windows and in the dark spaces between.

At home, the washing machine and dishwasher were throbbing. Donna was out. She had cleaned up the vomit on the landing, in the Ottoman thing, and the bathroom, leaving traces only in the breaks in the tile cement. She had done enough to make the place look like there had not been a party. Ashley did not care by then. When Mrs. Meydel got back and got going on it, and for sure by the time her dad and Janet returned, the house would offer no trace of its temporary occupation by the barbarians.

An ever-so-slight smell of weed. Horrible stuff. Donna? She supposed so.

Ashley had had a late night and a busy day and craved her bed. Despite the evidence, she still had the feeling she had not slept in it the night before. She wondered if she had sleepwalked and fretted the whole night, turning her life over again and again in her mind.

14

In the middle of that night, Ashley awoke breathless, fixed on the memory of a visit to Washington DC to the Montpierres, her mother's side of the family. She dreamed of Sally Hyde infrequently. Maybe she had been dreaming of this visit in particular. There was no other explanation for the vivid pictures in her head.

She was eight. Her mom's cousin Solange, a straw-haired woman with anxious ever-moving features, was showing them a photo album. Ashley was feigning interest. There was a photo taken at a wedding the year before at Firemont's run-down Dominican church, the whole company with bride and groom at the center, the men's dark suits dandruffed with a ton of confetti, the company ankle-deep in the stuff. Solange said, "That's you there, Ashley." Ashley glanced at the picture. Solange's finger rested under the image of a small girl at the front in a white dress. Ashley had said a polite *oh, okay*, but her mom cut in at once to say no, it wasn't Ashley. The incident had stuck in her mind and come to haunt her sleep, Ashley realized, precisely because her mom made such a big deal out of it.

"That's *not* Ashley." Ashley remembered Sally Hyde strident, her voice on the edge of something too mysterious for Ashley to grasp.

"Looks like her," somebody said.

"Hey." Ashley remembered her mom's eyes flashing and hostile, searching out the source of the voice. "I know my own kid." That voice was unnatural, auguring an argument.

"Sure looks like her," somebody else dared. Ashley got the impression the voice was her dad's.

"No." Sally Hyde turning, chin out, eager for a challenge. *"No–it isn't."*

The face of the kid in the photo was blurred, but her elaborate hairdo was clear. It was one of those creations that would last only as long as it took to do the photos, braided into elegant little ropes and pinned up around her head; it was ridiculous to make a kid look like that. Ashley's mom and dad were in sharp focus. There were a load of the Montpierres and seemingly random five-towns people like Mrs. Lynch, the meals-on-wheels lady, some of the old women who tended to the church and some of the Dorn family from Firemont, who were the church trustees. There was Martin Ferrie, in a military dress uniform. Ashley tried to cast her mind back to the wedding, but she and Donna had been taken to a *lot* of weddings; they all merged in uncomfortable clothes, ridiculous pomp, rich cake, ugly kids and lame speeches, music and dancing.

"Ashley couldn't go," Sally insisted during that DC visit. "Chicken pox. And we thought Donna ought to stay quarantined too. But anyhow." All those years on, Ashley got a sense of them all looking warily at her mom in the hopes of a good moment to move on from a conversation of no consequence. "I know my own kid." This was the crux of the thing for Sally, Ashley could now work out. "And that's not her."

"Sally's right," somebody said at last. "I remember now. That's a different kid."

Either back in the memory of real life or in Ashley's dream, another voice pitched in, "That's that kid that disappeared."

Ashley remembered tears of frustration in her mom's eyes as she stabbed questions at them: how *dare* they talk about some *other* kid? Who *cared* about some *other* kid? They looked at her, shocked, though some of them, Ashley could now conclude, surely recognized the obsession a gram of coke could lend to a rant. Sally stood and smiled at last, surveying them all, silent. It was her way of shaking up the Montpierre squares, those DC dullards, Ashley realized all those years later.

The Hydes dropped out of touch with the Montpierres after Sally's disappearance. Adam Hyde confessed to Ashley that he had never got along with them, anyhow. They resented him, he said. "New money," he explained eventually. "The Firemont Montpierres were old money, and old money people despise new money people–in fact they despise anybody who has to work to make money. Not that they had a dime between them, like all those old families in Firemont. They soon moved over to pool their pennies with the DC Montpierres."

Ashley felt herself falling back into sleep, blasted by those ancient memories, not of the wedding itself anymore, nor of the mystery kid who may or may not have disappeared. She thought of her mom, off her face, and the rest of the Montpierres disapproving.

In her mid-teens Ashley went through a phase of badgering her dad with her suspicion that her mom ran away to reunite with the Montpierres. Eventually he unearthed copies of missing person reports filed by him and those same Montpierres, yellowed articles from newspapers plus a sensationalist resumé cobbled together by a true crime rag. There was even a report from a private detective at a level of fee-justifying detail, but adding nothing. Even so, Ashley had never shaken the suspicion that her mom was in fact in DC.

It was revived as she sought sleep again. Even as she drifted off, she was bugged by the aching childishness of it and yet drawn into the small ray of hope it pretended to offer.

15

The next morning the house phone trilled. Ashley ignored it in case it was her dad-possible-or Janet-unlikely enough to be more or less impossible-or Mrs. Meydel-likely. When she checked, there was a message from the Barnton vet's receptionist, asking her to call as soon as she could.

She and Donna argued about which of them was going to retrieve the cat. Ashley had taken Araby to the vet's, though, so as far as she was concerned it was up to Donna to go get her back.

Donna *really* had to be at school, she reminded Ashley, because she was caught in some kind of truancy report system. It triggered if she was absent from any lesson, and how it worked was that there would be an immediate call to the parent.

"There's no parent here," Ashley reminded her. "And anyhow, I meant you do it after school. Obviously."

Ashley got an odd flashback from the middle of her night: that wedding photo from the eighties, the girl with the blurred face and the absurd hair, a kid who disappeared. She saw her in her sister's face for a second.

Donna was talking at her. Ashley offered her a not-my-problem expression. She said, "Whatever. But I can't go-really, I can't." It was genuinely out of the question for Ashley to go; she was due in to do a day's work at Ancestor Farm.

She was too preoccupied with her mom in that scene with the DC Montpierres, with distant weddings and missing persons, to work out at once that Donna's reluctance to go to the vet's was sparking a good idea. What Ashley *could* do, of course, was drive to the farm–of course she could. As she would be picking up Araby on the way home, it was another legitimate use of her dad's car. And anyhow, it had not occurred to her dopey sister to point out that she wasn't a signatory to the credit card in any case. Ashley made it look like she was giving in to Donna, telling her, "Okay, listen. I'll do it. But you owe me one."

"Cool."

"A *big* one."

Donna was too busy not to agree, tied up in the complicated business of getting to school without Mrs. Meydel to remind her where she had put her stuff, or to feed her whatever was for breakfast. At least that would save Donna having to head to the school WCs to throw it all up. She was going through a bulimic phase. Ashley was only slightly scornful of this, as she had been through one herself.

With Donna gone, Ashley relaxed. She did not have to be at work till ten. When she had a car, she didn't mess around bringing her work clothes in and changing; she wore them. Accordingly, she put on her skirt, blouse and apron. She tied her hair up. She could have left the shawl and bonnet till she got to work, but put them on for old time's sake; the sight of them gave people a start and a laugh at stoplights.

The phone went again, the readout showing the vet's again. Ashley let it trill. The receptionist left the same message. Ashley could not stop off at the vet's first and bring Araby in to work with her. She was pretty sure eighteenth-century sculleries would have featured a cat, even if just to terrorise the mice, but the twenty first century was full of laws governing workplaces, animals and hygiene. She would just have to fetch Araby after work. It would be less complicated if she just went there, rather than called.

She picked up her dad's car key, tossed it and caught it. Then something pricked into the lightness of her mood and she stopped, got an inkling of bad news, a bad day. She did not know why, and because it lasted only a second, she let it pass, and barely had time to be afraid of it as she got out the door and walked round to the garage.

16

W hy did Ashley, daughter of a household accurately described as new money, and a lot of it, do a
minimum-wage job? Nobody she knew understood why she
worked at Ancestor Farm. She did so because it was useful in
a number of ways that had only become clear after she had
been there a while. The year before graduation she blundered
into it as a volunteer during Christmas break, one of a number
of local enterprises into which the school railroaded students.
It seemed more interesting than making up auction hampers,
helping deliver the eccentric Mrs. Lynch's meals-on-wheels
service, or sorting the seasonal onslaught of charity appeals
at the Postal Service. The school described the initiatives as a
chance to get involved in the real world; that claim deserved
the ridicule it attracted. She resumed the Ancestor Farm job as
a part-time worker after graduation. The pay was not an issue
for Ashley, who lived in a world in which people wouldn't even
get out of bed unless obscene sums of money were on offer.
That was *her* version of the real world. Her keeping at the job
actually took more effort to explain than to do the work.

She had wavered over giving it up, but there was a stubbornness in her that kept her there whenever she thought
of Janet sneering, Donna rolling her eyes, her dad citing it
as a criticism of his ability to provide–joking but serious really–and until recently Michael Stambolisky patronizing her.
She also realized at some point that she had gotten to like
the farm because it was not home and was not college. It was

not Michael and his world, nor the catty world of her drifting friends and fixed-in-place neighbors: it was, partly, hers.

Ancestor Farm was a time-warp of Americana faked from props, costumes and facades. It was raised on the grounds of a onetime lunar park whose attractions had pressed permanent patterns into the ground and poisoned the surrounding land. As long as Ashley was one of the museum's living waxworks, nobody could get to her. She used it as a way of keeping up with her studies; the farm was rarely busy, and then not for long, and Ashley was left alone to sit and study, free from distractions.

She kind of liked her boss. He was a refugee from academia called Edmond Demonte. He had given up tenure in George-town, specializing in what he called 'vanished peoples'-Etruscans, Hittites, Romans, Byzantines, and others-and was full, if prompted, of stories about his travels in the areas those peoples had once occupied. He dismissed the papers he had written on them as meaningless; there was nothing, he told Ashley, like being among their ruins, watching from the heights they once held, resting hands on the structures they built. He thought true Americans were among the vanished peoples of the planet. He didn't mean Native Americans, occupying but never seeking to own the land before it became America. Ashley did not quite get that, but was happy to take his word for it. His theories filled shelves in the libraries of several universities and she did not envisage tracking them down and reading them unless she got a few months to spare.

Another good thing about Ashley's place at Ancestor Farm was its lack of responsibility. Unless something went horribly wrong, she would get through her studies and one day be a doctor. She had no starry eyes about such a career, recognized that it was going to be unglamorous and full of responsibilities to people at their ugliest and saddest. College was a drag, home was a drag and her lack of a social life caught her attention only to vex her, so her day at the farm featured a window into a kind of nothingness she craved.

She worked there on Mondays, as college took up Tuesday to Friday. She had been scheduled for a day off as she was owed a day for covering for her co-worker Francie at the weekend, but Francie was out yet again.

Francie was a disorganized single mom, short and skinny, with dark eyes on an odd slant, like one of the Roswell aliens. She was pretty in an uncaring, unconventional way that Ashley kind of admired. She had an air of quiet authority unfortunately canceled out at once by almost anything she said.

She had done a year of college, she claimed, but, not dedicated enough to keep up the lie, admitted to Ashley that she had hardly attended, with the excuse, "Who's got the *time*?" As if to make up for the holes in her education, Francie tried to sound educated–too hard, Ashley realized, having wondered what made talking to Francie so irritating. She said, *albeit* when she meant *although,* said *plausible* when she meant *feasible* and *entitled* when she meant *obliged.* It wouldn't matter if she said the words once, but when she got hold of a word, she did it to death. When she talked about others, like her ex and father of her kid, the kid himself, her friends, her family, or social workers, she often dubbed one of them, in the course of the increasingly convoluted conversation, as *yours truly.*

Francie also said *ex-sedera* a lot. When people questioned her rendition she explained, "It's, like, *Latin*?" She did it once too often to Mr. Demonte, who knew a bewildering number of ancient languages. He finally snapped at her, "The word is *etcetera.*"

She looked at him and said, "*Totally.* That's what I'm *telling* you."

Francie was still likable. Mr. Demonte suffered her absences in good humor, though he once commented to Ashley that it was feasible, or plausible, or both, that Francie timed her absences for when the farm would not be busy. If she thought this was going to make the other workers feel grateful, she was wrong; it meant that she missed out on cleaning, always done in visitor downtime. Francie's initial reaction to Ashley losing first one car, then another, had been one of annoyance that Ashley therefore couldn't give her a ride home to Aliceville anymore when they worked together. Francie's own car had been repoed the year before–spectacularly, by all accounts.

Seeing the expression on Ashley's face one time when she turned up to find Francie a no-show, and that she was going to have to do the cleaning alone, Mr. Demonte reminded her gently that the job was a passing thing for her–and very grateful he was, too–and she would one day escape it. People like Francie were not so lucky. "Please be kind to her," he urged Ashley. "Even though... you might very well want to, uh... *kill* her."

Mr. Demonte had probably once been handsome, despite his protuberant septum and slightly hooded eyes. Middle age had bent his back a little, thinned his hair, and dulled his teeth to an un-American off-white.

He was decked out in his usual work garb, a cross between a gentleman and a hands-on farmer. He greeted Ashley with some puzzlement, as he was expecting Francie, for whom he often had to run through the dress code when she turned up with patent heels and nails done in the absurd fashion of the nail bars in Aliceville. Ashley suspected Francie decided not to turn up precisely because she'd had a showy nail job at the weekend and wanted neither to hide it with gloves nor fade it prematurely with cleaning materials.

Mr. Demonte was soon back in his habitual control. "Wristwatch." He tapped his own wrist but looked at Ashley's. It was her turn to be puzzled, as she had just put her watch into her apron pocket. Then she remembered she was wearing an ASPCA wristband–Janet had hundreds of them at home, leftovers from a failed attempt to get her viewers to buy them. She had put it on, she guessed, in an unconscious desire to show she was in support of the protection and care of animals for her visit to the vet's, which was... weird. It was soon stashed in the apron pocket, where she also had an mp3 player, two coursebooks, a notebook, several pens, two bananas, her cellphone, her keys, her pocketbook and the key for the Chrysler.

Visitors were encouraged to ask questions. When they did, Ashley was supposed to stay in character as she told the group about her dreary chores rather than say, "What does it look like I'm doing, Einstein?" Elderly tourists were the worst, veterans of a thousand visitors' centers and determined to squeeze their whole five dollars' worth of reduced rate out of their visit. Junior school kids were the best as long as the teacher had gotten bored and lost attention–they usually had by the time they reached the scullery. When kids dutifully followed the questions on their worksheets and asked Ashley what she was doing, she sometimes popped her bubblegum and told them she was waiting for an online shop. It passed the time till she could get back to her college books.

Ashley's day passed in the illusion of a forgotten corner of the eighteenth century, with cows lowing and sheep bleating out back, and chickens clucking, with recordings of them for when they didn't feel like it. Mr. Demonte had opposed this move by the museum board, recognizing it as the first nail in the coffin for the funding of the two cows, four sheep, and changing cast of chickens leased from a nearby farm, and for the two workers who dropped by twice a day to check on them. Mr. Demonte had spent many days on the phone negotiating about this. He still sometimes went off on a rant about the tight-fisted bastards who expected the entire eighteenth century for a few measly bucks, yet didn't want to fork out to buy the animals' demonstrably free-range milk and eggs at cost.

When the visitors' voices faded, Ashley replaced them with music under her mob cap, something classical she had stumbled across on the Internet and could not put a name to. It was dreamy and spiky, and accompanied her at the end of the day up the track to the parking lot tucked away behind the visitors' center.

The picture she made as she pulled the car key out of her apron pocket and beamed the doors open lent her a secret smile: eighteenth-century farm girl, not only with all her teeth but about to get into a Chrysler PT. It would have been confusing for a time traveler who might land at that moment. It was not quite so amusing when she saw herself reflected in the car's shiny surface. She banged her forehead, appalled at her stupidity. Her plan had been to collect the cat then go for a long old drive and stop for some food, maybe. Araby would not have minded; tough luck if she did. But Ashley had been so pleased with having the car and not having to wear her everyday clothes that she had forgotten to bring them with her. Now she would have to reclaim Araby, dump her home, change clothes and, if Donna was home, sneak out again for a drive. She pulled her bonnet off with force and scraped her fingers when she snapped the elastic band off her hair. The music was annoying her, and she cursed softly. She pulled her earphones off and scrunched them into her apron pocket, reaching a hand in to turn off the player.

A sound nearby: like the shuffle of a footfall on dirt. Ashley turned. Nobody there, and yet she got the feeling she often got around the five towns, that somebody's eyes were on her. Out back of the museum fallow fields spread out under the sunlight of the late afternoon, but there was a darkness in the trees beyond that merged them into the surrounding woods. There were stagnant pools in the woods that went deep into the earth, so Ashley had heard, and lost tribes of hillbillies hidden out since the Civil War. She thought she saw a movement in the trees and started, spooked. She wanted to laugh the feeling off, but the only thing that moved her shoulders was a shiver at the top of her spine. It was a marvel that Francie and some of the other workers stood there to smoke. In the time it took to smoke a cigarette you could be snatched, and vanish forever.

Still feeling observed, she got into the car then pulled out of the lot and onto the highway in the direction of Barnton.

17

There were a few people in the vet's waiting room but they were subdued and occupying their own spaces; the evening before, it had looked to Ashley like the Sick Pet Club. She got them all united in a stare as she swished over to the desk in her big skirt and shawl, the ribbons of her cap trailing from her apron pocket.

The receptionist welcomed Ashley, her smile professionally pleasant. It was a different girl to that of the previous evening. This one wore glasses that were too big for her face. Her smile dropped when Ashley gave her name. "I left some voicemails with you." She sounded professionally pissed. Ashley deflected the comment with a tight little smile and a slight movement of her hand to suggest that, as she was there, the messages were no longer germane, so why even mention them when they both had an evening to get on with? The girl said, "Doctor would like to see you."

Ashley wondered why nurses and receptionists dropped the article before the word *doctor*. She didn't ask why, instead said cheerily, "Hey, there's nothing wrong with *me*." That was worse, if anything. The receptionist's expression said she had heard that gag twenty times that day alone. With a sweep of her head, she bade Ashley follow her. There was something about her that Ashley not only disliked, but feared: she had dropped her professional face just long enough to show one to Ashley that had more than the hint of a real-world sneer on it.

The girl led her through a corridor with its own unsettling environment: an odd mixture of antiseptic and pet smells, alarming red safety warnings and yellow bins marked with a skull-and-bones and the words *used sharps*. A bit like her joke to the receptionist, Ashley thought. She put on a smile she didn't feel like wearing.

She was agitated at the idea of their keeping Araby in for longer and at having to drag out to Barnton again. It was no big deal after a day listening to music, reading, and being a prop. After an early start and a full day at college, though? A *pain*.

The vet was in his mid-forties. He had sleek black swept-back hair reminiscent of a rocker from the fifties. The look on his face was grim out of habit, Ashley thought later, as if all the bad news he had to give pet-owners outweighed the good. The colors of his eyes didn't quite match, she noticed. He was inviting Ashley into his office. He was all red-rimmed stare and teeth on the corner of his lower lip. Something in him promised a frank discussion that would help Ashley forget the small worries and would, she sensed, wipe that ragged smile off her face.

18

Ten minutes later and two hundred dollars lighter, Ashley stood on a street crowded with small-town rush hour, eighteenth-century scullery maid clutching a leaden Dolce and Gabbana bag. Traffic made its noises and people walked around her all in a blur.

The only figure to break her out of her absorption was in uniform. It belonged to a parking attendant. A beetle-browed Black woman, short but with big hair on which her cap perched precariously, she had her little machine out, a finger poised over it. She also had her eyes fixed on Adam Hyde's car registration. Ashley put her bag down and joined the woman in front of the car.

"You Amish people driving *cars* these days?" The attendant looked amazed. She abandoned the catch-no-eye stare that such unpopular functionaries assumed. Ashley kept a wary eye on the woman's data-entering finger. She explained the fancy dress. Then the usual kind of conversation ensued, Ashley's indignation turning quickly to pleading. The attendant's professionalism melted to Ashley's story the moment she pointed at the vet's and said, "My cat," and offered to fetch her bag from the sidewalk as proof of her story.

"Jeez, no." The woman put her machine to sleep. "You don't have to do *that*. Tough break. I like cats." She made a beaming face, which was... inappropriate, Ashley thought later. "But stuff sure happens to them. What was it?"

"Uh, a girl-cat," Ashley said, then realized that something else was required.

"Traffic accident," they chimed together, almost harmoniously.

"Man, I see it all the time." The attendant dipped her facial features and pursed her lips. "*All* the time, sure. Cats, dogs. Hey, squirrels."

"Squirrels?" Ashley put into the pause.

"*Oh* yeah. Sure. Saw a calf a couple weeks back, wandered out from a farm on up out along down away by the highway toward Greenton–you know the Brahm spread? Messy, messy roadkill–but *messy*. Huh?" She shook her head. She checked the near distance, as if she'd spotted something of interest there–a heinous parking violation or a brown bear getting creamed by a truck–and began to move on. "You be lucky now," she advised Ashley.

Ashley's grimace was meant to telegraph thanks and gratitude. She let the expression slide once her benefactor was a safe distance away. It was replaced with her face on the verge of a scream. Being lucky was far from her grasp.

When she walked back round to the sidewalk door of the car, Janet's fancy Dolce and Gabbana bag, the one with Araby in it, was not there. Ashley assumed calmly that she was going nuts. Why not? Then the calm deserted her. She could feel her nerves tensing for a blow and most alarmingly could hear her own breath. Hands trembling, heart jumping, she fumbled in her apron pocket for the car key, found it, dropped it, picked it up, then stuck it in the lock and pulled the door open.

She looked on the front seats, and on the back seats. Then under them. Where else? With a step back, and a deep breath, she opened the trunk. A quick check of the glove compartment occurred to her for a second. Then she got what she thought was a bright idea, even as a stripe of fear went all the way through her and made her shrivel inside. Had she left the bag down by the vet's reception desk when she paid, distressed by the vanishing dollars and the vet's words busy burning themselves into her head? Possible. Only one way to find out.

Ashley would rather have gone anyplace else or done anything else than walk back up that path and return to the vet's; she would rather have been spectacular roadkill, splayed across the road, guts on show like an animal ready for investigation on a lab table. She took in a gulp of air and walked.

She had not been gone long enough from the vet's for anybody to have forgotten her. For a second Ashley thought the receptionist was about to break into a giggle when she asked, her voice timid, if she had, uh, mistakenly left the–*her* cat behind. The question got everybody's attention. There were a few seconds of pregnant silence before the receptionist broke it with a very controlled *no* and a look that added *sister, you are a walking* cabaret. The girl's emphasis drew the vet back a step as he passed the inside doorway. He stopped and took a long look at Ashley. The nurse happened to be out near reception, too. She put on a face so unassumingly blank that it was pure derision. Ashley felt the Sick Pet Clubbers' eyes jetting acid at the back of her head.

The receptionist nodded through Ashley's explanation about having gotten distracted by a parking attendant. She knew that everybody there was wishing she could stop gibbering and leave. Fortunately, that was one thing she could do. She told her listeners that she'd surely put the bag–and stopped mid-utterance. "*The bag.*" The receptionist emphasized both words. "*Right.*"

She would check in the car, Ashley assured them, backing away and untangling a shoe from the lower reaches of her skirt. She would check, she told them again–she would... *do* that. When she got out the door and onto the vet's driveway, feeling in her apron pocket for the car key, she saw just how difficult that was going to be.

19

Barnton police station was fronted by a desk cop with an expression that could be described at a stretch as *technically helpful*. As Ashley waited in line, she observed that his face was formed of a granite statue's smile and dead grey eyes which he had trained to perform the trick of hiding whatever was replaying in his head while he attended to business. He appeared to agree with everything that was said with the phrase "Yeah, yeah, shouldn't *happen*," and ended each interview with the words "Well, see what we can do, huh?" He made them sound fatal.

When Ashley got her audience with him, it was not long before he was getting confused over the difference one consonant kept making. Ashley said to forget the cat and concentrate on the car. He set to it, bringing forth a new blank form with a flourish. The first thing he asked for was the registration number. When it became clear that Ashley didn't know it, impatient glances homed in on her from everybody in the waiting area. The cop was used to it. He said he believed her, *but*; he was not going to be able to file a report without that number. His eyes were already poised to welcome the man behind Ashley.

Nobody was allowed to use a cell phone in the building. The public phone in the lobby was being treated to astonishingly rapid Spanish by a very tiny woman with a very angry and deep voice. Ashley stepped out into the street and called her sister.

Donna said, "What's up?"

"Oh, I'll *tell* you."

"Tell me... what?"

"You'll love it."

"*What?*"

Ashley kept calm and asked Donna to get the car details. She listened to Donna recite them, checked and double-checked them and wrote them down. Donna sounded too distracted to wonder why Ashley would need those details. She also neglected to ask how things had gone at the vet's, so Ashley told her.

"Dead?" Donna said the word as if she had just learned it.

"Yeah. Donna–"

"Wait–what? How do you mean?"

Ashley was not sure how to answer this. She held the phone away from her ear a second and looked up along the street. The distant clouds looked like mountains. She felt as if she were climbing one. She re-connected ear to phone and said, "She *died.*"

"*Totally* dead?"

"Dead as in never-ever-coming-back-*ever* dead. Hey Donna, you want to know how she died?"

Donna did not sound as if she did. Even so, Ashley recounted the vet's pronouncement that Araby had died a genuine celebrity death: an overdose of a stimulant to her central nervous system, possibly cocaine. It was an event unknown to him in his twenty years of practice, so he had run more than the usual number of tests and analyses. Ashley had gone on the defensive to tell him that what he said was impossible. He widened his eyes at her and informed her it looked like they were having a perception conflict. But wasn't she just a *little* prepared to see his point of view and meet him at least half*way?*

"I *knew* it," Donna squealed. "I *knew* James and Shannon were holding. I just *knew* it."

A very unwise blurt on Donna's part. Later, Ashley was re-lieved; it meant that James and Shannon had not given her sister any of the stuff that had done for Araby. Right then, though, she did not want to know. Donna was going to have to be the one to make the explanations to Janet as to what had become of her famous cat, Ashley told her. She said Donna might also have to go on daytime TV to reveal Araby's fate to its community of square-eyed freaks, and that animal ob-sessives would stalk her to the ends of the planet forever. Of course, she was raging and bluffing. She wanted to tell Donna that she should not be hanging out with people who fooled with drugs, but it was off-topic for the moment. The way she felt right then was that her stupid sister could go to hell in whatever way she chose.

The thing disturbing Ashley was that it was, without a doubt, no accident. It wasn't like anybody had dropped a wrap through carelessness and Araby found it, clawed it open and snorfed it up in a fit of feline delinquency. Cats did not *do* that. Even if it had spilled out of the wrap there was no way she would have given it more than a passing twitch of the whiskers. No. One of those little bastard friends of Donna's would have had to... *administer* it to Araby somehow. And it had probably been James or Shannon, or both. Wasting a gram of coke in the service of a prank would be nothing to them. They also had the badness to go with it, and the nerve.

Ashley went back into the police station and waited in line again. At the desk, the cop filled out a sheaf of forms with the details of the vanished car. There was no point to it except to get that magic number Adam Hyde could pass on to his, as far as Ashley was concerned, useless insurance people.

"See what we can do." The cop was about to wrap things up with Ashley when he registered her appearance. "You Amish people are driving *cars* now?" he checked.

She gave him a long look that almost puzzled him. She could not be bothered to explain. She gathered her stuff together and turned.

"Hey, though," the cop remembered. "How about this cat?"

She told him it was okay. The cat was dead presumed missing and there was no point in looking for her, twice over. She had a vision then of the bag thief hefting his prize in his hand, turning a corner and pulling its zip open, and then opening the opaque little body bag inside. Even the thought of him jumping out of his skin barely made it down her face to make her smile.

20

Déjà vu: Ashley, outside the police station. No car, no cat and she wanted to cry. She was the closest she had come to unmasking herself and manifesting her private face, letting it all out and hollering out her misery. She was also dressed as an eighteenth-century scullery maid.

She summoned her dad's number to her phone. Her thumb hovered and she thought about it but snapped it shut, not ready yet for long-distance histrionics from her dad or Janet. No, it would be better to call them when she was less uptight. She pictured herself stretched out on the rug in her room, a cushion under her head and a couple of Janet's downers swimming through her system.

That corny substitute cat idea distracted her. From where? Some book, she thought. A movie? A common tale: parents out, cat dies somehow, kids replace it... somehow, with an identical cat-somehow, again. At the end the original cat comes back-Ashley forgot exactly how-nonchalant and inscrutable, and sees off the impostor, and the whole gang live happily ever after. Or at least you never get to see the bitching and recriminations that will go on. As a plan to fit Ashley's circumstances, it sucked for all kinds of reasons, paramount among them being that Araby would definitely not be coming back.

But that was what would make it work, she thought-would make it foolproof. No. Too many fools were involved, and she was the chief one. And anyhow, where was she going to get a substitute cat? Pet stores sold kittens, not full-grown mogs. Rescue centers vetted the hell out of you and it took longer than if you wanted to adopt a child. She guessed there were small ads all over the place for cats, but investigating them could take weeks. Ashley would have to face it: she was going to be the host of Celebrity Cat Killer Party forever, her co-hosts being Donna and her horrible pals.

Her phone jumped. She imitated it, then checked the number. It was a cell, no name. Not her dad, anyhow. And not Donna. It could *not* be Janet. Neither was it an Animal Rights group nor an alliance of daytime TV pet obsessives. Not yet. She answered, got a *hello* worked into a purr, and heard, "I'm calling to remind you about your appointment."

"Appointment?" Ashley shivered with a hunted feeling. "Is that the... vet's?"

"The *vet's?*" The hint of a patient chuckle. "No."

"Appointment, really?" Ashley was sure she did not have a dental or doctor's appointment scheduled. "For what?"

"This is Eliza." The caller had it rhyme with *Ebeneezer*.

"Eliza?" Ashley rhymed it with *wiser*. "Eliza who?"

"That's El-*eez*-a?" The correction was firm without sounding tetchy. "I am the fortune teller's factotum."

"The *fortune* teller? Hold on–the fortune teller's... *what*?"

"Her factotum," Eliza said calmly.

Ashley was familiar with the word and yet had not, to her knowledge, ever heard it before.

Eliza explained, "Dentists have, like, *receptionists*? But fortune tellers have factota."

"They do?" Ashley then remembered her rendez-vous with the fortune teller, made on some dark day she did not care to remember. She wondered what excuse she could make.

"They do." The voice sounded hesitant, as if afraid to detract from the harmony of the conversation. "Yes."

"What time is my appointment?" Ashley checked. "Remind me?"

"Last of the day?" There was a pause. "Six thirty. Are you going to be on schedule?"

Well, Ashley was about to say, *I thought you might be able to tell me that, having a fortune teller in-house and all.* Then she remembered that she had already pissed off one receptionist; a mighty revenge had been exacted and she would push her luck if she chanced it again. She was about to tell the fortune teller's factotum that she would love to come but unfortunately had a dead celeb cat and a stolen car and a potentially retributive step-parent on her hands. Not to mention the whole of the daytime TV-watching community, who would have nothing better to do–especially in the evening–than tar-and-feather her before witch-hunting her out of town. She also had the small matter of having to go bury an ax in her sister's head then disembowelling her nasty friends. And in any case, she was a, ahem, woman of science who, no longer being freshly dumped, had no use for mumbo-jumbo like fortune telling.

On the other hand this was, on balance, an even darker day than the one that had led her to such foolishness.

The fortune teller's factotum asked without impatience, "Are you there?"

"I'm here," Ashley said. "But, uh, look... Listen."

The doorway of a store flew open and let out a blast of hip-hop. A woman was yelling at a kid to get right back to her because the freaking bus was coming. People standing in line began to nudge Ashley forward. Ashley thought she heard the fortune teller's factotum say, "I'd really like it if you came," but knew she had to be mistaken.

In contrast to the deserted space of the day before, around Ashley teemed a street going nuts with the rush hour. Bus stops were attracting crowds and, as buses unloaded, adding to them. People with nothing to do but kill time were staring at Ashley Hyde, the personification of celebrity feline death in her archaic Americana maid costume. Small kids were point-ing and hoodied teens were laughing in an offhand way that had nothing to do with humor, and sensing whether even more fun could be had from her. She saw the Aliceville bus approaching. It slowed with a hiss of hydraulics and opened its doors.

"I'll be there," Ashley told the fortune teller's factotum. "Remind me, what's the address?"

She got on the bus, put a finger in her free ear and listened to Eliza's directions. Everybody on the bus was gawping, kids snickering and adults both amused and hostile. *Per-lease*, Ashley had the notion to say to them, *you all know about Ancestor Farm, and how the people who work there dress up in olden-dayz-ee clothes and all, huh?* But then, why *should* they know? The museum was an indulgence for bored schoolteachers and retired people with nothing better to do, not for the working stiffs and driven-to-distraction mommies of Aliceville and Barnton.

The way Ashley's life was going that evening, she wanted to hide away from it and miss the turns it might take. She later saw that at the heart of her decision to head for the fortune teller. It was a sidestep out of the way of the trouble coming at her. She was out of her depth, she realized. She was not in control. She put her head down and breathed deeply and sought some protection from the nightmare she was living through, knowing that there would be none, not on that bus, not under the gaze of a fortune teller, nor of her factotum.

21

T he bus was a sardine can full of people laden with bags and kids, most of them bellowing at one another or into cellphones. The small kids hollered and slurped food and drink made from pure color. Young guys played music from whatever gizmos they had, just loud and tinny enough to be annoying. They made it clear if they caught anybody's eye that they'd shank them rather than turn it down. Gaudy girls giggled and screeched.

Not looking at any of her fellow travelers, Ashley looked out the window. On the steps of Barnton's bowling alley, there was a gang of sour-faced kids, some of whom Ashley remembered from the party. The boys were poised on BMXs or tapped feet on skateboards. Donna's cat-poisoning pal Shannon Seeley was by a car, hanging with two older guys. Ashley thought Shannon was exactly the kind of tramp who'd get into stuff with guys to impress them before they consigned her to wet memories.

Ashley remembered Araby-how could she have forgotten her, even in ten busy minutes? It was a strange jolt of memory, as if from some hundred-year-old dream looking back from a lifetime. Poor little creature, knowing everything she needed to know all her life and then poisoned and faced with terrifying confusion, then consumed by it. It was too outrageous. Nobody should treat any creature that way, no matter how... unlikeable. Living her little life in control, then her feline brain exploding... imploding. Shannon and James were going to have to answer for it. Ashley's features set into the face. She was determined to show them, and soon.

Out there, other girls were making laughter and gestures, trying to draw Shannon's attention and favor. Ashley searched for Donna among them and was cautiously pleased not to see her. One girl, an anorexic fourteen-year-old who, Ashley thought she had heard, broke a bone in her hand while smashing open a condom dispenser, looked up as the bus moved off. It looked to Ashley as if the girl was blowing her a kiss with a sudden repulsive movement of lips painted vampire crimson.

When the bus stopped on the outskirts of Barnton, Ashley was six feet away from the picture window of a fancy burger bar. Framed: the Frenchie set from college around a table, performing laughter for one another. If any of them had turned, Ashley would have been revealed, a mouth-breathing outsider, watching. Their looks would have wormed out of her a sense of panic at being seen on the bus with welfare families and migrant workers, those unhealthy eaters, those conversation shouters. She sank in her seat and turned her face in.

The last fields gave way to the first few streets of Aliceville, Ashley saw Edmond Demonte standing on a traffic island. At first, it looked like a bizarre impression of him, a trick of memory or of the evening light. She realized she had never seen him dressed other than as Eighteenth-Century Man. In his plaid shirt and jeans and muddy gym shoes, he looked like a man adrift from his true time. He did not seem to want to cross the road. His hands were at his side and he was relaxed, watching not the traffic but something across the road. He turned his head toward Ashley and she turned hers away, but thought he saw her, and nodded, then wondered if she had imagined it. When she looked back, he was gone.

Almost at once, she saw Francie on a pedestrian path that, Ashley thought, angled off into a long-abandoned building lot fading into the fields. Like something out of a country song, Francie was plastered in vivid make up and pushing a baby carriage. Ashley did not need to qualify as a doctor to see that Francie was definitely not sick. Mr. Demonte was going to bring this very point up with Francie, it seemed plain. She may have thought about it a little more had she not seen Michael Stambolisky. The bus came to a stoplight and he crossed the intersection in his Porsche, a companion in the passenger seat. He was talking and waving a hand. Was that Chloe? Ashley was over him, of course–over Chloe too–well of *course*. She could think *whatever* to herself and curse them just for the hell and fun of it. Then her mind was taken off them entirely.

Because not far behind Michael Stambolisky, Adam Hyde's Chrysler cruised into the picture. In an effort to race the stoplight, the driver was going at a clip fast enough to close the slight gap with the preceding cars. Ashley jumped out of her seat, but by the time she got to the front of the bus the car had merged into the silhouettes made by the evening sun. The bus driver made a stony face; he was not going to open the doors on a stoplight. And what had she been going to do, anyhow? What, run down the street tripping over her skirt and shaking her fist at the thief like something out of the funny papers?

It was like the landscape was reading her mind and scratching through it to open up her cares for examination. None of it was a revelation to Ashley, so it just had to be the landscape showing her how smart it was, making its point; it was a vindictive place. She had always hated it. She loathed it all over again and vowed that she would leave, whatever occurred in her life. If Columbia fell through, she would go to New York anyhow, flip burgers or sew sequins, work in a bookstore–anything, as long as she was out of those five towns and away from the eyes that filled them, and the mouths that gave them their soundtrack.

22

A shley escaped from the bus in Aliceville's center. Sharing the fate of a lot of towns in the state, her life had been chased out of the place. It had been dumped five miles up the highway to a site reclaimed pointlessly from nowhere, and turned into the Aliceville Mall, already shabby and peeling. Left behind in the center was an open space interrupted by a concrete traffic circle. There had been an obelisk there–a Civil War memorial–but the developers had uprooted it and set it as the centerpiece of the mall, where it meant less than nothing. Aliceville looked like the kind of place where the garbagemen didn't collect but delivered.

Tattooed bald guys walked dogs who surveyed the world with an e-number hyper-awareness. Their escorts stopped to grunt and gesticulate heads-ups. Kids rode the sidewalks on bright, gimcrack bikes; they used them like mobility aids to save them the trouble of walking, Ashley thought, not fast enough to prompt exertion. Two groups of street drinkers, by that time of day bored with their own company, eyed passers-by. Ashley almost saw cartoon light bulbs splutter on over their heads as they yelled friendly but edgy obscenities at a dog walker.

She started to hope that she didn't stand out. Cue one of those same dim bulbs crackling over her head: she was Miss Arcane America. She heard the first guffaws and a shouted question as to the whereabouts of her horse.

Most of the storefronts were boarded up, but a Yo Chicken and a Sliza Pizza cast out odors of old oil, and light that clashed with that of the day. There was a dollar store, a thrift store and a twenty-four-seven behind an iron grille. There was a nail parlor called Some One Whose Beautyfull outside which its Asian girl workers smoked, their protective masks around their necks. The tattoo parlor was called Pain and Ink. There was also Aliceville Quizine, a store selling red plastic kitchen stuff. The fortune teller's factotum had told Ashley to look out for that.

Beyond it was a place with a purple nightlight in its storefront window. The door was black, but a sickle moon and a star glowed pale yellow on its center panel.

A feeling swelled up again in Ashley of the pointlessness of her venture. Though she had put it out of her mind, she remembered making the appointment for her reading from the secrecy of her cell phone and her room, not mentioning it to a soul. Well, she was done with Michael, and with Chloe, and she was over them both and back on track at college. She was in the middle of a very bad day, admittedly, but at least it was probably not going to get worse.

She heard a call: "Yo, Florence Nightingale." She did not look at her audience. They cussed, not *at* her, as such, but in a pointed way that made her feel like the sheltered farm girl she resembled. She hurried, her gait becoming stupidly dainty.

There was no *hope* of a cab on that street, and Ashley really didn't fancy wandering off the main drag to look for a cab office. The bus stop was across the street, and Ashley had a foot out on the pavement when a car shuddering with revs and bassy music and full of yelling boys made wind across her. It bust a plastic bottle on its way, and the explosion startled her. The car was up the road before she finished swearing. A turn back to check if she'd dropped anything out of her apron during her jump allowed her to catch the flutter of a movement in the fortune teller's window that, for a second, glued her to the spot, then got her walking back.

23

I n the window, a yawning mouth, the flexing of shoulders, the disdainful swish of a tail, and eyes that glowed amber for a second to appraise Ashley Hyde before they fixed on something more diverting. The background looked like an empty wardrobe covered in dusty, dark blue velvet. Five aces of spades lay on the floor as if dropped by a cardsharp. There was also a small plaster bust of a boy on its side and a square of embroidered yellow silk with loose threads and a tatty corner, like somebody had abandoned the making of a pocket handkerchief or a dicky-bow. Among these things lounged a cat who, if it wasn't one of Araby's nine lives, had to be a first cousin.

Ashley was drawn from trying to catch its eye again by the shout *Hey, Cinderella* behind her and then by the buzzing of the black door before her. It opened with silent magic. She stepped into a hallway whose lights were diffused from the picture rail of the interior walls. A veiled woman emerged from the darkness and bowed her head. She took Ashley's hand, held it in both of hers for a second, and said, "Welcome."

Ashley said, "Hi."

"I am Eliza."

"Right. The fortune teller's... fac*totum*?"

"Indeed." Ashley saw Eliza's dark eyes narrow as she registered that Ashley was dressed in the clothes of bygone America. "And you're Miss Hyde."

"Sure."

"I'm happy that you found us." The fortune teller's factotum was a cross between Philadelphia's Muslim women when they dressed for summer and the lead in an amateur drama of *Scheherazade*. And who said *indeed*, a word that English people used in old movies? Everything about this woman was pissing Ashley off–but then she guessed that whoever she met that evening would fall to the same level. What she really needed to do was forget the cats–all of them–and go home and sink a pill and sleep away her troubles.

Eliza handed her a business card on which was printed the single word *Tudora* in a luminous cursive script, *$40* added beneath it in shining ink. She asked, "Cash or card?" Ashley opted for cash. She could not help it, but let the words form in her head: she would be unwise to leave a record of her visit because she was planning on stealing–yes, the only word–the fortune teller's cat. They were stark, with the ring of the court-room to them.

"I will ascertain whether Madame Tudora is ready for you," Eliza told her, and she turned back into the gloom.

Ashley consigned *ascertain* to the spangly vocabulary with a roll of her eyes. Eliza opened a door that revealed another dim light, which helped Ashley orientate herself a little. She put her right hand out and found a door handle. It had to lead into the room in which the cat was doing its front-of-house act.

Ashley had not stolen anything since her shoplifting expedition with Sue Shah when they were eleven. She had never needed to, but, more pertinently, it was still sharp in her mind how everybody had looked at her and Sue in the store when they were caught, and in the office, as they waited for the police. There was also the cop's palpable annoyance at having her time wasted when she could have been out catching felons, plus the bitchily amused cast in the eye of the office girl her dad sent from the studio to pick her up. Not to mention Sue having been foolish enough to tell everybody at school about it when she could easily have kept it quiet. Ashley had suffered enough disdain in her life and did not need any more. However, it seemed at that moment that it was certain to come and that it was going to be a toss-up between getting a name as a cat thief or a cat killer.

She remembered Eliza telling her she was the last sucker of the day. In that case, she would surely deposit Ashley with her mistress and then leave. Ashley guessed that she could make some excuse to preclude the fortune teller following her into the room at the front. The inner door was opened. Her heart shaking, Ashley followed the beckoning hand of the fortune teller's factotum.

24

A shley could have made a good guess at what the fortune teller and her room would look like. It was a corny carnie sideshow tent but set up in the back of a one-time store. There were drapes around the walls, not to keep the light out–there were probably no windows in a store's back room–but to enhance the gloom. Low-watt bulbs were subdued further by fringed silk shades. Backlit from below there was a statue of a snake-handling boy on a short column, a ceramic hand with a blue glass eye in its palm in a niche in the wall, and, in another niche, brass scales. On the floor between the door and a round table lay a faded Turkish rug in red and black, woven blue eyes at the corners Ashley could see.

The fortune teller wore a tailored black linen jacket and a floral print blouse in muted greens and yellows, its collar fixed with a mixed metals brooch in the shape of theatrical comedy and tragedy masks linked grotesquely by one tongue. A green scarf covered most of her hair. She was somewhere in middle age, classically and timelessly striking looking: sharp-nosed, dark-eyed, full-lipped, a woman who, Ashley thought later, had mastered arts both graceful like, say, dressage, or sword fencing, and brash, such as flamenco dancing. Ashley had been expecting a batty old dame with unkempt hair and dirty fingernails. The fortune teller sat at the far side of the table, which was covered by a damask cloth.

"Ashley." Madame Tudora spoke quietly.

"That's me." Ashley approached. "So, uh, what's the... procedure?"

"Sit down." Madame Tudora waved toward the chair on Ashley's side of the table. "I'll be reading your cards." Her accent sounded almost English. Ashley was sure she had only glanced down for a second to orientate herself over the chair, but when she looked back there was a deck of cards in the center of the table.

"Not my palm?" Ashley did not know why she felt so disappointed. For a few seconds she was adrift from the script she had been rehearsing.

"No." Madame Tudora picked up the cards and fanned them, then reconstituted them into a block in front of Ashley.

The cards: a regular deck and not Tarot, disappointing Ashley further.

There was a movement behind her, and the fortune teller's factotum came in bearing a small tray. She bent down beside Ashley, revealed the tray as a tiny wooden table, unfolded its spindly legs and on it placed a fluted china cup of something that steamed. "Camomile," Eliza announced softly-camo*meel*, of course–and was gone. Ashley was not crazy about camomile tea, or any tea, but guessed that asking for a Dr Pepper would not have gone down well. The sweet steam wafted up to her face. Madame Tudora said to her, "You were the child who read."

"What?" The words were unsettlingly familiar to Ashley. "Who... *read*?"

"Who read," Madame Tudora repeated. Ashley remembered her tutor Mrs. Ensley reminding her of that. For a crazy moment, she thought this had to be the Jessicator in her evening job. "And you still read."

Madame Tudora no longer sounded English to Ashley, more like somebody who had acquired English, correctly and painstakingly.

She barely had time to reflect on this when Madame Tudora told her to cut the cards and keep at it until she was left with eight piles, and then to take the top card from each. Madame Tudora stashed the remaining cards to one side. She told Ashley to take a minute to look at the cards–she did not have to memorise them–and then to place them face down in a rough circle. They were a mixed bunch, and their numbers meant nothing to Ashley. She noted that the two eights and a two would have been good to hold in a game of Crazy Eights.

Madame Tudora took Ashley's attention away from the cards when she said, "There is a woman thinking hard about you."

"Right." A general enough thing for any fortune teller to risk, Ashley thought. "Who?"

"You have a sister? Whose name is... Begins with D?"

Ashley said, "Dorothy?"

Madame Tudora lowered her eyes and formed a smile she did not want to share. She did not need to say, "Oh come *on* – who's called *Dorothy* these days?" She was silent for ten long seconds. "*Is* that her name?" she seemed to be asking, although she put up a don't-tell-me hand. "Italian lady?"

"My sister?" Ashley was puzzled. "Italian? Oh." *Donna*: Italian for *woman*. Okay, she had fallen for that. She got the gloomy thought that Donna would never morph into a woman, just remain a child. The urge to ask Madame Tudora if Donna was going to die soon taunted her, but that made her superstitious in that environment, wary of prompting bad luck by talking such possibilities into being. She recovered her antagonistic mood, and asked, "What's my mom's name?"

Madame Tudora shut her eyes a second, seemed to be thinking. "Sarah," she said. And that was true. "But known as Sally." That was just as true. Sally Hyde had been gone a long time before Ashley found out that her mom had been christened Sarah. It was as if she had a secret name from another life.

Ashley was not sure if she dared ask the question that came to mind then but went ahead anyhow. "Where is she?" Madame Tudora looked the question back at her. "My mom?"

"I don't know." The look challenged Ashley to ask more.

"Is she the woman who's thinking of me?"

"I don't know."

"You don't *know*?" Ashley was torn between admiring the woman for her honesty and deriding her for her lack of finesse. "Is my mom alive?"

"There is a woman, indeed perhaps several women, focusing thoughts on you right now." Madame Tudora was looking at her own palm, Ashley noticed. She craned her neck a little to see if there was anything held in it. Madame Tudora caught that and held her empty palm up. She said, "Their thoughts are... troubled. I know that your mother is not part of your fortune at this time."

Ashley was not entirely surprised; her mom had not been part of her fortune for most of her life. She began thinking of all the women with whom she had had contact in the past few days. All her onetime friends at the party, for instance: the undercurrents between them would have made a few ripples in the ether, surely. There were the vet's receptionists too, and the nurse, the parking attendant, maybe. And Donna-Donna had to be thinking of her, even only to worry about what she was going to say to try to deflect blame for the fate of Araby.

"But... how do you know all this?" Ashley asked, flustered.

"Well." Madame Tudora laughed abruptly and looked a little surprised at the question. She said, "I'm a fortune teller. And now, concentrate." She cast her gaze to the cards for the first time and told Ashley to shut her eyes and place a finger on any card.

"Open them now, if you want." The woman had her own eyes closed, Ashley's chosen card in her hand. She held it up with the suit toward Ashley, a red jack. "A *man* in your life." The fortune teller's tone held what could have been a hint of mockery. "The knave of hearts. A romance." The old-fashioned word seemed ridiculous, but it cut into Ashley all the same. "Now finished."

"Yeah."

"And in... anger."

"Yes."

Madame Tudora opened her eyes and trapped Ashley's in them. She made a little pout, as if to inform Ashley that it had not been a question. "You were too young." She sounded disapproving, but it was probably just the unnatural precision of the woman's speech. "For this kind of man."

"Yeah." Ashley let her agreement out with a long breath.

"And so is your friend."

"Friend?" Ashley added Chloe Gustavson to the number of women whose thoughts might have been fixed on her. And so they should have been. *Bitch*, she thought–how could she have known the C, L and E were destined to be silent in Chloe's name–*bitch*. Bitterness welled up inside her with such acceleration that she felt a wave of the danger in it, and thought she was going to sit upright, make the face she glimpsed only in her most private moments, and cry.

"Whatever you may call her now." Madame Tudora nodded. Ashley stared. "He is a man who is not ready for his... relations with people to come to any satisfactory conclusion. I see it." Madame Tudora tossed the jack aside with a dismissive flick of her thumb. "And what I see is that, in time, he will look at you, this man, and he will realize that he was foolish to lose your love. And so will your friend."

"Will we be friends again?" Ashley was mad at herself for letting the question out. She and Chloe had shared a great deal of their lives. Ashley had a flash of birthdays, Christmases, Valentines, even, impromptu presents and in-jokes and kisses, dances, movies, trips out and trips away... all chucked in the air. Her question revealed to her that she was not over Chloe–not yet.

"I don't know." Madame Tudora's tone suggested a gentle annoyance. "But a fortune teller isn't required to tell you that you don't need friends who... betray you in such a way. Your future is full of friends. Perhaps you should choose them more carefully. Not in a... paranoid way," she warned. "Just... *wisely*. Don't stop trusting people. See if they can, in some small way, earn your trust. Now."

Businesslike, she turned three cards very rapidly and, hardly glancing at them, said, "Eight, two, eight," even though their order was actually two-eight-eight. "A significant number for you." She clicked fingers. "Not a house." Eyes closed, she nodded.

Ashley's fancy of laying out a perfect play in a Crazy Eights game was dispelled by the echoes of the jolts that had totalled her car that night on a corner in Falkender. The numbers, the way Madame Tudora ordered them, were from her Peugeot's registration. She hadn't had the Nissan long enough to remember its number.

Against Ashley's scientific view of the world, against her sense of logic, and her better nature, Madame Tudora was spooking her. "My car," she said.

"You lost that car." The fortune teller paused. "And you lost another," she added matter-of-factly. "But think of it in this way. You were unharmed. Think how many people are unlucky in accidents on the highway. Let me tell you that many people come to me saying, 'My husband, my wife, my child, my friend, dead on the road,' and how... empty their lives become. Their thoughts are roamed by... ghosts." Her use of the word sounded a little apologetic. "All because of cars."

"Sure." Ashley had put the loss of her cars into perspective the night Harold Shester exploded, but said, "You're right."

Inside, she was still on-mission. At the back of her mind there was Janet disguised as Maxine Wasserman and a million TV gazers and the cat-shaped hole that would appear in their universe if she didn't take steps to avert such a disaster: it would be *Night of the Living Pet-Lovers.*

"You'll get another car," Madame Tudora promised. "And soon, I think. They are things, objects." She gave them the tiniest sniff. "They mean..." She fanned the three cards in her hand, and almost before Ashley had registered the movement, they were gone. "Almost nothing."

From then on, Madame Tudora had Ashley nailed. Ashley's lack of friends came up, and her conflicted desire for them. Ashley's failing grades came up, and the danger they represented to her plans. The fortune teller assured Ashley that they would pick up. And New York? Yes, or a place very like it, there in Ashley's future. She sensed Ashley's fear for Donna's safety, and observed that Donna was at that moment very open to suggestion; Ashley should not be afraid to take control to make sure that her suggestions, accompanied with guile and a little gentle force, were the ones Donna followed.

Madame Tudora said that Ashley's future was shining; the lacks would be filled. Ashley would escape from the hurt in her life, would calm the forces steering her and go at her own pace. Ashley liked hearing all that, so it was only with some reluctance that she asked, "What about my... current problem?"

"Hmm." Madame Tudora picked up the final card, an ace of clubs. She studied it hard then took a long look into Ashley's eyes, saying, "The ace suggests that your problem will be solved if you do one very... *obvious* thing, and by the most direct way. Clubs are... *elegant.*" Having found the word, she let it hang, as if trying to decide whether it would do. "They bring elegant solutions. This doesn't mean that it will necessarily be a... *pleasant* way, or an easy one." It seemed as if the words displeased her because of their inexactitude. "It may involve some risk of... retribution." She seemed to like that word better, and nodded. "Possibly. Your father is absent right now."

Ashley was looking for the card. It was gone. She got the impression of a disconnected part of her mind having witnessed it flying off into the air surrounding her. The change of tack took her by surprise.

"Yes? He's away?"

Ashley nodded.

"Well." The fortune teller leaned back in her chair a little. Ashley got the impression of anybody at the end of a day's work, wanting to relax, stretch her arms, hook a thumb into her waistband and give it a tug. "Perhaps your problem will be solved when he gets back from Europe."

"How do you know he's in Europe?"

"Paris, Strasbourg... Geneva," came the answer, very slowly and deliberately. "Rome, Florence, Vienna? Vienna, I think. Kraków... Prague – yes. Brussels?"

Ashley nodded, but did not need to. Madame Tudora added, almost in a whisper, "London, England."

"You can see all that?" Ashley was pretty sure that the woman had recited her dad's exact itinerary, made those names greater and grander than ever in her odd, almost-European accent. She stared at Madame Tudora. "But how?"

"I don't know." The fortune teller, a fortune told, folded her hands before her with an air of finality, and Ashley knew that their session was over.

"Wow." Ashley knew she was looking impressed, if not amazed. She was both.

There was no more to tell, and nothing more to ask, for the moment. Ashley remembered that current problem of hers, and what the fortune teller had said about resolving it. She looked up. "Listen," she said. "Can I use your bathroom?"

25

Ashley's eyes had adjusted to the low light in Madame Tudora's room, so she felt at ease in the passageway. She ran her hand along the wall and found the door handle. She opened the door into a room busy with furniture, storage boxes, junk mail and flyers and bills and free newspapers and magazines, books, packs of incense, tins of cat and people food, some crockery, some cutlery and a life-size phrenology bust with its nose missing, on which was placed a wig of long black hair. On a desk perched a scruffy cube: a computer monitor, the words *St Agnes of the Oilfields* scrolling across its screen. Over the desk were shelves with rows of files marked, Ashley saw at once, with the names of local towns and neighborhoods.

The main sight, though? A young woman who sat on the arm of a cluttered couch, busy lacing up a shoe. Her head jerked up when Ashley came in and she broke her lace with a snap. She turned the startled look that invaded her flushed face into a moon-shaped grin.

Her name was Mary Dorn. She was one of the Dorns of Firemont, which had never meant anything in Ashley's lifetime; she had some idea that the family had once been big deal old money. The Firemont Dorns were a cursed and unlucky family, her dad had told her. They had blown fortunes on crazy spending and suffered bankruptcy and ruin, lawsuits, disappearances, fugitives, murder and suicide. Mary's dad was in jail for... fraud, Ashley thought, and her mom had died when

Mary was a kid. The Dorns had been friendly with the impoverished remnants of the Bouvier family back in the sixties or seventies and Ashley had heard that they had also had links to Charles Manson and his murdering girls.

Mary had been at Ashley's elementary school. Ashley recalled a bright, showy kid not restrained by the sorry figure she cut: raggy-haired, snot-nosed, dressed as if by chance, a distinct air of chaos about her.

Ashley had not liked her much but had always been aware of her.

What was left of the family rattled around the Dorn mansion, which had once stood snootily in its own grounds, but had been swallowed up by the expansion of Firemont in the sixties. People scoffed that it was only the housing projects around it that kept the decrepit old place standing.

Mary had gone to junior high someplace else or, Ashley had heard, not at all. Whatever she had done, the shine had been roughened off her by the time she resumed schooling at Falkender High. She had still been a smart Alice with a look that said she knew all the answers even if nobody would ask her the questions. She became one of those kids on the periphery, rarely invited to take part. Most of the kids, and some teachers, thought Mary Dorn was disturbed. If not actually nuts.

Despite her milk-white skin and blond hair, there had always been something about Mary that made Ashley think of the Black girls who congregated on Sundays at the five towns' evangelical churches. She had the same long fragile-looking limbs and flat chest, the same plastic barrettes in her hair, sometimes plaited elaborately, Ashley recalled, into works of ludicrous art. She had dressed like the church girls too: thin cardigan sweaters, faded or pastel, hard to tell, buttoned at the neck only, pale shapeless dresses with the ghosts of patterns, flat pumps she wore as late as possible in the year and her legs bare and veiny, when girls had been wearing pantyhose or long pants for two months. Mary Dorn was one of those kids always caught out when it rained out of the blue on spring or fall afternoons; no raincoat nor jacket, and sopping wet by the time she got across the campus, her fancy hairdo reduced to rat-tails, her dress see-through.

Ashley recalled Mary staring at her in class, turning away if caught, or smiling shyly. Mary Dorn's blue eyes were startling. Ashley thought this was a possible consequence of her habitual intensity, her eyes forced into wide alertness, but it had struck Ashley more than one time that Mary Dorn's eyes startled her precisely because they resembled her own. Once or twice over the years when looking in a mirror, worrying at a zit, brushing teeth or just gazing idly, she got the unsettling, strange thought, 'Just who *is* that?' and found herself thinking of Mary Dorn. Creepy.

In the fortune teller's storefront room, Ashley forced out a smile and a cheery, "Hey, Mary Dorn." She resisted adding, as the kids had done at school, *of the* Firemont *Dorns.*

"Oh. Hi." Mary looked Ashley up and down. "Ashley *Hyde*? Goodness me. I didn't recognize you."

"No?"

"No–goodness, no," Mary said. "Not at all. I haven't seen you for the longest time."

The dress and cardigan combination hadn't changed. Mary wore scuffed, clumpy shoes, one of them sorrier than ever with its broken lace. Ashley looked at a coat hanger on the picture rail. On it hung the remains of the fortune teller's factotum: a shimmery tunic dress with a print of jagged leaves, gossamer harem pants, a veil, a kind of headdress with plastic coins on it. Ashley looked at it long enough for it to be absurd that Mary's eyes were not drawn there too.

On the desk by the laptop, Ashley saw a contact lens case, and she also took a theatrical, piercing look at that for good measure. She looked down in search of curly-toed slippers and thought she saw the tip of one on the other side of the desk.

"Well, I recognize you." Ashley made the foolish face people made when they said things that didn't need saying. "So, then, Mary *Dorn*, what are you doing here?" Ashley put on a somewhat silly voice, as if embarrassed to be asking a question so directly.

"I'm, uh... I've got a... an appointment."

"Oh, you do?" Ashley dropped the silly voice. She looked hard at Mary Dorn.

"Yes." Mary's hand strayed toward the lens case. Ashley watched it. Mary drew her hand back and made a fist. "Yes. I... actually do."

"*Actually?*" Ashley let the word hang, redundant. Mary bent her head and nodded. Ashley persisted, "With the fortune teller?"

"Yeah." Mary tried to laugh. She made an aren't-we-girls-kind-of-stupid gesture. "But... I mean..."

Mary's smile became a misery. Ashley had seen it go that way just once back in school. The memory now came back to her: accurately suspecting Mary of attending to something off-topic, a teacher had snatched up Mary's notebook, and strange plastic confetti had fallen out of it, going all over the nearby desks and the floor. The entire class had collapsed into laughter. The teacher had thrown the book back down with some violence. Ashley was puzzled at the clarity of such a trivial incident in her mind then remembered the Washington Montpierres and the small girl in the photo who was not her–confetti everywhere, of course, some dreary wedding.

Ashley set her focus back to the present, latching onto Mary Dorn's faltering words and saying, a little harshly, "But... *what*?"

"Why are you asking me..." Mary fussed with her hair. "In that way?"

"What way is that?" A tremor in her guts revealed to Ashley that she was nervous. She was sure that Madame Tudora was about to come in to find out who was talking.

Mary's eyes mirrored Ashley's. Ashley was startled by them all over again.

Ashley said, "You need to go through the fortune teller's receptionist."

Mary dropped her smile.

"Her *factotum*," Ashley prompted.

Mary looked down at her nails. "I have an appointment," she repeated. She was about to add something else when she looked up and saw the determined set of Ashley's face.

"No you don't," Ashley informed her. "I was the last one of the day. Remember?"

"Remember?" Mary didn't know what to do with the word.

"Listen, Mary. I don't have a lot of time."

"Hey." A flush came into Mary's cheeks. "Just who do you think you are, barging in here like this and telling me..." The fight went out of her. Her eyes were no longer angry enough for it, her voice too low. "Well... what *are* you telling me?"

"I said listen," Ashley reminded her. "Or what I'm doing is walking out that door and, first thing tomorrow, straight to the local rags. And I'm sure I don't need to tell you that I have... uh, connections with people on TV." Ashley never thought she would hear herself say those words, but there they were. "You know all that." Ashley almost laughed. "In fact, you know everything about me, don't you? So are you listening, El-*eez*-a?"

26

By the time Adam Hyde and Janet Snyder got home to the dark, muted American burbs from the bright lights of their grand tour of Europe, nobody would have known there had ever been a party in the Hyde house. Ashley could rely on Donna not to mention it, not because her sister had suddenly gained the art of discretion, but because the present took up her entire her attention span. The party had been a dull old wretched old affair anyhow, utterly forgettable–the vindictive drama enacted at the heart of it remaining private. Donna had, appropriately, forgotten it.

A reunion, over-loud, crass. As the greetings were exchanged, Ashley got the impression that her dad had been so impressed by airlines' executive lounge facilities that he had forgotten the splendors of Europe's cities, their cute squares, bijou museums, hidden Leonardos, chi-chi town halls, even the wizardry of ancient clocks. She was taking part in the conversation simply to spot an opening for the spin she would have to put on the disappearance of the Chrysler; that was to be the only big event of Adam and Janet's absence.

The tacky presents were distributed; Adam Hyde was a naturally generous man but liked to accompany his largesse with hoo-ha. Ashley got a metal Mozart effigy stuck on a paper-weighting rock, a papier-mâché Rabbi puppet and a letter-opening knife with the Paris coat-of-arms. Ashley said, "Nobody gets *letters*, Dad."

"Bills, Ash." Adam Hyde pointed to the pile of them on the corner of the kitchen unit. "It'll open bills just as well, and when you start to get them, you'll be glad of it. You'll be able to stab the postman."

No news about the cat, of course; the cat was *not* news. There was nothing for Ashley to do. Events would unfold and she had to be ready both to react to them and steer them. A strange movement on the table: she nearly moved her hand away as if she'd been stung, but it was her hand that had made the movement. She was trembling. She put both hands on her knees.

The fortune teller's cat had passed with flying colors in front of Donna. Ashley was only cautiously cheered by this. It was fair to say that Ashley could probably have brought home a pipe-smoking albino orang-utan and told Donna it was Araby and she would barely have registered the substitution. Despite being told quite specifically during Ashley's call from outside the vet's that Araby had stepped onto the slippiest celebrity trail and done a full River Phoenix, Donna expressed only minimal surprise at the cat's resurrection. She had given the impostor a faint smile before getting distracted by something on her phone and forgetting about her.

Eagle-eyed Mrs. Meydel, though? Maybe she was just distracted as a premature grandmother–all new-baby-this and new-baby-that–but she had not missed a beat at her first sight of the little *doppelganger*.

Madame Tudora's mog had taken well to her re-homing. Ashley had used love and affection like lethal weapons to orientate the creature, followed by plenty of food. The cat was easy with Ashley by the time Janet arrived home and had begun to register both Donna and Mrs. Meydel as presences no longer worthy of scrutiny. She was a calm little thing. Araby had always been almost humanly nervous and uptight, a cat diva. The arrival of a bunch of new people was never going to faze the fortune teller's cat, nor pique her curiosity.

Mary Dorn told Ashley that the cat's name was Piska. "You're kidding," Ashley had said. "I mean, that is *so* not a cat name." It was though, Mary said, and exactly: it was Romanian for *little cat*. Ashley had re-christened her Araby 2.0.

On the evening of the homecoming, it didn't take long for Janet to ask, "And where's my special baby?" She walked into the lounge and called Araby's name. That was not going to cut any ice with Araby 2.0.

When Ashley had seen the cab arrive, she had put the cat on a small mound of Bouncy Cat Bix in her basket in the far reaches of the kitchen. Araby's small basket and blanket had gone with Araby and the luckless thief. Ashley had bought nearly identical replacements. Araby 2.0 wouldn't go near the large basket, maybe sensing the bad vibe in its abandonment, like a house in which an ax murder had happened. Luckily the vet's nurse had removed Araby's collar and name disc on the first visit and gave it to Ashley, swopping it for one similar to a hospital wristband. The collar would have taken some replacing, as it had been made by a jeweler and sported a ridiculously huge opal. Opal or not, Araby 2.0 hated it and tugged at it with a paw, but that, Ashley had had to whisper to her, was just tough. She only had to wear it until Janet had seen it anyhow; then she could claw it off if she wished–she could take it to the pawnshop for all Ashley cared.

Her dad and Donna were catching up, going, *Yah? Oh* yah. Oh *yah, rilly? Oh* yah. No, *rilly?* Ashley wondered how long they could follow the conversation before forgetting what they started off talking about. She went to join in this sparkling repartee and left Janet to repeat Araby's name in increasing puzzlement. Ashley heard her say very sharply, "*Baby!*" As Janet's perplexity was peaking, Ashley saw the cat's nose come round the kitchen door, her dark shape passing Janet unhurriedly. Ashley thought up some dumb questions for her dad and added some phony laughter, all the while with half an eye on the double act playing itself out a few feet away.

"Ex*cuse* me?" Ashley knew things were getting critical whenever Janet started with the two words she had turned into a weapon. "Ashley," Janet said quietly. Ashley, fully immersed in her role, thought, *oh, okay, why me, as usual*? "*And* Donna," Janet added.

Ashley volunteered to turn and ask, "What?"

Janet said, "I'd like for you to tell me what has happened to my cat."

Ashley could not look at Janet. She looked for the cat. She got the sickening feeling that she had deluded herself into missing something very obvious. Maybe the fortune teller had messed with her and hypnotized her: Araby 2.0 *was* a pipe-smoking albino orang-utan.

"*I* don't know." Donna locked onto Ashley's searching look and reflected it. "*What* happened?"

"Not only my cat," Janet warned. "But my public's cat." She tried to sound as if she were sending herself up whenever she said *my public*, but she didn't fool Ashley; Maxine Wasserman had taken Janet over and they both meant it earnestly.

"She took sick while you were away." The words had been gathered on the stage cue in Ashley's head, and burst out for their moment: a bout of flu, a visit to a vet's, transport, medication and home again in an hour. "It lasted like a *day*? She's fine now," Ashley finished. "Why? What's up?"

"Ex*cuse* me? *Look* at her." Everybody looked, then looked back at one another and made the faintest of movements with hands and shoulders. "Look how goddam *fat* she's gotten."

"Could be the medication," Ashley said.

"*What* medication? Where is it?" Janet held a hand out. "Show me. Where's the vet's report?"

Ashley sidetracked them with a rambling tale of how it had not occurred to her to look for details about Araby's regular vet. Of course she had a plan, and one that most non-domestic animal Americans could only dream about. Nor had she thought to contact anybody at the studio, not on a Sunday afternoon. Mary Dorn had managed to get Ashley a report on the Barnton vet's stationery that detailed treatment for the flu, plus a receipt. The small bottle of pills Mary gave Ashley would make any creature fart a bit if they had to be demonstrated–that was all. "How did you *get* this?" Ashley had asked, but Mary had said only that a girl had to keep a *few* secrets.

Janet fumed and looked from Ashley to Donna to the cat, then back to the bogus vet's report. Janet always looked at her most perplexed when facing a problem that could not immediately be delegated to one of her lackeys. It did not matter what the story was, Ashley kept reminding herself, as long as it got thoroughly confused. She introduced the vet's first opinion, the nurse's opinion, a rumor detailing a new strain of animal flu, and another in which it was reported that some cats did not get on with certain ingredients in commercially available food... Janet was not bothered about other cats. Desperate inside, calm outside, Ashley filled every second of silence with prattle. Janet was dismayed to see that the conversation was continuing without her questions being answered. She gave up on it at last. Thunder-browed, she declared, "You have ruined her."

Ashley and Donna protested. Their dad said, "Hey, Jan, I think that might be putting it a *little* strong, huh?"

"Ruined," Janet insisted.

"You could send her to a fat farm," Donna risked, and while Ashley and her dad giggled, Janet answered with a murderous look. "I mean, they must *have* one for cats."

"She doesn't *recognize* me," Janet said.

That was accurate enough. Ashley had to resist a smirk.

"Of course she does." Adam Hyde waved to Araby 2.0, who was in the hallway contemplating items of baggage, and called, "Don't you, baby?"

"She does *not*." Janet walked over and bent down to the cat. Araby 2.0 sent her a polite glance, then went back to her ruminations. "No. There's something weird here."

That was as close as Janet got. Ashley guessed that her stepmom would always know that something was up and that *something* had happened–Janet was not stupid–but she would have to live in ignorance of what it was. So would her viewers. It was better that way for all of them.

"The cat is fine," Ashley said. "I promise you." Sensing her moment, she took a deep breath. "However."

"What?" they all said. Even Araby 2.0 looked round at her.

"Well?" Janet prompted her.

"Something *did* happen while you were away." Ashley saw a *eureka* look come into Donna's face. Before a neon tube fizzed to life over her head to lead her to say, *Oh* yah–*the cat died of a coke blast at our party, but it's okay now because she came back,* Ashley said, "But not with the cat. It was the *car*."

Ashley didn't have to lie that much. She told the story of the theft more or less as it had occurred, missing out on that one important distraction of the cat. In place of the car, Ashley had a copy of the police report with its wonders-working crime number, plus a promise by e-mail from Mr. Kiss-of-Death-to-Young-Drivers Carr the insurance man to assure her dad that he was already onto it. It would not be long till Adam Hyde was back on the road, or at least out in the garage polishing a replacement till it looked like a distorting mirror in a sideshow.

Adam Hyde had a moment of gloom. It was quickly followed by a session on the Internet to check out the prices of cars. "Might even get you one, too," he said softly to Ashley without looking from the screen. "And how about Donna? She want one, too? Hell." Ashley forgot herself for a second, became a child and joined Donna in a squeal. "Let's buy cars," their dad said. "Whole bunch of cars."

"A whole *bunch*?" Donna checked, eyes wide with wonder.

"A *fleet*. That's totally the word for it."

Excluded from the excitement, Janet abandoned them to their window-gazing. The vacation over, she transformed fully into Maxine Wasserman. She got on her phone to worry underlings at home on their Sunday evenings with matters pertaining to the next day's show. There were cars to organize, guests to be collected, features to be coordinated, sets to arrange, props to be placed, hospitality to conjure up; it was the script of a Sunday evening cabaret familiar to the Hyde family. It had all been done, as usual–Janet's team being pros in an exacting business full of divas and coke-heads, dicks and deadheads–and yet the affirmative answers Janet repeated out loud never quite seemed to make her happy.

They sat down to the dinner Donna and Ashley–mostly Ashley–had rustled up. Their dad was his foolish, optimistic self again. He practised his vacation stories on them before wearing them out at the golf club and got up in the middle of the meal to load his hundreds of snaps onto the computer so that he could bore everybody rigid with them right after dinner. When her phone allowed her a break, even Janet tried to join in. Ashley only once in a while caught her staring across the room at Araby 2.0's sleek back, a puzzled and slightly wounded look on her face.

27

J anet's trip to tourist-town Europe evaporated in a five-minute TV wonder on *Morning with Maxine*, and on the same show Araby 2.0 was welcomed with gusto by her fans. That was one episode Ashley made sure to watch. The show's hostages out in TV Land texted the cat and e-mailed her. Some even phoned the show to meow that they'd missed her, under the impression that she too had gone on vacation. "No," Ashley told the screen. "*Much* better than that. She's died and been to Kitty Heaven and come back." Though the production staff had to hold her down at first, it didn't take Araby 2.0 very long to stop freaking out at the lights and noise and some of the most irritating people on the planet. Araby 2.0 was a wise little cat. She had been out in the big wide world. She had witnessed parades to her door of the lost and lonely, the bereaved and the desperate, of skeptics and believers, and had witnessed Aliceville's street drinkers amuse and destroy themselves out the window. She didn't *really* want to be cooed at by morons on Janet's show–what self-respecting cat *would?*–but soon settled down for her weekly ten-minutes of limelight.

A few mails and the odd call trickled in to the TV station, the gist of them being, *I know cats, and that cat is not Araby. What have you done with her?* They never saw airtime. Janet dismissed them as the ramblings of deluded people–like anybody sane would watch her show anyhow. All the same Ashley knew they were bugging Janet enough to make her look closely at the cat. Then she would look just as closely at Donna and

Ashley, unable to ask the right questions because she didn't have the imagination to think her way to them. Or maybe, Ashley guessed, Janet was possibly, and sensibly, afraid of the answers she might get.

28

Mary Dorn had the weirdest job Ashley had ever heard of. How it worked was that once she had dug around into punters' lives and supplied her boss with a few of their past events, they went away in the belief that the events she foretold would come true. Madame Tudora sold only good news, and everybody had something to look forward to when they walked out of her place. Was there any harm in that? Ashley swung between an uptight *yes* and a generous *no*. Nobody liked to be duped–true. Everybody liked to be spooked just enough to have a tale to tell, plus a little hope to take away.

Ashley thought of the evening she and Mary met in Aliceville. She could not help but laugh at herself. A confluence of Americana personified from lazy research: Ashley from a bonnets-and-shoe-buckles movie come to life, Mary and Madame Tudora from the sideshows of the Depression.

"Who *is* she?" Ashley soon asked Mary.

Mary did not like the question. She became absorbed, poked at the crust on her cappuccino then confessed, "I don't know." She looked sheepish; she might not have believed that either. "I answered her ad for a factotum because I liked the word."

"You're kidding." Ashley laughed, both delighted and scornful. "I mean–what, you've researched everybody in the neighborhood except *her*?"

"I call her Madame Tudora, same as everybody else. And that's cool. Know why?"

"Why?"

"I didn't realize at first." Mary looked as if she did not expect to be believed. "But I guess it's because I like the illusion as much as anybody."

"But there isn't any for you," Ashley said.

"There is *so*."

"You *know* it's all fake, though."

"Not a word we like." Mary eased a prissy expression into a smile. "No, listen though. When I'm in there with her I forget how we got there. I get to be part of the illusion and, while I'm there, I believe it. If I didn't..." Mary thought about it. "The picture would look just... *wrong*. Just a little wonky. You know what I mean?"

Ashley remembered enjoying the lights and the cards and the little smile Madame Tudora wore as she teased Ashley with her past and future. Even the tea, too, its sweet-smelling steam leaving an impression of haze; it had truly been a performance, her own private séance.

"How did she know where my dad went?" It was the first of many questions she would ask Mary about that night.

"*Morning Without Maxine*." Mary laughed. "There was a slot on the show every few days where she called to let them know where she was."

"Oh, God. And you had to watch it for that." If Ashley had been in the mood for vengeance, that might have been sweet revenge.

"I recorded it," Mary said. "I whizzed through it quick. It's not the... *best* kind of show, is it?"

"It's entirely awful. Wait, listen though, what Madame Tudora told me about my problem–she said to do the most obvious thing?"

"She was improvising. You can always do that with an ace." Mary put on a grave old-time-movie voice. "*Do the* one *thing, and the* one *thing only... You pull a two it's, like, you are at the fork in the road, so choose the best one.*" She laughed it off, self-conscious. "You get a three and it's... Oh, I don't know. It worked though, for you. Right?"

Sure thing, it worked: Janet Snyder was beginning to grow fond of Araby 2.0 and ceasing to look at her in puzzlement. Even Ashley had to remind herself sometimes that Araby 2.0's presence was her own little piece of theater. As a bonus, the cat was an upgrade: sweeter, calmer, quieter, and, sometimes, affectionate.

"*Right?*"

"Right, Mary. The cat was called by a Romanian name, you said?" Ashley's store of questions never ran out. "Madame T is Romanian?"

"I guess."

Ashley knew nothing about Romania. She recalled Michael Stambolisky's dad asserting that Romanian was not so much a nationality as a profession. She had not understood the re-mark, though it had both made her laugh and stuck in her mind to intrigue her.

"You really don't know?"

Mary moved her shoulders, smiled.

"Was she mad at you?" Ashley resumed. "About the cat?"

Back in that messy storefront room in Aliceville, Mary had put it to Ashley that it would be better if she brought the cat to Ashley's. Ashley had been suspicious of the idea at first, then had reasoned that if Mary thought Ashley was prepared to scatter their whole deck of cards, she would bring her, for sure. And besides, Ashley had no bag with her that night; the cat, scared, angry, maybe, at being uprooted from her familiar environment, might easily have jumped out of Ashley's apron pocket and gotten away at any point on the journey home.

"No," Mary said. "I told her about your problem. We're not sentimental about animals. We just went and got another. It's a good job for a cat. I wanted us to get a monkey." She giggled. "Put a little embroidered vest on him and a little fez-you know, those little round red hats the lodges wear? That would've been cool. A bit high maintenance, though."

"Sure. A gorilla might have been better, though–waving to its pals out that window."

"Totally," Mary said. "But anyhow–obviously–I told her about your plan. I mean, you never know."

"What?"

"She might really have the eye." Mary looked at Ashley, stern and serious, and made a fist with index and pinky fingers extended. "The power to *curse* your ass."

They tumbled into laughter, hands on each other's shoulders.

Ashley went for the odd night out with Mary and her notebook, into which she wrote down anything Ashley could remember about people in the neighborhood who might one day book an appointment with Madame Tudora. Nothing was too trivial for Mary's pen: a stray incident from high school, an opinion somebody had expressed, only once, or a stray thought out loud, a pause they made at a store window, an idle smile at a thing that pleased them, a turning-up of the nose at something that did not.

Ashley told Mary about Dru Kallista and her annoyance at Greek country customs. She mentioned Shoshannah Ross, panda-eyed with her excessive mascara. Sue Shah's shoplifting haul came back to mind–why? A puzzle, but Ashley itemized the things found in Sue's bag when they got caught: a snazzy notebook with a spangly gold cover, five pencils to match, a pack of sticky tape she'd possibly picked up by mistake. Matt Gadden would probably not be heading for Madame Tudora, but you never could know, and Ashley told Mary anyhow about the unbidden kiss she gave Matt from a sugar rush and the comment he made after. She joked that Madame T should remind him that *Nacho Breath* was an ungentlemanly thing to call a girl, even if he *was* only eleven at the time.

She told Mary about the wannabe French set at college and the laconic way they congratulated one another by chanting, "*Chapeau!*" That was apparently a French bike racing fan's way of saying, *I take my hat off to you*, but was weird in any language.

Ashley told Mary a lot of things about Chloe Gustavson–she could not help herself. There was the time some boy broke her heart and she cried for a week. She also spent all her waking hours pounding out Schubert's *Moment Musicale No 3*–two minutes lasting a whole semester–for a school concert she never attended because her dad took her skiing at the last minute. And about the time she lost her pocketbook in some mall and Ashley had to give her money to buy her mom a birthday present, a snow globe with the Liberty Bell in it which she promptly dropped and smashed when she took it home and got it out to wrap it. Ashley told Mary about the way Michael Stambolisky looked at Chloe at that party that first time they met and the way Chloe looked back at him, and how for thirty seconds Ashley felt like a stranger between them. She told her how she knew right then that Michael and Chloe would steal each other's hearts and leave Ashley's bruised.

Then she remembered, "But you *know* that part."

Mary said, "I did hear, yeah."

Ashley shook her head at the absurd wonder of it, trying to find just a little outrage.

And Francie; Ashley told Mary about her scatty co-worker. After all, she first heard of the fortune teller from Francie, but even as she was telling Mary to expect a visit from her there was a nagging fear at the back of her mind. She had not seen Francie since the night of her visit to the fortune teller. It seemed that nobody had. Francie had not shown for work. After some dissembling, her roommate Viv told Mr. Demonte that Francie was not with the ex with whom she had hoped to reconcile, nor was she at her folks' place in Lackawanna–she had called both to check. If Francie *had* taken off, Viv let it be known, she would be kind of put out–no, make that *very* put out–seeing as Francie owed her the best part of a hundred-buck loan plus a month of her share of the rent.

Mary asked Ashley about people's houses and apartments. Not being their friends, and not ever getting invited to their homes, that was one thing Mary could never know; she truly had no idea. She bade Ashley tell her anything, just shut her eyes and remember. "*Anything?*" Ashley checked. So she brought to mind gaudy, frayed floral drapes, family photos with crud in the filigree frames, the badly-placed table in the hallway on which sat badly thought-out purchases, like the white bust of some Greek god, the ashtray in the shape of Lake Manitoba, the Celtic cross with *Made in China* on its back. She added an exercise bike in a kitchen, a pool that was always the wrong shade of blue-turning-green, and not in the environmental sense, and one place in which the towels next to the bidet were in a user-friendly shade of brown. They thought about that one surprisingly often, intoned the words *eww–gross* like children and giggled about it, knowing it had already become one of their in-jokes.

Was it likely any of them would turn into seekers of fortunes and brave the center of Aliceville past the ranty drinkers, the dog-men and the sweaty gym-bag carriers, the girls, like Francie, in search of nail jobs, the loud boys in cars, the chubby ones on bikes? Ashley doubted it.

"You'd be surprised," Mary told her. "We get all kinds. It's not all lonely housewives and bereaved people. We get bankers, pastors, tax collectors, basketball stars..."

"Hit men."

Mary laughed, said, "Maybe."

"Serial killers."

Mary said nothing and looked away, the smile gone from her face. She looked up brightly and nodded, allowed, "Surely–why not?"

Ashley colluded with Mary's research for the fun of it. She enjoyed the knowledge that whatever she told Mary would go no further than the very people she was talking about.

She seemed to be static, to spend all her time with her head in books or forever writing out possible answers to possible questions in possible tests and possible final exams. She was stuck into a routine of college, work, sleep, study, then college again, and seemed to be frozen in place, destined never to move. But in fact Ashley Hyde was moving under the swell of a momentum that was so smooth she barely noticed it, truly spinning out of the loop.

29

Ashley was not sure if she had ever loved her sister–Donna was *not* very lovable–but she had always liked her, for sure. That was actually better. She had a stark picture of Donna flunking her life away and the world disdaining and dismissing her. She had to change that picture.

Madame Tudora's advice had stuck in Ashley's mind. She got tough with Donna over those friends of hers. Then she walked the walk and got tough with them.

She spied Shannon Seeley one night in the parking lot of a St Maz restaurant, Shannon having escaped her parents to sneak out for a smoke. Ashley screeched her car into the lot–the little Fiat convertible she had persuaded her dad to splash out on in the face of more sensible choices. She got out, left her door open and ignored the car hop's frantic waves. She strode over to Shannon and recounted as much as she could remember of the list Mary Dorn had given her; it detailed meetings between Shannon and James Dufrayne and various dog-walking men in Aliceville and Barnton who dealt weed, speed, and, Mary was almost certain, meth, if not heroin. Shannon's open mouth was silent. Ashley told her that if she thought she was going to drag Donna into her high-toned low life, she was crazy. "You're out of your league," Ashley told her. "And if you think you can get away with stuff like that you are more stupid than you look, I promise you." Shannon began to protest, but it faded in the face of Ashley's even-toned onslaught. As the cat had been resurrected, there was no point in bringing up *that* story, but the rest of it burst out of Ashley with a conviction that scared her. Maybe that was what would make it work, she thought later, invoking Madame Tudora: create an illusion, make it real. "And you tell James the same thing, and if he wants it clearer, I'll find him too," she warned Shannon. "Stay away from my sister, both of you." She backed off in case Shannon saw she was trembling. The car hop got a ten-dollar bill for his inconvenience, while the drivers in the small line that had built up had to settle for an apologetic wave.

Ashley also prevailed upon her dad to be consistent with Donna. If Adam Hyde did not want his younger daughter to pick up some dangerous habits, he had to give up a few himself–or at least refrain from talking about them, firstly like a high-school kid and secondly like they couldn't be avoided. Ashley was never sure how it was working but, gradually, something changed for the better in the relationship between their dad and Donna.

There was so much that Ashley had on Donna with regard to the death of Araby version one, that Donna dared not step out of line. Maybe that formed into a habit of its own. It was better than any habits Donna might have picked up with those estranged friends of hers. "You don't have to be cool at any price," Ashley told Donna when she lamented being frozen out by the cliques at school, at a loose end at weekends, or being sniped at. "It really doesn't matter. Trust me."

Ashley took her own advice and forgave herself for having been taken in by Michael Stambolisky and for having acted so la-di-dah with her one-time friends. She made no attempt to regain them. That would have taken years she did not have. She did not think any of them would forgive her for her disdain, not completely. And it was genuinely not so important, she realized, if she could forgive herself.

She eyed the croissant-eaters at college and found out that French cuffs were like regular cuffs but extended to allow for the old-fashioned oddities known as cufflinks–trinkets from a time before buttons. She approved, and bought eight double-cuffed men's white shirts slightly too large for her, plus four sets of cufflinks. She also took a shine to wingtip shoes and got a black pair, a tan pair, a pair in oxblood, and a pair in oak-colored leather with green canvas inserts. She abandoned her half-formed wish to hang out with the gang, though. This was not only the result of her being mature about it; the memory of one of them coming in that time wearing a beret had also had an effect. And were Maryjane shoes not just twee and girly? Bobby Dusenberg, taking up with some petite sophomore fashionista, also had nothing to do with it. If they had really been so great at anything they would have been at some swankier college in some swankier town. They just liked being the brightest fish in the little pond in the five towns. Ashley was happy to dart around its shallows a while and take in the peripheral sights without getting distracted by them. She sent Bobby and friends the occasional wave but knew she would leave them fumbling with their French, transfixed in the mirrors they held up to one another. Give them time, and they would be denim too.

30

Ashley Hyde last saw Mary Dorn as she drove her yellow Fiat through St Maz early one evening in late summer, not long before she left for New York. She was at a stoplight and took an idle look to her right. There sat Mary in one of those up-itself cafés, coffee in front of her, head bent over a notebook, pen poised.

Maybe it was a bizarre in-joke among habitual eavesdroppers: Mary's ears were sticking out. At first, Ashley thought her friend had had her hair cut short. Then she saw she had just fixed it close to her head in thin plaits pinned back over her scalp, pins and clips gleaming in it. Since their recent acquaintance, Ashley had only seen Mary with her hair in a sloppy ponytail. This new look was strange.

But it also looked familiar. Ashley remembered it from school, falling to ruin in the rain. She also knew then that her mom had been right about the kid in the Firemont wedding photo she had been shown in Washington all those years before: it was not Ashley at all–it was Mary. She had not disappeared, either, as one of the Washington Montpierres had recalled. Audacious Mary Dorn had just not shown up to school for all of junior high, because it slipped her dad's mind that she had to go.

Mary's mom had not been there to remind any of them about school because it was she who had pulled off the disappearing act. Ashley had done a brief investigation into the Dorns, just to return the compliment, and to check some of the wilder stories about the family. She found plenty of those, many sensationalist in tone, some questionable and frankly unbelievable. However, the disappearance of Mary's mom, Anna St John Rome Dorn, was as well documented as that of Sally Montpierre Hyde, and only a year before.

Sure thing, Adam Hyde recalled the Dorn woman who had gone. But if Ashley didn't mind, he'd had enough on his plate round that time. He had wanted to forget the cranks' bogus sightings, the half-formed condolences, the pitying looks, the papery presses on his hand from old ladies, the faces of flummoxed cops, both consoling and suspicious; he wanted to forget what a bad place America was in the dark, shake it out of his head and live in the light. And Ashley had to too, he added. Ashley shocked herself by agreeing.

So she imagined her mom and Mary's mom meeting up to set off for another life, laughing and free, shedding their fancy names and the stupid men to whom they had been tied: all that lay behind them as they sat sharing a milkshake. They were dressed in the awful clothes of the eighties, had the silly hair of the eighties, were tapping their feet to the terrible music of that decade and had a big brash car outside.

As Ashley watched Mary in the café, she saw that her friend wore an almost dangerous air of concentration. She was surely listening to the people around her. Maybe one of them had taken it into their head to do that unsettling walk through Aliceville for a reading with Madame Tudora. If Ashley was the kid who read, Mary was the one who listened; they had the two passive language skills sewn up between them.

They had shared evenings full of laughter. Ashley enjoyed being let in on some of Mary's secrets. She liked Mary's wide vocabulary and the eloquent, joyful way she used words. Mary was gentle, Ashley saw, and kind. She was generous and clever and, Ashley realized later, was her friend; she was the friend Ashley had been missing for much of her life. Mary's eyes would light up when she saw Ashley, and she laughed at Ashley's lame jokes, touched her hand to make a point. That was how friends acted and was what friends did.

Mary had always been on the verge of telling her something important, Ashley was convinced; there was something on her mind she wanted to spit out. Ashley did not know how she knew that without finding out what it was. She knew, that was all–real friends just *knew*. Mary never made a thing out of it the way people did when they were determined to give away something in the end anyhow. Ashley had spied it in those eyes that looked for fleeting moments like her own, and then it would disappear. The moment of revelation would be replaced by a joke, Mary going, "What's that?" and doing a tiny wave next to her ear and Ashley pretending she did not know and Mary saying, "A micro-wave," then going on as she always did, no pause.

"Is it something the fortune teller told you?" Ashley got bold and asked Mary once. Mary took it as a joke and covered her hesitation with a laugh and a shaken finger: *no*. "*What* then?"

"*You* tell *me*."

"You can owe me."

"What?"

"You can owe me a secret."

Mary threw her head back and laughed and said, "I'll think of one–one that'll thrill you."

That evening in St Maz, Ashley waved a micro-wave at Mary, who would only have seen it if she had looked up and out the window. Ashley thought of parking the car and going to join her. She slowed in search of a space but got hooted on. Nowhere; it would have to be the public lot and then the hassle of getting a docket and walking back. And she was sweaty after a day at the farm, disguised in those ridiculous clothes, and needed to get home and shower and change. Donna needed some help with her summer crammer school homework too, though Ashley was really just in the mood for lying on her bed, eating carrots and reading her book until it sent her to sleep.

A mental note prompted her to call Mary, and she did so maybe eight days later. She got Mary's voicemail and told it, "Hey, I don't know what to say. I'm going to Columbia. But you know that. You know everything, girl. Uh, Mary? You're the memory I'll bring with me." The words were something she might only have said to a machine. With a little laugh, she resumed, "Hey, you and the cat. You owe me a secret–I didn't forget. Be in touch, right?" She was glad she said those words, later–glad, but heart-broken sorry too, because Mary Dorn died early that October.

Nobody knew they were friends, so nobody told Ashley right away. Her dad mentioned it in an e-mail maybe two weeks after. It was an afterthought about how the Dorn kid–*the last of the Firemont Dorns*, the newspapers were calling her–had succumbed to some freaky heart condition that ran in the family. Ashley surely remembered her, no?

Ashley surely did. She spent a day in her room, curled up on her bed unable to eat or drink or get up or let herself sleep. With no desire to open her door, answer her phone, check her mail or go to classes, she became unaware of time. "Mary was my friend," she repeated to herself and the walls. That was all she was able to say before a corner of the darkness brightened, and she crawled forward cautiously to lift it up and diminish the shadows.

She was guiltily certain that, had she known, she would have been too busy with induction at Columbia to get home for the funeral. Mary would not have cared, but Ashley was still troubled. Who would have gone? Ashley wondered. Mary had known so many people, learned their intimate and, of course innocently random business, but nobody had known her.

Ashley had gotten to the online news report just before it was replaced. A boy's face looked cheerily up at her from a sidebar, and she was able to ignore him awhile as she read the few lines that told her that Mary's funeral had been held at the Dominican church in Firemont. There was a snipe that

Mary's dad–*comic fraudster Deedee Dorn* as they described him, after his courtroom habit of trying to laugh off the claims against him–had been let out of jail to attend. Ashley saw him in a photo taken at the service. He looked gray and sad, looked friendless and lost, anything but comic, and alone, even hemmed in as he was by a church crone and a prison guard; he looked *exactly* like a parent who had lost a child, which to Ashley had to be one of the saddest things in the world.

Her eyes were drawn, and in some irritation, back to the boy's face. The word *missing* was written above it. She saw that her neigbor Martin Ferrie had also gone along to Mary's last performance. He was a friend of the Firemont Dorns, she remembered, and recalled seeing him in uniform in that same wedding photo in which she and Mary had been mixed up for all that time in her head.

Missing, she saw, some boy, eyes full of sass, a kid–no, *the* kid from the St Maz College–and hadn't she forgotten the place already?–from the five towns bus, the St Maz mall, the night foolish Harold Shester reduced himself to a string of sausages. She remembered the kid appearing next to her as if by magic; now darker magic had made him disappear. Ashley's eyes rested on his face–poor kid–well, young man, still looking no more than twelve, all nerve and verve staring back at her.

She left him in his sidebar, and studied the blurred faces in the funeral photo. No evidence of Madame Tudora there, dark and enigmatic on a fall morning lit by low sunshine. Ashley wondered how her business would do now that she had lost her factotum. Maybe Ashley would visit her again one day, to see if she really had the eye. If anybody could, the fortune teller could recover Mary Dorn's untold stories, intact and perfect, and for Ashley only, from the smoke and mirrors and the world of the vanished, to guide her through the next phase of her life.

Part 2: Mary

I

The movement—she would never forget it if she lived to be a hundred. So many people and so much equipment, a living map of tracks and cables. *And* the hazards in the fuzz between the blinding lights and the shadows they created to elicit tripping, falling, and cursing; *fun*, Mary Dorn thought. She gave the word voice by clapping her hands. At a command—her clap, she was mistaken for a joyful second—the scene became quiet except for the hum of the fans.

An underlying smell of burning; Mary Dorn enjoyed it until it repulsed her.

She watched the visitors. One, an old man, eyed a young woman wearing only historical underwear, flouncy, frilly, and yet stiff and restricting. Another man, not so old, nudged yet another, drawing attention to the sight of yet another young woman, also in underwear from history books. Her face was upturned. As a make-up woman painted her bowed lips, her fragile, everlasting legs splayed because there was not enough room for them between the stool she sat on and the floor. One of the men mouthed the words *boy-oh-boy*. The other men beamed out *lucky-guy* smiles.

One of the visitors could have been picture-book handsome, Mary decided. He had brown hair ploughed into neat trenches by a comb. His clothes were pressed and new-looking. So were his even white teeth. When he caught the eye of one of the girls, he smiled wide and lines appeared around his eyes. There was an easygoing look to his actions and yet... Behind them?

Something Mary neither knew nor liked nor trusted. She had watched him earlier from one of the niches in the wall over the hallway. He came out of the ballroom and teased a bright blue pill from the top pocket of his sports coat, checked it, and necked it. He let out a long breath and then a loud, abrupt fart. He was pleased with it all, Mary gathered from the look on his face–the incoming and the outgoing.

Too many visitors, Mary thought. They were taking up space, getting in the way. She could not work out why they were there. Actors? Well, okay. Her house was crawling with actors because they were making a movie there, and you need-ed actors to make a movie, of course. The camera operators too; she knew from one of her dad's encyclopedias that you needed them for a movie. And sure, the same thing with the guys linked to their sound equipment by enormous head-phones and the ones who stood on ladders and erected towers of lights, and the girl wandering around calling out cues with a copy of the script. The make-up girls too, the caterers and the gofers. The visitors though, collars open, neckties loose, with their chicken necks and their dandruff, their spreading rear ends, the hair in their ears that had migrated from their heads, it beat her why they needed to be in her house.

After amusing herself with the lights, looking into them and enjoying spaced-out near-blindness, Mary got an inkling of the irreparable damage in them. She decided she had better watch the people instead, lip-read what they said, scoff at the things they did and put them aside in her mind to be marveled at or dismissed at her leisure.

One of the old-time underwear girls had let out a mouthful of cusses at Mary's dad, Deedee Dorn–Mary was not sure why. People were always swearing at her dad. It was ugly, and yet he did not seem to mind. Deedee's friends all swore cheerfully at one another. It was still ugly.

"Action!" The word brought the quietest quiet there could be. The lights in the center of the ballroom brightened, and

Mary felt a new heat from them. All attention was on the set. Even the visitors stopped looking at the girls for a minute and strained to see over the rigs and ladders, some of them on tippytoes.

Mary had heard the actors run through the dialogue several times. She had asked Deedee why they kept repeating the same things. "Even *I* know what they're supposed to say by now," she grumbled.

"I heard a thing about you," a man's voice said. It was the actor with spots that Mary had seen covered up by an inch of makeup.

She was sure he had gotten it wrong again. Forbidden to raise her voice, she settled for a hiss and an impatient gesture nobody saw.

The actress said, "What have you heard?"

"No." Another man's voice, deep and lazy. Mary craned her neck to see him. "Go again."

The clapper made its noise. "That's how you know it's a real movie," Deedee had confided to Mary earlier. He winked and pointed. "That what's-it-called there–that... *thing* that claps." She had indulged him. She already knew it was a real movie.

Mary looked round and saw the same visitor say, "Boy oh boy," again. He caught her looking. He poked his tongue out. It was light brown–coffee, disgusting. She returned the gesture.

After another moment of hush, the spotty actor resumed with the words, "I heard some *things* about you."

"What have you heard?"

There was a silence during which looks were exchanged, Mary sensed. The cue-girl said, "A *lot* of things." Mary knew her voice by then. If Mary were her, she definitely would have sounded more impatient.

The other man's voice called, "Again," and the what's-it-called clapped once more.

Deedee Dorn appeared behind one of the lighting rigs, noticed only by Mary. As he had promised her, he was in a stage cowboy costume, all big white stitching and string tie and brand-new tan leather. He also wore a sheriff's star. He caught Mary's eye and raised a finger to his lips. He snuck up on two of the girls in their strange underwear and put his arms over their shoulders. He said loudly, "You're under arrest."

One of the girls let out a toy scream and raised a bare foot. There was dirt on her sole. Mary had seen her picking her nose earlier.

The director yelled, "Cut." He appeared in a gap between the rigs. His face was young, though he was balding. He wore a blue Hawaiian shirt, white utility pants with lots of pockets, and orange socks with black leather sandals.

He marched up to Deedee and the girls. A head shorter than Deedee, he looked up at him, blinked, and said, "Could we get you out of shot *and* earshot?"

Deedee said, "Pip-pip, maestro. Sure thing."

Only the people close by could work out that their relationship was a friendlier one than it seemed. The visitors were too intent on the girls in the underwear to see.

Silence was resumed. Mary reached out and touched a clump of cables. It almost throbbed with warmth. She could smell more than the electricity; there was sweat and stale makeup and grease from the food they rustled up at the catering truck, burped out, or rising off heated-up clothes.

"Hey, Doctor Jekyll." Deedee did an exaggerated stage whisper and beckoned to the handsome visitor, who gathered the other visitors around him. Deedee pointed to the girls, who were filing into the hallway to flop onto chairs and *chaises-longues*. They fanned their faces and lit cigarettes. Deedee was in winking overdrive. Mary worked out that he needed the men's help; the extras needed to be kept occupied, and he could not entertain them all on his own.

Mary was puzzled and alert. The handsome visitor did *not* look like a doctor. And in the hallway earlier, his pill swallowed, his fart on its way up toward Mary, he had been stopped in his tracks by a low voice, calling him *Mr. Hyde*. He had made a strangely uncomfortable smile, waved a hand, and said only, "Oh, hey, Martin."

Mary had looked for old Martin Ferrie, but he was out of her sight. She was wary of craning her head too far out of the niche, remembering a spectacular fall she suffered the summer before while doing so. On that occasion, Martin had braced her ballooning ankle in wooden spoons and bound it all with a shredded shirt and driven her to the hospital, and reminded her that trying to see too much could be very bad for a girl.

In the center of the ballroom the lights were fired up again, and there clapped that clapper—a real movie back under way.

"I heard a lot of things about you."

"What have you heard?"

"You told the kid she was–"

"*Child.*"

Mary sensed the tension between the actor and the director. With the visitors gone, Mary was able to wriggle in closer to watch the scene. The ballroom had been cleared of all but a fluted column on which rested a broken bust from the garden, of a woman wearing a kind of headscarf. The spotty actor stood next to it in old-fashioned clothes, his hair greased back except for a hanging forelock, his broad-brimmed black hat in his hand.

"Kid, child." He sounded scornful. "What's the difference?"

The director said, "Uh, it's more archaic."

"What? More... what?"

"More... *redolent.*"

"*What?*"

"It's in the script," the actress said calmly.

She was on TV sometimes, Mary thought: a Latin brunette in her thirties with contrasty dark eyes. She walked unhurriedly back to her place.

"In the script," the director agreed. "Just *say* it." He stretched and looked up, looked around the room at the technicians and the cameramen, and nodded. "Okay." Expectant eyes in nodding faces. "*Roll.*" He said the word with such conviction that Mary knew they would get it right this time.

"I heard a lot of things about you."

"What have you heard?"

"You told the *chi-yuld* she was a *god*?"

"A *saint*. I told her a saint died the night she was born. And she came down to replace that saint."

"And what did she say to that?"

"She, uh, she wanted to know *which* goddam saint."

"So what did you tell her?"

"I don't know from saints. I mean, I could only think of famous ones."

"So why was that no good?"

"What, are you nuts? She wouldn't have replaced a famous saint, would she? She spoiled my entire... *metaphor.*"

"*Metaphor.* Right. But now look at her. How are you going to get her–and those crowds out there–to believe she *isn't* a saint?"

For a second, only the whirr of fans could be heard. Then the director shouted, "*Love* it. Everybody take five."

Mary busied herself with bugging as many people as she could during the break. The two actors sat on the rickety ballroom chairs outside the cleared scene, on the edge of the chaos and clutter of furniture, moved aside and put wherever it fit. Mary asked the actress if she was in any movies. The actress grinned and said, "Only this one. But if you watch your TV next week after midnight on the shopping channel, you'll see me in a *very* talked-about role."

Mary promised she would, even though the TV had gotten broken a few months back during one of Deedee's parties, or stolen. Again.

The script girl laughed when Mary asked to see the script. She waved her copy at Mary and said, "*You* don't get a veto."

"A what?" Mary saw only the title of the movie, *St Agnes of the Oilfields*, on the cover. She was not too bothered–she had lost interest as soon as her request was out. She turned and called over her shoulder, "I don't want one, *anyhow*."

The hallway was empty except for Deedee. Mary walked toward her dad, her mouth open. Deedee held a finger to his lips, sat on a step and put a hand out. He pulled Mary toward him and bade her sit next to him. He kissed her ear lightly.

"We'll stay down here for now," he said. "Don't want to disturb our backers."

"Backers?" Mary examined the word: not one she knew. And she knew most words.

A peal of laughter made its way down the stairs. Mary heard a dog growl, yet knew it was a man making the noise. She took a look up. On the mezzanine she saw a man, hunched, intent on the viewfinder of a hand-held movie camera. By the time she had drawn her dad's attention to it, the man had gone.

Deedee said, "Our money men."

"Money men." She examined the words a little critically. "What are they doing?"

"They're keeping the girls out of trouble, honey."

"Oh. Okay. But... *no*." She slapped him gently on the shoulder. "But I mean, why are they *here*?"

Deedee looked surprised at the question. "We're telling a story here, honey," he said. "Can't tell stories without money."

2

The stories were never far from Mary Dorn. They hovered in her head as she slept and she sensed them in signs around her, as if they were trying to reveal themselves. They often featured dark streets and cars, the swish of tires in the wet, and an unexpected visitor. Weren't they the most fun?

Some of the stories, she worked out, were left behind by visitors. There were often visitors to the Dorn house. Expected? Sometimes, she sensed, but often not. Mary lost count of them, but took their stories in and never quite let them out. Some families tell a suppertime story of a relative who found a purse that held nine hundred and ninety-something dollars and handed it into the police. The better tale is how that relative pocketed it and blew the money on a spree in Vegas. Others have an uncle, or an aunt, who robbed a small-town bank and lived on the proceeds or got a stretch in jail and forever felt foolish. Some have a grandpa who swam the Hudson in winter or walked the Mason-Dixon line for kicks, a grandma who gave Richard Nixon a piece of her mind as he approached his car, or kissed JFK as he approached his–or the other way round. Others feature a cousin spoken about only reluctantly, whose attempted burglary turned into a conflagration that maimed and traumatized, or a girl-cousin as removed as possible who, in a dispute over inches in a yard boundary, slaughtered a neighbor with a garden implement.

Mary's family, the Firemont Dorns, was full of stories, but one put all the others in the shade: the family was full of mass murderers. It was never related at suppertime nor at any other time, just festered in corners of the Dorn house, waiting for Mary to tease it out.

The junk in the upstairs rooms told a multitude of tales that distracted Mary from that story. Their associations, and the visions they gave her, kept her amused, perturbed, and sometimes awake at night.

She was six when she picked up a globe watch with letters etched into its back. When she opened it, metal and dirt fell out. Some years later, a Russian dictionary revealed those letters to her, spelling out X-E-R-S-O-N. Time meant nothing to her, and it was probably some years farther on that she discovered that her great grandfather's brother Emmett Dorn *probably* acquired the watch in the town of Kherson in a place called Ukraine, often with a superfluous and annoying *the* in front of it. That was how the stories began, Mary realized, from wanting to put the vagueness of probability or possibility into words that could be made concrete: one yarn had Emmett winning the watch in a card game, while another pictured him stealing it from an inattentive dandy or a dying soldier. The romantic one said he was given it by some love-eyed countess.

Mary understood that her great grand uncle Emmett Dorn liked acquiring things. She understood too that he had a fondness for telling stories. In another few years, it became clear that what he liked most was observing people, messing with them, and then killing them.

A tug on a closet door spilled out yellowed bridal dresses, lace gloves that went to Mary's shoulder, pink satin pumps Mary later associated with fetuses, all clinging to one another, and bouquets that fell to dust. She never got all princessy about them; they were sorry-looking things and nothing less. The passing of the years, and the photo albums she kept finding, made her aware of the Dorn weddings at the nearby Dominican church and of the Dorn honeymoons and Dorn divorces, the testimony to them all dumped in those attic rooms.

Caught in the eyes of those who had come before her, she ranged the photos on the floor, ventured among them and trapped herself. Then she glued them onto the wall around the games room door and made them into a collage that looked like a church icon screen. She could read little in those stark and haunted eyes, even on their wedding days.

Mary had a clear memory of only one wedding. Her heart went hollow, and she feared she could no longer breathe in if she let her breath out. "Wedding days sure are big days," was all her dad would say. It was plain to Mary that he was trying to make out he did not know what day she meant, and which wedding. *He* knew. Even absent-minded Deedee Dorn was unlikely to forget the day his wife disappeared. If he did, Mary was happy to remind him.

By the time she was nine, Mary was tired of weddings. She turned her attention to rusting shotguns, rotting cartridges and spills of powder, and picked up ragged hunting clothes. She thought about those poor animals, her predecessors and their guests popping up out of the vegetation to bring them their doom in tongues of fire.

She opened atlases that took up half a tabletop. They revealed maps of places that no longer existed: eagle-guarded empires of Germans, Austrians, Hungarians, Prussians, and Russians, the pink British one, the fragmenting and ever-shrinking Ottoman Empire, the Polish Corridor, Ruthenia, Bessarabia, Galicia, the Levant and the Holy Land, and others too many and wildly spelled to keep accurate track of. All the same, the names filled Mary with the desire to travel to impossible landscapes. One thing stopped her cold: the sensation that the people in those places had been helped into their disappearance from history by Dorn wiles, whims, and wares.

When Mary pushed a door that had been painted over, she went flying into a walk-in closet full of US Army cigarettes, rations and medical supplies, freezer boxes with hundreds of ampoules of morphine, and amphetamines in pill, powder, and syringe tube forms. She did not know what use any of it was, just one sure thing: it all looked toxic and misery-inducing. There were playing cards printed with the names of airborne divisions featuring Ronald McDonald's face stripped to the bone and his wish that the recipient should have a nice day.

Mary found a lampshade, a repulsive object, its design a smear bearing a resemblance to a sailor's head. It had been brought back from a Nazi concentration camp by a wartime Dorn. Years before that, she knew she had a bad feeling about it and stowed it out of sight until an article in an ancient copy of Life magazine revealed it as a tattoo on human skin; it was the day she learned the word *genocide*. She would never get at the meaning behind its ugliness. Who could want to keep a memento of a deed like that? So the next thing she thought of was how it had to go in the trash at once, right then, in the middle of the night. She put it there, then remembered where it had come from. She rescued it in the pale light of morning, the garbagemen noisy out in the street, and buried it in the yard. That was not right either, but all she could think of. Maybe it was the thing, she thought later, that brought bad fortune to her family once the Second World War was done.

In addition to the atlases, Mary had been doing a lot of searching in encyclopedias. New words flooded her head. She finally had to ask her dad, "What exactly is... murder?"

"Hey." Deedee Dorn tried to laugh. "You really don't want to know that."

Mary listened to the house, checked that her aunt Jude was out of earshot, and said, "What *is* it, though?" There were conversations Deedee's sister approved of and ones she didn't. Mary had the certain idea that this one would not come up to the mark. She watched her dad's expression patiently, feeling the force of his stare. He was trying to remember how old she was, she guessed. She risked, "I'm eleven." She *was* nine-and-a-half. It was not a big difference.

"Eleven or not, you really don't want to know." Her dad had resumed his easy manner. "Watch some movies," he advised. *Watch out the window*, he could have said, she thought later. *Rummage some more through the papers upstairs.* He said, "Think of something... uplifting. Think of... Michelangelo."

She wondered if he was challenging her. She adopted her look of scorn; Michelangelo was in all the encyclopedias. *Murder* was in them too, she guessed, and not far away, under M. She had known, anyhow–nine-and-a-half or not, eleven or not, it was difficult not to know what murder was in the Dorn house.

"And you don't fool me, young lady–you're ten." The call from Deedee Dorn was faint; Mary was already by then immersed in the study of murder. Later, exhausted by it, she lay on a bed and studied the ceiling of the one-time master bedroom: angels up there sporting Weejun loafers, letter sweaters, Levi jeans, Pendleton shirts and Fender guitars, daubed by a guest as pay for his board. He was the nearest the house would get to Michelangelo. He finished his work, then strangled a local child. He testified that the child had stalked him repeatedly, appeared at his window at dawn blowing a bugle and wearing a goat's head and had read thoughts in his head that no child should know. Previously of good, if casual, character, Mary guessed one day years later that he had been at those frozen amphetamines.

In a closet in that room a Gretsch guitar lay in its case, creamy and pristine, its fittings a dull gold. It was stolen from an inattentive Elvis Presley outside a Tucson venue as he signed his name for a crush of fans. Mary finally looked up a report: a slew of bug-eyed girls separated Elvis not only from that guitar but from his entourage, his jacket, most of his shirt, some of his pants, his wallet and much of his momentary dignity. Later, whenever she took out the guitar and caressed its curves, Mary thought maybe that was the moment Elvis realized he had ceased to be a man; he had become a phenomenon. She tried to imagine his fear and his sudden loneliness. She could not work out which of her relatives had grabbed the guitar, though it occurred to her later that such trophies were bribes or gifts, totems to appease the Firemont Dorns.

Mary was genuinely eleven when it occurred to her to wonder: was she beginning to know too much? Her head hurt as the feeling washed through her that there was so much more to find out. There was also the warning that once she knew she couldn't *not* know. She lay on a bed, swamped by her finds, the house empty below her. She was afraid to go back into those rooms and yet also afraid to let what was in them out of her sight in case it turned out she had imagined it all. So she went on wondering, but in the meantime, she thought it best if she just went ahead and found out everything there was to know then sorted it out later.

A sound from downstairs; her dad coming in. Or a repo man. A cop, maybe a burglar, an assassin. She picked up a Makarov pistol and weighed it in her hand. Mary never forgot that she had once saved the day with that gun, the first one she had found in the house.

Her dad was on probation. Her aunt Jude had told Mary she was not to speak to him without supervision. Mary was also not to let him up the stairs, was not to be charmed or cajoled by him, was not to give him any money, not that she ever had any, and certainly was not to accept any from him, though she sometimes did. The Makarov was for show. She would never shoot her dad. She may have shot a burglar but not a cop, definitely, nor a repo man, probably. No, the pistol just quieted her dad if he was being loud, because it reminded him that the Firemont Dorns had flooded the world with guns. Suppertime evidence of the family's weighty contribution to mass murder was guaranteed to get her dad's supper down his throat as fast as possible and to get him away from the table in double-quick time. But only if he was being noisy or acting hare-brained or was higher than any kite had ever flown.

As if the Makarov acted as a kind of key, once Mary unearthed it she found other pistols. They were formed of dull gunmetal or were gold and silver-plated–vulgar, tacky–seven-shooter revolvers like the Russian Nagant or one-blast Derringers, six-shot all-American cowboy Colts, and multi-lethal automatics. There were rifles too and a German submachine gun, a Schmeisser, a British Sten submachine gun, an old thing made of pipes. One of her favorites was an elegant Thompson submachine gun. There were M1 carbines and a Czech sniper rifle that looked both beautiful and deadly. The pinnacle of the art? A Kalashnikov.

They were just objects. Despite their associations, they meant nothing. It was the paper left behind that told the story of the Firemont Dorns. One day Mary Dorn would get through it all, learn it all and know it all and would, she always had the uneasy feeling, regret it all till she could find something to make her forget it all.

She stood in the kitchen studying a doodle that had caught her eye in the trash. She puzzled over it and impatient, finally, with the story it refused to tell, screwed it into a ball, and returned it to the trash.

There was a greater untold story that Mary wanted to uncover and she knew it lurked in America in the dark. She never quite got to fear the streets, the cars, that urgent sound made by tires, nor even the unexpected visitor, a man, she was sure, who came out of nowhere before you even knew he was there, did his dark place business swiftly and faded back to nowhere, but she was never comfortable thinking of them, either.

"I know the story," she told her reflection numerous times. She imagined her reflection saying back at her, "So tell it." Then she had to confess that she did not know it at all and did not want to, but that it would come in its time, along with the rest of those tales that spooked the house.

3

The crones of Firemont thought they knew the story of the Dorn family. Mary trusted this for years, then had a moment of revelation: the crones knew only stories. That was not the same. Rotund or rake-thin, neatly turned out in absurdly formal duds or Walmart comfy, the crones bore names and wore faces from another age, old documentary films and newspaper files. They had shopped for the Dorns, cooked and served the Dorn food, stripped the Dorn beds and washed the linen. They had snooped in the Dorn drawers and closets and rummaged through the garbage. They had forgotten their own stories.

By tradition the Dorns married in the Dominican church opposite the house, or got their inheritances reduced to a dribble. The crones gathered to watch the weddings. One said, "She may be a Dorn, but she's not as nice as the ten o'clock bride." Another recalled sniping, "Not even a five-hundred-dollar suit can make that fellow look like anything but a murderer in the courthouse." And from yet another, "Did you see Tyler the Smiler giving his daughter away again? He should stop giving her away and charge a hire fee."

"Your mother looked a picture, though," one of them told Mary. The woman stroked her chin, pretended to look away and cackled. "A very... *spirited* girl," another said. Mary also got, "Your mommy had a nice *smile*." Most of them didn't talk about her mother however, and she got the impression that Anna St John Rome Dorn had wound up 'best not mentioned' in their collective memory. Mary realized that she had carried a strange and unsettled feeling about her mother for most of her life, one that resisted being put into words.

Even with the promise of dollars, a gathering of crones was harder than herding cats, so Mary eventually sought them out one-by-one to gather their parts of the story. "You *saw* them," she kept saying. The crones saw the Firemont Dorns living and breathing, she meant, laughing and celebrating, caught them raging, spied them sad and gloomy. Mary envied them. "You saw into their eyes." The crones didn't know what she was talking about. It was white-iced cakes they remembered most vividly, fluffy white dresses, shiny white cars, the mayor schmoozing them in his pomp, Hollywood movie stars with charisma slapped on like make up, sprinkling the Dorn gatherings with glitter.

When pushed, the crones remembered blood on sheets and clothes. They remembered girls crying in the yard or the kitchen or the ballroom at four in the morning. They remembered potent powders in the drawers of bedside tables, hypodermics and tourniquets tossed in the trash, crushed glass ampoules, empty bottles on the floors. They remembered raised voices and the sounds of slapped faces, listened in on calls that included threats, pleas, excuses, declarations of fidelity and of the abandoning of it. One remembered a body in the pool, graceful, bobbing a foot below the surface, remembered its hair waving like sea grass. One recalled a pale form in red bathwater, yet another the stupefied look of a man who had gone too close to one of the open upstairs windows. They all remembered them being gone without the aid of the police or the wagon from the Barnton Morgue.

Mary noted all they remembered. Her pictures started to fill out but still she did not know the real story, nor about the paper trail that led to both mass and mundane murder. The crones could only tell Mary so much, so she stole keys and snuck into rooms, opened cabinets and closets and heaved valises and portmanteaux up onto beds. She opened them and pieced together the stories thrown up by the lives of the Firemont Dorns. She spent her nights keeping the Dorn ghosts from their rest until the light outside told her to go to bed or school. In this way she became the family curator, the discoverer of its secrets and the bearer of them.

Mary Dorn was the last of the Firemont Dorns. She intoned that to herself like some sort of mantra. It seemed pretentious; after all it was just a name. If she ever bore a child though, it would not be a Dorn. The Firemont Dorns would end there, buried in Firemont, with her.

4

Mary Dorn would never be tall, and her build would always be scrawny. She reminded herself of a teen from the black-and-white *Amazing Tales* comic books she found tucked away in random corners at home. Her skin had always been tight over her bones, her larger veins visible. Her eyes were blue, and not from Deedee Dorn, whose eyes were deep dark brown. Her face had features that her aunt Judith called 'fine' meaning not coarse but also, Mary thought, a polite way of saying *unremarkable*. She had bright blond hair, which was *very* un-Dorn. The Dorns were dark in almost any way anybody could think of.

Mary had no dress-sense as such, no style, as such, but mainly and truly-and honestly-no preference. She grew up thinking of herself as classic nerdy girl, neither from choice nor to make some kind of statement; it was just how she was. Just like Einstein, or so Mary read, she wore clothes that were not worth thinking about. If it was clean and to hand, she put it on. If it was old and if she noticed, she would chuck it. Thanks to the sweatshop labors of brown children in faraway countries, even cheap clothes seemed to last forever.

5

Mary's forebears had no qualms about chucking things. A theme Mary identified in her family's story was *waste*. From eighteen sixty-five to nineteen fifty-five the Dorns of Firemont had so much of everything that wasting it, it seemed to Mary, was compulsive. Mary thought their urge was like that of certain peoples in the Mediterranean and Balkan countries, who smashed the crockery in restaurants merely to show onlookers they could afford to replace it. This was noted, and in some grudging admiration, by that swashbuckling great-grand-uncle, Emmett Dorn. The great Dorn waste was revealed in diary entries and photos, press cuttings and invoices, lawyers' notes and copies of police reports. There were clothes worn once, and tennis courts played on once; there were church pews sat on once then reserved and empty forever. There were fancy *chaise lounges*, sprawled on once only. And there were promises given once and, once forgotten, goodwill used up, once only. There were women used once, then discarded. And servants paid once and, when they complained, beaten, just once. The fancy Dorn cars were driven once, run off highways and into cornfields, over precipices, or into swimming pools that were only dipped in one time.

'We are the real futurists,' Mary's great grandfather Theodore Dorn wrote to an aristocratic colonel in the Italian fascist army with whom he was on business terms throughout the nineteen twenties and thirties. 'Everything we do is ephemeral and may last only one day. That is the only kind of future we have the right to expect, the one we make, just for one day. You would be well advised to remember this in your adventures in Africa. When our civilized western world howls its opprobrium, and it will, it will be too late, and you can tell it, "That was yesterday, and is no longer remembered, or important. The future has left you behind." And by then you can give them something else to howl about. If this is your desire, I will supply the means. And, as always, on very favorable terms.'

So it was a search for novelty, Mary concluded, that gave the Firemont Dorns their attitude toward the disposability of objects, and of people. It was a quest to prolong the exuberance in a new day full of new sensations, a life lived in twenty-four hours then tweaked and lived all over again the next day.

'I like everything I do to be fresh,' a society Dorn was quoted on a society page reduced to a cutting. 'Fresh is my watchword.' There was a photo of her, Aleksandra Poniatowska Dorn, one of Mary's great great aunts, unsettling eyes piercing through those of the photographer toward a tomorrow that stopped happening for her when she was twenty-nine. The hole in her heart expanded just a fraction as she sashayed barefoot down a Tijuana street in search of either flour or flowers–that report, promoted to news rather than the society pages, had said *flours*.

Aleksandra had given up on society by then. 'You do a thing once only,' she told those society page readers. 'Else it's stale.' Her handwritten notes, married to the clipping when Mary found it, were actually finished. *Or it's as corrupt as my family.* Mary imagined Aleksandra's white-knuckle life, eyes straining, that hole in her heart growing a little with each anxious beat. *News to me she even* had *a heart.* Somebody had written in neat little characters in the margin of the clipping, possibly the Dorn she had deserted for a dope-dealing jazz guitar player.

A note found in the desk drawer of a bank employee under investigation for money-laundering read, *You will double cross me once, and once only*, or so it was claimed in a cutting from *True Crime* magazine. The note had been pushed through his mailbox the day before he was murdered. There was a photo of the note in the magazine, all precise characters. Mary tried to match them to a Dorn hand. It vexed her that she could not until she knew there was no need: that double *once* was better than a signature.

"Get fresh with me," Mary was told as a child, "and you'll do it just once, young lady." It was a litany from Dorn visitors of her grandfather's generation. Maybe they were on a search for quiet in the fast, noisy lives they once led. They never stayed long–their visits were primarily for reminding Mary's dad of their claim to the Dorn house. They stayed long enough to make known their opinion about the squalor and decrepitude of the overgrown tennis court, the collapsed stables, and the death trap swimming pool full of wires and weeds and an old Buick. "That used to be fields," they said, nodding at the encroaching housing projects. "Meadows," another would claim. "There used to be trees. We used to ride our ponies over there. Used to picnic right there." All true, but after a few years of this, Mary wondered why they used the exact words each time, and irritated them by completing their reminiscences in the pauses.

"*Was* it all true?" she checked with her dad.

"I guess." Deedee wrinkled his nose. "I can smell those damn ponies right now."

Nobody's disapproval was ever going to cow Mary Dorn. It turned her into the kind of child who sulked while smiling though, and who, free from attacks of conscience, placed dead rodents into water tanks to corrupt the supply and, on summer nights, strategically removed mains fuses, broke their filaments and replaced them stealthily to spoil everything in the icebox.

She sat over the staircase in niches that had once held busts and vases and watched the visitors huff and puff up and down.

She was invisible there. She made faces at them and dared them to look. She waved as they left empty-handed, weighed down by their unanswered questions.

In the story Mary was told, the Dorns who made the money had died out by the nineteen sixties or had gone cheerfully bankrupt or gone to seed or to hell, and the expertise had gone with them. That was not exactly true. What happened was that the government sent the CIA out to do the shopping, and they bought the Dorns. "The family was hardly a bargain by then," Mary's dad would one day tell her. "But it's always pot luck in the sales, huh?"

6

The Dorns' success stirred with Jeremiah Dorn, Mary's great great grandfather. He was born around eighteen thirty somewhere in upstate New York. He started out as an apprentice on the railroad, then became an engineer. His talents lay elsewhere, though. A faded collection of deeds suggested he made a killing in minerals when still young. Though there was little about him among the papers, Mary soon discerned ghostly scenarios picturing him buying up no-hope stakes from men at the ends of their tethers, then getting lucky with them, using the railroad like a train set to move those minerals, then buying or running off the competition.

By the late eighteen fifties, Jeremiah Dorn saw that a poisonous wind was diverting men's minds from commerce to politics. And from there? One destination: war. Mary's theories were doomed to remain sketchy; her great great grandfather was not a man who wrote things down. It hit Mary that he saw beyond a war between the North and South and worked out what a smart man might do. He knew that partisan politics was for the suckers who would end up in battlefield graves or maimed beyond repair. He saw that wars would come and go but that commerce would always be there.

He knew a war would require copious numbers of munitions, so that was where he concentrated his efforts. He dispatched agents to European gunmakers, chartered ships and trains, bought and built warehouses, formed a private army of men with black hats and bribed his way into contracts when force failed.

He followed the money and mainly sold his toys to the North. Evidence of sales to the South was circumstantial, and it seemed that many Southerners began the war fighting with fowling pieces abandoned by the British in the previous century. Mary found traces of Jeremiah's doings in the odd Southern triumph, however.

Though he wrote nothing down, Jeremiah left marked railroad timetables, hotel and restaurant bills, copies of invoices, floridly scribed gentlemen's agreements, and handwritten squares of onionskin paper that served as deposit slips and statements from a bewildering number of banks, all of them either north of the Mason-Dixon line or in London, England. On no piece of paper from Jeremiah's time was the word *gun* written—rubber, yes, kapok, canteens of cutlery, bales of paper, timber, and all manner of useful things, but never guns.

With Jeremiah's papers spread over the floor and with Shelby Foote's three thousand-word *History of the American Civil War* in front of her, Mary figured out that every significant battle won by the Union was one in which Jeremiah had replenished the Blues' stocks of arms. For nearly all the North's big victories—the battles of New Orleans, Shiloh, Vicksburg, Gettysburg, Atlanta, and any of the sea battles—the paper located Jeremiah wining and dining in towns in which the Union's chiefs were billeted either just before, just after or, occasionally, during those battles. The papers showed extra laborers and dock workers hired, trains diverted, delivery schedules, and payments, a lot of payments. These patterns showed till about midway through eighteen sixty-four. The South was as good as beaten by then, its precious slaves all but emancipated, though not welcome in the North, its other denizens doomed to everlasting redneck hurt.

Buried among the papers was a large photo of Jeremiah with verdigris and rust around its edges from where it had been fixed in a frame. He had unruly dark hair only barely tamed with pomade. His lips were thin and colorless and hardly there, those of a man who never smiled. His black eyes were unsettling in the way they trapped the viewer's.

After the Civil War Jeremiah married one Agnes Volkender, whose family owned tracts of land in both Prussian Pomerania and Pennsylvania. Why they settled on Firemont was not clear to Mary from the Dorn papers. It was slightly elevated and had either been the site of a firewatch tower or a gun emplacement. Knowing the family's history of starting fires rather than stopping them, it had to be the latter, Mary thought.

Five of their nine children survived childhood. The three girls were tamed, sent out on approval to other families, and married off. They were subsumed into those families, and their particular Dorn lines died out and eventually became Barrymores, DuPonts, Fishers, Bouviers. Mary spotted the odd report of Dorn wilfulness in their doings from time-to-time but it was not only the photos of them that were faded; their very substance had vanished, and Mary never felt moved to investigate them farther.

It was the two Dorn sons she was more interested in. They were instilled with Jeremiah's view of the world and unleashed upon it.

7

Jeremiah Dorn was a good example of what his second son, Theodore, Mary's great grandfather, was fond of referring to as a jack. It was the jack in the pack who determined the outcome of the play, Theodore said, not the king or queen, who had too much at stake, nor the joker, who was too frivolous. It was the jack who sought fortunes with nothing to lose and took the risks. Maybe it was the jack in Jeremiah that got him arming the South from time to time in the Civil War. It was a risk, but allowed him to keep friends all over the continent and, after the war, to trade its length and breadth.

Theodore incorporated a jack into the Dorn logo until the First World War when the selling of munitions was still seen as a laudable and thoroughly American thing to do. Once the customers were revealed to be shadily UnAmerican, the Dorn name was dropped from the logo to leave only the jack, with the name of St Vitus written on one of his hands.

By the nineteen twenties there was no logo, the brand hidden from all but those in the know. The business profile puffs–*Dorn, an all-American venture, furnishing freedom and independence*–toadied by Hearst newspapers from the drafts Mary found in Theodore's own hand–petered out. She imagined that even bought-off press barons would have fought shy of publicizing any Dorn venture by the twenties, left with something like: *Dorn guns, putting the roar into the twenties, Dorn bullets, drowning out all that jazz.*

8

Jeremiah's first son was Emmett Dorn, born eighteen seventy-six. His motto, embossed onto business cards, was, *Be bold, or stay home.* And he was, and he didn't. He became a professional loose cannon, answering to no government, system or family. His deeds may have included impregnating a concubine of Turkish sultan Abdul Hamid in Istanbul and murdering a eunuch in the process. He *may* have finagled sponsorship from the Greek War Ministry for agitating in favor of Greek independence in Turkish territories, then spent the money on travel, wine, women, and casinos. He *may* have assassinated a Prussian official in Paris, fixing it so that a wine merchant from Herzegovina got the blame, freeing a good-looking and well-off widow to marry into the unbeheaded remnant of the French aristocracy. By accident or mischievous design, Emmett *may* have exposed a plan by European spymaster Sidney Reilly to steal French naval defense plans from an office in Marseilles, nearly getting Reilly killed in the process. There was also evidence that Emmett supplied Serbian nationalists with guns, possibly including the one that *may* have started the First World War when the Austrian archduke Franz Ferdinand and his archduchess ventured unwisely to Sarajevo and got shot on St Vitus' Day nineteen fourteen.

Emmett Dorn wrote a book which survived as part manuscript and part typescript, pompously titled *An Emerging History of the Balkan States at the Start of the Twentieth Century.* Mary thought a more accurate title would have been *Foreign Women*

I Liaised With, and Their Relatives who Wanted to Dismember Me Until I Shot Their Faces Off. Mary thought it began promisingly, with the words *The Balkan peninsula is named after the Turkish word for honey, which is* bal, *and the Turkish word for blood, which is* kan, *but how I figure it is the way its people seem intent on destroying one another and the civilised world, it should have been called Kankan.* Unable to resist a tale worth telling, the book revealed that Emmett soon eschewed the politics and concentrated on the can-can in music halls, the chasing of women, and in turn the chasing of Emmett by various husbands, fathers, brothers and enraged villagers. The book finished with a pessimistic note to the effect that a guy couldn't *do* anything anymore without the entire world getting on his *back* about it. Mary was shocked as well as entertained by his deeds. In service to the privileged position of being Emmett's book's only reader, she sometimes kidded herself that she believed a single word of it.

Despite his qualifications, nobody saw him as fit to head the Dorn family. He was too arrogant for diplomacy and did not see the need to explain himself to anybody. For a man with such a lot of explaining to do, this was a genuine flaw.

Emmett's gift for improvisation deserted him when he followed another man not seen fit for anything. By the time Emmett ran into the Turkish general Enver Pasha, Enver was wanted by European powers for the genocide of Armenians in Asia Minor. His own people also wanted to talk sternly and excitedly to him about his careless loss of the entire Ottoman Empire. The last anybody heard of Emmett Dorn was that he accompanied Enver and his ragtag army in a suicidal assault on a Soviet force in Bukhara, Central Asia. Everybody assumed Emmett's luck ran out right then along with Enver's though there were rumors, even when Mary's dad was young, that he had lived on somehow, some place, keeping a low profile. The idea of Emmett Dorn keeping a low anything made Mary laugh, though a part of her wished he had survived and, his face as old as time, walked up to the house and pulled on the bell to ask for a glass of something in exchange for a tall tale. Mary would have welcomed him in though she would have kept her Makarov pistol close, and made sure she saw him off the premises before it got dark.

9

Jeremiah Dorn's second son, Theodore, charmed anybody who would listen into believing that he had invented the modern world single-handedly. With only a little help, he claimed, he'd forced it down the throats of Americans.

Mary's great grandfather was obsessed for a time with the possibilities in photography, and his patronage certainly brought the art forward. He put money into researching the improvement of sights for sniper rifles and for the camera technology used in spotter planes in military reconnaissance. As he headed his memos, there was *plenty of scope for development*. Mary guessed both the puns were pardoned.

As a by-product of his research, there were thousands of images of him made. It was a new ether for him to dominate with his frank stare and vulpine grin. So there he was at the party he threw every twenty-eighth day of June, St Vitus' Day, his nasty joke to celebrate the time Serbian fanatics killed that foolish Austrian archduke and his wife–with or without the help of Emmett–to start that war that did so much to prompt a spike in the Dorn fortune. And there he stood, grinning with society gals and flappers, and with poets and writers–F Scott Fitzgerald for one–with artists–there was Picasso–with scientists, dictators, madmen, megalomaniacs. There too with Prince Feliks Yusipov, no longer welcome in his native Russia, a photo cattily captioned, *With fey old Felix, telling everybody how he killed Rasputin. Again.* Theodore's bodyguards tried to blend in, though in fact they were sometimes caught in the background, looking as incongruous as gorillas in tuxedos, moonlighting from gangs like Al Capone's and Meyer Lansky's. They all went on to careers that ended in the stark high-definition of press photos, eyes shot out in diners and barbershops. Mary's great grandfather was pictured shaking the hands of fascists as he ensured that they could cut down Africans who came at them with spears. In one he was standing with the Duc D'Aosta, who lived in a bad-luck palace built by a hapless Hapsburg in border city Trieste, its white battlements in the background, its curse just bouncing off Theodore Dorn.

Despite the charm, Theodore Dorn was the family's first mass-murderer, Mary realized. She had to allow that Jeremiah Dorn had not seen his work as murder; mass murder was simply what men did, mindlessly and thoroughly, in the nineteenth century and in all the centuries before. Theodore Dorn had been educated though, thought himself sophisticated, she assumed–evolved, even–but none of that stopped him furnishing the means to perpetuate the barbarity of those earlier centuries, and at a price almost anybody could afford.

10

U nder Theodore Dorn's leadership, the Firemont Dorns supplied every faction in the fourteen-eighteen world war and in the civil war that followed the Russian Revolution. When the US entered the fray of the European war, then the business had to become slightly more discreet.

It was Mary's grandfather Tyler Hudson Dorn who pointed out to his father that they did not always need to be haring around the globe to pitch sales. With the Vollstead Act prohibiting alcohol, there were men at war all over America, and vast private armies in need of private arms. Mary's granddad also pointed out that the mobs had well-established networks of routes, friendly cops and politicians and shipping and trucks that could be used. They also had expertise and an endless and expendable source of manpower.

It was easy to get them as customers. Some of them owed Theodore Dorn for a multitude of favors. Whenever they forgot this, Tyler was good at reminding them, at first with a friendly overture. If that was rebuffed, he arranged for them to sample the merchandise at a range that proved to be fatally close.

As Theodore's number one son, T H Dorn was establishing his credentials. Theodore had always maintained that there would be no passengers in the family business, no matter their pedigree. Tyler won his first *coup* from his connections with the Prohibition mobs, supplying the Irish in their war against the British–"Ousting the Brits is a great American tradition," he was fond of declaring–and then against one another.

Maybe because there had been nobody to contradict him, Theodore Dorn had seen himself as a gentleman. Tyler Hudson Dorn had no such pretensions. Mary's grandfather adopted a direct approach and got rid of those not amenable to it. He was almost certainly involved in the murders of several Irish republican idealists who were getting in the way of buying arms from America, liberal journalists, including newspaper editor Walter Liggett, and trades union activists, and he had enough law enforcers in his pocket not to care who knew. He did it systematically and ruthlessly, joked about it in indiscriminate correspondence, and logged all the expenses in his accounts.

Gentleman or not, Theodore Dorn had been the soul of urbane discretion as he plied his repugnant trade. Nobody, as far as Mary could find out, tried to do him any personal harm. On the contrary, there were five attempts on the life of T H Dorn. In nineteen thirty-eight a bomb destroyed a corner of a New York restaurant, killed seven people and injured twelve more, but left her granddad shaking plaster from his shoulders and yelling that he needed a refill in his port on the house. Another try in the mid-forties saw two bodyguards filled with bullets, but Tyler standing unscratched. He had calmly shot the assailant, whose gun had overheated and jammed. "Should've bought it from me," he jested later. A nineteen forty-nine car bomb gave him only whiplash injuries, and he still managed to drive it some of the way to his doctor till its wheel rims gave up the fight. A shotgun attempt in nineteen fifty-four offed the unlucky occupant of a barber's chair, a slot given up by Tyler, who wanted to finish a leisurely breakfast next door. Maybe it was this kind of luck that made friends and enemies alike dub him Tyler the Smiler; maybe they just liked the rhyme.

The last attempt wiped the smile off his face. A sixteen-year-old prostitute stabbed him in the ear with an ice pick. She said at her trial that she was having an off night. It was not a very agreeable way to go, but then T H Dorn was not a very agreeable man, so it suited him. Mary thought that, had he not been quite so involved with that last assault on him, if he had read about it or had it told to him as a suppertime story, he would almost certainly have roared with laughter.

Mary was glad she had never known him, that her grandfather was nothing but paper and stories.

II

She never stopped following that paper. As far as she could make out, it was after the Korean War that the cracks appeared in the Dorn stronghold. A poet and soldier called Kalashnikov had come up with a weapon that was reliable and cheap and, most importantly, thoroughly of the East. The Eastern Bloc of communist Europe was too tightly sealed to allow private enterprise from American patriarchs, its armaments business sewn up by the Russians and the Czechs. The guerrilla peasant armies that sprang up in Asia were good at fixing the junked weaponry left in their hills and jungles after the Second World War. They were also content to trust in the haphazard, and in a whole lot of gods nobody in the West had heard of. Peasant guerrilla armies in Africa were also into improvisation, which took a man with a gun, and a god, a long way.

Tyler's sleepless hands-on approach had covered a raging paranoia. The result? He peopled his business with yes-men unfit to run it once he was gone, so it spasmed into free fall. The paperwork for those years was crazy and proved too much for Mary when she first found it. It took her years to work out what had been going on in her family after the Korean War. One thing was clear though, and that was Tyler's lack of a suitable heir.

12

The splendid figure intended for a man christened Dominic Damian Dorn was known to family, friends, admirers, enemies, bookies, Internal Revenue men and police departments as Deedee. He got a bad write-up in the Dorn papers, the suggestion being that it was under him that the business sank to rack and ruin. In truth, none of the family's leading lights were destined to stand up well under the process of order that Mary imposed on the papers and artifacts. The Dorns preferred chaos, she recognized, and that was because within chaos almost anything could be hidden. The difference between the chaos in which Deedee lived his life and that of his father, grandfather and great grandfather, was that they knew what had to be hidden; Deedee assumed that if he could not see it, then nobody else could, either.

There were a lot of letters to Deedee from, mainly, female relatives. They conveyed complaints about allowances not being paid, school fees not being honored, cello and driving lessons canceled because of non-payment. Final demands for doctors' and dentists' bills were often enclosed alongside catty reminders about how such pledges to pay were made in perpetuity with Theodore or T H Dorn. 'After much discussion,' one letter began, 'it is felt that the business–OUR FAMILY BUSINESS–is being MISMANAGED. And we would like to PETITION that it gets put into COMPETENT hands at once. You are ACCOUNTABLE.' Whichever distant Dorn had written this was out of the loop, because the Dorn business of supplying men bent on murder with the means to do it had long been in the hands of people accountable to nobody.

By the mid-fifties, the Dorns had been more or less forced into partnership with an entity it had been sure to always keep at a polite distance: that was the US government, represented by its intelligence community. It liked to do things in ways more mysterious even than God. Its people had their own ideas about who should be able to buy guns and who should not. It was ostensibly like any of the country's institutions, with a clear hierarchy. Under the surface, however, it operated like a medieval court; there were power struggles between factions, and faces in and out of favor influencing events with blackmail and backstabbing, to see that their cronies came out on top in the fight against non-Americanism, both domestic and overseas.

Some of T H Dorn's new friends in intelligence had seen that the success of their activities would hinge on supplying worldwide anti-communist forces with weapons. To this end, they had gradually taken over the management and networks in the Dorn business. Once Tyler was gone, the rest of the family was on borrowed time, and its access to family funds was cut off. In exchange for large injections of laundered cash, disappearing almost at once into the great Dorn waste, Tyler had signed away deeds and given powers of management to a range of individuals representing some very questionable state organs.

If Mary's dad had nurtured any ambitions to take a role in the family business, he would have been disappointed. But in fact Deedee Dorn had shown no aptitude for arms dealing and, from his late teens, an active distaste for it. That had suited everybody.

The youngest child and only son, Deedee was born in nineteen forty-nine, the runt of Tyler's litter. Mary's dad's sisters were her batty aunts. Alïce (pronounced Ah-*leese*) was born in nineteen thirty-five, and Naomë (to be said as Nah-oh-may) two years later, and there was war baby Serä (sounded, at her own insistence, as regular *Sarah*) in nineteen forty. Mary's Aunt Judith was born on Victory Over Germany day in forty-five and, as if to celebrate this, was spared the foisting upon her of a pointless umlaut.

The aunts had dropped out of family life and stopped visiting long before Mary was born. Apart from Judith, they all made written complaints that the house no longer felt like their home, and that they did not feel welcome there among interlopers from state security factions, and the distinctly odd people with whom Deedee had filled his life.

What Mary knew about the aunts came almost entirely from the Firemont crones.

Her Aunt Alïce's quirk was either losing things or breaking or spilling them, often right after being told it was crucial for her not to spill, break or lose them. She managed to mislay her passport at the New York docks on the day of a trip to Europe; she enjoyed the sight of people running around trying to make things right. She also stumbled into a priceless crystal sculpture her dad had been given, either as a gift or in settlement of a bet or debt. It had been placed as the centerpiece at a party so that T H Dorn could swank to a lot of artistic types he had invited. Mary imagined her aunt's girlish pleasure at the smashing; Mary was envious of witnesses to the slo-mo fall, and the smithereens. She wondered at the courage it must have taken to go ahead and do it just out of sheer cussedness. Alïce married five times, and Mary wondered if it was because she kept running out of things to break, always in need of a ton of new wedding presents in crystal and china.

Naomë pretended not to be able to hear. The endless visits to hospitals and specialists grabbed her, as did seeing them all perplexed at her status as a medical mystery, and the ensuing waste of time and money and resources. Thin as a stick, she was beautiful in a hard, angular way that suited the times she grew into. She became a fashion model in London, England and then a society hostess, whatever that was. Her name turned up in an English scandal called the Profumo Affair, after the government minister who lost his job because of it. There were a thousand black-and-white portfolio photos of Naomë in the attics. Just when Mary thought she had seen the last of them, she found a handful more, her aunt's eyes big and spaced out, hair shorn into a severe boy-bob, in Mary Quant, in Dior, in the miniest mini skirt and the skimpiest bikini.

Serä's thing was being late, making people wait, or just being absent. She got off on people not knowing where she was or what had happened to her. It backfired on her eventually. She was late for a plane to Hawaii for a vacation with some friends and had to get on the next one. That crashed, leading to her permanent absence, and making her forever late.

Mary's Aunt Judith's vice was stubbornness, Mary was told, to an abnormal degree. If she decided to do something, it would be done. She might change her mind about it later. She might even admit it had not been the smartest thing to do–like the time she stole a visiting senator's amphetamines and car and, both suitably fueled, joyrode it non-stop across the country to Los Angeles then called to apologize and to ask should she drive it back or did they want to collect it... or what. Her demeanor was taken to be sinister and malign, so the crones avoided her if they could, though said she was the only one of them to ever be polite. Judith disappeared in the late sixties and became a focus for both frustration and admiration in the family. She had been the sister closest to Mary's dad. Deedee told Mary he felt betrayed for a long time. "They all disappear," he lamented, if he was in the mood. "The people I care about–all go, one by one by one by one."

Deedee Dorn made the simplest thing into a maze from which everybody around him struggled to escape, long after he had walked free of it and forgotten it, fixed on devising the next maze. That was not a quirk; it was how he was. It was how he grew up in the paranoid household of Tyler Hudson Dorn, and he knew no other way to live his life. His eternal, foolish optimism seemed to Mary like some incurable disease.

She remembered the mazes, her dad building his walls and driving her crazy. She remembered being out in the yard hiding, or in the streets of Firemont in the punishing rain or blinding low sunlight of the winter, being rescued by crones and taken into their homes until they could ascertain that it was safe for her sanity to be allowed home. They were helped in this by a family friend; he would appear at their doors smiling and hoping it was a convenient time to let them know that the Dorn household had regained blissful order and that he would now be glad to take Mary off their kind hands. He would thank them, take their wrinkled hands in his and palm them some cash for their care and their trouble. His name was Martin Ferrie.

13

There were no crones in residence, nor even in evidence, by the time Deedee Dorn occupied the house as heir and head of what was left of the family. By the age of twenty he had dropped out of several colleges, lost uncountable jobs and drifted away from several relationships that had been unnaturally intense and serious. He had also squandered a fortune on objects he had lost and trips he could barely remember, both physical and mental, and was in debt to individuals and institutions to the tune of sums described from mere thousands to hundreds of thousands of dollars.

On the wall of one of the upstairs rooms, Deedee once graffitied. *I remember only ideas and sensations.* Full of them, and burdened by not much else, he had presided over a haphazard household.

By all accounts–none of them, as far as Mary could make out, completely unbiased–the Dorn staff in those days included at various times Cold War refugees, possibly Cubans, possibly Eastern Europeans, and at least one man from China who claimed, for ideological reasons, to be either Japanese or South Korean. There was a Gypsy woman who, Mary saw written in an unknown hand, made things happen, *from the mundane to the magical*, which may or may not have included dealing in illegal drugs and the poisoning of a Congressman's secretary-mistress as an aide-mémoire to make sure that a vote or veto went a certain way.

Mary's dad's priorities were drinking beer and smoking weed, snorting speed and listening to jazz and then, later, loud electric pop music, and partying as much as he could. Consequently, the household was in a permanent state of motel-like flux. Any direction Deedee Dorn's life took was steered by those ideas and sensations of his and by whoever proved the strongest in leading him on. These included stoners who partied manically or were too zonked even to raise their heads. Another companion was a writer called Zig Berkowski, a minor star of the late Beat Generation, who scribbled or partied once he broke out of extended states of melancholia. There were several groups of Arabs active in Palestinian politics, who partied infrequently, then fell prey to revolutionary or religious guilt and would withdraw to their room to plot, usually following lengthy, ranty phone calls from other revolutionaries. For a short time, there was a minder from some sect Deedee had gotten mixed up in, who partied whenever he forgot not to.

The stoners were early hippies, cursed with the insight to know that flower power was never going to change anything. They bitched at one another about who was to do the household chores; it being plain that the Dorn staff, whoever they were at this time–Mary was never able to get any sense of chronology–were not going to be clearing up after them. They bitched about these things so long that nothing ever got done, and in that time the house acquired a patina of squalor it would never manage to shake off entirely. They went on a lot about the natural way of doing things and about being respectful of the environment and yet ate cold soup or beans out of the can and then tossed the can onto the piles of garbage that accompanied them everywhere. Though they left a mark on the house, their numbers were depleted by getting caught shoplifting and arrested and needing to be bailed by parents, swiftly followed by haircuts and minimum wage jobs. Overdoses saw a few of them off into hospitalization and the use of parental medical insurance. Some of them found the necessity to head at once for Canada rather than Vietnam, very often following a seemingly friendly conversation with kindly visitor Martin Ferrie. They were also overcome every now and then by the realization that Deedee's generosity was tempered by the erratic Dorn finances.

One group of house guests included Charles Manson and his pals. Fortunately for Deedee, he had no big money to be fleeced out of, and Charlie had not yet worked up the balls for his *kill the piggies* kick. Mary imagined the scorn a man like Theodore Dorn would have summoned up at the idea of Charles Manson: her great grandfather had courted Mussolini, Franco, Hitler, Stalin and Chiang Kai Shek, and would have regarded Charlie as a laughable amateur. And in need of a haircut, too, which he later got, of course, on the state of California's dollar. She pictured the Manson family in the house, but knew the place was safe from them, and so was she; they could leave no imprint on it.

Zig Berkowski set a few of his stories in the *decaying, squalid, small-town pile belonging to an old patrician family way past its days of influence and glory.* Ingrate, Mary thought.

Like the stoners, the Palestinians also suffered from an encounter with Martin Ferrie. After some bizarre information ending in them meeting up with Israeli agents disguised as other Palestinians, they were returned to their troubled country in pieces.

Martin Ferrie saw off the wavering cultist too, and returned him to his cult HQ with, Deedee claimed, minimal bruising.

"Who *is* he?" Mary finally had to ask her dad.

Deedee smiled and, surprised, said, "Well–you know old Martin."

"Yeah." Mary knew old Martin. "But... I mean... *what* is he?"

Martin Ferrie had been in and out of the Dorn house ever since Mary had been able to remember anything. He had been a friend, an uncle, a savior: he had taken Mary to the hospital when Deedee and his friends had been too stoned to notice that she was walking around the house with a bright red hot fever that might have killed her, and another time with a broken bone in her ankle after a fall. He helped Mary with math, with reading and with drawing, and taught her how to plot a line on a map using compasses, told her about George Washington crossing the Delaware and Paul Revere's midnight ride. He mended stuff, such as plugs for appliances and the broken fuses for the icebox. He organized shopping deliveries when Deedee and those friends had failed to notice that nobody had eaten anything in days. He booked exterminators for the rats and the insects and got crones in on cleaning blitzes, ordered like military campaigns. Mary knew old Martin. And yet she did not know him at all.

"How do you mean?" her dad asked back.

"Why was he always here?" She thought about it. "Why *is* he always here?"

"What?"

"What's his... *connection*?" Mary clapped, as she often did when she found a hard-won word.

"He looked after us," Deedee Dorn reminded her. "He looked after your granddad. Then he kept an eye on us. You *know* all that."

Did she? Mary was never sure. Instead of knowing, she just had the feeling that she ought to have known, but did not. She knew only that Martin Ferrie had been in the backdrop of her entire life. For the first time, it occurred to Mary that it was not she alone who knew everything that had gone on in the Dorn house and family; others knew more, and Martin Ferrie knew more than even they did.

"Martin... *loves* you," Deedee declared. "He loves us, all of us."

Mary found herself in the unusual position of having no answer to that.

With Martin Ferrie's aid, peace descended on the house whenever it was required, but there was never any order to it, as far as Mary could ever make out. Her dad would appear out of the chaos of a six-month binge spruced up in suit and tie, hair cut and neat, clutching a new briefcase. He would be ready to set off on another business venture, but it was all whim and fancy, Mary came to understand, all circumstance and happenstance.

There were certainly times when Dominic Damian Dorn was, for a while, in a house empty of all but his new wife and daughter. He looked at Mary, Deedee said, and remembered he had a family to raise. His devotion to this was sincere, but always in passing, leaving him to concentrate on his latest money-making, and wasting, scheme, his eyes distracted by fluttering, faraway dollars.

14

Martin Ferrie's name began to come up often in the Dorn correspondence, the deeper Mary dug into it. It eventually came up on the Internet, once Mary had caught it up. Martin Ferrie was a star of websites applauding or raging about the US intelligence community. They had a conspiratorial, paranoid vibe to them and often verged on the hysterical, which was why they were relatively easy to dismiss as convenient fancies.

In the years between the dusty Dorn papers and the web, Mary had often found herself thinking about Martin Ferrie. When she thought about him, the repulsive lampshade came to mind–Mary was not entirely sure why; Martin was too young to have been in the Second World War. He would have been there in spirit though, she was sure.

Mary knew Martin Ferrie had often bailed the family out of trouble–she could not help but know that–but still associated him with some of the ugly incidents that had happened in the Dorn house. She stopped listening for his name in her dad's rambling reminiscences. She stopped marking it in Dorn correspondence too, but would click on a search engine history drop-down menu and see it, a remnant of her past curiosity and of her family's curious past. She would immediately close the window, but sensed that Martin Ferrie was a man who could not be stopped by closed windows, nor even doors. Not even if they were triple-alarmed and locked.

Mary did not need reminding that Martin Ferrie had worked for Mary's grandfather T H Dorn in some capacity, whenever the other duties that claimed him had allowed. She had some idea that his association with the family started then. She had always known that he was ex-military, and part-time or full-time CIA, and as such was involved in anything the US was doing that was, or could become, incendiary. Those wild-haired bug-eyed fast-fingered men on the Internet backed all this up, those few banal facts repeated. Even though scant, they expanded to fill Mary's head. Martin Ferrie was related to Mary, as far as she could make out, by marriage with a distant second cousin of hers, one Dorothy Dorn, who had died not a year into the marriage of a condition brought on by a hole in the heart–the Dorn hole, as Mary came to think of it. At the time, Martin Ferrie was in some Cambodian jungle and did not hear of her death for months, just kept sending her letters and waiting for replies that would never come.

Back in the civilization of the five towns, Martin Ferrie had seemed unable to settle down again. He had become a permanently distracted man. That led him, Mary saw finally, to become even more closely related to her.

15

Mary's mother was called Anna St John Rome. Mary never saw her name written as Anna Dorn, except in early newspaper reports of her disappearance, which happened when Mary was eight years old.

Mary remembered her, of course. Anna was tall and good-looking and, as far as Mary remembered, wore long dresses and skirts and smelled of lemons. She spoke softly. She never got angry but did get into silences that seemed unfriendly and defensive. Mary remembered her being silent when she should have been talking, remembered her staying in her room when she should have been outside it, joining in with things.

Mary did not remember being distressed by her mother's absence, just, sometimes, puzzled. Maybe that was one thing she shared with Martin Ferrie, as she waited for her mom to come back. She wrote no letters but sat still for days, she believed, weeks, even, doing nothing but think up ways to please and delight Anna when she returned so that she would not want to go away again.

A lot of the time, life was fun with her dad and his friends. Deedee Dorn allowed Mary to live the kind of life that just... occurred. Her dad cared about her, of course, and he cared *for* her too, in his own way. Mary never felt neglected or endangered. She never felt suppressed or repressed. She remembered she was motherless only when those interfering Dorn visitors vented at her dad about it.

Mary Dorn was living a life described, at various times, as *neglected*, *feral*, most inaccurately–just a buzzword–*wanting*, whatever that meant, *not conducive to becoming a citizen*, whatever *that* could ever mean, and *prejudicial to her development*. All the same, she was defying science, or social science at least, and developing anyhow. Under her appearance of ratty hair and patched-up clothes unsuitable for any small girl, not to mention the dirt that held them together, Mary was usually healthy and clever enough to defy the descriptions.

Some of these were from letters Deedee received from concerned visitors and some from the observation of curtain-twitching neighbors. Mary was unaware of the storm these comments made. She was able to get her own food, as she was sometimes the only one who remembered she needed it, often living on boxes of cereal with milk that was curds and whey, packets of cookies, jars of dried coconut and mixed fruit pieces, sugar and flour–*ingredients*, basically. She could also get up late and stay up late because nobody reminded her not to do those things. She could sit in the little library and read all day and all night, encyclopedias and dictionaries, mainly–storybooks did not interest her–anytime in the week.

She more or less lived in the summer house at the bottom of the yard in the summertime and fantasized that she was exploring the Amazon rainforest or Robinson Crusoe–that story had somehow made an impression on her as the name of the island, and she was always slightly disappointed as an adult that it was not.

Mary Dorn lived her own life, but she knew instinctively that she needed a mother. Everybody needed a mother, she sensed, whether they knew it for sure or not, and Mary was lucky enough to have one find her.

16

As the house raged around Mary, or even when it was quiet, she kept up her habit of sitting in the niches on the wall over the staircase. Mary saw a lot of things from up there that she was probably not supposed to see. Though it seemed kind of normal at the time, she later wondered why her dad's guests picked the hallway to enact scenes of mind-altered free expression, dope deals and consumption, sexual satisfaction or failure, arguments of the heartfelt or plain drunken variety, and just one time, mercifully, violence.

Mary kind of liked the free expression. It consisted of pairs of men, mainly, trying to work out the minutest shades of meaning from what was actually incomprehensible–she first heard the names of Nietzsche, Aleister Crowley, F Scott Fitzgerald, Bob Marley, the Cumberland Gladiator and Top Cat from them. One time, a man just repeated the words *fucking mayonnaise* for an hour. The words held Mary in a trance. When she came out of it, she remembered that she had once eaten a jar of the stuff, culminating in a midnight yawn of yellow spew that lasted on and off till dawn. Others sat or sprawled around saying little, but, "This is in*tense*." The drug and sex scenes were repugnant but also kind of funny, the repetitions, the wide eyes and open mouths, the grunting and squealing. The arguments mostly made her laugh too; they were no more than obsessed bickering, and petered out in confused amiability. Except for that one time.

It was a scene that gave her nightmares for a long time. There were no raised voices to announce it. One man followed another into the hallway, saying nothing, and beat him up mercilessly. He knocked him onto the floor but even then did not stop. The other man screamed like an animal caught in a trap. Mary never wanted to hear that sound again. The beaten man had only one shoe on, she remembered later. She felt sorry for him for that reason alone. She stayed petrified in the niche, stone silent, and never remembered how she had gotten down from there.

The next morning, the antagonist was up, being suave and loud over brunch in the ballroom. When Mary thought of him later, she had a picture of a man from some earlier time: greased-back hair and sideburns, the white collar of his shirt out over that of his sports coat. He had foxy features and eyes that were wild and bright, hungry for sensations. Mary walked into the room right up to him. She had to stand in front of him for a minute before the conversation stopped.

She remembered him then, fluffing his lines and holding everybody up, making that clapper keep clapping. His zits were more under control, but he was the spotty actor from the movie that had once been shot in that very room.

He leaned down, set his face at her, and said, "Well hello, little lady. Is that another sweet roll for me there behind your back?"

Mary said, "What you did was dirty." She remembered the word being difficult to say, due to nerves, maybe–maybe anger–and it coming out all southern: *duddee*. "It was dirty," she repeated. "Dirty."

Some of the people in the room tried to carry on with their conversations. An olive-skinned woman with a badly-done punk hairdo giggled and looked at nobody. She said through a wonky grin, "Wild, huh?" Without looking at her, Mary remembered her–the actress from that same movie, who calmly delivered her lines each time. Mary did not take her eyes off her quarry, but was aware of others nudging one another. There was a sneery guy in a bathrobe, too young to be balding though he was. Mary remembered him too: the director of that very same movie, acted out in that very same room. *St Agnes of the Oilfields*, she remembered, but did not let the words distract her. There was a pot-bellied Indian guy with bad teeth. There was an anorexic Oriental girl with speckly skin, who chewed on one of her bangs and held a full glass of juice in front of her, as if unsure whether to drink it or talk to it. Maybe one or two others, but they were the ones frozen later in Mary's memory.

She said, "That movie wasn't real."

The company exchanged puzzled looks.

The thought occurred to Mary right then. She had no idea why anybody should make a phony movie–what was the purpose of such a thing?–nor even how she knew that. The thought glowed in the center of her mind, but she was busy, and forgot it for a very long time.

The violent man tried to laugh Mary's words off. When she persisted in standing there before him, he used language inappropriate for a ten-year-old to hear. Mary was able to paraphrase what he said as: "Take a hike, kid. Go play with your dolls."

Mary did not. She refrained from a haughty dismissal of the idea of paltry *dolls*, when she had entire attics full of *stuff* to amuse her. Instead she took a look at her dad and, good old Deedee, he stepped up to the plate and told the man not to talk to his daughter that way. Then he told him to leave. The man was scornful. He clattered his coffee cup down and stood there looking fierce and indomitable. At that moment, Mary feared more violence and more of the nightmares that had plagued her sleep, more of the sight of blood and the sound of a fist on the bones of a man's face.

"Get out of here." Deedee looked round at them all. "All of you," he decided. "The party's over."

The violent man took a step toward Deedee. Mary pulled out the gun she had hidden in her bathrobe; it was the trusty Makarov pistol she had taken a shine to. The sight of it got the violent man pausing and, in reflex, raising his arms a little. He nearly risked a grin, then surely remembered where he was–America, where small kids with big guns had been known to blow big holes in small men. Maybe he remembered too that he was in a house with a history of arms dealing. A drop of sweat from his brow hit his prominent upper lip, and he shook his head and turned away. He made a brief, impatient appeal to Deedee and then to the room.

Mary kept her eyes fastened on the man, but was aware of the looks going around; those well-fed breakfast expressions were fading. Even her dad looked alarmed, though he had to know that the guns in the house were ornamental, broken or decommissioned.

"You looked crazy," he recalled for Mary.

"I was trying not to blink," she said. "That makes anybody look crazy."

"Yeah, but..."

"What, Dad?"

"So does an old Russian gun."

That day in the ballroom, coffee cups were dropped with porcelain chinks, and cutlery tinkled on plates. It was remarkable, Mary thought, but they were all heading for the door.

Maybe that was the Dorns deep inside her, she thought, years later; maybe she became a true Dorn at that gun-toting moment.

With the place to themselves, Deedee got Mary to put the gun down. He hugged her and pulled out a chair, swept crumbs from it and the abandoned makings of a joint, patted it, and bade her sit. "You saw that... *thing* yesterday?" He sounded fearful, almost tearful.

Mary could not know it, but it had been the sole topic of the gathering's thoughts at their breakfast, if not of their words.

The violent man was a bad hat, not just an actor, but a bit of a gangster. The other man in the hallway was too, but a conman, a wit, a poet, the kind of man often used by Zig Berkowski in his stories: clever and quick with words, though a loser all the same. The violent man had been on the end of the other's sharp tongue and had neither understood it nor liked it. He had taken up the last resort of the man with no words. Mary would have a horror of violence from then on. "What kind of human being wouldn't?" she would demand of her friend Ashley Hyde, years later. "If we resort to violence as a matter of course, we're no longer human. We're animals. Or robots."

That was at the heart of the untold suppertime stories. The Dorns had furnished the means for the thuggish people, the men without words, to take over the world. Of course, at the end of the story, they were just that bit too stupid to manage it, but peace could only be achieved with even more violence, so the thugs dragged the world down a notch with them and made the good guys a little less human.

"You were not supposed to see that." It sounded like Deedee was ticking his daughter off till he said, over and over, "I am... truly sorry." Mary knew that. She told him so. "Truly sorry, really, truly sorry." Mary told him she knew and told him again.

"It was *dirty*," she repeated.

"*Duddee*," he quoted, and they came close to a laugh. It was at such moments that Mary loved her dad the most. The fecklessness she sensed in him–she knew that word–faded. She ignored the smell of morning whisky on his breath and knew that he would be undergoing a revelation–an *epiphany*, he called them–and would be on the wagon for a while. "They're gone," he began to repeat. "They're out of here. They're done. They're gone. Done. Gone." Mary liked the slow poetry of the words. She sat there leaning on her dad, a tingling feeling in her head and down her spine, telling her that life was about to get better.

"You'll make new friends," she observed cheerfully. "You always do."

Deedee looked at her. He tried to fix on the mood behind the words.

Mary meant them, but had a vision of those future friends, she swore to herself later: wasters and losers, pointlessly handsome young men and ornamental young women, shrouded in the painfully hip clothes of the time, presided over by their ridiculous hair. She did not dislike them in advance, but, for some achingly odd reason, she felt just a little sorry for them.

17

There was nothing quite like a pistol for clearing a house. Deedee's friends were leaving as ordered, but they bitched about it at Deedee and one another as they packed. They used the phone to call taxis and other friends where they would go freeload, and bitched about them too.

They challenged Deedee with statements and questions. One said, "This is how you treat your friends, huh?" Another offered, "Dude, that kid is disturbed." A woman catted at him, "Tail wagging the dog round here, huh? Some *party*, Deedee." The balding guy whined, "You've gone straight, Deedee–I always knew you would."

The Indian guy came and stood in the doorway, looked at Deedee and opened his mouth but was unable to speak. He cast his eyes down, clenched a fist and vanished. He came back wearing a trashed leather jacket. He did the same thing for a minute, looked as if he were about to leave again then said only Deedee's name.

Deedee didn't look at him, said just, "Bye, Bob."

"You're my friend, Deedee," the Indian guy said.

"Sure thing."

"My friend, right?"

"Pip-pip, Bob, sure enough. Go already though anyhow, huh?"

As the man vanished for the second time, Mary noticed that he was wearing blue suede shoes, pale enough to highlight a tomato-red stain on one of them. She found out later that he was called Bob Shawadi and was, he claimed, America's only Indian Elvis impersonator. He had been one of the victims of Deedee's attempts to break into the music business. Deedee's publicity-hunting strategy of booking Bob onto spots in redneck towns where the cowboys would hate him had been proven to be all sensation and hospital visits and no substance. Deedee had confessed himself convinced by Bob's talent, but unable to do anything with it.

"A-hula hula-hula," Deedee sang softly. Mary joined in. There they sat singing nonsense amid the debris. "Middle-period Elvis," Deedee tried to explain.

He smoked furiously. Mary picked up a book and read a few lines out loud in the hope of them bringing unexpected wisdom. She munched on abandoned toast. She looked out the window and commentated occasionally on the activities out there. She kept coming back to the song, just when Deedee was hoping she had forgotten it.

Out the window, she saw the violent man shoving one of the Turkish rugs from an upstairs room into the trunk of his car. She told her dad, and he looked pained. He picked up the Makarov and weighed it in his hand, but put it down with an air of distaste. He smiled to himself in what Mary would always remember as a seething, self-hating kind of way.

18

A woman arrived amid the turmoil of Deedee's friends in transit. She was petite and tan and unsmiling. She carried a small travel bag and, under her arm, that same Turkish rug that nearly became contraband. Mary saw at once that the woman had retrieved it from the thief's car. This alone was enough to intrigue Mary. The woman dumped her bag in the doorway and put the rug down. She unrolled it with a flourish, tapped its curly corner with the aid of her foot and tilted her head and took a squint at it and nodded, satisfied. Mary saw it properly for the first time, all the intricacy and wonder and skill and art of silk and dye, a watchful blue eye woven into its center and at each corner.

When Mary sent her a questioning look, the woman said, "That's *my* rug." She cut all the questions dead and said, "Deedee, why are you letting these people steal our stuff?"

That was a good question, but Mary's dad ignored it. His face broke out in a wide smile that dismissed all his worries. "It's true." Deedee Dorn sounded ridiculously happy. He nudged Mary. "It *is* her rug. Our great uncle Emmett stole it from a sultan. Or so he said."

The name Emmett rang a bell with Mary. She was not entirely sure what a sultan was, but the achievement sounded dramatic. Caught up in the excitement, she said, "Wow, Dad, *wow.*"

"Mouthful of palindromes." The woman took a long, close look at Mary, then stepped over and put a hand on her shoulder. There was electricity in her touch, Mary fancied. It gave her a pleasant jolt that made her let out one of those child-screams, forceful but fleeting.

"I hated her for getting that rug," Mary's dad said. "But not for long. Look at it. Tatty old thing."

They all looked. The rug's five eyes looked back.

"I only wanted it because she wanted it first," Deedee confessed. "My sis." It was almost an afterthought. "Mary, say hi to your aunt Judy."

Deedee and the woman moved toward each other and hugged. Mary hovered beneath them. She said, "What's a palindrome?"

Her aunt made space and drew her into the hug. "I will tell you," she promised. And Mary never forgot the word *palindrome*, nor who she heard it from, nor where they all were, their exact places in the ballroom–she would never forget that day at all. "I will tell you a lot of things." Mary believed her, but laughed.

Her aunt Judy's accent was strange. She knew why Mary was laughing, Mary could tell, but did not care. Mary knew from that, right then, that they were going to get along. She knew somehow that her dark aunt had come back to stay, to be with her and her dad and to give them some shape to their lives. She had no idea how: she just knew, and that was all that mattered.

Mary was not sure whether she had ever been unhappy, but sensed then that her happiness was about to take on extra momentum and steer her. She stepped out of the triangle they had made and pulled the Makarov out of her pocket and raised it over her head. She was aware of Deedee grinning and of her aunt pointing, open-mouthed but wordless. Deedee was saying, easily, "No, it's not loaded."

The Makarov did not have a hair-trigger and was sturdily made for Russian soldiers who lifted barrels of pitch with a finger and ate nails for breakfast.

"And anyhow," Deedee was saying. "It doesn't even–"

Mary bit down on her lip with the effort, supported her elbow, didn't quite aim, and pulled that trigger. The explosion of energy startled them all, as did the falling spits of plaster from the ballroom's frieze. Four hands reached over Mary and wrestled the gun out of her hands and she stood, disarmed but giggling. She jumped for joy. She saw a ring of faces drawn to the doorway, stragglers from Deedee's departing friends; they scrammed at once when Mary turned and caught them in her triumphant gaze.

When Mary's aunt took her by the hand and led her up the stairs under the niches to a bathroom to give her an industrial-force scrub, Mary did not holler. Even when it became clear that her aunt was going to cut off all Mary's hair then smother her scalp for an hour in nit-killing lotion that stank of gasoline, Mary made no protest. That day was the start of something new. Nothing else in Mary Dorn's life was going to be as important for a long time.

19

In April nineteen sixty-eight Judith Dorn, in her final year studying philosophy at Paris's Sorbonne University, got distracted for a minute on a boulevard by a Gypsy guitar player. Either as an *homage* to her aunt Alexandra Poniatowska Dorn or simply with a deep-seated wish to escape the way her life was going, she took off with her guitarist to lead a shambolic traveling life. She missed summer term and her exams and the student riots; she occasionally felt wistful about all of them.

Some Gypsies told strangers that they were from everywhere or no place at all, but events led Mary's aunt behind the Iron Curtain to the Romania run by the *Conducator*, Nicolae Ceaucescu. At the time, he was a hero. He had distanced his country from the Russians, made friendly overtures to the US and schmoozed western leaders. More importantly, people had work and food and heat and light and clothing and were happy, as far as they knew. "Romania seemed as good a place as any to be," Judith said.

Mary thought her aunt's accent was how a well-educated foreigner would speak English. Judith had stayed in Romania for over twenty years. "I never forgot English," she told Mary. "Of course not, though I did hear of people who claimed they'd lost their native languages entirely. But I hardly spoke it. There was nobody to speak it to. Now the whole world speaks English. Badly. But not in those times. And not among the Gypsies, hardly even now."

Aunt Judith's Gypsy was called Tudo, short, just about, for Tudor. He also had a secret name known only to his mother, or so he claimed. He used another few names, for people to whom he owed money, for policemen, for communist party informers, for officials and judges, and anybody else who got on his case.

Judith summed up the Gypsies thus: people who got equally exercised by profit, loss, birth, death, justice, injustice, the rise and fall of regimes, nations and empires, and by the sudden appearance of a goat at their gate or a chicken in their doorway. They cared not about money but about the idea of it. The same went for truth-whatever they decided was the truth, at any time, was the truth, for the reassurance of it, for the fun of it. "This does not make them bad people." Judith wanted to be sure Mary knew this, so she told her often. "Or stupid people." Mary took her word for it; the Gypsies did not sound much different from her dad.

"Tudo was an amazing guitar player," Judith told Mary. "But his kind of music went through a bad time in the seventies. Everybody wanted beat music, electric guitars, drug music, loudness. In Romania there were a lot of amazing musicians, but to get anyplace at all you had to be exceptional. And they were all exceptional. They also don't go so crazy for guitars over there. They like violins. And cimbaloms, they love those."

"What are they?" It sounded like a fruit to Mary.

"Cimbaloms were invented one day, or so Tudo said, when a Gypsy broke into a mansion to steal a piano. He was too mean to ask a friend to help because he'd have to share the profits when they sold it. But the piano was too heavy to lift and transport on his own. Of course it was. That's not stupidity," Judith broke off to reassure Mary. "That's optimism. Anyhow, so he gradually broke off enough parts to make it light enough to carry. A cimbalom is like the board of a piano with the strings exposed." It was news to Mary that pianos had strings at all. "You hit the strings with little metal hammers, so you get tone and percussion all at once."

"What kind of sound does it make?" Mary asked.

"Like somebody hitting piano strings with a hammer, of course. An unsettling sound, kind of creepy. But glorious, too."

"So Tudo didn't play guitar in Romania?" Mary had to steer her aunt back to the story sometimes.

"No. No opportunity. I sometimes think he played the guitar only so he could go to Paris one day and impress a girl. He had a very special guitar," she reflected, almost to herself. She would often do this. Mary worked out later that it was her way of not crowding the conversation and inviting Mary into it. If she showed interest, her aunt continued. If not, she went back on track and Mary only remembered later what had been said and would be intrigued, then bring it up herself another time. In this way, some of their conversations went on for years.

"How was it special?" Mary was thrilled at the idea of things or people described as *special*. She had not been exposed to too much advertising at that point, or the fact that *special* could be a very overused word.

"Well, at one time the guitar had belonged to the greatest ever Gypsy guitar player of all time."

"Really? Who was that?"

"A Belgian, called Django."

Mary did not believe that the greatest ever of all anything could have come from a place as no-account as Belgium. A session among some encyclopedias soon told her that Belgium had produced Adolphe Sax, who invented saxophones. Maybe not the most famous person called Adolphe, but the only one you could introduce to your parents without them reaching for a gun. There was also Jacques Brel, the greatest ever European songwriter not from Britain, and Tintin and his dog Milou, the greatest ever comic book characters. The greatest ever racing cyclist and the one with the most consonants, Eddy Merckx, was also Belgian. And aunt Judith was right: that greatest ever guitar player Django Reinhardt was indeed Belgian, and invented his own style of jazz.

"So it was a valuable guitar?" she pressed her aunt.

"Ostensibly."

Mary knew what that meant. She raised a hand to stop her aunt from searching for a different word.

"In fact, priceless."

"But?" Mary had gotten into the natural rhythms of Judith Dorn's stories. When things seemed to be going well in them, Mary often sensed a *but*.

"But not exactly. The big problem was that only very exceptional Gypsy guitar players could play a guitar like that. The next problem was that no Gypsy would be able to afford a guitar with such a pedigree... such a... story attached to it."

Mary nodded.

"The other problem was that no Gypsy on earth would believe that Tudo's guitar was what he said it was. Even the suggestion of it would have gotten him beat up by any Gypsy he approached with that story. Only a *gadjo*–a non-Gypsy–would believe it. What Tudo needed was for some *gadjo* to come strolling through the *mahala* one day–the Gypsy quarter–who was well-heeled, liked jazz and was able to listen to a story and believe it. Though that was about as unlikely a thing to happen as an elephant falling on his head, Tudo lived in hope of that for a while. We were going to sell the guitar for a load of money, go out and celebrate and smash a ton of plates, drink proper champagne and not home-made, and–"

"Wait–what? Plates?"

It was then that Mary learned that it was the custom among people of the Balkans to celebrate the end of a meal by smashing all the crockery, just to show they could afford to replace it. "A terrible waste," Judith said, but Mary was dwelling on repeated assurances in Emmett Dorn's Balkan saga that *a lot of plates hit the deck that night*. She was reinforced in her conviction that not all learning was got from books, not even encyclopedias, and that you had to keep an ear open and an eye out for the random.

"Hey."

Judith snapped fingers in front of Mary's eyes and brought her back to the present. Mary said, "So what happened?"

"Well... We never did drink that champagne. I've forgotten. One day the guitar was there and the next time I looked it wasn't. If he made any money from it, I never saw any."

"But was it true? *Was* it the guitar once played by this guy... yes, *Django*?"

"Tudo wouldn't have lied about something like that."

"But that's so unfair."

Judith Dorn laughed long and hard, but told Mary nothing more. Mary learned a lot from her in this way, to get the truth of something from a laugh or from silences with characters of their own, mere looks on her aunt's face.

"Anyhow, he forgot the guitar and went on making a living in the usual ways."

"What ways were they?" Mary already knew from the family history and from all the Dorn ventures that making a living, whatever it might be, was a fraught thing.

"Too numerous to recount. And, in any case, not discussed in front of women. Let me tell you, Mary, as a woman, you have to find out things for yourself. Nobody is ever going to tell you."

"*You* tell me, though."

"Don't be so... *literal*." Judith's look of annoyance was brief, then became a smile.

Tudor was daring, Mary's aunt's tales revealed, and cunning. "Unfortunately," she admitted, "he was daring when he should have been cunning, and cunning when he should have been daring. He died." That was the conclusion of that story, though Judith hinted that his death was untimely and needless, in the pursuit of an illusion whose real truth came home all too suddenly. When he died she saw it as a sign that she should give up on the Gypsies and on Romania too, and come home.

Everybody had given up on Romania. It had long been a totalitarian jail, with little food, light, heat or decent clothing, and few happy people. Nobody cared or remembered how the *Conducator* had rescued them from the Russians; they had empty bellies and misery.

Mary's aunt told her very briefly what communism was. On paper it was great, but people could never live up to its ideals. Because of that, like everybody in America said, it was a bad thing, she agreed–but at least she had lived through it to gain the authority to say so. The end of it was not good for people in minorities, like the Gypsies; it spelt nationalism and chauvinism and what Mary heard as 'petty, bourgeois' spite–her aunt said it was the worst spite there could ever be, the spite of seven-year-olds in full-grown adults. "You know that war going on right now?" Judith nodded toward the table at a newspaper, the word *Srebrenica* bold and terrible in its headline. "Over in Yugoslavia?" Mary did not, but would soon dismay herself and learn. "Same thing." Nobody seemed to have thought about conflict amid the celebrations of Christmas nineteen eighty-nine, only the Gypsies, watching their TVs and shaking their heads but, Judith said, also being pragmatic enough to go out into the good-natured crowds to entertain them with music and dancing bears, look at their palms and tell what could only be their good fortunes.

"Regimes don't matter to Gypsies," Mary's aunt told her. "Whoever the government is, they're going to be mean to Gypsies. But with the communist government gone, it meant everybody else was going to be mean to them, too. I couldn't live among mean people. And also, with Tudo gone, I didn't know what I was going to do there–I didn't want to marry his brother."

"No, sure–*what?*" Mary laughed, not sure what she had heard.

"It was a... traditional *gesture*, that was all. I *think* it was, anyhow. But he already had a wife, and three's a crowd. And anyhow, she was a bitch. And he had bad teeth and... casual body hygiene, and his kids were brats. So it was time to travel. It was time to come home." Judith startled both herself and her niece with a finger pointed at Mary. "To you and your dad and the funny little lives you were leading."

"And to get your rug back," Mary reminded her, and clapped excitedly.

"That was the most important thing," Judith seemed to agree. "And I was just in time, right?"

20

Before the arrival of her aunt, Mary was tended intermittently by crones. She was washed more or less thoroughly by their snaggy old hands, made vaguely presentable, and dressed and beribboned in a style, it was plain from photos, belonging to decades earlier.

She had carried out her life under their watchful eyes till they got forgetful or slept or strayed or fell prone to the distractions of advanced age, hostage to urinary infections that bred hallucinations. They were content to let Mary commune with fantasy playmates to replace those she had left behind in reception class and to let her sit in the moldering summer house and read encyclopedias and atlases. They took her to the stores and to church. When her dad's parties looked like they were getting out of hand, they brought Mary to their overheated homes, tucked her up on their sofas, or gave up their beds for her. "She never asks about her mother," Mary distinctly remembered one saying to another in a tone of either wonder or disapproval. One time she was sure she heard one of them answer–and Mary could tell she was being mischievous–"Nor her father."

Mary's mother had been a dreamer, the crones said. It sounded like a compliment for a while. Like Mary's dad, Anna St John Rome had been the neglected youngest child of a Falkender family with fortunes similar to those of the Dorns: not exactly gone, but certainly hard to find. Her string of names had an illustrious and romantic ring to it. Mary thought her mom would have had to be a dreamer with a name like that.

Mary liked the name Anna being a palindrome and became obsessed with saying it, writing it and thinking of it.

The St John Romes had made a pile out of importing materials used in mining. Their business had gone pear-shaped not due to any acts of God but down to bad judgement, mismanagement, corruption and theft. They paralleled Mary's family in that way too: the expertise petered out and the dreamers were left in charge, though not for long.

Anna was weak and sickly, Mary was told. She had lost her dreams, and her senses of humor and loyalty, once she found herself marooned in a family whose woes were worse than those of her own, and with a man whose attention never fixed on any single thing long enough to appreciate it.

She had run into Deedee Dorn at a dance someplace. She had liked him because he was the most stylish man there and also because he made her laugh. She also liked him because she had been dying to try cocaine all through her nineteen years, and he appeared to have a bottomless supply of it.

Deedee rarely wanted to talk about Anna. Among the things he said were that he and Anna had *got on*, and that she laughed easily–something that attracted him to people, often with dire consequences–that she wasn't stuck on *things*–she liked to *do* something rather than *have* something–and that she was not one of those home-maker types. And not snooty, he told Mary; she got on with anybody, got on their level quickly. She was accommodating. "Maybe that was the problem with her," he said, once, as if he had never thought of it before. "Yeah."

"How, Dad?"

"Yeah."

"I mean, why?"

"*Yeah.*" Deedee waved absently at Mary to be quiet, as if thinking hard about what he was saying and not wanting to be put off. But there was only that one affirmative word which, at the sixth or seventh repetition, became meaningless.

Judith Dorn tried her best to be kind about Mary's mom. "I'd like to tell you some great things about her," she said. "But I didn't know her. She was pretty. I know that much."

Mary knew that too. There were boxes of pictures of Anna, plus cuttings from the local rags that featured her. Her mom was indeed pretty. That satisfied Mary for a long time, as she masqueraded as one of those annoying small girls who thought being pretty was the sum of it all. Being pretty, though, she found out, was actually just one of Anna St John Rome Dorn's flaws.

21

Mary lived a different life once Judith took over her care. It was framed by routine to replace the chaos of her earlier years. There was school again, with early rising, early bedtimes, regular meals and two hours of homework at night. Mary sulked and sometimes raged and rebelled, but even she had some inkling of how much better she looked and felt, and was unable to disagree with any of it.

Her dad still had pals to stay. As ever, they brought their pals, who in turn drew dealers, fences, repo men and lawmen. Deedee still threw parties, and they still went on for days. Once the drugs were done, though, and the laughter and goodwill gone, Mary sensed anger and irritation in the air, the ennui of failure and abandonment. Deedee walked around elated or sat in his room in a ten-day gloom once the party people were gone.

Judith fixed things so that Mary was hardly aware of the life Deedee persisted in leading. She did this partly by physical separation. She moved herself and Mary into five rooms on the second floor of the house, plus two guest bathrooms, one of which she turned into a kitchen. On both Deedee's and Martin Ferrie's dollar she got workmen in to extend the widow's walk outside onto a staircase, so that neither she nor Mary had to go into the main house unless they wanted to. Judith set up a schedule for Mary to see her dad, and in this way injected some order into his life too; Deedee knew that five times a week he had to be spruced up and ungloomy enough to walk up a flight and spend time with his daughter. Often he was indeed vaguely spruced, but fizzed with cocaine when he failed to banish his blues naturally. On these occasions, he often had pockets full of cheap magic tricks that rarely went right, though they astonished Mary and made her laugh just the same. He dug out the house's historic guitar and sang Elvis songs, sometimes in an exaggerated Indian accent, the chords barely keeping up with his voice. He made mutant balloon animals. He brought bats and balls and dragged Mary and Judith downstairs to the ballroom and got them playing a strange cross between baseball and tennis. He would sometimes keep up an exhaustive patter, as if playing to a crowd.

He was watched closely by his sister, and sometimes coldly. The visits would occasionally end abruptly, Judith declaring, "That's enough." She would escort him downstairs. Mary would hear their voices pitched in arguments or confession, then hear laughter, and a hint of reconciliation.

Mary liked the high-adrenaline comedy of such visits, but began to prefer her dad when he was not effusive and hysterical, never knowing exactly what made the differences.

Judith changed their environment upstairs by getting all new furniture. The first thing Mary noticed was that the sofas and armchairs did not smell of *bed*; the furniture in the rest of the house had had people sleeping on it so long it took on a smell Mary later associated with motels. Mary's new life had a fresher smell, she realized. So did she after a while, and she held her hands up to her face in shame when she remembered all the wrinkled noses she had once caused to come to school colleagues, teachers, storekeepers and even among travelers on the local buses.

22

Mary asked her aunt what her life had been like in Firemont before she chose another life and, like a girl in a picture book, ran away with the Gypsies. Judith said, "I honestly can't remember." Mary guessed that she did not want to; it was disrupted by the collapse of the family. Judith told Mary a few things she could probably have worked out, about private schooling, horse riding, skiing, tennis, summers at Martha's Vineyard in a Dorn house now long repossessed by some bank, and trips to Europe. Mary had to grow a little before she was told her aunt's tales of how all of these pleasures were either curtailed or phased out alongside the paranoia enveloping the family.

By the mid-fifties, the Dorn house had become a CIA safe house–its very own mansion–a fortress inhabited by armed men. There were visits from government officials and long discussions accompanied by cold food, beer and staccato laughter.

There was the more or less permanent presence of Martin Ferrie. "Who *was* he?" Mary asked.

"Well." Aunt Judith tried to keep her face impassive. "You know him."

"Yeah." Mary thought *not* this *again* and replied with some impatience that yes, of course, she knew old Martin. She thought she had heard old Martin's car pull up the night before, and his step on the porch, his knuckles on her dad's window, his low voice. She had stood on a chair, wanting to watch him leave, but had been unable to see him in the dark. "Sure. But I mean, *what* is he?"

Martin Ferrie had inquisitive eyes. He often seemed to stand still and stiff and tall and straight with his hands at his side like a cowboy in a movie–no, in a video game–about to draw a gun. Mary would watch him absorbed in something, a tabletop doodle, maybe, and she would swear that he could see her, without looking. When he smiled at Mary she was sometimes only able to summon up in return one of those smiles so fleeting and reluctant that recipients get the impression they imagined them.

He was their friend, she knew–there was no doubt about that–so she was sometimes puzzled as to why his presence was so unsettling.

"Believe me," Judith said. "He was the only friend the family had, once my dad was gone and the money with him. The house became a grim place. All these... unpleasant men everywhere. And they changed all the time, and because we were away a lot–at school, or on vacation, whatever–we'd come home, get to the gate in a cab and they'd be reaching under their coats for guns. Some of them could barely speak English. It was a bad place to be. And only Martin put them right."

Judith had been too young to hold any appeal for her older sisters; they had ignored her, if not actively disdained her. The only creature in the house to appreciate Judith's attention, once the Dorn pets had died off, was Deedee. Judith was both attentive to and protective of him, because he hardly ever saw his father, and their mother Pecunia spent most of her time in the heart of her own family, fed up, as her letters would show, with the eccentricities of the Dorn fortunes and the peopling of her home with unshaven men in bad moods. Finally she became forgetful even of her children. She turned her back on the life she had made with Tyler Hudson Dorn–*who could have dreamed up such a man*, she wrote to Judith one time, *with no soul, and no wit unless it was cruel, and no idea of how the* people around him could *feel*; all of them were filtered through his narrow prism.

There were stories of how Pecunia ruined a party when she attacked a politician with a parasol. Mary grew up abhorring both violence and politicians, nor was she keen on umbrellas, but she would still like to have been perched up in one of the niches, watching that. Another time, Mary's grandfather spent an evening yelling at exiled Russians and Cubans and having every insult and snipe interpreted word-for-word in two languages. Mary would not have minded seeing that, either. Other scenes relayed to her by her aunt were uglier, though. In the kitchen, an exotic-sounding visitor–Uzbek, or Tajik, or Kazakh... or Georgian–got himself into a genuine Wile-E-Coyote accident and shot himself in the face while cleaning a pistol. Senators' aides sought out empty rooms in which to rage, tremble and cry. A man ran out into the front yard to scream that he had been robbed and ruined and began taking off his clothes, screaming that the family may as well have the shirt off his back, too. Judith looked at Mary in alarm as Mary saw the comedy in it, and laughed. A German bodyguard had whacked the ten-year-old Deedee hard over the head when Deedee rode a tricycle into his knees, resulting in Martin Ferrie dragging the man around a corner of the house to beat the living daylights out of him. A Nicaraguan maid who spoke not a word of English smashed Judith's tiny record player to pieces with a metal ladle when Judith put on a tune called *Lipstick On Your Collar* one time too many.

"How did that song go?" Mary distracted herself with the question. Her aunt obliged her with a hummed answer. Mary was not impressed by the performance. "Goodness," she said. "It all sounds really... *unhappy* and horrible." There were surely happier stories in the house. They had to be there someplace, and Mary resolved to find them, though at the same time she knew there were none, not really. She decided not to change the habits of her short lifetime, though, and to search anyhow.

23

Despite missing most of junior high, Mary still gained a haphazard education. Her knowledge was encyclopedic–literally, most of her reading having been from encyclopedias. There was a downstairs room half-full of the things, a remnant from one of her dad's ventures.

It was no use asking Deedee about his attempt to go into the encyclopedia business. Also off-topic were any mention of antique clocks with plastic innards, hundreds-of-years-old musical instruments made in Taiwan, a machine for keeping baby milk at the correct temperature at all times, a device for fixing the telephone on the shoulder for those who really had to keep two hands busy while talking, 3-D cameras the size of small televisions, and a whole lot of other junk.

Mary found a hoard of photos of Bob Shawadi doing Elvis Presley, many of them featuring that stolen Gretsch guitar she had unearthed. There were also printed tickets for shows that had been cancelled, letters from various record companies about Bob, largely of the opinion that Deedee had to be having some sort of weird joke with them and, okay, it was funny and all, but if he bothered them again they would have the law on him. There were several letters too from Elvis Presley's lawyers, threatening to sue should Bob ever perform any of Elvis's songs live.

Deedee had briefly been the singer in a band called The Windy Popes, though there was a trace of them in Deedee's recollections only if she pushed him. "I moved on. I was Mr.

Twenty Per Cent, girl," he'd spin it. "I say let the vain dupes do the performing and preening and pouting." His other venture into the music business was the management of an all-girl post-punk band. After using up names that record companies and venues refused to see printed or in lights, like the Cliterati, the Malice Bands and the Angri-Las, they settled on the name The Parma Violents. They had a minor local hit with a tune called *Christmas Sucks Without Drugs*, fifty copies of which had their own corner of a room, along with the usual press cuttings, photos of scowling girls with guitars and a press release promising the imminent release of a tune called *Thanksgiving Turkey Blues*. It seemed safe to say the Parma Violent girls were not keen on holidays.

Part of the trouble with any of Deedee's schemes for making money was that, once a flush of enthusiasm was levelled by the practicalities of business, Deedee lost interest and claimed never to remember any such scheme. He was able to laugh off the Parma Violents when Mary mentioned them to him, narrow his eyes and say, "Oh... *them*," and wave them away. "Those crazy *girls*? Oh... God, yeah. I can't *remember* them, even."

Mary named them all, counting them off on her fingers. Deedee acknowledged her with the faintest of smiles. Mary asked, "What about Bob Shawadi?"

Deedee tried the same frown and wave, the same words, the same smile, even, until Mary reminded him that even she had once had a sighting of Bob. "Yes," she said. "The day Judith came back."

"I think you're mistaken, honey."

"The day the man tried to take the rug your great uncle Emmett stole from a sultan." The day she saved with her Makarov, she meant, that scene that lived in her head, and never changed. "You know, when the horrible man–"

"We don't talk about Bob anymore," Deedee said. "We just don't, honey." He hesitated, said, "Bob got into trouble for doing... a bad thing."

"What bad thing?"

Deedee shook his head, and decided to bore Mary out of her interest. He said, "Income tax evasion," and let out a little laugh.

His ploy worked. "Okay." Mary's acquiescence got her dad grinning until she said, "What about the encyclopedias, then?" and he tried to find his frown again. He saw a man in a suit, a startling image of himself in car windows, an ingratiating expression on his face that even he did not believe in; he saw a shopping cart on fire in a layby, encyclopedias burning bright, all that knowledge, carbon on the wind.

"People don't want knowledge," he sometimes said. "They know it all. They *think* they do, anyhow."

From the encyclopedias, Mary's knowledge occurred in alphabetical order. It ranged from the fanciful to the fascinating to the banal, and was therefore useful sometimes, but mostly not. It certainly seemed to be disconnected from whatever any teacher wanted Mary to learn, and did not endear her to any of them.

Other children were also averse to Mary's knowledge; those interested in gaining their own knowledge were sheepishly on the side of the teachers while those who were not could not have cared less. Mary's enthusiasm for learning suffered cruelly at school.

Judith showed Mary early on that she was never going to learn all she could from encyclopedias. "Do you know what *nuance* is?" she asked Mary. "Is that word in that fancy vocabulary of yours?"

"No." Mary never tried to fake it if she did not know but always felt tragically disappointed with herself. "*Nuance*?" She shut her eyes, shone a flashlight into the corners of her head in an attempt to light up the word where it had settled. "Hey, don't tell me. No." Mary crushed her fingers hard into her palms; it was a way to avoid stamping her feet or crying.

"Oh, you can look up what it means, alright," her aunt said. "But it's *people* that teach you nuance. That's how it sticks in your head. It's not a picture on a page, or a line in a book. And where do you find people? Yeah-at school. You don't have to *like* them. It helps if you do, though. And you'd be very wise to."

Mary remembered some of the kids at high school from her time in reception. On her return to full-time education, she had greeted them like she had seen them only the day before. That did not go down well. Many had genuinely forgotten her and anyhow they were all too cool for this nerdy kid, had all their friends already or had an eye on the friends they wanted to have.

"Mary Dorn," she used to hear them sneer at school, "of the *Firemont* Dorns." That was not something Mary ever said-of course not-and she had never heard her dad or anybody else in the family say it. By then she had seen it in old newspaper cuttings, written by fawning society page reporters with nothing better to do, covering those stupid Dorn weddings and small-town charity bashes. Mary knew the jibes passed on to her at school had been brought back to life by parents or more likely grandparents. That told her that people stayed bitter and stupid and prejudiced all their days. There was no answer to the jibing, so Mary did not try to find one. "Maybe it's affectionate," both her aunt and her dad told her, but they were just reverting to Gypsy optimism on her aunt's part and things-you-tell-kids-for-the-hell-of-it on Deedee's.

Nobody at school had any feeling for Mary Dorn that could have been described as affection. She only occasionally felt sorry for herself over it; deep down she did not care. She was a Dorn-a true Dorn, she never forgot, had pointed a gun in anger that time she saved the day-and she was thick-skinned.

She was also learning that her own company was the one she would be in most, so she had better get to enjoy it. She was never at a loss for anything with which to occupy herself, either at school or at home. The things Mary was interested in, she knew by then, held no appeal for other kids.

The teachers never grew to like her. As she had spent most of her life among adults, albeit adults with a distinct air of Peter Pan about them, Mary had too easy a way with those elder-and-better pedagogs, or so they complained to her dad. He put on a give-the-kid-a-break face but promised he would 'talk' to her. He did not; he had no idea what their beef could be.

She was bored at school more or less all the time, her mind a long way from where she was. Her declarations that she knew stuff got withered out of her with all those *oh-no-not-her-again* glances. Tests turned out not to be a good means of strutting her stuff; they never asked questions she was interested in, nor ones to which she knew the exact answer. So she learned the stuff the teachers wanted her to learn, eventually, because she wanted to at least get them off her back. She also did it partly for her dad and her aunt. It did not matter that her dad was uncritical; if Mary's report card had said she cut a kid in half with a chainsaw, Deedee would have told her she did great.

Nor did it matter that Judith didn't give a damn for what teachers thought–and never showed her face at school–but she often reminded Mary that a girl had to fit into the world for her own sanity. In the margins of Ceaucescu's Romania among its minority people, Judith Dorn had seen what happened to children who refused to fit in. It was okay for adults, she told Mary; they made their own choices and their own escape from them. "I stayed in Romania for love," she confessed to Mary. "And love is great, and all, but it's a foolish thing. I loved a foolish man and became a foolish woman because of that. But not forever."

Those words caused a small jolt in Mary's mind, telling her at that moment that she would never love any man. Later, she sensed that she had always known it. She did not feel adrift from the idea of love; it was just men–she would be bemused and mystified by their love, Mary knew, and *would* escape it.

"But it was my choice," her aunt said.

"What?"

"Mary, all I'm saying is that you got to fit in before you know how you can get out. If you're out from the beginning, you have no idea of what you're trying to escape from. Trust me."

Mary read up on Romania. Because she made connections, she read up on communism, got to the Russian Revolution and skipped to Karl Marx sitting in libraries, and got bored. Her mind fast-forwarded her to read up on the countries that had made up the Eastern Bloc, in Eastern Europe and the Balkans. She read up on the wars that came to life in the Balkans and about the Ottoman Empire, the Turkish people, then the Central Asians, then Eskimos, then the Native American people of her homeland, till she was looking at a photo of a Navajo blanket that looked almost the same as a rug woven in Turkey. That was probably how in a school test she would be asked a question about George Washington and end up writing an answer about the fashion for wearing wigs in Europe, or how false teeth were invented. Mary made connections, but often found herself adrift in them.

Mary thought the kids at school, and some of the teachers, were afraid of her. She had no idea why. It was not like she carried her Makarov around with her, but there was no need; she was a Dorn, and the Dorns had flooded the world with guns, had prompted the St Vitus dance of murder and made it an everyday event. That was where the disdain came from, she guessed, some kind of bravado, a touch of defiance. Those grandparents who passed it on to the kids at school were from the time of T H Dorn, that overbearing gangster who got rid of people he disliked and lorded it over those he wanted to hurt. Their defiance was different though; it was petty, and ridiculous. Mary was a Dorn, sure, but she had been tipped out of a different mold. She would one day find out just how different, and so, she hoped, would they.

24

Mary recalled her dad as a man of many guises. Depending on his mood, Deedee would appear in the clothes of the day, a flamboyant, piratical and, it must be said, ridiculous eighties look: hair coiffed, shirts frilly, shoes suede and pointy. More often than not though it'd be the bluejeans and cheesecloth shirts of an earlier age. On the odd occasion it might be those of a different age altogether, suited and vested like something out of some old movie, hair greased back, two-tone shoes all shined.

Much of the time, however, he was the man in pajamas. He sat in his room, drank sometimes, smoked a lot, and watched a lot of TV. He said once, "TV is good. You know why? Because you can always find something to laugh at on TV. Even if the rest of your life doesn't give you anything to laugh at. You can watch TV and laugh. That's why TV is popular. It does what psychoanalysis can't do, and makes sad people laugh."

"Why are you sad?" Mary asked him, though she was old enough and canny enough by then to sense that there were all kinds of reasons why her dad should be sad. She also knew what psychoanalysis was.

"I'm not *sad*, honey." He pointed. "TV. I'm laughing."

Sometimes he played with his grandad Theodore Dorn's gold-plated revolver. It was a Russian Nagant pistol and had been intended as a gift for either Lenin or Stalin or Trotsky, or any of the others–they were the only ones Mary could remember from those murdering despots in Soviet Russia–he had to schmooze so he could offload guns. Theodore had never gotten very far with any of them, so in the end it had suited him to stay with the fascists. He had not understood the Russian mentality, Mary worked out, which was that they were not going to pay the going rate for anything because, in their forced labor camps they had a captive army to produce goods for nothing and what was more would give their lives up to do it. The fascists had been the ones with an itch to fill the world with lethal flying lead.

Maybe the TV kept Deedee laughing, but there was also his unblinking optimism that the good times were not far around the corner. That was something he could never persuade himself not to believe, and that was why Mary and Judith never worried too much about the presence of the golden gun.

25

As if one man of many guises in a house was not enough, another took three-dimensional shape in Mary's appraisal of her family history. Her labor followed her into her teens with the stark truth that the Dorn household had featured Martin Ferrie from the late fifties on. Mary knew that from Judith and, much later, from her dad, but the telling pointer to his presence was his appearance in the correspondence of the Dorn company under Tyler Hudson Dorn and in that of the shadowy men who eventually took it over.

Mary cut through a fat taped-up legal file one day and got wedding confetti bursting out of it. Across the floor it went, to be trapped in the gaps in the boards, in her hair, her shoes, her toes, in the hem of her skirt. After some initial amusement and a token attempt to clear some of it up, Mary did not let it distract her from the file's contents: Martin Ferrie's correspondence in his tiny, economical script. There were letters he had written returned to him in pique, disgust, or in one telling case mockery, from various women. She found traces of old Martin's work everywhere, in doodles on paper he had picked up, it would seem, at random–stray envelopes, bills for water and power, flyers for doomed local businesses–noting men's progress, Mary soon saw, and foretelling their endings. They appeared to be labors born of distraction, but there was an edgy creativity in them too, the work of a driven man who was never quite still, whose brain would never let the rest of him sleep.

Mary knew old Martin. From that moment, it was young Martin she became obsessed with. The more she learned about him the less she knew, his features fading to the pulsing glow given off by a ghost.

Among the Dorn papers, the flimsy copies told a tale of a troubleshooter who was, if required, a maker of troubles. Whenever those movers and shakers behind the Dorns had a problem, they scrutinized it and got Martin Ferrie to deal with it. Reports of everything from civil unrest to trade union activity to lone individuals writing complaints to Congress featured scribbled notes in different hands, saying, *Consult Ferrie*, or *Give it to Ferrie*, or the friendly but stark *Martin*. Then the references were shortened to the plain *MF*, and then just *M*, his name disappearing as his presence among the Dorns grew. After the late fifties the same hand would write *BPWD* over the reports. Mary was puzzled by those new initials. She thought at first that Martin Ferrie had failed in some way and been replaced, but context hinted that the initials also referred to him.

She covered pages with possible words that would unlock them, such as *Big Problems Will (be) Dealt (with)* or *Bad Prognosis, Will Disappear* or *Beg Pardon, Washington–Done* or *Bid (for) Possible Weird Death,* and a hundred others. She wrote them backwards and used synonyms and ciphers made from the letters, but never found anything that would reveal their meaning to her. She sensed that she ought not to ask her dad, or her aunt; how would they know, anyhow? And supposing they knew, why would they tell her?

Whatever it meant, Mary's reading revealed a pattern of big problems dealt with, prognoses that could certainly be described as bad, people who disappeared and Washington getting its apologies and its work done. There were also a few weird deaths in the stories. Some of the people mentioned in the correspondence had drunken road accidents and took drunken midnight swims that ended in drowning and fell down lift shafts while drunk and ludicrously, when drunk, got caught in heavy machinery. Whatever the BPWD meant, it all seemed to lead to alcohol, to trouble, and to Martin Ferrie.

The family had a lot of work on its hands in the fifties. When most Americans thought the war ended in nineteen forty-five, the men behind the hijacking of the Dorn company knew it was just beginning. They were paranoid visionaries, men who thought in terms of loving Old Glory and fearing the red flag of the Russians and their satellites. They were big boys who rallied round their flag and decided that, if anybody was going to screw up the peace, the US would screw them up more. They did not only take over arms businesses but bought pharmaceutical, engineering and science labs, cornered markets in medical and building supplies, agricultural aids and transport and kept a deep Santa's cave from which to hand out to the good kids and withhold from the bad ones. Mary read some of this from the correspondence then used libraries and then Internet search engines, once the world around her had evolved to cater to her curiosity. She was in the middle of some document saved in a seemingly-forgotten corner of Netscape Navigator when it hit her mid-sentence that, for a time, these mischievous operations were run from the house in which she lived.

The house was good. She had to keep convincing herself. It was hers, in some way. It would never do her harm.

It was scattered with that tiny confetti, a sign, she realized, of her investigations. She found some pieces in the washing machine. She found one in a shoe. She rolled it up between thumb and forefinger, let it unroll and saw that it was inscribed with impossibly tiny numbers. She had a memory of old Martin doing the same, spied through the kitchen window, a motionless man studying the tip of his finger.

As far as Mary could piece it together, Martin Ferrie started off as a regular soldier but excelled in undercover activities in various 'theaters'–the Dorn correspondence of the time was full of an odd language which verged at times on the Shakespearean, cautious and eloquent in its own way, almost hip and at the same time quaint. Throughout the fifties and sixties, Martin Ferrie built himself a reputation as the go-to guy for what looked like some very questionable acts. He worked for T H Dorn as a 'consultant strategist', whatever that was. He acted as a bodyguard for him, though obviously was not there when Mary's illustrious grandpa got stabbed by a tiny slip of a girl and, presumably, showed a last vessel-popping expression of outrage.

Mary worked out that a figure very like Martin Ferrie intimidated senators on both sides of the house whenever an election came up or a bill was under way that might interfere with the Dorns' CIA-related business. This man was ghostlike in a fog of acronyms and initials, with his CIA and NED, taking AA (appropriate action, apparently) and, it appeared, sometimes LSD. He seemingly also influenced the awarding of sales and manufacturing contracts in the US and overseas among friends and enemies alike, and of permits to do business in little nooks and corridors barred to those with no green light. He worked for Robert Kennedy against Aristotle Onassis and for Onassis against Kennedy. He was on the sidelines of schemes to oust Fidel Castro–Mary checked the dates in the correspondence with reams of published materials–and almost certainly took part in a plot to end John F Kennedy's stay at the White House. Whether it was the one that actually cut short that ill-starred residency or not, Mary found impossible to work out. Martin Ferrie certainly contributed to a climate in which killing a president became an achievable idea.

When Mary saw the movie *Apocalypse Now*, made a few years before her birth, she was on the point of giving up on it when she saw a scene of a man in a shirt and necktie ordering an assassin to *terminate, with extreme prejudice*. The actor didn't look exactly like Martin Ferrie; it was more his manner, and the fancy language, that got Mary sitting up listening, disturbed, to the night-shaded house around her, poking once more through its secrets etched onto paper. She shuddered to think that the BPWD had lived in her house and received orders in its rooms, that he had orchestrated some of these deeds from its phone, even that he had, in his amphetamine wakefulness, got up at night to pull cartons of orange juice out of its icebox.

He was still there–of course he was. She knew old Martin. His visits followed a pattern, like a piece of music. The prelude was the hiss of the electronic gates, then the rumble of one of his cars on the mud out front and the noise of a car door shut gently once he'd parked. The next movement was his entry into the house, and he would stand in the hallway and take a long, look around–Mary had seen him do this when she sat in the niches over the staircase. Then he would find Mary and make sure he greeted her and, later, Judith, who had looked on his visits with a politeness verging on the unwelcoming. This had stopped once Judith cut them off upstairs; Mary had several time heard voices raised in arguments between old Martin and her aunt on this very subject.

Martin Ferrie would see Deedee. They would drink, if Deedee was drinking, and would content themselves with tea if he was on the wagon. They would talk in low voices. Martin Ferrie would stay an hour, or two, maybe.

Mary had learned not to ask about him. Her questions made Deedee antsy and evasive and made her aunt moody. They just said, "Well, what *about* him? You know old Martin." She once plucked up the courage to go downstairs and ask Martin Ferrie outright what those letters BPWD stood for, but it had taken a long time–she had been amazed at the gap between her resolve and her steps–and he had gone by the time she got there.

Her investigations showed that Martin Ferrie was a man who was often gone by the time anybody wanted to talk to him: Senate committees, veterans' associations, coalitions of mothers of disappeared and displaced persons in Central America,

insurance companies, district attorneys, embassy representatives–all had wanted, at various times, to talk to a man who,
under a variety of names, bore a striking resemblance to the
Firemont Dorns' very own Martin.

Mary found out that Martin Ferrie's association with her
family had not stopped at his semi-official functions under T
H Dorn nor under his bigger, cleverer friends in government
agencies. Nor had old Martin been content to remain as a
family friend. One day, Mary found a bundle of confetti-strewn
letters addressed to him by Anna St John Rome Dorn. Out of
all the things Mary found in the upstairs rooms, these were
the ones that truly made her regret her inquisitive nature at
last. They made her want to have her tapes erased. They got
her gloomy and depressed and to the verge of anorexic, the
edge of suicide. The letters went from the flirtatious to the
strangely boringly pornographic, then ended abruptly with
a scornful pity that was languid and not angry, calm rather
than anguished. They also went through the last years of the
nineteen seventies. T H Dorn's BPWD, it was starkly plain to
Mary, was her real father.

26

Mary came to understand Martin Ferrie's appeal for that dreamy mother of hers. Mary's great grandfather Theodore Dorn had at one time bored everybody in earshot by repeating his theory that the best military people were romantics and dreamers. He lauded all those fascists and Nazis and Falangists in their fancy uniforms and with their parades and flags and searchlights and banners, because only romantics had the vision and optimism to wage wars. They were also gripped in the belief that they were destined to be the last ones standing unscathed, high boots shining, medals and sabres glinting, tall and terrible, faces covered in blood and scars but triumphant. Mary's mother had lost whatever comfort there may have been in her own dysfunctional family with all its fancy names, only to be stranded in the Dorn house with a man whose attention was in a million irretrievable pieces. She had dreamed of opportunities, to do anything but stay in a crumbling house and be part of its furniture and legends. Yet there she was in darkened rooms behind drapes, creditors prowling the outside and Deedee's impromptu bug-eyed friends haunting the inside.

Martin Ferrie, Mary had always known, kept one eye perpetually open for an opportunity. It did not matter how busy he was fixing things for the Dorns and the CIA; he was a jack in the pack, an improviser with a contingency template for anything that might turn up.

When Mary was old enough to know such things, Judith told her that Martin Ferrie found it difficult to keep his pants on whenever he drifted within striking distance of a vulnerable woman. She said that, not long after she had come back from Romania, he had come on to her. She had cooled his ardor by inviting him to her room for a drink spiked with something that made him fuzzy and limp and harmless. An expert spiker himself, he knew what had happened, but too late. As he passed into a haze he grabbed hold of a moment of clarity to declare that now the wars were over and Judith and her kind had won and banned the bomb, why not forget those allegiances of their stupid idealistic youth and have a good old middle-aged romance? It was all grand declarations with him—Judith said this was at the root of all of Martin's attraction to causes—and the scary thing about them was that they could either be acted on or just laughed off, and still retain equal weight. She reminded him that she knew damn well that he and his kind had only brought the bomb underground, sensibly deciding they had better have a planet left to fight wars on, if they were smart about it.

Judith said that the declarations of men like Martin Ferrie were easily dismissed. But if only one in ten marks fell for them then the other nine brush-offs were forgotten; that was a classic jack's *modus operandum*.

From the correspondence, Mary saw that her mom was not the woman for either Deedee Dorn or her real father; Anna St John Rome Dorn would belong to no man. When Martin Ferrie got tired of her heavy-duty melancholy he claimed the call of his other business and at the same time took up with another local woman. Mary's mom wrote him and told him to be happy until he got further distracted, until even more business took him elsewhere and, finally, until all the bad things lurking in his conscience made their way out and drove him off a cliff.

Mary was too young to be finding all this out—she was fourteen by then—but one thing was always crystal clear to her:

Martin Ferrie was not her dad and never would be. He was just her father, a banal matter of biology.

27

T his change in Mary's paternity sent her through a phase of disdaining Deedee, despite her good intentions. She yelled at him once, "You're *not* my father," though it was nothing other than the marking of one sorely vexing moment out of many. She saw a blink of hurt appear in Deedee's face before he disappeared back to his business. Nobody could hate Dominic Damien Dorn, and Mary knew that. It was a quality he had, even a mystique, that took him a long way in life in the absence of money, talent or demonstrable success though not, in the end, quite far enough.

Mary's Dorn grandmother Pecunia wrote letters to her children–it saved her from ever seeing them, Mary concluded–in which she praised, castigated, or indulged them, all with a practiced weariness. In her last letter to Deedee, she struck a note of worrisome truth. *You are not as clever as your sisters*, she wrote him. *But even you will see that this family is no longer a going concern. DD, find your own way and pray that charm still works in these cynical times we live in.* It was a horrible thing to write. When Mary showed it to her dad, he said, "Your granny told it like it was. After a while, nobody dared ask her anything. They didn't want to know the answer."

The illustrious Dorns that preceded Deedee knew that you did not achieve success on charm alone. You had to be ruthless too. You had to shake the hands of men you had ruined, lend them handguns and leave them alone with them. You had to then turn up at the funerals to smile gravely into the eyes of their widows, promise you were there for them, and not blink an eye. Deedee could never have done that.

Mary's father could, and surely did.

Mary was old enough to fight her indignation and to refrain from showing Deedee the letters that had toed and froed between her mother and Martin Ferrie. That did not mean she was not at times tempted. Deedee knew anyhow–of course he did. When Mary's father made his infrequent friend-of-the-family visits bearing gifts and checks, when he bent down to Mary and murmured, "And how's our girl?" and mirrored his eyes briefly with hers, Deedee never turned a hair.

He did not flinch from being a father, either, though his style was open to criticism. Deedee would have loved Mary, and neglected her, whether she had been his or not. Not vindictive, he forgave everything and everybody, and was therefore puzzled when the world failed to adopt the same approach to him. From both her dad and her father, Mary learned that this kind of romantic optimism was fine in its own little way, but no way to live a life.

Martin Ferrie cut a lonely figure on his corner in Falkender, Mary thought, out on his porch through the summer months, a soda in his hand, a book on his lap, his radio on low. Surveillance cameras were trained on the street, she suspected. What else? A loaded handgun nearby at all times, the shrubbery full of man-traps or, for all she knew, grenade launchers. He had no doubt made a lot of enemies among adversaries and organs of the state alike, and he was a survivor, scarred but intact. Mary wondered why he bothered though, just to live that silent life devoid of the company of his fellow creatures, welcoming them with bright eyes that were dark at the core and, ultimately, closed. Mary felt nothing for her real father. It was the substitute she would continue to love.

28

L oving Deedee Dorn had always been difficult, and it never got easy. When his business stopped taking him away, or when the fallout from it stopped secluding him in his room in front of those TV rays, he reached for that golden Nagant revolver that had belonged to his grandfather. He pondered its interrupted destiny as a gift for tyrants and thought about its chambers and channels.

One day Deedee leveled it at two policemen that came up the path armed with their own pistols and, just as deadly, warrants. He got them on the retreat in double-quick time in the first place and on their radios in the second. Realizing how absurd a siege of the Dorn mansion would be, Deedee pointed the gun at his temple and pulled the trigger. He laughed when it stalled on the rust that had built up in its mechanism over the years–no gold in there–and tossed it. He went to pack a bag and groom himself carelessly for his hands-up walk outside to face the forest of non-rusty firearms pointed his way.

Mary partly believed what her dad told the courts: he had been misled by partners and duped by middlemen, persuaded into unlawful actions by both accountants and lawyers, remaining ignorant of laws pertaining to the movement of money and declarations of profit liable to taxes. Only partly, though. It cut no ice at all with judges and appeal judges, who refused to be sidetracked by Deedee's lawyers and described him as a 'corrupt and wilful Walter Mitty', with a warning to jurors not to be taken in by his charm. It was the wilfulness they should focus on, the investors Mary's dad had ruined, and the taxpayers who suffered Deedee's financial shortcomings for an astonishing twenty-five years and still counting.

There was also the not-so-small matter of how Deedee raised money for a movie that was never going to be made. For a time during the court case, the movie *St Agnes of the Oilfields* was much quoted, then revealed to be just that title plus a few pages of script. The fraud was the least of it. In supplying his backers with girls, one of them under the statutory age of consent, Deedee was on an additional charge of importuning under the Mann Act. The only film in any camera that day was used to record a few clandestine minutes of the backers' sordid orgy in the upstairs rooms of the Dorn mansion, which led to the more serious charge of blackmail.

Of all the bad and the ugly Dorn people, makers of mayhem and mass-murder, Deedee was the only one with a spark of gentleness and decency in him. And yet? The only one ever to stand in front of the law. It was not fair.

By the time Mary was eighteen, her dad was a full-time absentee. For a change, she knew where he was, a guest of the state in the Lehigh County Prison in Allentown. She placed calls to him one time a week, wrote him once a fortnight and visited him once a month: once, in true Dorn fashion, and once only. All of these communications were fronted by a persona she put on to let him know that she and aunt Jude were doing fine. Typical of Deedee, he was content to hear good news, and never asked how and why.

Martin Ferrie sent them checks through a law firm in Philadelphia. They covered food and utility bills and left a little to splash around. The one time Mary got taken by a mood that made her tear one up and throw it in the trash, her aunt calmly phoned her father to request a replacement. "Deedee is gone," she had to remind Mary.

What she meant was that Deedee's haphazard provision from the random savings scattered among twenty-odd bank accounts was all swept up and accounted for and, of course, still found wanting. It was the missing funds they were all interested in. Deedee had been able to offer only a grin to answer their questions–hell, *he* didn't know about any missing money; if he did, he would have spent it. He also recounted his patchy memories of trips and kicks and parties, goods and chattels and food and drink and nights out on towns whose names he could no longer remember, with friends whose faces too had faded. His stories drew such cheer and laughter when read out in court that the judge only reluctantly ruled them as inadmissible.

Deedee was good at absence, Mary decided. It was the only thing he was ever good at. It was the only thing her family had ever done well, whether they did it to themselves or forced it upon others through the mechanism of that mass murder with which they furnished the world.

29

Mary's flawed and pretty mom had nearly always been absent. Mary remembered her-of course she did-but she was mainly photos and stories until Mary found her letters. Mary had a mental picture, clear as any of the photos of her mother, of Anna St John Rome Dorn at her dressing table wrapped in a towel, make up spread out in front of her. She was staring at the mirror, a picture of stillness Mary dared not disturb, even as an excitable and curious child, and one she found almost impossible to disturb even years later. She could not make it move in her mind. She recalled her mom clinking a glass at a party in the ballroom with a man in a green uniform; it might have been Martin Ferrie. Mary remembered her mom murmuring at her to go to sleep, but it was as if she could not really see her; Mary had felt like an invisible doll, and had begun making faces at her mom, getting no reaction. And there was her mom watching silently as a hairdresser plaited Mary's hair and pinned it around her head-they were going to a wedding at the Dominican church down the street-puzzling Mary with her silence.

Mary remembered her mom getting into a car immediately after the photos were done at that same wedding, a cab, she thought. It was the last time she ever saw her.

"She went back to her family," Judith told her. "Or so I heard." Deedee had always parroted a version of the same thing.

"What else did you hear?" Mary grew up to ask her aunt, many times, with increasing eloquence or impatience. Judith finally cracked and yelled at Mary to put it to rest. Judith had a drink, or so Mary thought, and calmed down and sat down and sat Mary down and told her one of those suppertime family stories. It featured the crazy St John Romes of Falkender, dispersed to California, New Mexico and, Judith thought–though it hardly mattered, with plenty of states to choose from–Louisiana. There were Anna's unsatisfactory stays with various sisters, Mary's distant and unknowable St John Rome aunts, and maybe brothers, Mary's uncles, who all had preoccupations of their own. The final tale was of Mary's mom joining the remnants of a hippy commune in Washington State and then heading to Alaska to join another commune, where she almost certainly didn't survive her first winter.

"What, and that's *it*?" It was too up-in-the-air for Mary as a story.

"That's it."

"But why would she go there?" Alaska to Mary was as foreign as Mars. "I mean, why would *anybody* go to Alaska?"

"I don't know."

Mary wondered why anybody would go to Romania, too, but that had been answered with the almost meaningless word *love*, and she needed to stay on-topic.

"And what–she just... vanished?"

"America is an enormous place," her aunt reminded her gently. "People are always vanishing."

Mary knew that. She saw pictures of the vanished all the time: newspaper ads and features on news bulletins, flyers tacked to trees, on the sides of milk and juice cartons–sad and lifeless things. She knew those people were never going to come back: the posters had nothing to do with hoping, only with coping.

Mary had three parents, near or far, and none of them any use to her. She looked through the Dorn papers and wanted, for some time, to burn them all. She concluded once again that there *was* such a thing as knowing too much, that you *could* stray into being too smart for your own good, and that she had foolishly crossed that line and could never step back. She withdrew into an orphan's sulk. She imitated her dad and sat in her room, stared at the walls and was sure at times that they were creeping toward her.

30

Mary wondered what had made her father careless enough to foul his own doorstep with his indiscretions. He was jaded, she guessed. He was a man who had lived on his wits for decades by the time he invited her mom for a spin through his world. With the power of the Dorns gone, Mary guessed that he saw no need to watch his back anymore. There was nobody with the button-pushing presence of T H Dorn to fear; there was only Deedee, the runt of the litter. It was the arrogance of a strong man among the weak, but to Mary it was a failure. Maybe she had watched too many old movies, but to her, it was the job of the strong to protect the weak.

Maybe Martin Ferrie's vanity led him into thinking he ought to inject some backbone into the family. It was not true, in any case: Deedee Dorn had flair and the ability to rise to the moment–a lot of the aggrieved witnesses at his trial had attested to this. All he had lacked was that final-strait winning streak and that had often been down to bad luck or maybe hesitation, a spark of sympathy for his victims that proved fatal to his luck.

Martin Ferrie's confettied letters both to Mary's mom and to the other local woman he had sweet-talked into a liaison, made pointed mentions of the end of the decade–the nineteen seventies–and how it was a portentous time. They were on the cusp of changes, a chance to take stock and reflect, grab chances and follow them up, look forward to a time *without consequences, but full of consequence.*

Sarah. The name glared at Mary. Long before Mary read the letters she had seen it doodled it onto any documents at hand, as if some lovestruck fourteen-year-old had wormed his way into the Dorn papers.

Mary's father had achieved a lot in his adventurous life. If the BPWD correspondence tallied correctly with the published sources, somebody very like the Firemont Dorns' old Martin trialed napalm and Agent Orange during the war with Korea in the fifties. He had a part in the killing of a liberal US president and countless less consequential people. He poisoned Laos's major rivers. He aided in the destabilization of peaceful nations in Central America and the Middle East. He assassinated the Bulgarian ambassador to the US. He advised on the destruction of several African economies. None of it was anything he could write home about, literally, so others had written it for him. Only a part of it was in boxes in the upstairs rooms at the Dorn house; much of it inhabited corners of the Internet under the custodianship of swivel-eyed obsessed conspiracy geeks that nobody would believe–sure, but that didn't make it less true. "Give it to Martin," they said, and they did, and they pushed his buttons– *Button Pusher, Will Do*, was *that* what BPWD meant?–and he did his stuff. Martin Ferrie had nothing to call his own that had not been achieved on behalf of a tiny version of America represented by groups of sinister men in those corny wood-paneled rooms they loved. Maybe by the time he was seeing the mysterious Sarah he was regretting the murderous life he had led–*this gray world I inhabit*, as he wrote to her in a heartfelt letter full of what seemed to be genuine contrition.

Mary avoided a letter-by-letter comparison for a long time, but was compelled into one. She saw that she had been right: the dates on the letters from Anna St John Rome Dorn and Sarah had begun to overlap. Then their contents had reflected this three-way split of affections and remonstrances.

Each of the women had, for whatever reason, returned all the letters Martin Ferrie sent her. The flings had ended, so why did they not just burn them? And why didn't *he*? Their lovelorn correspondence was dumped unceremoniously among the Dorn papers along with other random stuff once in her father's possession, the remnants of his part-time life among the Dorns.

Mary's attention was sidelined by letters from his Vietnam comrades to their wives and families, last messages he had not delivered. There were also scribbled notes from State and War Department cronies exchanging cryptic in-jokes about collapsed economies, fouled rivers and jungles, and those now-buried enemies of the US. Martin Ferrie had kept carbons of provocative letters he wrote to the press expressing exaggerated liberal views on issues like the military, abortion, welfare payments and overseas aid to developing nations–all causes in which he played a large part in stunting; he had a lot of fun with them.

These monuments to his guile, to his passions, triumphs and failures were in a tatty cardboard suitcase in a dusty attic. He had been unable to bear parting with them, Mary guessed.

Mary found out that Sarah had been from a clan of solidly respectable one-time landowners who made a plodding living out of real estate and industrial developments: the Montpierres. She junked both names to become Sally Hyde when she married Adam Hyde, an up-and-coming writer for TV who blundered into a talent for production of daytime TV fare for housewives, children and imbeciles.

Mary remembered Sally Hyde. She noticed her at school, dropping off her two daughters. She would see them at the mall or out in town and, one time, in Falkender Park, before Montpierre Holdings bought it up, bulldozed it and overnight stuck light industrial units on it.

Like Mary's mom, Sally Montpierre-gone-Hyde was pretty. She was fragile and porcelain-skinned–almost ornamental.

She looked kind of vacant, kind of dreamy. She was able to carry girlish clothes off-ankle socks, Mary remembered, the brightest white, which to Mary looked ridiculous on anybody other than junior school children; Mrs. Hyde had managed to make them look cute.

The patterns Mary made out disturbed her, but she could not unmake them. She did not feel pleased about them, nor want them. She wished she could unknow everything, and sometimes idly wondered if there was a pill she could take to make that happen. Her father could surely have found one, she thought, somewhere in his icebox.

Mary did not remember the older Hyde girl very clearly from her time in reception class, but once she got to high school she was in classes with her. Ashley Hyde was serious and humorless, Mary thought, wrongly. Ashley was focused, and very direct.

It wasn't that Ashley disliked her, Mary could tell. No antagonism; she did not look at Mary with disdain, like some of her friends. Unlike the other girls, Ashley Hyde did not roll her eyes when Mary drew attention to herself in class with a rambling, irrelevant answer that nobody understood except the teacher. Possibly worse: she never gave Mary a thought. Mary fretted about this for at least a semester.

They should have made a connection. Mary looked at Ashley Hyde a long time. She saw the ghost of Ashley in the correspondence between her father and Sally Hyde, saw her features between the lines. She saw the spikes of alarm in the words, of fear, accusation, of a clinging to a doomed relationship. Her father had been looking for another wife, and the continuation of his name. It was never going to be Anna St John Rome Dorn but, Mary got the feeling, there may have been a time when it could have been Sally Montpierre Hyde. Despite his part in the mass-murder of whole populations in the emerging world, Martin Ferrie was in part an old-fashioned romantic, ridiculous though that seemed, and wanted nothing more than to run away with the lady of the manor and live a quiet life raising tolerable-looking children.

Mary thought how he had sought to strip them of their illustrious names and reduce them to common old Ferries. In Sally Montpierre, Mary saw a woman who would lay low this poisoner of rivers, deforester, killer of presidents, with simple words in a small collection of letters, the last few of them so dismissive that Mary almost felt sorry for the man who had to read them. She saw the slow-burning anger of a woman not afraid to stick up for herself, and of a powerful man cut in two by her decision to shove him out of her life and get back onto the life from which he had sidetracked her.

Martin Ferrie had deposited his share of Mary inside her mom, and she got the surest sense, even before she became a friend to Ashley Hyde, that he had performed the same service in the Hyde household. Mary saw a faded picture of herself in Ashley, and knew she was another of her father's indiscretions come to life: Ashley Hyde was Mary's half-sister.

31

Mary's discovery of Ashley's status came too late. She had gone through a phase as a pre-teen of wanting a brother, preferably–a sister, if she had to. The want had worn off after a time, with an acceptance of the loneliness of being in a house full of adult strangers whose attention only rarely strayed her way. It had also receded, she thought, once she instilled herself back into the world of school, peopled as it was by kids who were as unimpressed with her as she was with them.

The day after Mary put it all together she could not stop looking at Ashley at school, which at least got her addressing Mary to say, "What are you looking at?" It was genuinely inquisitive and not the way the question usually sounded. Mary loved Ashley for that alone. "Your eyes," she could have said. "Your lovely blue Ferrie eyes." One answer to give would have been, "My half-sister. What are *you* looking at?" Then they might have gone off to a quiet corner for Mary to change their lives, and they might have laughed at the wonder of it all. Or Ashley might have gone into stone-cold shock and challenged and deflected the whole thing away.

It would have been nothing, probably, compared to the challenges both Adam Hyde and Martin Ferrie might have set it. Mary got an inkling of harsher words than Ashley would think up and of lawsuits, and violence. Right at that moment, the difficulties involved in saying any of this occurred to Mary, and never left her.

One way to *not* get a smile from Ashley was to mention the TV dynasty or, more accurately, the alliance between the man she thought was her dad and onetime popstar Janet Snyder, who masqueraded as daytime TV host Maxine Wasserman. Just as Mary never mentioned that she was one of the Firemont Dorns, Ashley Hyde refused to acknowledge her TV connections and stonewalled both kids and teachers if they were mentioned.

Mary heard of bad blood swilling around the Hyde-Snyder household, between Ashley and her stepmom, not to mention between Ashley and her sister Donna. Even without the interloping of Martin Ferrie, Adam Hyde and Sally Montpierre had not had a happy marriage, by all accounts. People said that Sally had been a wild child in several US cities as she grew up and took too much acid in the sixties. Martin Ferrie had not been the only guy to beat a path to her affections. She sounded to Mary like a slut, basically. In the photos of her that Mary tracked down later, she looked either out of it or angry at the many small-town-news events to which she accompanied Adam Hyde.

Martin Ferrie lived on the same street as the Hydes. He had a one-storey pile that took up a corner. He was the affable retiree who attended neighborhood charity drives, barbeques and pot luck parties. He cracked lame jokes with passers by. Mary thought of his eyes on his daughter every time she left her house. It was freaky that he looked on Mary in the same way, and more than a little repugnant.

Such a thing would make any... *normal* man sad, she thought, prompt him into guilt, at least. Not the Dorn family BPWD. Of course not; their old Martin, if the correspondence was to be believed, and the theories of paranoid men who frequented chatrooms and made black-backgrounded websites, Mary's dear father had been the scourge of peoples, of entire continents. Why would he care?

Mary wondered what had happened to Ashley Hyde's mom. She assumed that she and Ashley's dad had gotten divorced to make room for Janet Snyder. It did not take Mary very long to find out that Sally Montpierre, just like Mary's own mom, had disappeared. Those few words reeled around her head and reverberated, and never really left it.

32

In the old Hollywood movies that played day and night in the Dorn house as long as Deedee managed to keep hold of a TV, it was the norm that the ogre got the girl; all the leading men were so old, and the girls so young. Even so, Mary found it difficult to grasp that her vivacious, pretty mother could have fallen for Martin Ferrie, a man with twenty-two years on her. She saw from Anna's letters that Anna regretted marrying Deedee. What woman wouldn't, Mary had to concede, a man unable to fix on anything a sane woman could consider seriously. He was also letting the Dorn house, his inheritance, crumble around him under the weight of freeloaders and inaction. Anna was stuck there as the place darkened and decayed, damp infesting the inside, the weeds overgrowing it outside.

Martin Ferrie was a man of action, Mary understood. She tried to picture him in his mid-forties and sat up abruptly, mouth open; she had seen no photographs of Martin Ferrie among the hundreds in the house. There was one in her head all the same, of a man in uniform behind her on the steps of the Dominican church in Firemont, at the wedding of some couple she could not remember, Anna St John Rome Dorn on one side of him, Sally Hyde on the other. That missing photo may have been all in her mind, but she saw Martin Ferrie as he was back then: tall, and straight-backed in his dress uniform, his hair buzzcut, eyes clear and blue and steady, teeth brilliant white.

It was plain from the pages Mary read that he gave Mary's mom money. *What*, Anna wrote once, *you robbed a bank with dollars in it for a change, and not pesos?* And Sally Hyde, too–he gave her white gold: cocaine, so much that she asked him if it was property of some corrupt Third World government, asked if he meant her to buzz forever, burn bright and never come down.

It occurred to Mary that he made himself absurd with his generosity, that it had made the two women despise him. Just a little, but enough. It was strange that he was unable to see this, until it dawned on her that he could, that he suffered their scorn and their abandonment of him, and put it down to experience. There was no way that Mary could imagine Martin Ferrie being down, or depressed, being wounded; he was full of arrows and bullets, but invincible.

Mary drew the obvious conclusion that Anna had left, unable to stand any more of either of the men in her life. Sally too; she had revealed Adam Hyde as wanting–he sounded like a piece of work, indeed–then found Ferrie ridiculous. She too had gone: the start of a pattern. Mary imagined the two women junking their useless men and reclaiming their fancy names, meeting up to take revenge on the spaced-out Deedee, the cheesy, embarrassing Adam Hyde and the double-dealing Martin Ferrie.

She imagined them in their new lives, giggling, drinking, toasting each other, hidden in plain sight, safe and happy. And not in Alaska.

The dates did not add up, she found out later. Anna disappeared on the day of that wedding at the Dominican church that formed the backdrop of her picture of Martin Ferrie. Sally had stuck around another year or so after that wedding, increasingly cranky by all accounts, stoned or coked off her face. There were shopping sprees for useless things then their return to stores. Rows in the streets at night with Adam Hyde drew small-town talk, as did quarrels in fancy restaurants.

On an occasion that made the local newspapers because it ended up in a minor charge, Adam Hyde's working lunch with celeb Maxine Wasserman was interrupted by Adam's future-ex-wife, plates smashed and a punch thrown at a head waiter.

Silence had followed the disappearances, of course, and not mourning.

They were dead though, Mary knew, when she was old enough to know, when she had put the pieces together in the right order–dead. Surely. She had learned the word *murder* at nine years of age and it had followed her ever since, etched into the attics and corners and carpets of the Dorn house, in its papers, in its people who had lived through its lifetime. But who would do a thing like that?

Not Deedee, Mary decided quickly enough. He was incapable of hurting a soul, physically, anyhow. She had a flash of Deedee's violent pal–him, maybe, even though he had caved in at the sight of her little Makarov... but he had been too late to the house. Bob Shawadi was a candidate, she guessed. She remembered a hungry, nervous look in his eyes, his Adam's apple moving rapidly, a red-brown stain on one of his blue suede shoes. Deedee had said he was trouble, but in all seriousness she could not really fit him to the disappearances.

Killers walked among them in their sleepy towns, it was clear. Killers sat on their porches, Mary assumed, just like non-killers, turned up to neigborhood barbecues, and made the same lame jokes each summer.

Killers sat in the kitchen studying tiny, numbered pieces of confetti caught on the tip of a finger, looked up, and smiled unsettlingly but said jovially, "A wedding? And I wasn't invited?"

Would old Martin have done such a thing? When Mary pieced together all the things he had done in the field he was good at, it was a possibility. But could a man murder even one woman he loved, let alone two? Mary was too young to ask the question and find an answer that was near the truth–she had never been in love, after all. She would one day ask Judith, who would almost laugh, and tell her she had better go find a man and drive him nuts to find the answer to that one.

33

Mary saw that Ashley Hyde did her best not to stand out. She did not do sports, and scraped top ten grades, nor was she ever the life and soul of the party. That was her way of being cool, Mary thought, and it became fixed as an influence on her; it made her decide in her last two years of high school that she too would fade into the background and make an effort at becoming an enigma. Without her rambling recitations, the beam on her face, her offers of unwanted help, Mary faded so thoroughly that she felt largely invisible. When she did talk, kids looked at her semi-politely but were already turning away, an ear out for a better conversation.

Mary realized that her invisibility served her enjoyment of observing people. All the better, she could do it without their knowing, hearing all they said. She was a genuine product of a house full of secrets, and eavesdropping not only appealed to her, but she seemed to be good at it.

She had always had an aptitude, even a talent, for listening to people but seeming not to. As a kid, she had sensed when her dad or one of his friends, or Martin Ferrie, or Judith, wanted to say something she was not supposed to hear. She developed a way of looking absorbed in something, a way of seeming as if she were suddenly far away. They went on talking in the belief that it was safe to do so. When they did that silly *pas devant les enfants* thing, in words or gestures, they were not fooling Mary. They also forgot that she had a ridiculously large vocabulary for a child. In this way, she picked up a lot of random information, about the wider family and its history and concerns, about her dad and his ventures, about the neighbors, about the little world around them in the present and past, and about the big world that stretched away out there.

As the world did not want to listen to her, Mary thought she would pay it a compliment it did not deserve: she would listen to the world.

Since her discovery that Martin Ferrie was her father, she no longer had the fact that she was a thick-skinned Dorn to fall back on–yes, she was the last of the Firemont Dorns, and yet was not a Dorn at all: she was a walking paradox. She was part Martin Ferrie and part Anna St John Rome and yet, to the kids at school she would always be Mary Dorn of the Firemont Dorns, this tainted figure from the five towns' tittle-tattle tales, their grandparents' prejudices, and their parents' petty imaginations.

Just because it seemed plain that Ashley and Mary were never going to make a connection, it did not mean that Mary's obsession with her half-sister subsided. Her serious listening began with Ashley and her best friend, Chloe Gustavson. Mary was jealous of them, of course. Just because she was resigned to being friendless and sisterless, it still burned her inside.

Chloe was blonde and dynamic, accomplished at soccer and skiing and on something scary like the clarinet or the oboe–something wooden and black and misery-inducing, anyhow. She and Ashley had been pals at reception and then at junior school, one of those in-each-other's-pockets friendships that boys were afraid of, which girls did so well.

The first thing Mary's eavesdropping revealed was a tension between Ashley and Chloe. There were conversational impasses, or a hurt puzzlement when one refused to be anything other than wholehearted about a remark the other had made. Mary thought they were friends out of nostalgia by that point, because it was unthinkable for them not to be friends. Mary was happy about that. She should not have been, probably.

In the final year of high school, Chloe Gustavson had a sadness in her eyes when she was with Ashley. It was the sadness of being eclipsed and of knowing that nothing could be done about it. It may have been to do with the clarity that Ashley was going to do something meaningful with her life: she was going to *be* somebody and what was more was going to do so without once mentioning her family connections. Chloe was not, and she knew it.

They had always been as good-looking, well dressed, and as intelligent as each other. Then, at the start of their last fall semester, it was obvious to Mary that, somehow, Chloe had become coarser looking, more brashly turned out, and plain old clever-clever, rather than intelligent. Mary sensed even then that Chloe was going to break her half-sister's heart, just out of a compulsion sparked by envy.

34

The resemblance between Ashley and Mary was marked, if only transparently, when they were at junior school. Mary remembered a shocking moment of revelation. They were five, maybe six years old. They were being herded in from the yard at the end of recess. They both tried to squeeze through a gap, like that tired old Laurel and Hardy gag: they were stuck. They glared, not in anger, just mutual embarrassment. They each knew they had to breathe in to get out. Mary looked in Ashley's eyes; they looked like her own–it looked like a mirror. They got out of the gap and walked on, looking back at each other, then were broken out of this by the clap of a teacher's hands. Mary believed that, had that not occurred, she and Ashley would have become friends at that moment, inseparable forever.

She also half-remembered an encounter with Ashley that never happened. She was eight at the time. Ashley was supposed to be going to a wedding to which the Dorns had also been invited. Not a Dorn wedding–there were no Dorns left to be married in Firemont's Dominican church by then–but Deedee knew the groom from some business venture, and he was marrying a Montpierre, a cousin of Ashley's mom.

Mary could not remember how she knew Ashley and Donna would be going. Nor did she remember why they did not go, in the end. That day was taken over by another event: the last time Mary saw her mom.

Mary was unhappy with that photo in her head, and how it changed with the fluctuations of her imagination. She decided to track down the real photo from that day and to find any photos she could of Ashley from that time when they were stuck together at recess for a second.

She retrieved a school photo of herself from the attic and set about contacting the photographer whose name was stamped on the back. His name was Frank Lynam, and he was based in Barnton. It turned out he had died.

Mary found his son in the book and called him. Frank Junior had not gone into the photo business, so it looked like a dead end. "Anyhow, why?" he asked. It was lucky he did. Mary told him she was looking for local school class photos for some vague college project thing; she made it sound boring enough for him not to want to question her. He suggested she contact one of the local newspapers, as they published school photos on their slow news day pages, and might have a store of them. Mary had already thought of that, but was certain they would not have kept photos going back fifteen years. Frank Lynam Junior said he could give her the name of one of his dad's old contacts at one paper, but that he would need to go look it up and call her back. Without much enthusiasm, and a little down about a perfect plan gone to nothing, Mary gave him her number.

Frank Lynam Junior called back not two minutes later. "An idea," he declared.

"What?" Mary was the one with the ideas, and had come to distrust those of others.

"Corner of my garage," he preambled. "Piled with my dad's work."

"Okay."

"Sure to be some school photos there."

"Sure."

If Mary wanted, she could have a rummage. If she *really* wanted, he suggested, half in cheek, half as a joke, Mary

302

thought, she could take it all off his hands and give him the space to put his kids' damn bikes, the videotapes he would surely never watch again but wanted to keep anyhow and the old lawnmower he was holding onto in case the new one blew up.

Frank Junior seemed slightly shocked at the speed with which Mary took up his offer. Within the hour she arrived at his place with a guy called Henry Claddach, the son of one of the Firemont crones, who hired himself and his pickup out to do handyman jobs if he was sober. People said Henry had spent his life lifting and moving stuff. A lot of it not his own, Mary surmised, from the police mugshot look of him. She and Henry, but mostly Henry, cleared that corner of Frank Lynam Junior's garage in a quarter hour flat and were gone.

Mary shut herself in one of the attic rooms for an everlasting week with the photos and their stories, unable to tear herself away from them. She was unable sometimes to look at any one photo properly, always taken by the next, and thus was led back and forth through the years they summed up.

The entire life of the five towns was in those photos, and Mary got a tangible sense of it pulsing away in the past, pushing at the fabric of the present. Those photos lined her dreams and daydreams and stopped her sleeping, all the scenes of schools, weddings, first communions, bar mitzvahs, saints' days, Christmas bashes with scary Santas, Asian festivals full of sareed women under ethereal lights. In between feasting there were car pile-ups, construction site accidents, fires, scenes from police-and-gangster shoot-outs too gruesome to make the papers and people on their way to the courthouse to disappear or outside it, exonerated or fined and laughing it off. The fishing catches, the competing dishes in cookery competitions, lodge meetings, fundraiser fun days and folk dancing contests were fascinating in their own way and at least raised Mary to a laugh. She also got to appreciate the men in suits and neckties or groovily unsuited and tieless through the nineteen seventies, the women in hats or revealing elaborate hairdos, big sixties and long seventies hair, and the kids in formal clothes and slicked-down hair, or jeans and sneakers trying to look mean and edgy.

And out of the frames leapt Anna St John Rome before and after she became a Dorn, frowning, with a feral intelligence, half an eye on the lens. Dominic Damien Dorn, there he was too: sharply suited, standing up to give a toast. There was Sally Montpierre, intense, pale and leggy, hair carelessly shoved to one side, braless in thin dresses. There was Adam Hyde, looking by turns goofy and manipulative.

And there was Ashley, never casting her eyes at a camera, cool and contained, oblivious to the intrusion or pretending to be invisible.

Nothing had been too trivial for the eye and lens of Frank Lynam. It was a gallery of the banal and yet all captured expertly–lovingly, even–something captivating in each frame; Frank had been an artist. The out-takes told the most fascinating stories. Mary specially loved a groom caught making a slobby lip-licking face, a kid who turned at the wrong moment and made his head a blur of startled alien eyes and mutant, toothy mouth, the father of a bride with his glasses halfway down his face, subjects caught unkindly by the angle or the light, a dish that didn't make it to the news because its creator was caught in the act of spilling it onto the floor mid-flourish, and a mayor showing all his gappy bad teeth instead of the tight-lipped smile he put on to kid the world that his teeth were all-American white.

There was Bob Shawadi, headlining some bash as Elvis, holding that purloined Gretsch guitar stashed in the Dorn house. And the girls of the Angri-Las, scowling and moody, dressed like bank clerks or Mormons then in their later incarnation as the Parma Violents, all ripped jeans and leather, a little older, looking a little more sick of the crass music business, adrift from Deedee's slapdash management and casting out alone to make it big or head for obscurity.

Mary saw Bob again under a long name from the Indian sub-continent. He was also under arrest, suspected of abducting a girl and of trying to abduct a boy, accused of actual violence and intended extortion; put-upon Bob with a cop-donated black eye, arraigned, no guitar, not singing. And poor Bob outside the courthouse, acquitted for lack of evidence–grudgingly, so too nervous to smile, too antsy to believe he was really free.

Most sets of photos and negatives were in their own envelopes with the name of the subject scrawled on the outside. This information was sometimes precise, such as *Nellie Klein's ninetieth birthday*, or it was vague, like *Draper party, winter*, or *Barnton High, summer*. Sometimes Frank Senior had included a cutting from the newspaper, or simply a torn-out page. In later years he had lost interest, Mary assumed, or it had all gotten so commonplace to him and he had relied on invoices to aid his memory.

Mary's family ghosts came to life again among Frank Lynam's photographs. There strode the farther-flung Dorns visiting town to petition Tyler Hudson Dorn on various matters, Mary guessed. They did not look happy to have a camera pointed at them and sure enough one out-take showed a bodyguard approaching the camera, a hand up, a look of intent on his face. There they were again at the Dominican church for the funeral of Tyler the Smiler: Mary's aunt Judith, her aunt Alïce, maybe eyeing things she could break, and that had to be Naomë in the silent world of her own making, and an empty place denoting Serä, who was either just plain late or forever late by then–Mary could not quite remember. Her dark aunts, and–at *last*–a man to guard their bodies for them: old Martin, the BPWD.

Scribbled or neat, marked precisely or vaguely, it was a selective history of the five towns and their people from the mid-fifties to the mid-eighties, which just about included the young Ashley, and Mary.

Mary had to remind herself that she had only wanted to see a few photos to check out the resemblance between herself and her lost half-sister. Because of the nature of the photos and the sheer volume of them, it was about two weeks before she finally did that. There were plenty of school photos and, because Ashley was Adam Hyde's daughter, a lot of photos of her at live broadcasts from the malls, Christmas lights switch-ons, Halloween, Thanksgiving bashes and New Year countdowns: Ashley smiley, Ashley bored, Ashley dutiful, suffering, blank-faced.

Mary spread the photos out and looked at them a long time. It was disturbing but fascinating to watch herself and Ashley ageing on the ballroom floor. Mary was sure more than ever that she and Ashley had a parent in common.

Just biology, she reminded herself all over again. It did *not* matter who supplied the cells and the juice. Their connection was DNA, a thing that could not be seen or quantified, a thing that made no difference to their everyday lives. Mary wished it could have been as simple as that. She pretended to be happy to have that part of her curiosity satisfied but there were all kinds of things that were still bothering her.

She looked at the enormous pile of stuff that now filled up most of one of the upstairs rooms. She wondered if there was anything else she could do with it.

35

At school, Mary tired of listening to Ashley Hyde and Chloe Gustavson. Their exchanges were funny in a not-so-funny kind of way, and kind of tragic–though "Not tragic like when you lose your *lipstick* tragic," to quote some girl Mary had heard on a bus one time–in that they were unconsciously signaling an end to their friendship. When Mary found herself struggling to remember the tragedy or the comedy within it she wrote the exchanges down as soon as she could so as to render them faithfully, pauses and all. And then, because they were not the only interesting kids in class, nor the only ones to have tragi-comedy in their exchanges, Mary began to write down other kids' utterances.

At the back of her mind when she started this was a courtroom doodle she found crumpled in a briefcase filled mainly with legal papers verging on the incomprehensible. They dealt with lawsuits brought against the Dorn family, concerning evasion of personal and company taxes, bribery of state officials to gain financial and commercial advantage, the breaking of arms embargoes in various countries and the theft of State Department documents pertaining to Dorn affairs. As a side-issue there were other charges, involving perjury in earlier trials and intimidation of witnesses. The doodle pertained to a trial involving money laundering done by a man doing it on behalf of another man also doing it on behalf of some other man, linked ultimately to Tyler Hudson Dorn. It featured an almost abstract diagram of a courtroom, with a judge, attorneys, a stenographer, the jury, the defendant and a changing cast of witnesses. Whoever had done it, surely from the public gallery, had drawn in vague heads and shoulders among the benches and written meticulous, neat little sentences to represent what they were saying. Most were verbatim absurdities, such as: *On noticing the proceeding of a preceding suspicious fiscal event, the procedure was to proceed with the procedure* (bank employee). Mary liked: *The teller was imbued of the opinion that the payee was exhibiting a nervous disposition* (assistant bank manager). *The accountant never closed that account on account of an account of his unaccountably premature death while on vacation in Florida* (Dorn employee) made her roar with laughter she recognized at once as unseemly. She was also very fond of: *These guys started a paper trail that literally covered the office with snow* (police witness).

She could see why whoever had compiled the doodle had thought those utterances worthy of the written word. They came up so often that the scribe had to write smaller each time to fit them in and had criss-crossed them too. Mary photocopied parts of them and enlarged them to read them better. It was one of the oddest documents she had ever seen. She looked the case up: some judge had been out to get T H Dorn through one of his employees or a hired hand, with the possible collusion of some of the security forces, already with their hooks into the family enterprises. Newspaper records revealed that within a year of the case, after which directors of a company linked to the Dorns were fined peanuts and forbidden from trading in certain stocks in certain countries, four of the people with star roles in the case were dead–five, if Mary counted the accounted-for accountant. A chill passed through her. She looked at the doodle in a different way. The doodler had been posted in the public gallery to decide who ought to pay the price for carelessness or duplicity later, in a dark place away from the courtroom's formal justice. He had made up his mind, Mary thought, then settled back and amused himself with his doodling. She wondered if she ought to throw the doodle away, wondered if it was bad luck to keep a thing like that in the house–like the tattoo lampshade–then figured that most of the Dorn paper could be described that way. It was only dusty paper; it had no juju other than the thoughts it had fixed in Mary's mind.

The handwriting was small and spare and neat; it was her father's. She was not surprised.

Following in his footsteps, she amassed a collection of copybooks filled with the things her classmates were saying in their unguarded moments. She abandoned the copybooks and adopted Martin Ferrie's handiwork to make a loosely-shaped diagram of the classroom. Once she had nailed one that was good enough, she photocopied it to use over and over. Anything that took her fancy went into the diagrams, the unintentionally funny, the genuinely absurd, things that sometimes should have stayed secret. The phrases formed a map in her mind, and she pinned her diagrams onto the walls at home.

"What *is* all this?" Judith was amused and curious. It was only her question that prompted Mary to give them a name.

"They're… whisper maps," she thought up. She felt it was a magic moment, from the kind of magic that only her aunt could work, because if Judith had not been there and if she had not been interested enough to ask, Mary would never have known what to call them. "It's what people say," she said. "So it tells you, in some way, what they think."

"What people?" Aunt Judith studied one closely. "This is your classroom at school?"

"Yeah."

"Interesting, Mary." Judith read a few, and laughed gently. "But are you sure you should be putting kids' names to these things?"

"No." Mary thought the names spoiled the look of the maps. "But I'd never remember them all if I didn't." There was a logic there that Judith could not disagree with. In time, Mary hardly needed to put the names to the whispers. She could identify most of them by the words alone. She still did it, though. She recognized that she had a mania of some kind, driven by a fear of forgetting.

She soon got bored with the format. The things the kids said were no longer that interesting–it was the making of the maps that interested her most and the process, the act of witnessing, eavesdropping, scribing. The nature of the maps changed. Soon the kids' names featured entries like how embarrassed one was because the rain washed the gunk out of her hair and made it look a mess for the rest of the day and how she fiddled with it the whole day long; how ashamed another was because some boy caught her looking at him in *that* way, but she denied it and none of her friends believed her and despised her for getting caught out, and another who got yelled at in science class for bouncing a tennis ball on the table and the teacher made him look *tiny* and he knew it and looked like a frightened little boy and no tough kid; and yet another, who looked great on a skateboard for seconds till she crashed and broke a front tooth and if she did not remember it all her life, then everybody else would: nothing monumental, just things that made Mary laugh and taught her something about people whose actual nature was always out of reach.

After a year or so, Mary had a pile of the maps so big she would have needed to clear out another room if she wanted to pin them on the walls. She no longer did them every day, did a weekly resume of incidents that had stuck in her mind, did them more out of nostalgia than anything else, and finally abandoned them for a bigger world, out of whose cacophony she separated the speech and sound.

36

Mary was on a bus one day when a guy got on at the Blue Posts Hotel in St Maz. He knew the driver, and did not sit down but lingered by the driver's grille and talked. He was middle-aged and kind of down-at-heel and had an old rocker's fifties hairstyle gone salt and pepper. He was kind of muscular but also kind of fat.

Mary gathered from what he said that he worked in the kitchens at the Blue Posts. She listened harder when he said, "And he said to me, you know, George, you haven't had a day's vacation for three years, am I right, and I said to him, don't I know it just, was what I said to him, and he said to me, George, he said to me, we got to talk about you taking a vacation." Mary knew from his demeanor that he was letting everybody in talking distance know he was never going to get that vacation; his manager was going to bring it up in another year's time but only to say the same thing. Mary saw that George did not care. He didn't *want* a vacation, had no place to go and no money to spend and nobody to go with. He was Georgie No-Pals, the working klutz who could be exploited to work Christmas and New Year's and Easter and Fourth of July and Thanksgiving forever and he was happy with that, or not happy, maybe, just... *safe* in the routine of it, the gathering of the gratitude. George was the first non-school character to get an entry on Mary's whisper diagrams. He was hardly whispering, which was the reason she could hear him, but she was not going to change the name of them just for him.

A day or so later, she was killing time in a burger joint in Falkender–it was a summer day and she did not want to go home right away. Her dad was going through a distressing period prompted and exacerbated by a storm of subpoenas and visits to and from lawyers, which made waves up through the house and got Judith down to remonstrate gently with him. These instances often ended with Deedee crying loudly on Judith's shoulder. He was feeling the walls closing in, Mary guessed, and there was something about it that, for the first time in her recall, made the house an uncomfortable place. She was sitting there–not exactly minding her own business, as it was fair to say that by then Mary Dorn minded anybody's business but her own–and listening to a nearby couple. The guy was English. Mary learned at once that he had been in the Army, the English one presumably, and that he was a tough guy, though he didn't look it. He was rambling out a tale of how he had gotten into a fight in a bar but only hit his antagonist twice. "Left, right," he told his companion. "Good, night." He put the pause in to get it to scan that way. That alerted Mary to a man trying too hard. Mary watched him staring at his woman companion, blinking, gratified to have told his tale but also, Mary sensed, afraid. Of what, she was unsure. She knew little at the time about how some men related to women. The Unknown Soldier was number two on Mary's diagrams. She listened hard for his name to come up. He said his companion's name a lot–it was Ellen–but she didn't say his.

Another joint, a pizza one this time, and another day, brought the third outsider to Mary's diagrams. He had a low growl for a voice. He was thin and wrinkled, late middle-aged and distinctly sickly-looking, with a mop of too-dark hair that made him look like an animated leather wig stand. He wore a striped polo shirt that was three sizes too big. His captive dinnertime audience was a boy of maybe fifteen. The growler was explaining the Second World War to him. All of it, it seemed. Mary did not think he'd get too far into it before dessert. He said the words *Ax-us Pow-urz* repeatedly until they sounded ludicrous, as if he had invented his own language.

Mary morphed into a full-time eavesdropper and turned her attentions, and her ears, to strangers wherever she found them, picked out the things they said, wrote them down, and gave them a lingering life in her maps. They were beginning to look like weirdo works of art, partly because Mary filled them in with descriptions, times, dates and places in different colored inks, a technique, she was uncomfortably aware, favored by crazy people who wrote to public figures about conspiracy theories. She tried not to let that bother her.

She was watching one couple having an exchange when she realized that she knew the woman from someplace–almost. It bugged her for days until she worked out that she had seen her in photos in Frank Lynam's collection. She had featured in a spread in a local rag twelve years before, having won a scholarship to Yale. Mary was therefore able to add the woman's name to the *event*–she knew *event* was too pretentious a term for them, but *occurrence* and *instance* were also kind of fancy. And took longer to write. The woman's name was Susie MacShane. Hers was not the first name on the maps–George the washer upper kept that distinction–but it was the first full name, and the first connection to a life beyond Mary's eavesdropping.

From then on she took out Frank Lynam's photos and cuttings and kept them out. She studied them obsessively. It was strange, but from the first day she recognized people from them, in Firemont, in Falkender, in St Maz, Barnton, Aliceville, wherever she went. A pram-pushing woman had been a junior chess champ. A guy in the line at a burger place in Barnton once got to the finals of the National Spelling Bee. A man Mary saw hosing down his yard in Falkender was awarded a medal for bravery after he rescued a child from drowning in the Potomac on a daytrip to Washington. The woman she saw locking up the kindergarten in Falkender was wrongly accused of stealing from thrift stores by some crazy manager guy who stalked her. She made ten thousand dollars out of it for defamation. A mechanic in a car service joint in Barnton had gotten run out of the US Army for selling supplies past their sell-by date to trailer park families near the base. A Hispanic junky who hung around outside Wal-Mart to panhandle had once been a home care worker for senile old people; she and four of her colleagues had been convicted on charges of burglary. What they had actually done was use their keys to go into the homes of the most bed-bound of their clients and use the rest of the house to hold parties, in a bid to escape the restrictions of the tiny studios they shared. Mary also spotted a man who went down for a year for imposture of a surgeon at the Barnton General Hospital; bizarrely, he completed a disturbingly unknown number of successful operations. His defense was that they were 'small stuff', like appendectomies. He was dressed as an airline pilot when Mary saw him, and carried a pilot's case. She watched, fascinated, as he boarded the airport bus from Barnton. Mary collected their photos together and followed up their stories with visits to the newspaper library. She sat in the dark reading the microfilms, fascinated at the tales she saw unraveling.

The subjects of her investigations made their faces in Mary's head, replicating those spread out on the tables and floors at home. They came to her in dreams, aged before her eyes, or reverted to when they were twelve and appeared in the news for winning a swimming competition. They went from peaceful forgetfulness to the day they stood outside the courthouse looking sheepish and contrite, swearing never to get involved in anything shady again.

Mary's obsession was getting worse, she had to admit. She had two rooms full of photos, and her maps. They were driving her nuts. They were not just lying on floors and tables and chairs and up on the walls; they were filling shelves warping in the center in a Tower of Babel in her head.

Then one day out of nowhere, Mary hit on an idea that would justify her encroaching insanity or in any case put it to some use. She overheard Ashley Hyde remark in class to Chloe Gustavson that it would not take a fortune teller to tell you something so obvious–she forgot what Ashley was pointing out in this catty way.

Mary thought Ashley was wrong there–she thought: a fortune teller was exactly what people needed, to tell them anything they wanted to hear.

37

E veybody should have had a fortune teller to help them see all the things they wanted to see, Mary decided. There was an artist's impression of a fortune teller's tent in one of her dad's encyclopedias. She wore a headscarf and gold earrings and had a shine in her dark eyes, a hand raised over her crystal ball. A believer sat before her, entranced. Everybody should get the chance to be entranced, Mary thought, just one time in their lives. They should have the opportunity to walk out of a fortune teller's tent full of optimism and hope. What did people walk toward, as they went about their everyday business in the five towns–work, family, commitments, or no work, no family and yet commitments just the same–burden, anyhow. How about the swimming champ she had read about who, at twelve, won the county competition for his age-group–what else happened, and what did he do after that, and where did he go? If he was still trudging round the five towns, parking lot to office to home to shopping mall to car to home, why not look in a crystal ball and tell him he would be the guy who would go on to save people from drowning one day?

"You were good in the water," Mary heard herself telling him. "I sense that you were swift as a... salmon." That sounded lame; if salmon were that swift they would not have ended up on dinner tables so often. Maybe a shark, though uglier, would be better. "I sense an episode in your future," she would say, eyes shut or glazed, hands on her crystal ball, "when you will need to be swift in the water again. I sense an... *urgency.*"

Her hands would be held up to her head by then. "*Yes*, an emergency in the water. I can't see the... exact nature of it. But you will survive it. And others will survive it because of you, and a man will come to shake your hand and tell you that you brought him back from the brink of watery... nothingness." Okay, that might have been laying it on a *bit* thick, but it gave Mary an inkling of how the deep parts of her mind were working. She would be the fortune teller. She would be Madame Maria, from... Romania, maybe, and the most harm she would do would be to get a guy back in the pool one time a week. It was perfect and, like the best of perfect plans, was too good both to be true and not to be.

38

M ary had flunked school spectacularly, and because of that she missed out on college. For some time she took jobs in that black hole that swallowed small-town girls, and went *into retail*. Those store jobs sapped her sense of optimism till it showed in her face, went into her bones and gave her a sense of almost suicidal ennui. "I don't think you're cut out for retail," she was told, twice–in exactly those words in two different places and from two different manager-types. She had never been rude to customers, even when they deserved nothing better, never made a major mess-up, neither with stock nor an order, nor with money received nor passed back in change. There was simply something in her demeanor that cast a pall of gloom over those places in which she was stuck for a working day. Mary saw that as clearly as those unimaginative managers.

Part of the way she was had been passed on from her dad, a willingness to vamp it, and part from her mom, she guessed, a tendency to drift in her mind, get transfixed by its distractions and daydream vividly enough to let the dreams take over her entire being. Maybe she had also inherited her great aunt Agnieszka Poniatowska Dorn's fatalistic optimism–off to Mexico with a dopehead musician; how was that ever going to work out? Or maybe there was some of Judith's spontaneity, agreeing to a twenty-five-year sojourn among the downtrodden people of a failing state and ideology. Maybe Mary's fortune was going to be to steer into the unknown and take whatever came as her life, roll with it or sink under the weight of it.

When retail gave up on her, she began a stint as a temp for an agency pool of receptionists. She worked at four different health centers, two hospital outpatient units and three dentists, covering all the five towns. She amassed a collection of three hundred plus floppy disks' worth of medical and dental records. For good measure, she also filled in at the new library in St Maz and collected more disks that told her not only people's reading habits but gave details of all their changes in address over the years. She made her own notes on people's sometimes extraordinarily lengthy comments to her on how a particular book had made an effect on them.

She also remembered the crones; they had never been far away, after all. They were not just old now–they were ancient, and could not remember much of their day-to-day present. Mary knew from her time as a doctor's receptionist, however, that a lot of old people remembered things from years back very clearly–useless things, random things, things that made no sense to any outsider–and she put this to the test by getting the women to just sit there and babble. They talked out strings of fascinating inconsequence, weapons-grade trivia, came out with the most amazing instances of the banal, of the barely perceptible, perfect little vignettes of moments in the five towns captured in time and, more prosaically, by Mary's pen.

Mary had never been able to make people happy, she had long realized, whatever she did. She made them uncomfortable or got them sneering, or pitying. If she told their fortunes, a little of their past to encourage them to believe in a little bit of their future, then they might go home happy after their encounter with her and stay happy, at least for a little while. Mary thought, in a world of such drudgery and sorrow, a little while of happiness was better than no while at all.

39

Mary asked Judith to tell her about the Gypsy fortune tellers she had known. Judith laughed and reminded Mary that there was nothing to tell. "There was nothing for *them* to tell, either," she also reminded her. "They'd look at a broken-shoed miner's wife in an area where there'd been a coalmine disaster and tell her she'd come through a time of pain and tragedy and poverty and bad luck. The woman would nod–yeah, holy *cow*–that's *right*. Then the teller would say she'd be out of the doldrums soon, and approaching a time of prosperity. There was a wedding coming, wasn't there? And of course there always was, because they all had a part in all the local weddings, even if it was just to pause near the little wooden church and follow the procession a little."

"Like our crones," Mary said.

Judith smiled faintly and told Mary she should not call those dignified old dames that.

"The teller would make the woman feel like she'd be the guest of honor at the wedding. Because there was a part of her that wanted to be, she'd get all fired up about it and believe it and walk away with her head high even though nothing had changed in her life and nothing was going to. That was all it was, a repetition of commonplace wishes. Why, do you think Americans believe all that kind of thing?"

Mary thought Americans believed in the unbelievable just as much as anybody else. What about all those missing people? They were never coming back. And yet Americans put their photos on the sides of milk cartons, on walls, on trees, on TV even, clinging to the tiniest hope. It was a shame, but there it was. She thought Americans always had the unattainable in mind, and kidded themselves as much as anybody else that it was just waiting for them to reach out and grab it. What else kept the US in its state of optimism? Mary thought Americans had a rosy and romantic view of themselves and their place in the world, oblivious to its disdain. Finally, she thought Americans had brought enough of the old world in Europe with them to have a store of superstition, keeping them believing. You only had to attend a church service and see them trapped for an hour in beliefs as ancient as the Roman Empire. You only had to open a book of urban legends to see that Americans had a crazy thirst to believe in the spooky things that disturbed and excited them at the same time and kept them walking around city streets at night with one eye out for the darkness and the werewolves, vampires, kidnappers and killers that it hid. Sure, Mary thought: such people would love seeing a fortune teller.

They would love it because the teller could remind them of the things they had done in the past, or the feelings they had. They did not have to be anything monumental. It could have been one afternoon when they stayed off work and they were scared of something: "Let me see now," Madame Maria would tell them. "I'm getting seventeenth May here, maybe two years ago..." But they got over it and on that afternoon they... lost wisdom but got wise, and started to smile again. Did that ring a bell? "Yeah-oh, really? You had your wisdom teeth out, right." The date would ring a bell, and the event. They would be so impressed with that, they would believe the rest, the fortune they would come into one day and the pretty girl or handsome man they would marry, plus the fine big two-storey house they'd live in. That time they read a book by... "Now me, I don't know much about books, but I'm getting a name here, would it be... John Irving? And that book affected you, is that right?" Or how that time they went to the doc because

322

they had this thing wrong with their... hmm, hand, near the hand? Wrist? Bugging them for a year and they thought it was osteoporosis, but it turned out to be repetitive strain? And a few weeks' rest cleared it up? "Is that familiar?" They would love it. "And you have a daughter, right? Letter C? Is it Clare? No, oh Clara? Well, *Clara* is going to get married, and soon, and it's going to be a big day, and you need to prepare to hit the stores and be picking hats out right this minute."

"Goodness," Mary said to Judith. "It will be so... easy." Her aunt looked at her hard. "And it'll do so much... good." That made Judith laugh a little, but also made her look at Mary strangely the whole evening.

The next afternoon, after a trip to one of the Asian stores in Barnton, Mary came down the stairs dressed as her idea of a fortune teller and got Judith squealing with laughter. Mary took a look in the ballroom mirror and knew nobody would believe a word she told them about their fortunes. In her shimmery tunic, gossamer harem pants, patterned headscarf and ridiculous curly Aladdin slippers, she looked like a kid who had raided the dressing-up box. She pulled out the crystal ball she got at a hippy store, held it in her hands and it looked like an overgrown glass baseball. Her aunt bade her hand it over, then threw it up in the air, passed it skilfully through the skeleton of the chandelier and caught it with a flourish. After a moment of anxiety, Mary laughed too, then–she had to–pulled the scarf off her head and sank into an armchair.

"It's a start," she said, and her aunt said it certainly was, then went back to making dinner. Judith hummed the way she did when she wanted to lighten the atmosphere after she and Mary had quarreled or, Mary had noticed, when she knew they were going to.

"I can do it," Mary told Judith over dinner. She had pulled out the encyclopedia with the picture of the fortune teller's tent and, as she had about fifty copies of it, she tore the page out to show her aunt.

"And in a year you'll have paid for your tent." Judith still thought it was kind of funny. "And your crystal ball." She looked at the picture. "And your little pillar there, with the bust on it. Hey, you could get a small orchestra to play outside."

"Okay."

"Some spooky music." Judith hummed a tune from her head.

"Okay, Jude. Alright."

They finished their food, and Judith made green tea and they watched a documentary about a kid who lost his memory in an accident and was, a year on, learning stuff he had learned years before. It was dull and sentimental, and anybody with half a brain watching could see that the kid was in no way ever going to regain all of the knowledge he lost and do whatever it was he dreamed of doing. It was a dumb illusion, but it left a good feeling behind it. That was what Mary wanted to do; it coincided with what people wanted. As the credits rolled, Mary noticed that Ashley's dad Adam Hyde was one of the production team. She reflected how that was the way to make an illusion into reality: production.

Adam Hyde was just a name to her. Martin Ferrie was the father figure in Ashley's story, and Mary had never really thought about Ashley's substitute dad. She just knew him as some guy who made terrible TV programs. Then she remembered him: a man on the stairs as she watched, dropping a blue pill into his mouth, letting some air out the other end as if to make room for it. Adam Hyde had been the handsome visitor the day they pretended to shoot the movie–not Doctor Jekyll, as Deedee called him, just Mr. Hyde.

"Pitch that tent in our front yard." Judith resumed the conversation. "And then nobody'll guess it's you, huh?" She had heard it all before, Mary realized with a sickening feeling in her stomach, from Deedee; he was going to wow people with this or that and hoodwink them or just charm dollars into flying his way in exchange for snake oil medicine. "You're your daddy's girl, alright," Judith said softly, like she was reading Mary's mind.

That hurt. Piqued by Judith's words, Mary left the table and left her aunt to it, stormed up to bed and lay in the dark, resisting the sound of humming from downstairs. She slept on her angst and on her plans, but also on the remains of her optimism–a hard old pillow.

40

Mary found out that she owned the house and that she had done so ever since she had been eleven, but *de facto*-that being lawyers' fancy way of saying *in legal fact*-since turning eighteen.

"You could turn it into a hotel," her dad told her. "The Dorn Hotel. I can see it now." Mary believed him. The place had been like a hotel most of her life. "Do it up, make it nice but keep some of the oldee-worldee charm for the guests."

"Sure, Dad," Mary said. "I could mount guns all over the walls, huh?" Deedee almost smiled at that. She could have put lampshades made from human skin in all the rooms, too, she thought. Syringes. Notes warning guests that they would be billed once and once only. Stories circled in newspapers that pertained to mergers and acquisitions, murders, and executions. "Put an encyclopedia in every room instead of a Gideon Bible, huh?"

And her father as the doorman: Martin Ferrie, like something out of *The Addams Family*, intimidating the guests in, threatening them out. Once in, once out.

Deedee said, "It'd be a classy establishment. You'd make a good hotel keeper."

"Is that supposed to be a compliment?"

"That's my girl," was all Deedee said to that.

"How are things in *this* establishment, Dad?"

Deedee was going to survive jail, Mary figured, and this had raised her spirits. He was in a block with a lot of other white-collar criminals who behaved themselves impeccably, mainly to avoid a change of accommodation to the less forgiving areas of the pen. He was doing some honest work for a change, making stuff like cartons, blankets and bags used by famine relief agencies. He was keeping regular hours, avoiding the booze that circulated, eating a regular diet, if not a particularly healthy one and, as had been his practice all his life, exercising as little as he could get away with. He was making friends among his fellow crims and among the guards. Mary got the idea he was happy in Lehigh. That was a good thing, because it was going to be home for a few years. He would not just survive, she felt sure, but would thrive.

"Child," Deedee said. Mary had gotten up to go. A guard was waving at them from a booth on a level above the visiting area. Mary did not remember when or why Deedee had taken that up–he had never called her that when she was a child, a *de facto* child. "You'll be okay, won't you?"

"Sure, Dad."

"You and your aunt?"

"Sure thing." Part of Mary was deep-down bitter–she wanted to remind him acidly that she had always been left to make her own way, and that Judith had looked after herself through twenty-five years in one of the darkest places in the world. "We're managing, Dad." Mary laughed. "But if we need any help we'll be right here banging on the door for you."

41

The sensible thing would have been to sell the Firemont house and the land too, but right then Mary could not bear the idea. Whatever had happened there throughout the years, it was home, and it surrounded and protected her. She had plans only for all the secrets she had amassed inside the house.

She kept on at her aunt with her fortune-telling idea. She said, "We've got to make some money, Jude." Okay, the house was theirs–hers, whatever; ownership of a place like that meant almost nothing, except to lawyers and repo men–but they had utility bills to pay, food to buy, if they wanted to avoid being revealed in the local press one day as two batty dames who lived in the dark in rags and starved. Deedee's money was gone, repossessed by creditors, taxpayers and, no doubt, lawyers. The Dorn riches, begun all those years back by Jeremiah Dorn and ritually squandered by every Dorn ever since, had well and truly vanished. "And telling fortunes *will* make some money. You know it."

Judith had grafted through the years she had been back in Firemont. She had been a private nurse, a lady's companion, a dog-walker and sitter and a clerk in an all-night convenience store. She had done any kind of job as long as she could be left more or less alone when she did it. This may have been a reaction to living among the Gypsies who, as Mary understood it, were the last true community in the world, with the downside that nobody among them had a private life.

"We can *do* it, Jude," Mary insisted. She gabbled away: they could set up a tent in one of the upstairs rooms, fill it with suitable... stuff–the junk people expected to see–and fake the atmosphere they expected. Mary would research the people who booked a session, recount enough about their past to impress them, dress in the expected clothes, make mumbo-jumbo noises, look in her crystal ball and see a bit of good news about their futures. She would send them away happy. That would easily be worth what–twenty dollars? Thirty? Forty even, for especially good news, and if the research revealed that they were loaded?

"We can do it," Mary assured her aunt. It was simple: in being wise about the past she would appear to be wise about the future. She would be a force for good and happiness and be renowned for her expertise. *So* simple.

Judith nodded slowly. Mary giggled with nervous joy till she realized that her aunt was scoffing at her plan all over again in her cautious, kindly way.

The chief drawback, Judith pointed out, was that everybody would know it was Mary, just from the location. "Where's your credibility?" she asked her. Mary was not sure what she meant. "Where's your... plausibility? It's a con game," Judith said, starkly. Mary was about to argue the opposite, but could not help but agree. "Listen," Judith said. "If you're offering a service as a... plumber, let's say, what do people expect?"

"Wait–what? A... *plumber*?"

"For example. They expect a guy, first of all, right? Not a girl, and not a boy–no, hear me out. Not a boy. Some kid turns up says he's going to fix your water supply, you go, 'No, sorry, kid. Go away and play. You don't look like a plumber to me.' He could be the best plumber in the world–child prodigy, learned it from his master-plumber dad instead of going to school, whatever. But you want a guy. People expect him to come in a truck, right–not on the bus, not in a family car, maybe. No, listen. They expect him to bring a bag of tools. They expect him to look at the problem, make plumber-type noises. Then he fixes it. Or not. It kind of doesn't matter in a way, long as he looks like he's fixing it. And that, basically, is how a lot of plumbers operate. They get away with being bad plumbers because they look, talk, and act like plumbers."

"Okay." Mary was starting to see what her aunt meant, but was full of foolish Dorn optimism that could get anybody over any obstacle if they tried hard enough. "I agree. But–"

"Do you understand, though?"

Mary was beginning to think she did. She remembered the first time she joined an online hacker community, the questions she had been asked and the off-the-cuff answers she gave, which led her to be thought of firstly as a cop, and then as a mere voyeur, preceding firewalls and ejection.

"People go to a fortune teller, they have certain expectations too. And there's another thing. I told you, I *knew* fortune tellers in Romania."

"Sure," Mary said, excited. "So what did they do?"

"Well, one thing they *didn't* do was go up the street to the local town to tell fortunes. You know why?"

"No," Mary said. "Why? I mean, what–they traveled miles away to do it?"

"Yes, of course they did. Gypsies *have* to go miles to make a dollar, so that's what they do. You ever hear anybody telling you Gypsies are lazy, they're wrong. Gypsies work very hard to do what everybody else does easily."

"Why, though?"

"Well, look at it like this. A woman from the village seeks out suckers to get their fortunes told, what do you think the suckers are thinking? They see the old woman who lives up the road in the *mahala*–I mean the Gypsy quarter–see her each day doing her shopping, or whatever, haggling over a few... carrots, shuffling along on her bad feet, right? They're not going to believe she suddenly has the magic eye to tell fortunes. She's just some old lady they see all the time. I mean, sheesh, logic alone should tell them that no penniless old dame, anyplace, is going to have such a thing as the magic eye, let alone one who breaks her back for a few cents each day, and trudges by on the backs of her broken old shoes."

"Right." Mary guessed she knew then what Judith meant.

"So nobody is going to come here and believe you've, what, installed a fortune teller in a corner of the ballroom? Same height and build as you? Same voice, and the same... *look* as you, no matter how many fancy clothes you put on. No credibility, Mary. And to pull off a con, you need it. You knowing the people around here, and their business, works in your favor, sure. But it works against you too."

And Mary was crestfallen and speechless, because of course her aunt was right and, even though she had only recently formulated her idea, she thought it had been in the back of her mind for an eternity, shining out hope.

She had wanted to give Americans their own spooky suppertime stories to take home with them. Now they were not going to get them.

"And anyhow, fortune tellers don't use crystal balls," Judith added, uncritically. "At least, I never knew one who did."

"They don't?" Mary was genuinely surprised, which snapped her out of a sudden and sulky lack of interest. "What do they use?"

"They read palms." Aunt Jude held up one of her own palms, its lines captured in the light for seconds. "Or cards."

"Oh, I know. Tarot cards."

"No, just cards. A regular deck."

"I thought Tarot cards were fortune telling cards, though?"

"Sure. But using Tarot cards is just... *trying* too hard. An ordinary deck is all you need."

"But how do *ordinary* cards work?"

"How?" Judith laughed brightly. "Mary, they *don't* work. *None* of it works. Whatever cards you use, you make stuff up. Or, in your case," she said, thinking, "you don't have to. It's good," she said, as if it was the first time she had thought about Mary's scheme. "But no matter how much you know, and how much you say, you're still Mary Dorn from the Dorn house in Firemont, and they'll know you're Firemont Mary Dorn and they're not going to believe a word you say and, just say some do, for argument's sake, in time, one of them will work out how you do it. Sure they will. You'll tell them something you learned, and something will go click in their minds and they'll remember that you were there in the background, hazy, maybe, but there, listening and it'll all come back to them clear as day."

"Goodness," Mary said. She felt stupid for even having considered the idea. "You're right, Jude. It'll never work."

"Never, Mary?"

"Wal-Mart are hiring, I hear." Mary got up, grabbed her things to take them up to bed with her, and fixed for a second on a dreary vision of form-filling, and a strangely liberating one of taking all the paper and photos from the rooms upstairs and burning them. There was also her eagerness to get to sleep and have another dream, fix on it, chase it, let it draw her on. "I'd better apply."

42

J udith Dorn stood in Mary's bedroom doorway. She did not put the light on. She knew Mary was awake. She took a few paces and stopped at the end of Mary's bed.

"Never say *never*." Judith's eyes shone briefly. "It's a grand idea."

"Sure," Mary said. "Thanks."

"It deserves to work."

"Yeah. I know."

"And it will," Judith said.

Mary was silent for seconds. She said, "What?"

They had to go about it the right way, Judith said. No greed, she said, no big money. It was in seeking to push the limits of a good thing that landed her Tudo in jail, twice, she said and, Mary got the impression, killed him finally. They would refrain from the exploitation of gullible people with money, with grief, with a lack in their lives of anything else, Judith said. They would pull off the small con and draw a line under any further relationship with the suckers. They were not to get too clever, she said, they were to stay modest; they did not want to attract professional sceptics–there were an awful lot of them around, she said.

"Goodness me." Mary was sat up on her bed. She was excited, wide awake. "What else?"

"You go to college."

"I can't do *that*." Mary looked hard at her aunt; Judith was serious. "To do what?"

"We'll think of something," Judith promised. "Something useful, something practical. For when this crazy scheme blows over or you get tired of it."

"What, though?"

"Mary, you can do anything, child."

"Really?" Mary waved the idea away with that little word, but then knew she would keep the thought in mind, and was worrying already about how it would come to bug her. "Okay. Sure thing. College. I'll go. Whatever. But we'll do it?"

"One more thing."

"What?"

Judith Dorn would tell the fortunes, not Mary. It was a deal-breaker, she warned. She was corrupt already, she confessed airily. She was old, she had lived. She had stared at the walls of a jail, she said–no, she was not about to go into the details, not right then; they were trivial anyhow: the authorities jailed the Gypsies for their own spiteful, self-serving reasons. The thing was that she would relay the lies. In that way, Mary would save her soul.

"My *soul*?" Mary laughed. "Oh, come on, Jude." Neither of them was overtly religious, so it was not worth arguing about and yet they did, until Judith reminded Mary that she knew exactly what they were talking about.

"The things you find out will be the truth," Judith said. "You handle the truth, Mary. I'll tell the lies," she repeated. "In the future, you'll want to do, and be, something else. The transition will be easier if you stay as you are. No." It was almost the end of the discussion. "The Firemont Dorns have told enough lies, used enough smoke and mirrors. It ends with me. You'll be my back-pocket witch doctor."

"Your... what?" Mary was halfway through a laugh at the strange phrase.

"A thing my dad used to say." Judith put on a growl of a voice; it had a quality of determined alpha-male petulance. "*I need a*

BPWD. It meant some extra help, was all, to do anything he couldn't do himself."

Mary was stunned at hearing the phrase she had seen written down throughout the later correspondence concerning her father: Martin Ferrie had been Tyler Hudson Dorn's back-pocket witch doctor. Too old to delight in the solving of the mystery, she sensed disappointment rising in her.

"I don't want to be called that," she said, quietly.

"It's a mouthful," Judith observed. "You'll have to be my factotum, then."

Mary looked up, frowning: another word she did not know. A smile seemed to be expected of her, so she put one on though her face only gradually made it plain that she liked the sound of *factotum.* She was sure she would not mind being called that.

"Hey, come on, Mary." Mary had never noticed before how... *authoritative* her aunt sounded. Her voice was harsh, it was knowing, it was confident–it was plausible and credible, and Mary believed in it and was cheered by it. "I'm the fortune teller. You wouldn't expect me to have a *receptionist,* would you?"

Also by Nick Sweeney
Laikonik Express
The Exploding Elephant
A Blue Coast Mystery, Almost Solved
The Émigré Engineer
Cleopatra's Script

Enormous thanks to Paul Lyons, my eagle-eyed reader, and to Geoff Nicholson and Joel Turner for their continued support and friendship, only some of it purely literary. Thanks too to John Maxwell O'Brien RIP, for his scholarly words and inspiration. Thanks and gratitude too to Stacy Brevard-Mays and the team at Hear Our Voice for making this book shine.

About the Author

Nick Sweeney's books include a hapless lover's jaunt around Poland in Laikonik Express (Unthank Books, 2011), an opportunist's wander into the wrong part of Silesia in The Exploding Elephant (Bards and Sages, 2018), and a look at the genocide-surviving gamblers of 1960s Nice in A Blue Coast Mystery, Almost Solved (Histria Books, 2020). The Émigré Engineer (Ploughshares, 2021) is about a man who escaped the bullets of the Russian Revolution only to find plenty more in Prohibition America. His Rome-set thriller Cleopatra's Script was published by Golden Storyline Books in 2022. He lives and works on the North Kent coast of the UK. More than anybody ever needs to know about him can be found at http://www.nicksweeneywriting.com

Printed in Great Britain
by Amazon

39729330R00199

Deal Makers

How intelligent use of contracts can help you sell more and deliver better

Tiffany Kemp

Deal Makers

First published in 2013 by

Anoma Press
48 St Vincent Drive, St Albans, Herts, AL1 5SJ, UK

info@anomapress.com
www.anomapress.com

Book layout by Neil Coe.

Printed on acid-free paper from managed forests. This book is printed on demand to fulfill orders, so no copies will be remaindered or pulped.

Printed in Great Britain by TJ International Ltd, Padstow, Cornwall

ISBN 978-1-908746-73-3

To Simon, Albert and Evie

Praise for 'Deal Makers'

"What a wonderful and hugely practical book. I have run my own business for 25 years but learnt so much from just the first few chapters!

The quick summaries are extremely helpful for reminding you what to look for. This is a book that should permanently live on your desk, and be given as a must-have to anyone who touches your contracts."

– Jo Haigh LLB AAT ACS CF,
Corporate Financier, Partner FDS CFS

"Many sales people find contracts intimidating, or something to be avoided until the last moment. They are often hard to understand and full of unpleasant threats. Yet there are some who use contracts to establish competitive advantage and sustain positive relationships. This book will equip its readers to grasp these benefits, turning the contract and its negotiation into a tool for winning. Read it now!"

– Tim Cummins, President, International Association for Contract & Commercial Management

"Tiffany's book is like a Swiss army knife: it contains plenty of tools and you may find yourself using one of them every day. Resourceful sales people will soon have it in their pocket!"

– Anne Jeanpetit, Contracts and Negotiation, Microsoft

"There are many books on the art and science of selling, but whilst hooking the fish is one thing, landing the catch is another. In this book Tiffany aims high and delivers pragmatic guidance on securing the contract and building relationships, both within an organisation and with its customers. She does not shy away from explaining notoriously knotty issues such as limitations of liability and contract indemnities. In her inimitable and open style, Tiffany draws on her experience to convey the messages in a remarkably concise, clear and memorable way. Lawyers, both in-house and external, would be well advised to encourage their clients' sales team to read and digest this!"

– David Berry, Partner, Charles Russell LLP

"In my role I have an increasing level of responsibility for the agreement of our contracts. Before reading this book I felt I understood the contractual terms involved but was aware that I didn't have a great depth of knowledge regarding the cause and effect of each one. The book certainly helped on that front, but its greatest value to me was in setting out how useful an understanding of contracts, and the actual document itself, can be in the sales process, as opposed to a necessary evil that will only cause problems when you thought the end was in sight.

The clarity and logical sense this book applies to each aspect of the contract document made it both an enjoyable and enlightening read."

– Daniel Hosking, Account Director, Questers Group

"I thought I knew this stuff, until I started reading. This book was a great refresher in parts, filled in some gaps and exploded some myths.

As someone who has to manage the tensions within bid teams, as well as with external parties, I can see me handing this out as a form of 'marriage guidance'."

– Liz Benison, President, UK AND IRELAND, CSC

"A concise and user-friendly introduction to dealing with Business Contracts in laymen's language. Invaluable for anyone involved in the contract negotiating process, helping them to decide when external legal advisors need to be involved and how much can be safely dealt with internally. Lots of useful summaries and all the key issues are covered in a clear, easy to read manner."

– Peter Lingham, Managing Director, The NAV People

"As someone who normally cannot get going with 'self-development' books and whose mind normally wanders off to other things, I can't actually stop reading! I'm taking so much on board, thanks to the blend of language, examples and stories. Genius!"

– Amanda Beswick, Account Director

Acknowledgements

This book would never have existed without the help and inspiration of a great many people.

My fabulous mentor, Jo Haigh, first made me wonder if I could write a book and then encouraged me to get on and do it. Thanks to the wonderful team at Devant, especially Alison Taylor, Janine Scott and Roger Huckerby. It has been with great delight that I've seen each of them absorb, adapt and challenge my contractual philosophy, constantly pushing me to think harder, analyse better and communicate more clearly.

To Tim Cummins and the lovely team at IACCM, thanks for your research, analysis and insight. You've put structure, process and hard evidence into the mix to show that commercial management is a profession that adds real value to business.

For the kindness of Abi Clark at Hiscox, who single-handedly navigated the stormy waters of corporate red tape to secure permission for me to use the Hiscox insurance policy drafting, I am eternally grateful. I'm sure I don't need to remind readers that policy details may change, and the text I've used here is extracted from a particular policy that may not resemble yours!

I would also like to thank my fantastic reviewers, each of them incredibly busy and knowledgeable individuals who generously gave their time, wisdom and insight to help me make this into the book you have in your hands. Their feedback and comments were invaluable; any errors that remain are entirely my own.

Thanks to: Liz Benison and Tig Matthews of CSC for their insights into big-company contracting; David Berry of Charles Russell LLP for reminding me of the perils of 'lawyer bashing' and keeping me on the straight and narrow; Robert Coles for his valuable input on structure and flow; Peter Lingham of The NAV People for his practical view on what matters to a technology business; Daniel Hosking of Questers Group for agreeing to be my 'guinea pig' perfect reader and doing such an excellent job of it; Brian Perfect of Salesperson Centric for his perspective on the role of the contract in complex sales management; Amanda Beswick, Paul Moore, Di Cronin and Sue Holly-Rodway for their keen observations and honest feedback; and my grateful thanks to Alison Taylor for managing to temporarily forget she's a contract expert in her own right and review the book from the perspective of a National Account Manager.

Finally, I'd like to thank: my husband Simon for picking up everything else while I wrote, and for his unerring support and encouragement during this process; my children, Albert and Evie, for their enthusiasm and interest in the wonderful world of contracts, for reminding me it doesn't have to be complicated, and for agreeing to share their pocket money contract with the world; and Mindy Gibbins-Klein and her team at Anoma Press for their splendid book midwifery skills.

Preface

Have you ever experienced a sinking feeling when your client (your lovely, dear, wonderful client, who really wants to buy from you, loves your product and thinks you're the best thing since sliced bread) says:

"We're just waiting for feedback on your contract from Legal, then we can press ahead with the deal."

It's the moment when years of sales training, wisdom and experience sit back and say... "Over to the Sales Prevention Squad!"

The mention of Legal, together with the words 'your contract', frequently signals the grinding to a halt of the sales process. Worse still, it means that the sales process has stopped being a 'sales process' and has become a 'contracting process'. And that means that you, as the sales person responsible for shepherding this deal over the finishing line, have lost control.

Why is it that contractual issues can quickly become 'deal breakers'? And why do they so often crop up at the very end of the sales cycle, when the pressure of both your company's and the client's expectations pushes you to agree to terms that don't really work, just to get the deal closed and the project started?

That's where this book comes in. The sales person's involvement in contract negotiation varies across organisations – from taking the lead (and even doing it all themselves) through to a marginalised position, sitting on the sidelines and hoping that Legal don't manage to lose the deal for them.

The challenge is that sales professionals invariably have little or no formal training in contract law, leaving them vulnerable and exposed when participating in negotiations.

In fact I'd go so far as to say that most sales people see the contract as something to be endured in order to get to a signed order, rather than something that adds any value to the deal or the sales process and to building positive, lasting commercial relationships.

My view is that we're missing a trick by treating the contract as an afterthought and the process of getting to contract signature as an ordeal. Used well, the contract (and the process of negotiating it) can be a positive aid to the selling process.

Since I founded Devant (a commercial contract and negotiation consultancy) in 2003, I've worked with sales people across multiple industries, negotiating many hundreds of deals. I've trained sales people and project managers on the essentials of contract law – and I've seen how those who initially viewed contracts with a combination of suspicion and boredom have embraced them as useful selling tools.

By getting to grips with contract language and taking an alternative view of how the contract is used in the selling process, these sales people have become professional 'deal makers', far less at the mercy of the contracting process. They've recognised how tightly bound their own wealth and success is with the success of the business, and have been able to take action to influence both of these in a positive way.

Helping you make better deals

You will see, as you work your way through the book, that there is a heavy focus on the sales person's perspective, even though performance in many of the areas we'll examine is outside the sales person's direct control. You'll also notice that some of the content falls into 'sales 101' territory. While this isn't a sales manual, it's necessary for us to look at some key sales activities (like identifying wants and needs, for example) and apply these to the contracting process in order to see how to tackle contract negotiation effectively.

However, it's not just sales people who have a narrow view of the contract and the role it plays in making good deals. Many lawyers, finance folk and even company directors and CEOs are equally guilty of viewing the contract as a necessary evil – something to be signed as quickly as possible and then put in a drawer and forgotten. The product marketing team, project managers and delivery managers sit even further away from the contract, often seeing it as nothing to do with them.

Whatever your role in the business, you can benefit from having a better understanding of how contracts work and what they can do for you. In the process, you will gain a different perspective on each element of the sales and delivery process and how they fit together, helping you appreciate the value of your own role and those of your colleagues.

So the main objective of this book is to act as your personal guide to making and delivering great deals and to fostering profitable and mutually beneficial commercial relationships.

What do I mean by great deals?

A great deal is one that:

- Delivers what each party was expecting

- Doesn't result in disputes

- Leaves both parties happy to do business with each other again

Contracts are not just legal documents

As you work through the book, you'll see that we examine the deal from a number of different directions. This is because each contractual relationship between you and your clients has a number of components, each of which contributes to the success or failure of the outcome.

These contractual components can be broadly described as:

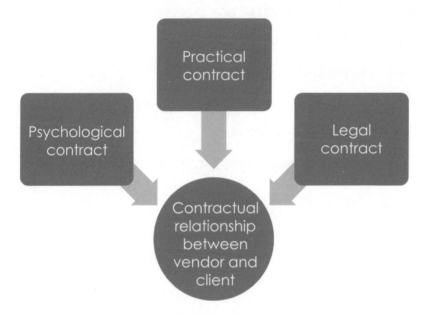

While many of these components interplay throughout the contracting process, they are largely reflected in the structure of the book as follows:

a. The **psychological contract:** Chapters 1, 2 and 3 set out the key players and how they should be working together, examining their expectations of each other and the relationships between them. They look at common problem areas and how to make these relationships more effective. These chapters also introduce the contract document itself and the role it plays in deal making. Chapter 4 looks at the importance of understanding the client's expectations, and chapter 12 comes back round the loop to see how we use what we've learned to negotiate and reach signature of a contract that works for both parties.

b. The **practical contract:** Chapter 4 takes the client's expectations and compares these with what you are actually delivering – probably the most important thing to get right in any contractual relationship. Chapters 5, 6 and 7 cover the remaining practical elements of your relationship, exploring the detailed nitty-gritty of what has to be done to make the deal work.

c. The **legal contract:** Chapters 8, 9, 10 and 11 cover the more technical legal elements which you might previously have considered to be the 'main contractual points' – but which you will quickly realise make up only part of the overall commercial relationship. These chapters go into some detail about how the 'legalese' works and what it means to you, helping to develop your legal vocabulary so that you can work more effectively with your legal counsel to make the best deals for your business.

When reading these chapters, please bear the following in mind:

(i) while most of the information in this book is universally applicable, the legal points in this section are considered primarily from the perspective of English law. Other legal systems may look at things differently.

(ii) this book describes the legal principles involved in commercial contracts, and how they apply in a general business context. Each particular situation has its own history and set of facts, which will impact on exactly how it would be treated in a court. This means that you should always take specific legal advice when considering your deal, and should not rely on this book as a substitute! This book will, however, give you the language and the tools to request advice more clearly, understand it better and use it more effectively.

Developing your contractual competence

As you'll see, there are a number of exercises throughout this book. These are designed to help develop your contractual competence by applying what you're learning to your current business environment.

How?

Using a combination of:

1. **Reflection** – asking you to think about how you do things at the moment and whether this meets the needs of your business, your clients and the deals you're making.

2. **Analysis** – examining how the principles you've learned could be applied to different case study situations.

3. **Action** – working with other members of the deal-making team to develop more effective ways of working and tools to help you deliver great deals.

While I know you're busy and unlikely to have the time to work through all of these in detail, you'll get much more out of this experience if you're able to complete them all. For maximum benefit, use the exercises as the basis for an internal development programme, involving all of the different functional areas in your review of how things work at your company and how they could work better.

You can download the e-workbook that accompanies this book by visiting www.dealmakersbook.com and following the links. The e-workbook contains extra material, templates and tools to help you complete the exercises and get the best possible value from them. Better still, it's free to download for purchasers of this book!

I wish you successful selling, straightforward and pain-free contracting and many happy and profitable commercial relationships.

Contents

4 What you're selling should match what the client's buying

5 Help your clients make the project a success

6 If you want your commission, help your company get paid!

7 The way you deal with problems shows your true mettle

11 A whistle-stop guide to the 'legalese' at the back!

12 Manage the contracting process to improve forecasting

Onwards and upwards

About the author

1

The Sales Prevention Squad is on your side!

This book will help you structure, negotiate and close better deals.

It will help you work more effectively with your internal resources, turning deal blockers into facilitators. It will help you build stronger, deeper relationships with your clients, establishing your reputation as a person of integrity and intelligence. It will enable you to become a more credible business person, supporting the growth of your career both in sales and in senior management.

How can you achieve all of these things?

Approach this book with an open mind. Be prepared to see things from the other side – this is one of your strengths as a sales person and it will stand you in good stead here too. When I say 'the other side', I should point out that there are many 'other sides' to consider as you work through the sales and contracting process. We'll be looking at each of them here and the contribution they can make to helping you close deals.

Invest time in thinking through the exercises. I know time is always at a premium and you're impatient to start seeing results. The exercises are designed to lead you along the path to success, building on your understanding of your business and the people within it, and developing your appreciation of the world your clients inhabit. Complete them all in order if you possibly can. Have fun. Remember it's only business! I look forward to seeing you on the other side.

Those who sell and those who don't

In any serious business there will be those who sell and those who see their role as keeping the sales people out of trouble.

If your business is very small or in the early stages of its development, it's possible that your directors see any sale as a good sale. If this is the case, you can skip the rest of this chapter for now, as the Sales Prevention Squad has not yet arrived. I say 'yet' because they always turn up eventually – usually as the business reaches a more respectable size and its shareholders begin to think about preparing it for sale, floatation on the stock market, or significant growth and investment.

For businesses that care about risk, that seek to ensure they'll be able to deliver what you sell and make money from it, the Sales Prevention Squad is an essential part of the team.

Barriers to selling

So who are they, and why do we call them the Sales Prevention Squad?

The Sales Prevention Squad is made up of all those members of your own company who could stand between you and your sale. They might be able to do this by delaying the supply of information you've asked for, withholding approvals, or asking you to achieve the impossible in terms of what you must get the client to agree to before your deal will be given the green light.

Legal and contracts

Top of the leader board in the Sales Prevention stakes are legal and contracts. You may have separate people (and departments) for these two roles or they may be performed by a single individual, outsourced to a law firm, or absorbed into the role of Commercial Director, Finance Director/CFO or even the Managing Director/CEO in smaller businesses.

However this function is delivered in your business, you'll almost certainly have felt the pain of a rosy-looking deal grinding to a halt when contracts are exchanged.

Perhaps you send your contract out with your proposals, and don't mention them again until the sale is agreed. The client is ready to give you a purchase order, but warns you that "If you insist on having us sign your contract terms, there will be a long delay while the contract goes through legal." If the client is a multinational, particularly if it has a US parent company, you might find your buyer desperate to go to any lengths to avoid sending terms to 'the lawyers at head office' – an outfit that seems to be the deal-killing equivalent of a black hole from which nothing ever returns.

It's just possible that your client quickly reviews your terms and returns them to you with a few mark-ups and comments on areas of concern. Then the ball is back in your court, and you must navigate your own legal and contracts process to deal with those issues and find a way to signature.

In the worst-case scenario, the lawyers of both sides engage in a long, drawn-out exercise of unarmed combat. Casualties of this contractual warfare can include goodwill between you and the client, mutual trust within your own organisation, hitting your quarter end target, and even the deal itself.

In the early days of my business, I was called in to help a vendor negotiate a deal with a large US corporation. I discovered that the negotiations had already been going on for over a year when I joined the team. They had stalled when the lawyer who was supposed to be supporting the vendor had so incensed the client's negotiation team that he had been asked to leave the meeting. The client refused to negotiate with him, or even have him in the building, because of his arrogance and confrontational attitude.

Fortunately, this sort of behaviour is rare these days. The 'race memory' of the sales profession is long, though, so that we're tempted to assume all lawyers are Sales Prevention specialists. And that means we're less inclined to involve them early in a sale and work with them as constructively as we might.

Many years ago, I moved from Bid Management into the role of Commercial Manager for the EMEA subsidiary of a large US software company. Our clients were telecoms operators and their contracts were often long and complex.

I'd got up very early to accompany the salesman on a 6.00 a.m. flight to Paris for a contract negotiation meeting with a prospect whose custom he was trying to win. Despite several calls and emails, the salesman had declined to participate in a planning session with me, so all I had to go on were the latest drafts of documents exchanged. During the flight and the taxi ride to the prospect's offices, I attempted to engage him in conversation about the opportunity, the prospect and the outstanding issues. All efforts were met with stony silence.

Despite an awkward start, it turned into an excellent meeting and we made huge strides towards agreement. In the cab on the way back to the airport, I asked the question: what had I done to upset the salesman so much? It transpired that he'd viewed my attendance at his meeting as the 'kiss of death' for his deal, expecting that going through the contract with the prospect would kill the relationship. Understandably, he wasn't a big fan of having someone he saw as the chief representative of the Sales Prevention Squad interacting with his prospect!

Fortunately, the success of that meeting turned things around between us, and I was pleasantly surprised to receive a call from him a few days later announcing that "we" were off to Bratislava to see another prospect in a week's time. I asked why he was so keen to involve me early, given his reluctance with the previous meeting.

The answer was one of the moments that inspired me to write this book. "It's simple," he said. "Now I know that having a good conversation with the prospect about the contractual stuff can help me close the deal faster. OK?"

Finance

Before you can agree the deal, you must obtain financial approval for the forecast cost, revenue and margin calculations. You may have to consider revenue recognition, and how the company's cash flow will be protected during the term of a long contract. The finance team can act as part of the Sales Prevention Squad, or can be remarkably rash when a deal is presented as being 'strategic'.

In my experience, describing a deal as 'strategic' translates into: "We're unlikely to make any money from it, but want to do it anyway." A high volume of 'strategic' deals is obviously bad for business, and the job of the finance team is to keep the company solvent, with enough working capital to grow and meet its objectives. So a certain amount of Sales Prevention from finance should be seen as a good thing rather than a bad one.

The detail of financial matters is beyond the scope of this book, but there are plenty of good books explaining 'finance for non-financial managers'. I strongly recommend that you familiarise yourself with how the numbers work. Such familiarity will help you build strong internal relationships and smooth the progress of your deal, particularly when taken together with the skills and knowledge you will gain from this book.

A good grasp of the numbers will also help you deal with the client's own financial Sales Prevention Squad, by enabling you to put together a winning business case for your product or service.

Another good case for getting both finance and legal involved early was demonstrated by a recent deal that one of my clients was trying to close. We'd been working on the contract for several weeks when their customer asked if we could change the contracting entity on their side to be a small but related company with few assets and an unimpressive balance sheet.

This changed the riskiness of the contract significantly and meant that we needed to take a fresh look at the invoicing and payment structure, to protect my client in case this small company had liquidity issues.

Fortunately, because we were working closely with the customer's FD, we were able to propose an alternative mechanism that protected my client's cash flow without imposing unpalatable guarantees on their customer. As a result, this change of structure only held up negotiations for a short while, and the deal was closed with very little delay.

The Delivery Team

Number three in the Sales Prevention Squad ratings for project-based sales is the delivery team. While the delivery team can be a sales person's greatest asset, providing pre-sales technical support, input to bids and proposals, product demonstrations and general credibility during the sales process, this isn't always the case.

Have you ever been frustrated when the delivery team tells you that something your client has asked for "Just can't be done" or (more commonly) "Can't be done that quickly, or for so little money?"

The temptation is to take the delivery team's time and cost estimates with a pinch of salt. You know how good they are at working miracles – they're unlikely to need all the contingency they've added. So there's no harm in pulling dates forward a little. Or agreeing to stick to the original delivery dates, even though there's no sign of getting an order for another few weeks at least, and you were supposed to have started work on Monday...

Generally, though, the delivery team is your favourite member of the Sales Prevention Squad as it's the one that contributes most visibly to helping you win the sale.

Product Marketing

If your business sells standard products of any description, you'll probably find that the product marketing folks occupy the position on the Squad filled by the delivery team in project-based businesses.

The marketing manager or category manager may have strong ideas about how to sell each of the products they are responsible for, and the sort of deals that are acceptable. If their focus is on volume and margin, you may find yourself at loggerheads when you try offering non-standard terms in order to win a new account.

When it comes to increasing the flexibility and commercial options available to you, making the product marketing team your friend is a good move.

EXERCISE 1:

Consider how you work with the legal, finance and delivery or product marketing teams in your organisation. Download the e-workbook from www.dealmakersbook.com for a template framework to guide your thinking.

The Squad are there to keep you out of trouble

It is not uncommon when complaining about the Sales Prevention Squad in general (and 'legal' in particular) to be told that "They're there to keep the company out of trouble." The implication of this is that if you fail to involve them appropriately, the company will end up in court, or insolvent, or worse.

While this might be true, I'm not a fan of broad-spectrum scare tactics; the fact that many businesses survive for decades without once experiencing litigation means that this sort of threat is seldom very effective.

So let's look at how your legal team can help you do better deals that contribute to the company's commercial health and keep you out of trouble at the same time.

Your contracts should reflect reality

The first thing you should expect from your legal support is that the contracts they draft reflect the reality of the deal you're doing. This means that they should accurately capture the mechanism you'll use for placing and accepting orders, for delivering goods and services, for accepting them, invoicing and getting paid, and for dealing with any problems that arise.

There's a strong tendency in many businesses for the contracts used to be disconnected from the way the business works. Sometimes this is because the contracts haven't been revised for years and still reflect an old and outdated mode of operation. Sometimes it's just because the contracts have been prepared on the basis of how a 'standard' business works, without reference to the people who sell, deliver and support products and services in this particular business.

EXERCISE 2:

Have you sat down and read your company's standard contracts? If not, now's a good time. Get comfortable (I find tea and biscuits helpful at this stage) and arm yourself with a red pen. Now review the terms (on paper), marking any sections that either (a) you don't completely understand, (b) don't reflect the way the company does business, (c) frequently cause problems with your clients during negotiations, or (d) have been the cause of disputes in the past. Download the e-workbook from www. dealmakersbook.com to help you complete this exercise.

Your contracts should help you get paid

From your clients' perspective, the job of the contract is to make sure that they receive what they expected from the deal. From yours, one of its main functions is to help you get paid when you've delivered what you committed to deliver.

If this doesn't happen, then you really might find yourself out of a job. As the old adage goes, a business can survive without profit, but without cash it's dead. So securing cash flow is essential.

Your legal support should help you assess your contracts critically to ensure that you will be paid as much as, and when, you're expecting.

And that's essential to make sure that you receive all the commission you're expecting – and that you never have to experience the indignity of commission recovery if a deal falls through!

Your contracts should keep your company safe

Although things rarely go to court, you still want to make sure that if you're using a contract, it'll protect your business if the sticky stuff hits the fan. And this is certainly where your legal support will feel most at home. Keeping you out of trouble, and preventing you from exposing your business to unnecessary risk, is what many lawyers believe their main role to be.

Unfortunately too much risk-sensitivity can lend to their 'Sales Prevention' credentials, resulting in advice that just about everything you might ever want to do will subject the business to too much risk.

As you work your way through this book, you'll discover the issues that genuinely create risk for the company and those that are red herrings – legally heavyweight, but less significant in terms of actual profitability and risk management. You'll also learn the language of contractual and commercial risk so that you can discuss these issues productively with your legal support as a valuable part of your sales process, rather than 'Sales Prevention'.

You may be perceived as a 'lion hunter'

In the same way that you look across the fence to those in the legal, finance, delivery and product marketing teams, they're looking back at you and drawing their own conclusions. It's worth taking a few minutes to see yourself as they see you, so that you can address any misconceptions that might be impacting the effectiveness of your relationships.

Depending on the size of your business, you may draw your technical sales support from a dedicated pre-sales team, from the delivery team or from the marketers. Whoever supports you, these product and service specialists are often the ones to convince the client to buy from you – it's their ability to answer questions, demonstrate product and interpret requirements that underpin your own selling skills.

Their view of sales, however, is sometimes less than flattering. You may have heard the old story about the salesman and the engineer who went lion hunting together, which illustrates their feelings well.

A salesman and an engineer embarked on a joint lion-hunting trip. After trekking across the savannah without sight of a lion on their first day, they put up their tent and ate a hearty meal in front of a crackling campfire. In the early hours of the following day, the engineer was roused from his sleep by an almighty racket – squeals and roars, loud shouting and the sound of undergrowth snapping.

Moments later, the zip on the front of the tent was undone and the salesman flung a live and very angry lion into the engineer's lap. As the zip closed behind him, the engineer heard the salesman shout back to the tent (as his feet pounded off into the bush). "This is a great process!" called the salesman. "I'll catch 'em and you skin 'em!"

If the phrase "You catch 'em and I'll skin 'em" has ever rung in your ears as you left the domain of the product team after sharing news of your most recent win, this book will help you improve your reputation among your colleagues.

The Squad needs you too

As your company's sales representative, you are the engine of the business. If you fail to bring in the orders, nobody else need bother to turn up. I am mentioning it here because although most sales people are well aware of their importance to the company's very existence, if you spend any time around lawyers you could be forgiven for thinking that sales people are the scourge of the earth.

Sounds a bit harsh? Sorry – and apologies to the forward-thinking lawyers reading this book.

But generally speaking, it's true that legal and commercial tend to have a pretty low opinion of sales as a function. Much as sales might be frustrated with the Sales Prevention Squad, the Squad themselves will have their own problems with you.

Recently I did some research using LinkedIn discussion groups to see what sales and legal teams thought of one another across multiple industries. The feedback from the lawyers was not uniformly bad; there were several who felt that their sales resources were well informed, mature and commercially aware. But there was an overwhelming view that sales people would 'sell their own grandmothers' to win a deal, and this meant they should be kept well away from contract negotiations as they were not to be trusted.

Whether you find such feedback insulting, amusing or merely frustrating, you will agree that it is not conducive to productive working relationships.

One of the aims of this book is to equip you with the tools, the vocabulary and the understanding to engage with your own Squad in a positive way. You will become one of those 'mature, commercially aware' sales people that legal and commercial like to work with and see as an asset to the contract negotiation process. And if you already fit in this category, you will develop your knowledge of the contracting process and the legal tools at your disposal to help you secure better deals – faster and more profitably.

Learn all you can from them

The great thing about technical and product experts is that, generally, they love to share their expertise. While making client presentations may not be their thing, talking with you over a coffee or a beer about the ins and outs of ERP solutions or fuel cell technology counts as 'down time'.

Make the most of this enthusiasm by asking sensible questions and learning all you can – not just about the product or service itself, but about how it's delivered. Ask what goes wrong and what makes a great client. Find out their idea of the 'perfect project' and discover what you can do to shape the opportunities you're working on to fit this ideal.

Don't oversell

By learning about the capabilities and shortcomings of your product or service you'll be in a great position to sell what your company is able to deliver. I'm sure I wasn't the first (or last) salesperson to present 'vapour ware' at a client meeting, knowing full well that it didn't *quite* exist yet in the form I was describing so confidently. The trick is to make sure that your product and service experts have bought into the vapour ware before you pitch it to a client.

If you're in a product business, overselling is more likely to occur in relation to your company's delivery capability than to the capability of the product, which will probably be well defined and understood. Nobody will thank you for selling 20,000 units for delivery next week if the next consignment of stock isn't due in until the week after – and is already spoken for by existing customers!

In particular, setting expectations that you and the team will be able to meet, *without* committing everyone's evenings and weekends for the next year, will make you much more popular. Bear in mind that however great they might be at pulling rabbits out of hats in a crisis, product and delivery teams rarely appreciate being asked to do it on a regular basis.

Preserve your safety net

If you treat them well, don't overcommit, ask intelligent questions and engage effectively with your product and service specialists, they will be your biggest asset. They will make you look good in front of your client, helping secure future sales. They will dig you out of holes when you need information for a proposal, or support with a presentation or demo at short notice, even though they are not your direct reports and they have 'day jobs'. In short, you need this team on your side. Take care of them and treat them with respect.

Life's too short for internal battles

We've established that you really do need the resources around you to be on your side, working with you to close successful deals. So why is it that many sales people feel their internal negotiations with these teams and their management are often tougher than their external ones with the client?

Some organisations have well-designed structures and processes that govern the way in which sales engages with marketing, delivery and legal teams and make sure it gets what it needs, when it needs it. Perhaps yours is one of them. If it is, review those processes to see how well they're working for you. If it's not, maybe now is the time to take a fresh look at how you use these resources in the sales process and see if there's a better way.

> **EXERCISE 3:**
>
> Using your notes from exercise 1, write your own 'vision statement' for your engagement with legal. Describe the world as you would like to see it, with a client-focused legal team that trusts you and makes a positive contribution to sales. Download the e-workbook from www.dealmakersbook.com to help you complete this exercise.

One of the things we'll do as we work through this book together is to explore different frameworks within which you can work towards successful sales that deliver great project outcomes and happy clients. Whether you have little or no legal, marketing or delivery support and need to become self-sufficient, or you have extensive resources at your disposal, either way we'll help you close great deals, faster.

Contracts can help you sell

This statement may come as something of a surprise. If the Sales Prevention Squad is largely concerned with getting 'watertight' contracts, how on earth can a contract help you sell?

Trust me. To show you how, I'm first going to tackle one of the big misconceptions of selling and contract negotiation.

Leaving it to the end of the sales process slows sales down

There is a comforting familiarity in the standard sales process. You start off with prospects, you explore need, build rapport, establish value, exploit your competitive advantage and slowly guide the prospect to the point of becoming a client.

Then, when the client has decided that you are the one – they want to buy your product or service and you've more or less reached agreement on the price – the subject of the contract arises. There are a number of different forms of contract which we'll explore in more detail in chapter 2. Depending on the one you use, you might find you can 'slip it past' the client so that they accept your terms without really noticing. If the deal is big, the value is high or the project is complex or high risk, though, chances are that you will have to put the contract squarely on the table and ask the client to sign on the dotted line.

It is at this stage that many sales that had been marked down in the forecast as being 'likely to close this month' start to slip. Why? Because things move beyond your control.

Throughout the sales process, you'll have been working hard to develop relationships within the client organisation, understand their decision-making process and selection criteria, establish timelines and work within them. Part of your job as a sales person is to *manage* the sales process, and hopefully you'll have been doing a reasonably good job of this.

But when the contract hits the table an entirely new cast of characters (or sometimes just a single, but troublesome, new character) becomes front of stage. Worse still, you have little or no relationship with these people. You don't know what's important to them, what their priorities are or how much weight their opinion carries within the organisation. You don't know what their workload is, or how high up their list your particular contract might be.

In short, it is at this point that the sales person frequently loses control of the sales process.

What does that mean for you? It means that at each pipeline review your ability to say with any certainty whether this deal will close this week, this month, this quarter or even this year becomes questionable. It means that the resources that had been 'pencilled in' to deliver your project start to get poached for other projects. It means that your sale, your commission and your credibility start drifting.

One of our clients, an email marketing solutions provider, was pleased to come to the end of its sales process, and passed its contract across to the new customer for their review. The contract had not been built into the sales process, and no mention had been made of how it would be reviewed, negotiated and agreed. As a consequence, the contract negotiation has now been going on for over a year and although there is little of significance outstanding, both parties seem to have lost the will to see it through. Worse, delivery of the project started some months ago so that the contract process has been sidelined.

While the delivery relationship goes well that's not too much of a worry, but if a dispute arises there will be problems ascertaining what should happen next and which terms apply. This could cost the client dearly.

Because the negotiation has been going on so long, the sales person who was involved in the original discussions has moved on. This opens the company up to claims that the sales person made commitments that are not reflected in the documents, and increases the risk of not having a signed contract in place.

Use the contract to build your relationship towards the sale

There is another way to use the contract that doesn't rely on leaving it all to the end and trusting to luck that the other side will sign it quickly.

In our approach, the contract forms one of your initial sales documents. How does that work?

Think of the contract as the documentation for the deal itself. This means that as you structure your deal you're putting together the building blocks for the contract – and the deal and the contract should work in harmony. By using the contract as your 'crib sheet', you can get it out of the cupboard and contributing to your sale early on.

If your contract is written properly, it should describe clearly:

- What you're selling

- How the client buys it

- How you deliver it

- What you need from the client in order to deliver it properly

- When the client should pay you

- Which elements of risk you believe your company should take and which should be the responsibility of the client

- What you'll do if things go wrong

If your contract doesn't do all of these things, it's time to have a conversation with whoever's in charge! But if it does, it's an invaluable guide to putting a strong, mutually beneficial deal together.

So a good contract will explain to your client how you work and how they should engage with you. It maps out the sales and delivery journey and demonstrates to your client that you've done this before – you know what you're doing and what sort of issues arise in projects of this kind. They're in safe hands. And it provides the prompt for talking through each of these issues with your client in the course of the sale.

Your contract should make it clear to the client what's important to you as a business and where your boundaries sit. By putting this on the table early, you have plenty of opportunities to explore any mismatch between your and their priorities and expectations and to work to find solutions (more on this later).

What if it's too early to 'talk contract'?

Depending on your own business culture and that of your client, it might prove rather a challenge to start waving the contract around before you have an agreed sale. The client may be very reluctant to engage their own legal resources until (a) they're certain they want to buy from you and (b) all of the main deal points are hammered out.

So does that mean that the contract stays in its box until the deal is done?

Not necessarily. It does mean that we need to take a slightly more abstract view of what we mean when we talk about the 'contract', though. In the next chapter we'll be looking at the contract as the 'User Guide for the Commercial Relationship' and you'll have the opportunity to create your own User Guide to help you through the sales process. Your User Guide will pick out all the key commercial points of your deal (broadly along the lines of the list above).

This means that, even if you're not comfortable wheeling out the contract itself, you can still use the contracting principles described here to help you work through the issues that are important to your commercial relationship, before it's time to sign on the dotted line. And when you do finally put your contract on the table it should be an easy ride, as you'll have already discussed and addressed the important areas that really matter to you and your client.

EXERCISE 4:

Think about a typical client for your business. Describe your sales and contracting process from their perspective. What is specific about your product or service, or the way you deliver, that would be helpful to share with your client? Download the e-workbook from www.dealmakersbook.com to help you complete this exercise.

Importantly, engaging early with your key contractual points also helps to build integrity. There's nothing guaranteed to shatter your carefully nurtured client relationship faster than suddenly telling the client that the intellectual property they thought they were buying from you will only be licensed. Or that you absolutely can't give them more than a 30-day warranty when they were expecting three years. By being open, and encouraging discussion of contractual issues throughout the sales process, you can deal with issues in a positive way exactly as you would if they were technical or specification issues, or other buying signals.

I have a client that came to me seeking dispute resolution assistance as it frequently had contract disputes with its customers. Rather than just tackling the disputes as they arose, I looked at the way in which the company sold and delivered its products and services. It became clear that the sales people were not using the contract to help them sell, but were passing it across the table at the last possible minute for the customer to sign.

Not surprisingly, the customer didn't pay much attention to it and then, when things went wrong and they learned that certain tasks they had assumed would be performed by their supplier were actually to be done by themselves, they felt let down. Even though this was clearly set out in the contract, because the customer's obligations hadn't been drawn to their attention, and had been rushed past them, the customer lost trust in their supplier.

My team worked with the supplier to develop tools that helped its sales people explain to new customers how the contract works, and what each party's responsibilities are. They now have very few disputes, and those that arise are generally with old customers who pre-date this new sales process.

Risk costs money

The other challenge that you're presented with, if contractual issues don't hit the agenda until the price and deliverables have already been agreed, is that you've effectively removed a key 'leg' of your negotiation strategy. You're sending your contract negotiators into battle with one arm tied behind their backs.

Why? Because risk costs money.

If that sounds like a strange thing to say, think about your home insurance policy. You pay money to the insurance company each year so that they'll accept the risk of your house burning down, being struck by lightning or suffering a flash flood. Let's say that to rebuild your house in the event of a disaster, and refit it with furniture and belongings, would cost about £200,000. That's quite a big risk to carry and you probably don't have that sort of money sitting around 'just in case'. At the same time, chances are your house won't burn down, be struck by lightning or suffer a flash flood. The probability of any one of these things happening is quite small. Your insurance premiums are set so as to balance the potential cost of a disaster against the likelihood of it occurring, with a reasonable margin on the side of the insurance company.

If you pay £600 a year for your house and contents insurance, that's the cost your insurers have allocated to the risk that your house might burn down or suffer equivalent damage.

Transposing this into your business, many of the provisions of your contract will be there so as to make it clear which party bears which risk – whether that's risk of your products failing, or risk of the client using more copies of your software than they've licensed. Swapping a risk from one party to the other is equivalent to moving money in the opposite direction.

You can use risk as a positive aid to selling. If you understand the value your client attaches to a particular risk, you might decide that it's something your company is prepared to accept as part of this deal. Taking the insurance example, you could say that you will accept liability for rebuilding the client's house if it is damaged by fire or flood.

If you've costed that risk at £600 per year (the amount it costs you to insure against it), but the client values it at £200,000 (the cost of rebuilding), you can see that you have an opportunity to obtain other concessions, including on the price, in exchange for taking on this risk for the client.

Understanding the trade-offs between risk and cash is a key part of the skill of the effective contract negotiator, and it is one that you will develop as you work through the material and exercises in this book. But if cash (in the form of the price) is already fixed before any discussion of risk has occurred, you reduce the options open to you in negotiations and also reduce your odds of achieving a deal that works well for your company.

Engaging legal early makes 'closing' easier

You might think that contractual issues are inevitably 'bad news' and that you don't want to put anything in front of the client in the early days that might put them off buying from you. I can understand this. Until the client is reasonably convinced that yours is the product or service they'd like to have in their business, you can't expect them to be enthusiastic about investing in the legal process.

If legal resources are at a premium in their business, they may be unwilling to engage them until all of the major deal points are agreed and they are close to being ready to sign. So how can you engage the client's contractual engine and take control of this part of the sales process?

Even if detailed contract negotiation is not on the agenda during your sales process, by using your User Guide to flag up issues that are relevant and significant as you discuss the different areas of the deal, you'll encourage your client to start warming up their own legal resources, alerting them to the possibility of a future deal and enabling them to consider issues that might cause a challenge if not raised until the last minute.

For example, a discussion about how you will be able to install your products at the client's offshore oil platform would enable you to mention your warranty provisions. You could explain how long a warranty you'll give for these products and whether, under the warranty, it's your responsibility to come to site and fix problems/replace units, or the client's responsibility to ship faulty units back to you for repair. If your standard warranty is 'return to base', but the client wants 'repair on site', you can use this as an opportunity to up-sell a more comprehensive servicing and spares package, perhaps including some training for client staff in how to replace faulty components.

If you uncover a showstopper during these discussions, it doesn't have to be tackled then and there before proceeding. If you and the client are both comfortable that there is a good fit between what you're offering and what they want, you can agree to take discussion of the showstopper offline. This gives each party the opportunity to explore alternative ways around the issue, including different commercial models, and find a way forward in the spirit of team working.

Sometimes an apparently major issue can be resolved by restructuring the commercial elements of the deal to shift risk from one party to the other in a way that both are comfortable with. If you encounter this at the last minute, however, you'll find that both parties have already obtained buy-in to the current commercial structure within their organisations, and change is a psychological as well as a practical problem for them. By finding these things early, you give yourself the best possible chance of reaching an amicable and mutually beneficial resolution.

Chapter 1: Quick Summary

- The Sales Prevention Squad appears when businesses need to manage risk in new deals

- Legal, product marketing, delivery and finance teams are all there to help you close deliverable, profitable business

- Get to know them and when to use them

- The contract has some important tasks – to reflect the reality of how you work, to help you get paid and to keep the company safe

- Your company's product and service experts are a valuable resource, so treat them well

- Much as you might have negative preconceptions about the Squad, they are likely to have low expectations of you

- Understanding the business implication of contract terms will increase your credibility with the Squad

- If the business is to thrive, you need to work together

- Keeping the contract to the end of the sales process will slow down your closing

- Sharing it at an early stage helps you build strong client relationships

- Because risk costs money, agreeing the price and deliverables before you've agreed the contract terms limits your negotiating options

2

The contract provides your 'User Guide' for the relationship

The very word 'contract' is fraught with negative connotations. Much like 'legal', it can throw otherwise sensible people into paroxysms of anxiety. The threat that things might 'get legal' or that 'we might have to revert to the contract' is guaranteed to raise hackles and create tension in any commercial relationship. So it's not altogether surprising that contracts aren't viewed in the warmest of lights by those whose objective is to build, develop and retain cordial and productive commercial relationships between organisations.

Contracts are just tools – how you use them is up to you!

Despite this bad press, contracts are, when all is said and done, just tools. The question is, how will you use this particular tool and will you be its master or vice-versa?

It might help to think of your contract like a particularly fast, high-spec motorbike with a gloriously throaty exhaust, a thumpingly powerful engine and nice fat grippy tyres.

If you know how to ride a motorbike, and are confident that you can throw it around twisty lanes safely, it can help you get from A to B faster and in much better spirits than your car. If, however, you have never ridden a motorbike before, or your experience is limited to a rented moped on holiday, climbing aboard this machine and dropping the clutch is likely to land you in a hedge, a wall or some similarly uncomfortable location at great speed. It could even prove fatal.

Similarly, if you're not comfortable with contract language, or the contract you have to work with has (metaphorically speaking) a rattling exhaust, slippery tyres and an underpowered engine, attempting to use the contract to drive your commercial relationship is likely to get you into trouble. So, dodgy metaphors aside, I hope you can see that if you want to be able to make good use of your contract, a certain amount of knowledge and skill is useful, and that once you have those, the scope of benefits available to you increases enormously.

The contract as door stopper

If you're not really sure what to do with your contracts, you can always put them in a cupboard and forget about them. Many companies take this approach. They spend a considerable amount of time and money negotiating their contract and then, once it's signed, they never look at it again.

Imagine doing this with the motorbike described above. You've spent ages specifying exactly what you want, saving up, arranging the insurance – and then you tuck it up in the garage, providing a home for spiders.

Your contract is capable of much more interesting and useful things than just holding the door open or insulating the attic.

The contract as insurance policy

Many business people I speak with tell me that their approach to the contract is to "Sign it and stick it in a drawer – if you ever have to take it out again, you know things have gone badly wrong."

They view the contract as an insurance policy that should be stored in a glass case with a little metal hammer attached and labelled 'in case of emergency, break glass'. They believe that contracts should not be bandied around in healthy commercial relationships and that the appearance of the contract is a signal that the relationship is on the ropes and you should call in the lawyers and prepare for a fight.

These people will have paid little attention to the main body of the contract, but will have focused mainly on the limits and exclusions of liability (see chapter 8 to find out what these are about). Rather than concerning themselves with making sure the deal doesn't go wrong, they will want to cover the company's back in the event that it does.

Another way of describing the 'contract as insurance policy' approach is as a 'box-ticking exercise'. You may have encountered (or even espoused) this view in the past, where those running the business are aware that they 'should' have some terms and conditions in place because it's something that 'proper' businesses do. But beyond that, their expectations are low and they view contracts as all being much the same with few distinguishing features. As a result, they may source their terms and conditions from the internet, from their competitors, or from a previous employer, (sometimes) remembering to change the name at the top of the document to reflect their company branding.

The problem comes when something does go wrong, and they pull the contract out of the drawer with the intention of relying on their 'insurance'. On closer inspection, they realise that the terms and conditions they've used don't reflect the way they do business. As a result, the remedies in those terms are not available to the company, since it hasn't served the correct notices on the other party, or complied with other obligations set out in its own terms.

In my many years advising businesses on contract disputes, I have often seen examples of companies in dispute who start out thinking they are entirely in the right, and should be entitled to seek a contractual remedy from the other party. After looking through their documentation, it becomes clear that this isn't the case. They could have used the contract to their advantage if it had been drafted to fit the way they did business, or if they'd actually followed and complied with its terms themselves. Since they had, instead, taken the 'insurance policy' approach and just stashed the contract in a drawer without reading or acting on it, they had effectively forfeited the right to rely on its terms.

The contract as weapon

The other use to which contracts can be put, and the one that is often at the forefront of a new client's mind (particularly if you're selling complex solutions, outsourcing or some similarly risky and high-value service or product set) is as a weapon.

If this is your intended use, then thicker contracts are better – they deliver a more satisfying 'thwack' when rolled up and used to beat your opponent around the head. Joking aside, the thicker the contract, the more opportunities there are for spelling out the dreadful and expensive consequences of different kinds of failure.

In its use as a weapon, the contract offers many targets. Liquidated damages (see chapter 8), also euphemistically known as 'service credits', can be used to punish poor performance against Key Performance Indicators (KPIs). The KPIs might include speed of response to questions, resolution of faulty products or problems or delivery of products. They could relate to the number of errors in performance of certain tasks or the delivery of certain services.

The thing that all these have in common, though, is that they are focused on punishing failure rather than rewarding success. If you're a parent, own a dog, or manage people (sorry for grouping these together, but the same principles apply), you will be aware that positive reinforcement of good behaviour is a more effective motivator than punishment of bad behaviour, and is likely to deliver more positive outcomes overall.

As you may have noticed, I am not a big fan of the 'contract as weapon' approach, and believe contracts can contribute much more profitably to our commercial relationships if used in a more proactive manner.

EXERCISE 5:

How are contracts used in your business? Think about when they are introduced into your discussions with prospects and clients, who initiates the contract discussion, and whether you usually do business on your terms or the client's terms. What would you consider the main purpose of the contract to be? Download the e-workbook from www.dealmakersbook.com to help you complete this exercise.

Relationships need rules

The concept of the contract providing everything you need for the User Guide for the commercial relationship is core to this book and to our approach to contracting. The relationships your business has with its clients, suppliers, partners, resellers, distributors, sales agents – and even with its staff, like you – are all commercial ones in that they involve people doing work or delivering products for money.

You may feel that commercial relationships don't need a User Guide. In your experience, it may have been the case that all parties to each agreement your business entered into were absolutely clear and of one mind with regard to what they were supposed to do, and not to do. You may have found that any disagreements were quickly resolved by frank and honest discussion between sensible and mature adults.

If that's the case, I'm really pleased to hear it – but you have been lucky.

In the early days of my business, I encountered a man at his wits' end – we'll refer to him as Steve. Some years before, Steve had been asked by his best friend (who was also best man at his wedding) to leave his secure job in a logistics company and start up on his own. The friend (let's call him Mike) had a business syndicating tenders for the airline industry. Mike would receive, through his extensive network of contacts, invitations to tender for the supply of a variety of products and services to airlines. He would source suppliers and would act as the prime contractor, pulling together offerings from other businesses and wrapping them up in a proposal for the airline – and, obviously, would make a good margin on the deal if it went ahead.

Mike was having difficulty sourcing a supplier for airline 'snack packs' – the little bags of pretzels, nuts and other nibbles that you receive with your drink on a flight. With his encouragement, Steve quit his job and started a business preparing airline snack packs. Mike drove opportunities his way and the company did well, hiring staff and leasing a warehouse and packing facility to support the growing turnover.

When Steve was two years into his ten-year lease, Mike's wife was made redundant from her high-powered job. At a loose end, it occurred to her that she, too, could run a business making airline snack packs. So she did. Almost overnight, Steve's orders dried up. He had no direct contacts with the airlines, as all of his deals were made through Mike's company. He had no sales team, no client relationships – in short, no pipeline and no obvious means of securing one.

Despite the close personal relationship between Steve and Mike, when large amounts of money were involved Steve found his friend was no longer willing to talk to him. The loss of the friendship was a huge blow – but not as big as the loss of his business and livelihood, having to make his staff redundant and figure out how to escape from the remaining eight years of his lease.

Implied rules – the danger of the psychological contract

In the story above, Steve had fallen foul of a concept known as the 'psychological contract'. More widely researched in the context of employment contracts, where it is used to describe the unwritten expectations that employers and employees have of their relationship, it applies equally to business-to-business commercial contracts.

Steve's expectation was that his best friend could be relied upon to act in a fair and reasonable way. If asked, Steve would have said that there was no way Mike would have deliberately taken action to cause Steve's business to fail. The psychological contract that

Steve thought he had entered into stated that Steve and Mike were 'partners', acting in each other's best interests. Unfortunately, Mike believed their contract was quite different; his view was that each of them should be looking out for their own interests, and that if an opportunity arose to profit at Steve's expense, simple friendship should not get in the way of business.

All too often, we enter into a psychological contract – either in the absence of a written contract or in addition to it. We expect certain behaviours of those we do business with which are not written down in any document. Similarly, we might hold ourselves accountable to standards higher than those in any contract or brochure. Generally this is a good thing – but if the parties have differing understandings of what that contract states, missed expectations and conflict can result.

By setting the rules of the relationship down on paper, both parties have the opportunity to scrutinise them and see if they agree. If not, it's possible to negotiate and reach a set of rules that both are comfortable with. Most importantly, at the end of this process both parties share a common understanding of what those rules are, and what is expected of them.

Express rules – encouraging good behaviour

When training animals, good trainers use 'shaping' techniques to reward and encourage good behaviour. These consist of rewarding the animal each time it does something in the desired direction. Not surprisingly, this technique is slow and painstaking. Fortunately, with humans we're able to move things a little faster than this by explaining what sort of behaviour we want.

If we use our contract to describe the behaviour each party expects of the other, we increase the chances of that behaviour occurring. So if we write that all change requests have to be signed by a project manager before submission, we're more likely to see signed change requests than we are if this doesn't find its way into the agreement.

The other benefit of having written rules for our commercial relationship is that they enable newcomers to understand quickly what they should do, and how they should behave.

Particularly when your contract is intended to last for a long time, the original team on both your side and the client side is likely to change. Relying on what the individuals who signed the contract in the first place understood to be their obligations becomes less and less helpful as people leave and join, and the memory of what was agreed becomes more fragmented.

Creating your User Guide: the three main functional areas

A contract doesn't have to be long and complicated to be effective. The key thing is to make sure that it covers the three main functional areas. In my company, Devant, we refer to these as the Three Triangles, and they form a good basis for both the contract itself and for your User Guide:

Devant's 'Three Triangles™'

Who does what, when?

This is the section where you document the 'doings' of your deal – the nuts and bolts of what will be done, by whom and when. It's the area where most disputes occur, so is essential to get right. In your high-level User Guide, this section will contain a summary of what you're selling and how it's delivered, and what (other than money) you need from the client in order to deliver it. You'd expect to include ownership of intellectual property in here too, if it's an issue that's important to your deal.

We'll cover the topics of what you're delivering, and what you should expect from the client, in chapters 4 and 5. In chapter 10 we'll take a detailed look at intellectual property and how it affects the deals you do.

When does payment occur?

This section is of great interest both to you as a sales person and to your company. But astonishingly, making sure you will get paid is not generally the highest focus for your lawyers.

While many different areas will have an impact on your success in getting paid, chapter 6 will explore the main culprits that you need to focus on in order to make sure your commission arrives in the quantities and at the times you expect it to.

From the perspective of creating your User Guide, you should focus simply on when payments will be made and what events each payment will be linked to.

What happens if things go wrong?

It may not come as a surprise to you that this triangle is generally the focus of most attention from lawyers during contract review and negotiation. There's a survey conducted every year by the International Association of Commercial and Contract Management (IACCM) which asks commercial managers which contract terms they spend most of their time negotiating.

The top two most negotiated terms, for many years now, have both been in this triangle. Concentrating on how to limit the risk to the business if everything goes pear-shaped is a good idea, as it may help to ensure that the company survives a contractual disaster.

However, if you agree that making sure everything doesn't go pear-shaped in the first place is a better idea, you can see that this intense focus on what happens if things go wrong could be counterproductive, and not the best use of time during negotiations.

So what goes into your User Guide under this heading? First, are there any areas that have caused you a lot of problems in the past? If those things happened again, what could you do to avert disaster, or to minimise their impact? This is the sort of thing we'd expect to cover in our high-level User Guide. We'll look at all the heavy-duty legal drafting that will be used to address these topics in the contract itself in chapters 7 and 8, but you should be able to pick out the key issues and summarise them in bullet-point form to help you through your sales discussions.

To show you how easy it is to use the Three Triangles to describe what matters in your commercial relationships, here's an illustration on a domestic scale.

When my children were six and nine years old, they decided they wanted regular pocket money rather than occasional hand-outs so that they could plan their spending and saving. We agreed that they would earn this pocket money by doing simple chores around the house, and we talked about the rules for how the pocket money would be calculated.

At the end of the discussion, Evie (then six) pointed out that we needed to have a contract so that we would all know what to do. So we did. Here's a scan of that original pocket money contract – it's still referred to from time to time when there's a disagreement about the rules. Over the years we have increased the number and difficulty of jobs, and the corresponding value of the contract, but the original deal still works!

Albert and Evie's Pocket Money Contract

This agreement is made on the 18th February 2007 between Albert, Evie, Mum and Dad.

1 Who does what, when?
   a. Albert shall:
       i.   Get drinks for everyone at meal times.
       ii. Clear the table and put the dishes in the dishwasher at meal times.
       iii. Put his dirty clothes in the correct washing basket each evening.
       iv   Tidy his bedroom and put toys away every day.
       v   Make his bed every day, and change it when needed.
   b. Evie shall:
       i.   Lay the table at meal times.
       ii. Put her dirty clothes in the correct washing basket each evening.
       iii. Tidy her bedroom and put toys away every day
       iv   Make her bed every day, and change it when needed.

2. When do they get paid, and how much?
   a. Each child shall receive pocket money equal to 50 pence per job completed for the whole week (i.e. for seven days in a row).
   b. Pocket money shall be paid on Sundays.
   c. If a child is particularly good or kind, then a parent may add ten pence to that child's pocket money for the week.
   d. If a child misses a job, then ten pence shall be deducted from that child's pocket money for the week.
   e. If a child is rude or unkind, then ten pence shall be deducted from that child's pocket money for the week.

3. What happens if things go wrong?
   a. If the dishwasher is full, Albert shall either put the dishes in the sink or stack them neatly and safely on the side.
   b. The children only need to perform their mealtime duties for meals that they eat at home. If a meal is eaten at a friend's house, the child should offer to do their mealtime duty there.
   c. If there is a meal that doesn't need cutlery, then Evie shall be responsible for setting out napkins and helping to serve.
   d. Toys that are not put away at the end of the day shall be confiscated for jumble or the bin.

Albert, Evie, Mum and Dad confirm their agreement to the terms set out above with their signatures below:

Albert: _____   Dad: _____

Evie: _____   Mum: _____

EXERCISE 6:

Take the copy of your company's standard terms that you reviewed for exercise 2. Write down the section headings (if there are any) in the order in which they occur in the document. Do they tell a story? Are they in the order that you'd expect to find them, in terms of the way things happen in your deal? Download the e-workbook from www.dealmakersbook.com to help you complete this exercise.

Your contract should be easy to understand!

Hopefully by now you can see the value of having a written contract that both parties agree applies to your deal and which describes the rules by which your commercial relationship operates.

If you've done a good job of creating a nice, practical, commercially-focused User Guide to help you through the sale, the last thing you want to follow it with is a convoluted, over-complicated and over-confrontational contract document. If we do, the contract itself will fail completely in its role as the User Guide for the ongoing commercial relationship.

Whilst we know that our bullet-point level summary has to be superseded by a full contract at some point, we want this transition to be as painless as possible. So the contract itself should be easy to read and easy to follow, and it should be easy to find the things that are of interest to you and the client at any particular time during the deal's lifecycle.

One of the challenges with contracts is that they are generally written by lawyers, for lawyers. The logic goes that it doesn't matter if contracts use obscure legal language that only lawyers can understand, because only lawyers will ever want to read them.

Whilst that might be true (there aren't many non-lawyers who *like* reading contracts!), if the contract is to deliver on its promise of helping you have more profitable and successful deals, it needs to be capable of being read and used by the whole team.

Clarity of intent, thought and expression

Clarity of intent means that both you and the other party are clear about exactly **what** this contract is supposed to achieve. It means that you've agreed the objectives for the contract and have a common view.

Clarity of thought means that you've both thought through **how** the contract will achieve that intent. In other words, you've considered the nitty-gritty of what the commercial structure will be, where cash will flow and when, who will own what, do what and pay what.

Responsibility for these two steps rests with you, the sales person, sometimes with support from the marketing or category manager, the delivery team and/or finance. You might also have input from legal as you try to ensure that the structure and process you've arrived at is achievable legally.

To build your credibility with legal, it is essential that you have thought through these two elements in some detail, and ideally have discussed them with the other party, before approaching legal to ask them to draft an agreement for you. There are few things more frustrating for a lawyer than to be told "I need an XYZ agreement" with no information about how it is to work. We'll be covering the key components of your contract in detail in this book, to equip you to conduct this conversation effectively first time.

Once you've conveyed the intent and the 'how', it's then over to the lawyers to deliver the clarity of expression. This relates to the importance of writing the agreement in a clear and unambiguous way, so that anyone can read it and understand exactly what is meant.

Make it easy to navigate

There is much that your lawyers can do in terms of layout and formatting to make your contract easy to find your way around. Use of numbered sections with headings that group related topics together is one. While that might sound obvious to you in the context of sales documents, there is an astonishing amount of superstition (for want of a better word) around what can and can't be done when writing contracts.

Some drafters worry that moving things around within their template or legal precedent document will 'break' the contract and make it legally ineffective. While it is obviously important that the different provisions of the contract work properly together, and that cross-references are correct, there is no law to say that you can't lay out and structure your contract in a user-friendly, story-telling flow. So encourage your lawyers to make your contracts user-friendly and logical, even if that means breaking away from their tried and tested precedent documents.

How to make a legally binding contract

You may have heard the saying 'a verbal contract is not worth the paper it's written on'! While most verbal contracts are just as legally binding as written ones (with contracts relating to land being one notable exception), their terms are rather more difficult to prove. This (in addition to the reasons set out above) means that it is generally advisable that contracts are made in writing. However, it is important to note that being in writing is not an essential component of a legally enforceable contract, so don't rely on your verbal commitments being non-binding.

Offer, acceptance and consideration

The three main components of a binding contract are called offer, acceptance and consideration. The **offer** is an offer that is capable of being accepted without any need to specify additional terms. So for example, if I said, "You can buy my car if you like", that is not an offer in the legal sense; you would have to suggest an amount of money which we would need to agree before the deal was done.

Alternatively, if I'd said, "You can buy my car for £5,000, payable today by cheque or in cash", I would have made you an offer capable of being accepted. You would be able to say, "Yes, ok" (your **acceptance** of my offer), and hand over the £5,000 (which is the **consideration**, or payment for the car). We would then have a binding contract, and I would be obliged to give you my car in exchange for the £5,000.

Let's say you'd taken a look at my car and decided that it wasn't worth £5,000 – so your response to my offer was to say, "I'll have the car, but I'll only give you £4,000 for it." Have you accepted my offer? No.

That's right, you've actually made a **counter-offer**. At this stage, I could take my car off the market without being in breach of contract. By making a counter-offer, you are deemed to have rejected my original offer, which means that I am able to take it off the table and am no longer obliged to stand by it.

A counter-offer doesn't need to relate only to the price. Your counter-offer could have been, "Ok, I'll pay you £5,000 but I only have £2,000 at the moment. I'll pay you the £2,000 now and the other £3,000 at the end of the month when I get paid." Because you've varied the payment terms (I proposed £5,000, payable today) you have effectively rejected my offer.

Suppose you have a motorbike that you are looking to sell so that you can buy a car. Knowing this, I might make you a different offer: "You can have my car in exchange for your motorbike plus £1,000 in cash." In this example, the consideration for the car is made up of some money (£1,000) plus a motorbike. So consideration does not have to be cash only – it could be other goods, commitments, promises or services. The main criteria are that it should be something of value to the seller, and something that results in a level of detriment to the buyer.

Proposals and POs – the Battle of the Forms!

In many businesses, signed contracts are not the norm. Instead, the business will make a proposal or prepare a quotation setting out its offer. The proposal or quote may make reference to the company's standard terms and conditions, which may be attached or available to view on the company website or on request. The company's intention is that the proposal and the terms and conditions together make up the contract between them and their client.

This is fine until the client responds to the proposal with a Purchase Order (PO). The company happily accepts the PO as confirmation of the client's acceptance of the proposal and terms, and starts delivering.

What's wrong with that?

Most company purchase orders will state somewhere (often in small print at the bottom) something along the lines of: 'This purchase order is placed subject to Company's terms and conditions of purchase, available on reverse/ at www.CompanyWebsite.com /on request'.

So their PO is not an **acceptance** of your offer, it is actually a **counter-offer**, as it is made subject to different terms and conditions from the ones in your offer. If you then go ahead and start delivering, you are deemed to have accepted their counter-offer. So your company will then be bound by the client's terms and conditions, not your own – and unless you read the small print and follow the links, chances are you won't even know what those terms and conditions are!

This situation is referred to by lawyers as 'The Battle of the Forms'. Put briefly, it can be described as: 'He who lobs last, wins', as the last set of terms to be 'thrown over the wall' before the contract is made will be the ones that govern the deal.

So when is the contract actually made in a situation like this?

The contract is created when one party acts in such a way as to indicate that they have accepted the offer made by the other party. In the example above, this would occur when you started delivering against the client's PO. And if their PO terms and conditions were the last ones 'over the wall', they will be the terms on which the contract has been made, whether you were aware of the fact or not.

One way that companies get around this problem is to use Order Acknowledgements to confirm receipt of a PO, and to re-state that their own terms and conditions will apply to the deal. While this can help, unless you require some further form of acknowledgement from the client that they've received your Order Acknowledgement before you start to deliver, you'll struggle to prove that they 'accepted' your counter-counter-offer.

Confused? This can be an absolute minefield, and the safest way to be sure you know which terms apply to your contract is either to have a signed contract or to ask your client to amend their PO so as to refer to your terms and conditions rather than their own.

MoUs, LoIs and HoAs

You may well have encountered an MoU (Memorandum of Understanding), LoI (Letter of Intent), or an HoA (Heads of Agreement).

One thing these three sorts of agreements have in common is that they generally lack the **consideration** that's required to make them into a binding contract. In other words, the parties are not offering each other something of real value, that 'costs' them something to give. They are usually setting out general expectations of what the parties think is likely to happen, rather than firm commitments.

While this challenge can be got around with some careful drafting, you should be aware that many of these sorts of agreements will not be legally binding and you may not be able to rely upon them. If it's important that your company should be able to rely on one of these (for example, if you're planning to invest in equipment or development work in anticipation of receiving an order), you should take advice from your legal folk to ensure it will work as you expect.

Chapter 2: Quick Summary

- Contracts are tools that can be used as an insurance policy, a weapon or as the basis for the User Guide for your commercial relationship

- Good client relationships flourish in a structured environment, and a User Guide setting out the key points of the contract can help projects proceed well

- If you don't set out explicit rules for your commercial relationship, implied ones will govern behaviour – even though you don't know what they are

- Good contracts are clear and well written so that non-lawyers can understand them

- If your sales process doesn't lend itself to early introduction of the contract itself, you can create a brief User Guide summarising the key commercial issues

- There are three main functional areas of the contract: who does what, when? When does payment occur? And what happens if things go wrong?

- Contracts don't have to be complicated to work

- While verbal contracts can be legally binding, written ones are better because you can review and amend them, and it's easier to prove their terms

- To make a binding contract, you need to have offer, acceptance and consideration

- Relying on purchase orders to create your contract can create problems with the 'battle of the forms', where your terms conflict with those on the PO

- MoUs, LoIs and HoAs are not usually legally binding

3

The small print matters – so keep your lawyers on side

If everyone wrote clear, easy to understand commercial agreements, you might (with a bit of training and reference to books like this one) be able to do much more of the negotiation without reference to lawyers.

Until then, you will almost certainly need them at some stage in the process. And keeping the lawyers on side is essential if you want to close deals faster and maintain good relationships with your client.

'Small print' and 'legalese' are not helpful but they're still common

Contracts have an unfortunate but frequently well-deserved reputation for being impenetrable and the reverse of 'user-friendly'. While some companies have made huge strides in the readability of their consumer-facing terms and conditions, business-to-business contracts seem to be stuck in the dark ages.

Why lawyers like 'legalese'

'Legalese' is a word we use to describe the more convoluted and archaic terms you will encounter in legal documents.

Why do phrases like 'notwithstanding the foregoing' and 'for the avoidance of doubt', together with words like 'indemnify' and 'liquidated damages' appear in so many contracts?

Although these words and phrases might seem unwieldy, for lawyers they provide a useful shorthand that they know is likely to be understood by other lawyers. Trying to convey the same point accurately and unambiguously without using legalese can turn a sentence into a paragraph. Ask your lawyer to translate the legalese in the previous paragraph into more 'friendly' language, and you'll see what I mean.

Another good reason for using this language is that law firms have huge precedent libraries available to them which they use in constructing new agreements for you, and these are usually populated with old, tried-and-tested language. Using pre-drafted clauses that have been reviewed and considered many times before by other lawyers saves time and gives your lawyer confidence that the drafting is robust. That confidence is sometimes misplaced, as it's not uncommon to find truly dreadful drafting propagated merrily through many different agreements, but nonetheless it gives the lawyer comfort.

The least laudable reason for using such complex language is that it keeps lawyers in work. While any good commercial lawyer will strive to use drafting that is clear and meaningful to the reader of the contract, there is still a sizeable minority that feels threatened by such accessible drafting. By perpetuating the perception that contracts are dangerous and difficult, this minority ensures that business people remain reluctant to engage directly in the review and negotiation of their agreements, and keeps fee levels high.

Why some businesses like 'small print'

If you've ever signed a contract for a mobile phone, hired a digger or rented a car, chances are you will have encountered 'small print'. Typically printed in columns on coloured paper, the font size will have been shrunk so as to get the whole agreement on to a single sheet of A4 paper.

Did you read it all the way through before you signed it?

If you answered 'yes' to that question, you're in a minority that's probably in single digits. And that, of course, is one reason companies like it – by printing their terms in tiny writing they discourage anyone from reading them. That does mean that none of their clients know what their terms are (with all the challenges that presents), but there are companies that feel this is a price worth paying in order to avoid having any contract negotiations at all.

This can work if you're delivering a very standard commodity product, on very standard terms that are absolutely fair and reasonable, in a low risk commercial environment. Otherwise, it's just storing up trouble.

Many years ago I received an email asking, "Just how small can the 'small print' be, legally?" I asked what they had in mind, and the company sent through the terms they'd prepared.

The document I received covered a single side of A4 but, even when enlarged to the width of my computer screen, was totally impossible to read. I enlarged the font size to 7pt, and the text expanded to fill four pages. I think it's fair to say that it was too small…!

From a legal perspective, the terms must be readable in order for you to be able to rely on them. After all, if the other party has no idea what the terms state, it's pretty tough to insist they comply with them.

Dealing with 'client paper'

Of course, even if your own terms of business are beautifully drafted, and you know and understand them well, there's no guarantee you'll be able to use them for all deals.

If you sell to government or local authorities, or to very large corporations, it's likely you've had to sign their contracts as opposed to them signing yours.

Many contracts in the public sector are dreadfully complex, covering all sorts of eventualities that will not be relevant to the products and services you're selling. However, it is notoriously difficult to persuade public sector procurement folk to accept large-scale modifications to their terms.

While you're unlikely to have much luck getting large clients to redraft their contracts without the legalese and complexity they're accustomed to, don't be afraid to push back if the particular terms are not appropriate for your deal. Change will happen, and the more people challenge the use of over-complicated and obscure contract documents, the faster organisations will react.

In the meantime, use your legal support to help you unravel complex third party contracts, and translate their legally obscure terms into something the business can understand.

When I first started my business, I had a project helping a large telecoms company to renegotiate many of its IT and software contracts, to reduce ongoing support costs. During the course of the project I got to know some of their lawyers very well. I mentioned that the company's standard terms of procurement were very one-sided and that when I'd previously been working for a software company selling to them, we'd made a significant number of mark-ups to the contract.

The lawyer laughed. "I know they're one-sided," she said. "In fact, if we ever receive our terms back from a new supplier just signed, with no mark-up, I give them a call and ask if they took any legal advice before signing! There are a number of points in there that we expect to receive push-back on, and if we don't it rings alarm bells about the commercial competence of the supplier."

This book will help you understand key legal concepts and contract terms but it won't turn you into a lawyer!

You might ask why I'm telling you about the importance of good legal support, given that this book is all about helping you to understand legal terms so that you can negotiate effectively and close deals faster.

In answering this point, I need to be clear about the role you should be taking in contract negotiations.

As the sales person, your objective is to close good deals that your company can deliver and that make a reasonable margin, without imposing too much commercial risk on your organisation in the process. It's not to become a pseudo-lawyer, engaging in detailed technical negotiations about the merits of this drafting over that.

While you may have the legal knowledge and expertise to conduct the whole negotiation single-handedly (or the deal might be straightforward enough to enable you to do so), having access to expert assistance is essential. However good you might be, and however much detail I squeeze into these pages, there's no substitute for the years of training and experience that your legal advisors should have!

Your role in the contract negotiation process should be to facilitate and project-manage the negotiations, making sure that conversations are happening between the right people at the right level and are occurring in a timely manner. You should be seen as a problem-solver, encouraging both sides to examine the alternative ways forward so as to reach an agreement both you and the client are happy with.

Understanding the legal terminology, and its impact on your business, will make you much more effective at performing this role. It will make you less likely to overcommit to clients and better able to frame your company's reservations about certain contractual obligations in language that your client will understand.

Despite our best efforts, though, it will not enable you to pick apart complex drafting and identify legal risks that might only be referred to obliquely or might only exist in statute and not even be mentioned in the contract document itself.

If your lawyers trust you, life will be easier and sales will close faster

Being able to communicate effectively with lawyers (both yours and the client's) will also earn you respect and credibility and speed up the sales process.

Tell them what they need to know

As in-house counsel, and now in my role as commercial contracts specialist advising other businesses, I frequently receive requests for 'an agency agreement', 'a reseller agreement' or 'a software licence agreement'. These are generally accompanied by words along the lines of, "Just something simple and standard, please."

You can imagine how helpful this sort of instruction is. If you were building a new home, I'm sure you wouldn't say to the architect, "Just a standard four-bed detached house, please." You'd be specifying which bedrooms were to have en-suite bathrooms, the size of the main reception rooms, and all sorts of other details that would ensure you received a house that met your requirements. The same is needed when briefing your legal counsel about a new commercial relationship that needs documenting.

Back in chapter 2 we looked at the three triangles, describing the main areas of your 'User Guide'. These were:

- Who does what, when?

- When does payment occur?

- What happens if things go wrong?

At the bare minimum, these are the questions you should be answering when briefing your legal support. Using what you'll learn from this book, describe who the parties are to the contract and what each has to do to make the deal a success. Describe any acceptance process that might apply, and identify anything that might get in the way of your being paid. And if this deal has any significant or unusual consequences of failure, make sure your lawyer understands how these are triggered and how they will work.

Simply taking the time to brief your legal support effectively and accurately will make you their favourite sales person. And that means that when you need help resolving the final contentious point standing between you and that all-important signature, your legal support will be there to help.

It is well worth developing your skills in this area, as they will also stand you in good stead during contract negotiations. On occasion, you might negotiate a particular point with your client and reach agreement about how to proceed. You then pass your briefing back to the lawyer, so that he or she can update the contract. If you haven't done a good job of briefing the lawyer, the updated drafting you receive back might bear little resemblance to the deal you and the client had agreed.

When this happens, it delays negotiations as you go round the loop with your lawyer until the contract reflects what was agreed. It can also damage the relationship with the client if they feel that the inaccurate drafting was an attempt by your company to renege on the deal!

EXERCISE 7:

Use the template provided in the e-workbook downloaded from www.dealmakersbook.com to describe a new commercial relationship in terms that your lawyer will be able to use to create a suitable contract.

Explore solutions with the client and your lawyer

In your role as facilitator, you are able to explore potential solutions to contractual issues without committing. Having a good appreciation of the impact certain terms will have on the business enables you to sound out the other side for their willingness to accept different solutions. And being able to describe these clearly and unambiguously will speed the process of agreement significantly.

Never set expectations beyond your negotiating authority

Exploring these options with your own lawyer first is always a good move; one thing that is guaranteed to make you unpopular with legal (as well as potentially jeopardising your job!) is committing beyond your authority level.

If you find yourself in a negotiation where you've encountered an unexpected obstruction and want to test out the client's boundaries before going back to your lawyer or other approver, take care to manage their expectations as you do so.

Use phrases like, "I obviously haven't discussed this internally, and have no idea if it would be acceptable to my own organisation, but could you do Y if we were able to do X?" This enables you to 'float' possible solutions without setting expectations.

Do be careful though, especially if the client seizes on your offering, as it's easy for something suggested as a possibility to be remembered by the client as a concrete offer. Make sure you reiterate that, "I don't know if my company would be able to agree to this, but I'm happy to suggest it to them and let you know what they think." Ideally, you should try to have a couple of alternatives on the table at this stage so that it's clear nothing has been committed to.

Find the right way to engage with legal counsel – one that works for you and your organisation

Having ascertained that it is unlikely you'll be able to do without legal counsel altogether, we need to explore the different modes of engagement and see which will work best for you.

Letting them handle all contract negotiations

If you have a really great commercial lawyer or contracts specialist, you might be comfortable passing all the contract negotiation over to them.

This, however, is a missed opportunity. If you think back to chapters 1 and 2, you'll recall that working through the contracting process can help you build a deeper and stronger relationship with your client. Bear in mind that in handing over the client to a lawyer you're entrusting that relationship to them, so make sure it'll be in safe hands.

You also need to consider the availability of your lawyer and the priority of this deal to them. If they are busy with bigger deals or other matters, you may find that the negotiations drag on simply because your lawyer is not able to respond quickly to client feedback, or attend review meetings as frequently as required.

Using them as backup

An alternative is to have the lawyer as a key member of your team, but not leading the negotiations. In this role, you retain control of the timetable and ensure that things move forward at the planned pace. You are also able to use the opportunity to develop your client relationship, and explore solutions together with the client which will stand you in good stead for future sales.

Engage your legal support early, involving them in the structuring of the deal and identification of issues, and allow them to participate in your negotiation planning and to meet the client. This will enable you to benefit from their expertise and experience, which can guide you through those elements of the negotiation that you are able to conduct independently. And when you do need hands-on support from legal, they will not only be familiar with the deal and the issues, they will also be known to the other side and their participation will not be seen as a 'red flag' to the client.

A further benefit of this approach is that it uses less expensive legal resource, keeping down your cost of sale without exposing your business to unnecessary risk.

Using legal for reviews and background support

If you're very competent in the area of contract negotiation, this approach can work brilliantly. By using your legal support for occasional input and contract reviews, you keep the costs to a minimum.

There are risks, however. If you are a long way down the line with your negotiations before you ask for legal input, and the lawyer identifies a fundamental problem with the deal structure, or spots a concession you've agreed to that will impose significant risks on the business, you could be faced with the uncomfortable task of going back to your client to unravel an agreed deal.

EXERCISE 8:

Consider which of these three approaches is most appropriate for you, in your business. Why? Would you use different approaches for different levels of deal? Is your use of legal resources mandated by company procedures? If so, consider whether the procedures work well for you and your colleagues, or if there is room for improvement. If you've earned the right to be listened to, by taking time to understand the legal terminology and issues involved and considering the topics covered in this book, you may well be able to change your corporate approach to speed up the sales cycle and deliver better outcomes. Download the e-workbook from www.dealmakersbook.com to help you complete this exercise.

Chapter 3: Quick Summary

- Despite improvements in readability in some consumer contracts, business-to-business ones still rely on a fair amount of 'legalese'

- Legalese can make it easier to convey complex legal concepts concisely, but also makes it harder for non-lawyers to understand

- Some businesses discourage clients from reading and negotiating their terms by using 'small print'

- You might have to do business on the client's terms, which may be less friendly and well written than your own

- Although this book will help you understand contract terms, it won't turn you into a lawyer – so you need to keep your own lawyers on your side

- Learning what matters, so you can brief your lawyers effectively, will make it easier for them to help you

- Keep within your negotiating authority, but do use your new knowledge to explore possible solutions to contractual roadblocks

- There are several different ways to work with legal counsel: you can allow them to negotiate for you, you can use them as backup in your negotiations, or you can just refer to them for reviews and input as required

- Find the right way for you and your business

4

What you're selling should match what the client's buying

Most of the sales methodologies I've encountered in my career have been based around helping the client identify their needs, and then shaping these to fit what you're able to deliver.

Some approaches use neuro-linguistic programming to help you move the client from their left-brain (analytical) thinking mode into a more right-brain (emotional, creative) mode. This helps sell the client the 'bigger picture' – the benefits of and value added by the product, service or solution you're offering to them. It encourages the client to visualise the world with your product in it, and see how much better this is than the world they inhabit today.

While this can deliver excellent sales results if done well, it can also result in a dislocation between 'sizzle' and 'sausage' that leaves the client feeling unhappy and let down.

What do I mean by this? Imagine you were instructed to sell sausages at a country fair and were targeted on selling as many plastic-wrapped packages as possible each day.

Imagine your success if you put up a poster advertising 'Get your 20cm-long case in tubes of minced pork, fat, rusk and seasoning here! Only £2.99 for eight, wrapped in plastic wrapper and ready for your freezer!' Standing by your poster with a table topped with neatly stacked packs of sausages ready for inspection by any passing shopper, you're ready for action.

That's selling sausages. Or at least, describing sausages in a clear, accurate, left-brain fashion. And, let's face it, it is unlikely to be terribly successful.

Selling 'sizzle', though, is a very different matter. With your packs of pink, plastic-wrapped porcine tubes stored neatly out of sight under your table, you have set up a mobile grill on your table, resting on a fresh tablecloth. Your sausages are sizzling enticingly on the grill – as each one is cooked, you cut it into inch-long sections and position them on a plate with cocktail sticks at the ready. As passers-by stop to try them, their hands reach for their money as their mouth waters; before the sausage has even contacted their taste buds, the smell has hooked them on your product.

The no.1 reason for contract disputes

Over the years, those of us who watch cases coming before the courts have observed a depressing pattern emerging. Although the basis on which rulings are made varies, the vast majority of legal battles in the commercial courts originate from differences between what the seller believed it was selling and what the buyer believed it was buying.

In most cases, the seller was of the opinion that it had done everything it was obliged to do under the contract, but the buyer disagreed. The parties had plainly failed to resolve their differences through discussion (despite trying in many cases for years to do so), and each felt sufficiently strongly that they were right to risk the cost and effort of a court case.

These cases, however, are just the tip of the iceberg.

At two training workshops I was delivering recently I asked how many of the commercial and contract managers in the room had experienced contract litigation during their careers. Out of a total of about 80 managers, most of whom had been working in this area for ten to twenty years, only three had ever been involved in a litigation – that's fewer than 4%.

I wondered if this meant that all of the professionals I was speaking to had simply only ever experienced very successful projects. So I followed up by asking how many had ever experienced a contract dispute resulting from disagreement about the scope and deliverables of a project. Every single hand went up.

So although relatively few cases come to court, leading some people to say "We don't have contract issues", when examined more closely it appears that everybody has contract issues. It's just that some of those don't register as being contract related, even though they are.

Why does this matter?

Unhappy clients = late or non-payment

One of the first points in your contractual relationship where differences of opinion about scope will impact you is when a milestone payment is due. The client has one major opportunity to exercise power over you if it is unhappy with your delivery, and that is in the area of payment – and it's one that can be wielded relatively easily.

One company I worked with, a software business, had a dispute over payment of its initial invoice for a new project. I'd drafted their terms of business for them around six or seven years earlier, but these hadn't been updated for a while. They maintained that there were no problems, and the terms worked well, so we had left things alone.

In this dispute the invoice was for software licences, and it was issued and payable on the date of signature of the contract. The contract and its schedule were both very clear – the licences were delivered immediately upon signature, and the invoices were issued at the same time. I couldn't see what grounds the client had for refusing to pay.

On further investigation it transpired that the software the licences related to would not be delivered for several weeks. Indeed, at the time the invoice was issued it had not all been written. So how could the licences have been issued?

The company had followed a process it had used for several years without a problem. At the start of the project, it issued a 'Licence Certificate' to the customer, stating that this would entitle the customer to use the software as and when it was delivered, in line with the project plan. This 'Licence Certificate' was used as the basis for invoicing, helping to improve project cash flow while the software was being enhanced to meet the customer's requirements.

While the customer project staff which had developed the plan, and signed off the schedule, fully understood and approved of this mechanism, the finance person who was being asked to approve the invoice did not. From his perspective, the contract stated that licences would be delivered, and licences meant software. Licences without software were not licences and therefore could not be paid for.

To prevent this problem recurring on future projects, we agreed to amend the wording in the contract schedule so as to make it clear that the licence would be delivered in the form of an advance 'Licence Certificate' that related to a future delivery of software. The revenue recognition implications of this two-phase delivery also had to be considered, as an internal issue for the company.

So whether the client thinks you've under-delivered in terms of quantity or quality, or failed to achieve the objective they set out for the project, withholding cash is a way to make you sit up and take notice. They may have complained before, but it's when invoices start to be rejected that your organisation will really begin to pay attention.

What happens next?

Unhappy clients = dissolving margin

Few companies are so arrogant as to ignore unhappy clients. Generally, a business will respond to disputed invoices by:

(a) investigating the cause of the dispute, to see if the client's complaint is justified; then

(b) if they believe it isn't justified, trying to explain to the client why this is the case; or

(c) if they believe it is justified, proposing additional deliverables (of products or services) for no money so as to compensate the client, or offering a discount or credit note against the disputed invoice.

So regardless of whether the client is right or wrong, extra work is imposed on your company trying to get to the bottom of the dispute. And if the client is right (or at least, if they are not sufficiently wrong for you to put a compelling case and convince them), additional costs are incurred remedying the problem.

This means that even if you are in the right, disputes about whether you've delivered what the client thought it was buying will cost you money and eat into your margin. Doesn't that provide a big incentive to avoid these disputes in the first place?

Unhappy clients = poor sales prospects

You'll have heard, and probably experienced the truth of, the sales adage that it's much easier to sell to an existing client than to find a new one. Of course, this is only true if your existing clients are happy with the products and service they've received from you.

Disputes over scope and deliverables can sour an otherwise good relationship, and significantly impair your ability to cross-sell and up-sell into an existing account. They also relieve you of a potential reference client or testimonial that could have helped you sell into new accounts. For all of these reasons, it's worth putting some effort into making sure that your 'sausage' matches your 'sizzle'.

EXERCISE 9:

What are you selling? Write your best 'sizzle-free' description of what your client gets from you in a typical sale. Limit yourself to 100 words and be as crisp and concise as you can. Now speak to a project manager on your delivery team, or the product manager from marketing if you're working for a product company, and ask them to do the same. Do they match up? Download the e-workbook from www.dealmakersbook.com to help you complete this exercise.

Writing good specifications can be tough

There was an advertisement many years ago for a wood treatment sold by DIY chains, which stated that the product 'does exactly what it says on the tin'. Having that degree of clarity about what you're delivering is something to aspire to, but it's difficult with some products or services where there is no 'tin'.

If your product is a tangible, physical item and is mass-produced to an identical specification for all clients, creating a clear and unambiguous specification is not difficult. And if you sell a high volume of products, it's obviously worth doing – the modest investment in time will be amply repaid across your many sales.

Products that are very complex, and possibly heavily tailored to the specific requirements of the client, tend not to have extensive and detailed user documentation. What documentation there is will often be either sales-led and lacking in detail, or highly technical design documents that mean little to the user. Neither lends itself well to the role of 'tin'.

What does a good specification look like?

While writing a detailed product specification might not be your responsibility, ensuring that there is one is certainly in your interests. As well as providing a basis for sales and marketing literature to be created, it will help you get paid if the client can reference an agreed document to assess whether the company has delivered 'what it says on the tin'.

The first characteristic of a good specification is that it exists. You might find that when you ask about the product, system or service specification, vague murmurings are heard along the lines of, "Dave has something that we used last time, on the XYZ project, doesn't he?" Follow the trail – if you are passed from pillar to post, don't give up until you have a specification in your hand. If this doesn't happen, and you start to feel like a hunter of yetis, or Loch Ness Monsters, it's time to flag this up to the business and find someone to take charge of its creation – or explain to you why it's not needed.

When you have succeeded in tracking down a specification document, read it. This will be good for your overall education, so it is not wasted effort, but I want you to read it with a red pen in hand. Each time you read a section that is unclear, ambiguous or incomplete, squiggle in the margin that it needs more work. If you don't understand it, chances are others will also have problems – and misunderstandings with regard to the specification will manifest themselves in unhappy clients and the problems that brings further down the chain.

Be critical in your review of the specification. Use your 'sales waffle' filter to ensure it contains only hard facts – this is the place for sausage not sizzle! And generally, while sales people are great at creating 'sales waffle', they also have very sensitive noses to other people's – sniff out the waffle and give it a red-pen squiggle.

So a good specification will exist, be clear, unambiguous, complete and free of waffle and hyperbole. A good way to assess how effective it will be in helping you get paid is to ask yourself in each key functional area, "How would I show that the product/service has done this?" If you wouldn't be able to demonstrate that it had been done, it probably isn't clear enough.

What if we don't know what we're selling when we start?

When the details of the product, service or solution are not clear at the beginning of the process, it is important to agree a mechanism by which you determine whether you've delivered what you said you would. This occurs frequently, although by no means exclusively, with software development and systems integration projects.

This situation presents a number of issues, one of which is that despite there being no clear specification, the client will often have a fixed budget at the outset, based on the 'sizzle'. That is to say, they will have secured the budget by persuading their management team of certain benefits to be delivered by your offering, even if they're not sure exactly how this will happen.

It is essential that you keep a close eye on the 'sizzle' that the client is using to sell the project internally. There is a strong possibility that your success or failure will depend upon it – after all, if the project champion has secured budget on the basis that your deliverables will achieve a particular outcome, you will have a strong interest in helping the project champion look good. This may well involve extra expenditure and margin erosion for you if the outcome he or she promised their superiors was not achievable within the original budget.

I have a very successful software client that delivers complex enterprise resource planning systems. At the outset, their customers have a general idea of what they hope to achieve, but given the size and complexity of the organisation and the interfaces between existing systems and the new one, this is rarely specified in full at the start.

The approach my client has taken is to use a progressive, workshop-led route, loosely based on a 'rapid application development' or 'SCRUM' model. This enables them to use workshops to explore what the customer wants out of each section of the software, to discuss the capabilities and any limitations that might impact on how those requirements will be met, and to agree the deliverables. This is an incremental approach, with workshops continuing throughout the project as different modules are developed and delivered.

Because of the highly flexible nature of this model, the company very rarely does any projects for a fixed price. Instead, they will give an estimated range of costs. At each workshop they will make it clear to the customer what functionality is likely to be achievable within the estimated price. If the customer wants more, they are given the option to either pay more or reduce functionality elsewhere.

The approach used by this company works very well for them and for their clients, who avoid the high level of contingency fees that companies frequently have to add when offering uncertain scope against a fixed price. Some clients refuse to accept a variable price model, though, and insist on having a fixed price even though the scope is far from fixed.

One way to address this is to have an initial fixed-price 'scoping phase'. This enables your team to work with the client to try to bottom-out the requirements and understand what is really needed. One of the deliverables from this scoping phase is usually a requirements specification, which should be the basis for subsequent work. The other deliverable is generally a fixed-price proposal to deliver against that specification, which is now significantly lower risk as your staff have a better idea of what's involved.

Proposals, SoWs and Order Forms

Unfortunately, while you've done a great job in making sure you have a clear specification of what your company is delivering, there's still room for disaster to snatch victory from your hands.

Despite you having specified exactly what's in your metaphorical sausage, the client is holding tight to the sizzle you originally presented – in the form of your initial proposal, response to their Request for Proposal (RFP), or tender. As far as they're concerned, while it's all very nice to know about the precise quantity of rusk in your sausage, all they really want is for you to guarantee that the sausages you sell them will taste as good, and make their mouths water as much, as the samples you offered at the country fair.

This can be a challenging conversation to have. After all, the client argues, you're not going to tell them that you lied in your proposal, are you? Surely if you felt strongly enough to include the sizzle in your proposal, you can include it in your contract? So why can't the proposal/RFP response/tender be the specification that you agree to bind your company to deliver against?

It's hard to find a way out of this discussion without 'fessing up to the existence of sizzle. Or 'sales waffle'. Or 'marketing hyperbole'. However you want to describe it, it all boils down to the fact that in your proposal you will make subjective statements and assertions about the impact of your product or service on the client's business that may not necessarily be backed up by hard measurable fact. Or whose truth might depend on certain actions or omissions of the client themselves.

Most sensible clients will understand this. The important thing is to ask them if there are particular elements of your proposal that are essential to their decision to purchase from you. If there are, these should be reflected in the (more objective and less funky) specification document. If you're unable to commit to them in your specification, it's time to have an honest discussion with the client and re-set their expectations – *before* you've entered into a contract with them.

Having agreed (hopefully) that there are good reasons why the contractual document should be a rather dry specification and not a souped-up proposal, you need to agree exactly how it will be incorporated into your contract.

Back to the Purchase Order

One way to incorporate the specification in the contract is to have the client reference it on their purchase order. As you'll remember from the 'Battle of the Forms' in chapter 2, there are inherent dangers in the purchase order structure.

Provided you manage these, and advise the client that you can only accept a PO that references your specification and your terms and conditions, this approach works for products that fall into the 'commodity' category.

By this, I mean that they are not bespoke or tailored, and that they have a fixed list price, so that the only variable the client needs to set out on their PO is the quantity.

Proposals and RFP responses

Proposals? Don't go there. If you can possibly avoid it, don't include your proposal as a contractual document.

Why not?

Unless you are absolutely fantastically disciplined in keeping all sizzle out of your proposals so that they remain strictly factual, the risk of inadvertently making a contractual commitment that you're unable to deliver against is generally unacceptably high.

With RFP responses, check *before* you submit your response whether it will form part of the contract. If the client specifies that the RFP response will be contractually binding if they choose to accept your offer, you must go through it **before submission** with a fine-toothed comb and remove every iota of sizzle, hyperbole and sales waffle. This might be something better done by a member of the product marketing, delivery or development team – whoever is best at keeping you honest.

SoWs, Schedules and Work Packages

If this is a long-term relationship with a client to whom you expect to sell multiple chunks of products or services over time, it's worth signing up to some form of framework agreement with them. A framework agreement generally sets out the terms and conditions on which the parties agree they will do business, *whenever the client wants to buy something from the seller*, but it doesn't actually commit the client to buy anything in particular straight away.

When they want to buy some products or services, the client will execute some other form of document with you – something like a Statement of Work, a Works Order, a Schedule, or a Work Package (there are many different names for what is essentially the same thing). We'll refer to it here as the Buying Document. This document will contain the details of exactly what they are buying, when it will be delivered, and how much it will cost.

It is rare for companies to go to the time, trouble and expense of negotiating a framework agreement unless they have a particular requirement for products or services in mind. These agreements can take a while to put in place, as they'll be there for a long time and both parties have to be comfortable that they'll stand up to long-term scrutiny. So generally, when you're negotiating the framework agreement, it will be in the context of the first lot of products and/or services that the client wants to purchase from you, which will be set out in the first Buying Document.

The Buying Document must be written using the same terminology as the main framework agreement, and should provide values for any variables created in that framework agreement.

What do I mean by this?

I mean that if, for example, the framework agreement refers to 'Products', and defines the term as meaning 'Supplier's products as set out in the Schedule', we should make sure we set out details of the 'Products' in our Schedule, and that we refer to them as being 'Products'. This enables the two documents to work well together and to do their respective jobs as intended.

If the specification for your products or services is long, you may wish to refer to it in the Buying Document rather than including the whole thing in the framework agreement. If you do, ensure you use the correct document name and version number and/or date, when you reference it.

Find out what your client thinks they're buying

We've looked in some detail now at exactly what you're intending to deliver to the client, making sure that your product or service is clearly and unambiguously defined. We've agreed that while nobody would buy a sausage purely on the basis of its technical description, it is essential that we have that technical description as our main contractual specification.

Now we need to return to the 'sizzle'. Hopefully, by working through the process above, you've brought your client with you on the journey and they are happy with the contractual specification for your product or service. But the fact remains that we humans are emotional animals and often make even very technical buying decisions based on emotional drivers.

If we press these emotional buttons during the sales cycle, getting our client all fired up about the wonderful outcomes that will follow their engagement with us and then fail to deliver against them, the client will be unhappy.

We can refer them back to the contract and the technical specification, to say, "Well we've done what it said on the tin!" And we would be right. From an operational and legal perspective, if we've done our job properly we will have an unassailable position that would mean we are under no obligation to deliver extra products or services, or to offer discounts, or make any other moves towards compensation – because we haven't done anything wrong.

But what about the third component of our commercial relationship – the psychological contract?

In business, as in personal relationships, there is sometimes a difference between 'being right' and 'getting what you want'. Thinking about what the client believes is in their psychological contract with you can help you to get what you want much more effectively than just proving that you are 'right'. In this instance, 'getting what you want' might involve:

- A happy customer who will act as a reference client for you

- A happy customer who will give you good testimonials

- A happy customer will commit to purchasing higher volumes and longer term deals

- A happy customer will want to list more products from your range and will be prepared to invest in promoting them

- A happy customer who will **buy from you again**

You see the pattern? The contract can put you in great shape for getting paid and avoiding disputes. But if you want to maximise the 'love' and the added value it brings, a happy customer will require more than just strict delivery according to the contract.

What needs have they expressed?

During the sales process, your client will have expressed many needs and wants to you. Some of these might have been set out in their RFP or similar document. These needs are easy to deal with, as you will have expressly responded to them in writing to say whether you can or cannot meet them or, if you can only partly meet them, how.

If you've been listening carefully, you will have heard them express other needs to you along the way.

What's important to them, and why?

When we ask what's important to your client, we must remember that in any deal we seldom have a single customer to think about. Depending on the size of your client and your deal, you might have:

- An operational buyer – the person who wants to use your product or service to make their life or work performance better

- A commercial buyer – the person in charge of negotiating the contract and the price whose goal is to buy your product for the least amount of money and on the most favourable terms

- An executive sponsor – someone not directly involved in the day-to-day negotiations but who is an influencer in the client organisation and supports your product or service

- The board of directors – who are responsible to the shareholders for the success of the business and the share price of the company

And for each of these, there are at least two levels of need to consider: what the person in that role needs personally, to make them look good to their team, their peers and their superiors and to feel good about themselves; and what they need to achieve professionally, on behalf of their department, their business unit or their company.

Of these various wants and needs, many of the professional ones will have found their way into your formal discussions and documentation already. It is the personal needs that you need to identify and note, to see if you can satisfy them within the bounds of what you and your company can do.

What are they afraid of?

The flip-side of the question 'what's important to them?' is 'what are they afraid of?'

While this might sound like a strange question (we're not interested in a fear of spiders or heights here!) it often sheds light on objections that simply don't make sense to you. The reason for this is that people are sometimes unwilling to disclose their personal fears and worries openly, and will find other ways of dressing them up in an attempt to get you to address them.

What do I mean? Put yourself in your client's shoes.

Let's say that the last IT system you purchased for your company was an unmitigated disaster. It didn't deliver the benefits that you had assured your bosses would result from it, overran in terms of implementation time and budget, and suffered numerous bugs and setbacks. As a result, your last appraisal was not good. You know your business is looking to cut costs, and fear that if you mess up this particular new solution procurement and implementation your salary will be top of the list for cutting.

As a result, you become the most risk-averse client ever. You nit-pick over the smallest detail of the specification, and insist on huge liquidated damages (see chapter 8 for how these work) for any delays in delivery. Despite being reasonably confident in the ability and integrity of your supplier, you refuse to cut them any slack or leave anything to their discretion – everything has to be nailed down so that nobody can possibly say that you didn't follow the corporate process to the letter.

Have you experienced this kind of client? I certainly have, many times. If you can identify the source of their fear, you can address it directly rather than through the smokescreen of issues that they vocalise. In the example above, you might decide that now is the time to take this client to visit your last three happy customers for a one-to-one drains-up chat. This may do far more to assuage their fears than anything you could ever say to them directly. And your client might be more inclined to share their worries with another customer than they would with you.

EXERCISE 10:

How can you find out what your customer is buying? Look at each of the different levels of client buyer involved in your typical sale and list all of the different methods available to you for finding out or deducing what's important to them and what they are afraid of. Download the e-workbook from www.dealmakersbook.com to help you complete this exercise.

Value = meeting the right wants and needs for an acceptable price

In the current commercial climate, the word 'value' has become synonymous with 'cheap'. A supermarket's 'value' range will have the most basic packaging and will trumpet its 'no frills' credentials.

Some buyers (especially the commercial buyer or procurement professional) will see this as the only possible definition of value, and will always be looking for the cheapest option. Indeed, they may be targeted and measured on this basis in terms of their professional performance.

Your role as a sales person is, of course, to build the value of your offering so that your client believes that the price you're giving them is going to be a worthwhile investment when compared to the benefit they will receive from having your product or service.

This can result in trumpeting features of your product or service that, while they might be important to some clients, are of negligible benefit to this particular client, right now. When we talk about value as being 'meeting the **right** wants and needs for an **acceptable** price', we mean that we're meeting the wants and needs that are important **to this particular client, right now**, for a price that **is more than justified by the wants and needs that we are fulfilling**.

'Wants' versus 'needs'

I've talked a lot in this chapter about the client's wants and needs without really explaining why I'm using two words where one would do. From a negotiating perspective, the two things are quite different. How?

Imagine you've been walking across the desert for three days. Your water skin is empty and has been for the last few hours. You're feeling lightheaded and unsteady on your feet as the heat beats down on you. Then, through the haze, you spot a large silver shape on the horizon. As you get closer, you see that it's a refrigerated truck, and outside it sits a man on a chair, in the shade of an umbrella, selling bottles of ice-cold mineral water.

Unable to believe your luck, you stagger towards him, pulling your wallet from its pocket and pointing dry-mouthed at his wares. "Hello there," says the man, "a, bottle of water for you? Of course. That'll be £100, please."

OK, let's stop there for a moment. You want the water, yes? Do you need it? There's no other source of water in sight and you doubt you'd make it through another hour in this heat without a drink. So yes, I guess we could say you need it. Will you haggle? If you had the cash, I suspect you'd hand it over without a second thought. You might possibly haggle over the price of your second bottle once you've replenished yourself, but right now all you can think about is the feeling of that cool water slipping down your parched throat and soothing your aching head.

Now let's transplant the action to the high street of your local shopping area. You've been on your feet for hours and fancy some water. You pop into the first shop you come to and discover that a bottle of mineral water costs £2.50. 'Extortion!' you think, moving on to the next shop. You buy a bottle for £1.50 a couple of doors down, drink some and continue with your shopping.

What's the difference between these two scenarios? In the first one, your desire for water was indisputably a **need**. You had no choice – no alternatives. You had to buy that water, at any cost. This meant that from a negotiation perspective all the power was in the hands of the seller.

In the second scenario, you were able to choose between a number of vendors.

Price became relevant in your decision making, as the different offerings would each have met your requirements in a similar way. And if you hadn't found an acceptably priced bottle of water in either shop, it wouldn't have been the end of the world – you could have finished your shopping and had a drink when you got home. In this case, your desire for water was just a **want**.

So a **need** has a key characteristic: it cannot be walked away from, but must be fulfilled. A **want**, on the other hand, can be walked away from if the conditions of fulfilling it aren't right for us.

There's something else you will have noticed about these two scenarios. In the first, not only was the need for water something that couldn't be walked away from, but the buyer (you) had no *alternatives.* The presence of multiple alternative sources of water in the second example, any of which would have been acceptable, allowed you to base your choice on which was cheapest, or which had the nicest bottle, or whatever other criteria were important to you. You can see from this that having **needs** puts you in a weaker negotiating position. Creating alternatives increases the strength of your negotiating position – while you might still need water, you have a choice of vendors. You'd be unlikely to ever pay £100 for a bottle of mineral water in your local shopping centre!

Matching their wants and needs to your offering

So what does that mean to us as sales people? We should seek to understand which of the requirements that our client has shared with us fall into the category of needs, and which are just wants.

I'm sure you'll be familiar with this in the context of your sales training, and will be experienced at considering and developing the client's functional requirements in this way. Here, we're applying the same sales techniques to the client's contractual requirements.

More than this, if there are certain commercial or contractual requirements that your client has outlined as 'wants' that you think you are exclusively able to meet, you may try to convert them from 'wants' into 'needs'. So part of the sales process will be to find ways to emphasise the value the client would derive from having this particular requirement met, raising it up their priority list above some of the 'wants' that could equally well be met by your competitors.

Similarly, if the client has identified as a 'need' something that you are unable to fulfil, you might look at ways to downgrade this from a 'need' to a 'want'. For example, you might say that if the client buys your product, the impact of missing a particular service level will be negligible, so there is no longer a requirement to have an automated reporting mechanism for tracking it.

Ultimately, you might realise that while you can meet the client's professional wants and needs by delivering against your technical specification, some of the personal ones just won't be achievable.

But if you can find a way to do both, you'll be assured of a loyal and happy client who will not only recommend you in their current job, but will keep in touch and buy from you again in their next company.

Use 'acceptance' to check you've done what was agreed

At the start of this chapter we saw that disagreements about the scope of what was to be delivered formed the bulk of commercial disputes. For that reason, we've devoted many pages to examining how we can clearly understand and document what we should be delivering, and how we will go about making our client happy. If we've done a good job of this, managing the process to ensure we deliver what we said we would becomes much more straightforward.

The proof of the pudding, however, will be when we come to ask for payment – will the client agree with us that we've delivered what was promised?

We can use the contract to facilitate this by defining an 'acceptance' process and some acceptance criteria to be used within it.

Defining acceptance criteria

The acceptance criteria are the means by which we prove that we've done what we said we would, and they can vary in sophistication and complexity according to the type of product or service you're selling.

If you sell some form of commodity or standard product, where the quality of the goods is instantly visible and they either 'are' or 'are not' acceptable, it may simply be the *fact* of delivery that forms your acceptance criteria. So your acceptance process might consist of signing a delivery note to confirm that ten boxes of the product were delivered undamaged on a certain date.

Even if your product is complex but standard, you might still decide that there is no need for the client to evaluate its functionality or quality before they accept it; the fact that it is the same as every other one of its kind should be sufficient. So again, delivery of the product might be the only criterion for acceptance.

Alternatively, if there's a degree of customisation or tailoring involved for this product, or if you're delivering complex services, your client might be justified in asking to test the deliverables and evaluate them against the technical specification you agreed in the contract. As you've defined a nice, clear and unambiguous technical specification, this should be a straightforward process. Indeed, defining the acceptance tests you intend to carry out at the beginning of the project is an excellent way to confirm that both parties have a common understanding of the requirements.

One thing to be aware of when determining acceptance criteria in this scenario, however, is that passing all tests 100% successfully, with no problems identified anywhere, is not always necessary to get a product or project accepted by the client. If the solution is still usable even with a few errors remaining to be fixed over time (particularly if there is a warranty or some form of support and maintenance in place – see chapter 7), you might want to define categories for any bugs or errors that occur.

You could, for example, define a Severity 1 error as being something that renders the deliverable unusable, while a Severity 2 can be worked around with modest interruption to the ease of use, and a Severity 3 is a minor irritation or inconvenience that doesn't materially affect the performance of the deliverable.

Having defined your severity levels (or whatever you want to call them), you will then define your acceptance criteria according to how many errors at each level may exist in the deliverable(s) if it is (or they are) to be accepted.

So you might say that the deliverable(s) should have no Severity 1 errors, fewer than three Severity 2 errors, and fewer than fifty Severity 3 errors – or whatever is appropriate for the type of product or service you're selling.

This has the great benefit that 'perfection' is not the only way to a successful outcome. Given how hard perfection is to achieve (particularly if you're selling software, where it's more or less impossible), this comes as a great relief!

Defining the acceptance process

The process for determining acceptance must be considered in the context of: which of you is best placed to do this work, and what is the client prepared to pay for? It might be the case that you've done such a good job of defining the acceptance tests and the acceptance criteria that the client is entirely happy for you to carry out the tests on their behalf and present them with the results. If they want you to do this testing, they will need to pay for your time in doing so, but this may represent a more sensible approach than finding time and resources to do it themselves.

Alternatively, they might feel that they must test the deliverables themselves to ensure everything works as intended.

Either way, make sure you've set out a clear process for performing the acceptance tests and for fixing any problems that are identified, and re-testing.

Importantly, you'll want to set out any documentation that must be completed to prove or confirm that acceptance has taken place. This could be in the form of an acceptance certificate signed by the client, confirming that the criteria have been met, or a test results sheet illustrating that this is the case. The key thing is that you have whatever level of proof you require in order to be paid any sums that are associated with achieving acceptance as part of your payment milestones.

As part of this exercise, you should be clear about the timescales for acceptance – both in terms of when it's due to start and how long it may continue. You might also, at your client's request, agree to specify how many attempts at re-testing will be permitted before the client is entitled to terminate the contract.

From your perspective, too, it might be helpful to have this potential exit route available. While ideally you'd like to keep going round the acceptance-testing loop until you 'pass', there may come a point where you realise that some fundamental problem with the deliverable means that you will never meet the acceptance criteria – or at least not at a reasonable cost. The option of bailing out in a clearly defined manner might not be desirable but may be better than the alternative. This is something you need to consider in the context of the riskiness of whatever you're delivering, and the chances of your encountering a problem you won't be able to fix.

'Deemed acceptance' and why you need it

Defining a nice clear acceptance process is very satisfying and gives the feeling that you have neatly tied up the final part of your delivery process before you've even begun. Without some form of 'deemed acceptance', however, you will have left some loose ends that could unravel the whole idea.

What do we mean by 'deemed acceptance'?

If we are agreed that acceptance has happened when we've met the criteria defined as set out above, and not before, what happens if we never conduct the acceptance testing? This could happen because, for example, the client representative who was responsible for doing the testing is ill, on holiday, or too busy to do the tests. Or it could be delayed because another vendor whose product is necessary for your own product to be properly tested is late in delivering their parts.

In any of these cases, acceptance might be delayed indefinitely – and with it, any corresponding payment you might be entitled to 'on acceptance'.

The concept of 'deemed acceptance' is your safety net – your insurance policy against any of these things occurring. It is a way of saying that under certain circumstances, even though we haven't proven that the acceptance criteria have been met, we will consider the deliverables to have been 'accepted'.

This could happen if, for example, the deliverables have been ready for acceptance by the client for more than a certain amount of time, and the client has not notified you that they have failed acceptance. Or it could be that the client has started using the deliverables in its business, but hasn't bothered doing the testing or signing your acceptance certificate. Or, in the case of products that are just delivered and inspected for breakages or shortfalls, it could be that more than a certain number of days have elapsed since delivery without the client notifying you of any breakages or short-delivery.

EXERCISE 11:

In your business, how do you demonstrate to the client that you've done what you said you would? Refer back to exercise 9 and check each element of your 'sizzle-free' description. Are you making any promises that you're not able to prove you've delivered on? Are they promises that are likely to be important to the client? If so, talk to your product or project manager to see how you can show your compliance. Download the e-workbook from www.dealmakersbook.com to help you complete this exercise.

Chapter 4: Quick Summary

- Mismatches between what the vendor thinks it is selling and what the client thinks it is buying cause most contract disputes

- Some of this is due to the difference between the sales 'sizzle' and the delivery 'sausage'

- These disagreements might not always go to court but can result in delayed or reduced payment, reduced margin and poor sales prospects

- Creating clear specifications is important but can be difficult if you don't know exactly what you're delivering before you start

- There are techniques (like SCRUM) that help you agree specifications as you go along

- The proposal, statement of work or order form could be used as a specification, but you have to make sure any 'sales waffle' is stripped out before it becomes a contractual document

- Find out exactly what your client thinks it is buying, which won't always be what's in the RFP – look beyond the corporate, to the personal wants and needs of your client

- You can charge a higher price if you're meeting client needs that are very important to them

- 'Acceptance' is a useful way to prove you've done what you said you'd do

- Acceptance processes and criteria should ideally be defined in advance

- 'Deemed acceptance' protects you against delays in testing

5

Help your clients make the project a success

So far, we've looked at how we define exactly what we're going to deliver, and how we make sure that this matches up to what the client is expecting. Now we're going to take a look at the other side of the coin – one that sales people traditionally avoid if at all possible but which will deliver great dividends for you if you embrace it and do it well.

In this chapter, we'll examine what we want from the client in order to deliver successfully, and how this ultimately benefits the client every bit as much as it benefits us.

Understand who you're selling to

Before we start examining the client's obligations in detail, let's make sure we know exactly who we mean when we talk about 'the client'. This time, we're not going to look at this from a human perspective (the operational buyer, commercial buyer, etc., from chapter 4) but from a legal perspective.

Identifying the contracting entity

This can be harder than you'd think, especially if your client is a large blue-chip company. These businesses tend to be made up of multiple operating companies, all owned by a group PLC.

To identify a specific legal entity if it is registered in the UK, the first place to look is the Companies House website, which you can find at www.companieshouse.gov.uk. Enter the name of the company in the 'webcheck' page and it will bring up all the companies matching this name, showing you the company's registered office, registered number, and various details of its trading categories and financial reports filed.

When you ask your client the name of the legal entity that will be contracting with you, you may discover that they have no more idea of the correct entity than you do. Just by way of example, I've done a quick count of all the limited companies including the word 'Vodafone' within their company name. Excluding those that have been dissolved or closed, I counted eighty-two different legal entities. By the time you read this, that number will almost certainly have grown – and this only represents their UK registered entities!

Why does this matter? Well it's easy to be swept along by the glamour of a big-name client and not check out the details. What matters when it comes to contracting entities is their solvency and ability to pay your bills. Some well-known brand-name companies will have a number of 'shell' companies established which don't actually trade to any significant extent and have very weak balance sheets. Signing a contract through one of these shell companies protects the main trading entities since, if the deal goes wrong, they have the option of winding up the company to avoid liability.

Of course, I'm not saying that any of the UK blue-chips would behave in this way, but you need to bear in mind that if they chose to, they could! There's a common misconception that the PLC owner of a limited company is responsible for settling the debts and obligations of that limited company. This might account for the laid-back approach of some organisations when it comes to signing deals with no-name subsidiaries of big corporations, but it would be scant comfort if things went wrong and the parent company decided to let its subsidiary go under, rather than bailing it out.

So when you're about to sign your first deal with a big-name company, make sure that the legal entity you're signing with has the assets behind it that you associate with the brand.

Companies House enables you to download the accounts filed for a company, and there are plenty of credit-checking agencies that will provide an analysis of the solvency of the company for you.

If your client is registered outside the UK, your task becomes a little more complex. Not all countries have a central register of companies. Some, like the USA, have registers on a state-by-state basis, while others have no formal registration process. If you're contracting with an overseas entity, it's important to take local legal advice to ascertain that the entity you think you're dealing with actually exists and has a legal 'personality'.

Once you've ascertained exactly which legal entity you're doing business with, specify the full company details in your contract. So if there is some form of company registration number, make sure you include this in your definition of the client entity.

EXERCISE 12:

Choose a global blue-chip company that you either do business with currently, or would like to in the future. Find out the registered company details of its UK trading entity, and list as many of its related or group companies as you can identify in 20 minutes. Which ones would you be happy to trade with? What percentage of them are non-trading entities? Download the e-workbook from www.dealmakersbook.com to help you complete this exercise.

Group company framework agreements

From time to time, you'll really strike gold. When you've not only managed to persuade a well-known corporate to buy from you but they've told you they want a framework agreement so that any other group company can buy from you too, you know you've done well. Haven't you?

Of course, it's great that any company in the group can buy from you without having to negotiate a new contract. You just need to make sure that the agreement is structured so that:

a. you can vet any group company before you allow it to buy from you, to make sure it'll be able to pay and is a trustworthy entity to do business with; and

b. if you do decide to do business with the group company, it agrees to be legally bound by the terms of your framework agreement as though it had signed it with you directly.

If that doesn't work, you'll need to ask the company you've signed the framework agreement with to take responsibility, contractually, for any acts or omissions of its group companies. This is called a 'parent company guarantee', and provides you with a contracting party that can be held accountable for fulfilling its part of your deal.

Bear in mind, though, that generally speaking companies aren't too keen to give parent company (or sibling company) guarantees. If you're not able to either have a mechanism by which approved group companies sign up to your framework agreement, or get a solvent and stable parent or sibling company to take contractual responsibility for them, you might want to consider declining their kind offer of a group framework.

If you do manage to secure one of these, however, you have indeed done well!

It won't surprise you to know that companies that are part of groups ask for this 'group company' facility to be included in their framework agreements incredibly frequently. One client of mine, a software company in the financial services space, was asked to execute an agreement that included this provision with a member of a global group. In this case, the participation of the other group companies wasn't a theoretical future event; a total of fifteen separate legal entities in different countries, all belonging to the same group, wanted to buy software from my client under the same agreement.

The company's lawyers were rather bemused by my request that they either had to guarantee performance for each of the group companies, or ensure that each group company signed up to the contract individually when it bought software and services from my client.

I was able to explain the contractual challenges of having only one company signed up to the terms of the deal but lots of others able to take advantage of it. In the end, the main customer agreed to accept liability for ensuring that each of the group companies complied with the terms of the deal. It was decided that this was more practical than trying to get fifteen legal entities, speaking ten different languages in ten different legal jurisdictions, to agree to the terms of the same contract!

Lack of clarity about client contributions causes problems

I said at the start of this chapter that sales people traditionally avoid discussions about what they expect from the client. In my experience, they perceive this as something that will put the client off – as a barrier to the sale. While this can be the case if there's too much of it too soon in the process, *not* discussing it will damage the relationship even more.

"So you're *not* doing everything for me?"

If you sell a basic commodity product where you don't need anything from the client except payment, you can skip this section.

For the rest of us, the client needs to make some contribution to the process in order for the product or service to be delivered successfully. Certainly, there are very few complex deliverables that can be implemented by the vendor with no contribution of effort from the client – although some vendors will try to persuade the client otherwise!

So what happens if you've spent the whole of the sales cycle telling the client to "leave it all to us" but when the project starts they discover that you need them to provide you with information, access to systems, infrastructure, third party equipment or software...?

I have a client who sells stock management systems to retailers. When he first approached my company for help, he was experiencing lots of disputes. His customers would be told by the sales person that this system would make their life much easier, greatly reducing the need for manual stocktakes and reordering.

When the software was installed, the customers were dismayed to find that none of their stock items were recognised by the system. Scanning bar codes resulted in an 'item not found' error. The reason for this was that before the system could be used to its fullest, it needed to be populated with details of each stock unit, so that it recognised it when it 'saw' the bar code. In their eagerness not to let anything get in the way of the sale, the sales people neglected to mention this small detail to the client.

The result? Lots of disputes from disgruntled clients who felt that the system just did not work.

If it is necessary for the client to do some work in order to get the full benefit of your product or service, they will find out eventually. You could argue that you'd rather they found out *after* they'd signed your contract, when their money was in your bank account.

As you can see from the example above, this rarely works for long. Resolving disputes with dissatisfied customers is a distraction to the business of selling, costs money and takes time. Not good business at all and entirely avoidable.

When delays on their part result in delays on yours...

Another consequence of not discussing client obligations up front is that you have no remedy if the client doesn't meet them!

So for example, if you need the client to make available a key member of its staff to provide you with information or review your work before you continue with the next stage, what happens if they don't? You could have a team of people waiting to get started on Stage 2, unable to be used for other work, costing you money – and doing nothing because they're waiting for the client.

A software developer client of mine was finalising a contract with his customer, agreeing the payment milestones. Milestone 3 was linked to the delivery of a particular module of the software. During the final negotiation call we were discussing the target dates for each of these milestones. When we got to Milestone 3, the customer said, "Oh, we might have to push that date back because you'll need XYZ to finish that module and I don't think we'll have it ready by then."

Up until that point, we hadn't been aware that there was a client dependency for that milestone. Once we were aware, we discussed how my client would want to deal with any delays on the part of its customer. My client wanted to be sure it would be paid the milestone regardless of any failure to deliver the module, if its failure resulted from the client not delivering XYZ on time.

Fortunately, the customer agreed this was fair – primarily because the customer project manager was absolutely certain he'd have XYZ ready by the new target date – and this provision made it into the contract.

A couple of months later, Milestone 3 had come and gone, and XYZ still wasn't ready. My client was able to invoice anyway. Although they still had to complete the work when XYZ finally materialised, their cash flow wasn't compromised by the customer's delays.

You need to decide, together with the delivery team and finance, what your company would want to happen if the client failed to meet one of its milestones in the contract. It could be that they are still obligated to pay, as in the case above. Or you might specify that the client has to pay extra for the wasted time spent waiting for them to deliver.

Whatever remedy you choose, remember the old saying 'what's sauce for the goose is sauce for the gander'. In other words, don't be too harsh on the client in respect of their delays, or they'll be similarly harsh when it comes to yours!

Picking up the pieces the client has left behind

Your objective, of course, is to have a successful project, regardless of how participative your client is. In practice, this may mean that you find your business performing tasks that should rightly have been done by the client, because you hadn't told the client they needed to be done.

By failing to share with the client what would be needed from them pre-contract, you lose any moral high ground. If the task genuinely needs doing, but the client hasn't scheduled any resources for it and has none available, your project manager may be inclined to just get on with it and do the work so as not to hold up the project.

And what does that mean to your profit margin? By incurring extra costs doing tasks that should have been performed by the client, you'll be eating into your margin, making this a less successful deal than it could have been.

Your client will appreciate this conversation

If you can get past the emotional barrier to engaging the client in a discussion about what you need from them, you will find it a positive experience. As we discussed in chapter 1, these conversations can help to build a stronger relationship and deliver better understanding between you and your client.

It shows you know what you're doing

By setting out the tasks, people, resources and information you'll need from the client in order to complete this project successfully, you are illustrating to the client that you have done this before.

Engaging them in this conversation allows you to share experiences from previous projects, and explain how their participation will add to the success of the project outcome.

It helps the client to plan

If you know you will need two client testers for three days each during the last week of April, the sooner you can let the client know, the more chance they have to plan for it. If necessary, they can schedule other resources to back-fill the day-to-day roles of those who will be pulled out to do the testing. They can manage holiday approvals to ensure the relevant people will be available when you need them.

In many businesses, you'd be lucky to get a resource for three hours, let alone three days, without several weeks of notice. So why leave it until the last minute? Remember that you want to make your client look good; springing resource requirements on them at the eleventh hour will not achieve this.

It builds trust

Think back to the example of our client with the retail management system. How do you think their customers felt when they realised the system they'd paid lots of money for was useless unless they devoted a couple of weeks to populating it with data?

By being up-front about what you need from the client, you immediately establish yourself as a trustworthy and credible supplier. You can also position this as part of your differentiation from your competitors.

Explain to your client that many companies don't share this information until after the contract is signed. If you know that all of your competitors will require a similar level of client involvement, but the others don't talk about it, this can be a way to demonstrate that you really do have higher integrity than others in your market.

EXERCISE 13:

If your business is project-based, talk to your delivery team. What would they typically require from a client in order to make their project successful? Ask them to list their must-haves, would-like-to-haves, and nice-to-haves. If your business is product-based, do this exercise with the relevant category manager. Download the e-workbook from www.dealmakersbook.com to help you complete this exercise.

You can't rely on the client's good intentions

In many vendor-originated contracts, and almost all client-originated contracts, there is very little about obligations on the part of the client. An obligation to pay something, at some stage, is usually included – although even that can be so well caveated in some agreements that you might wonder if you'll ever see the cash!

Why is this the case?

There are a couple of possible reasons for this. Being generous, we could say that our relationship with the client is so good, and their interest in the success of the project is so strong, that we're sure they'll do everything possible to help. So there's no need to write this down in the contract, because the client's own self-interest is sufficient motivation.

Another possibility is that the client-vendor relationship is still (despite lots of marketing spiel and industry noise to the contrary) not based on a true partnership approach. There is still an expectation that the vendor does all the work and the client takes the benefit. This is the case even in many organisations that trumpet their 'partnership' with 'key suppliers'. And, not letting the vendors off the hook, there are many sales organisations that fundamentally mistrust the client and avoid any hint of team working so as to keep the relationship 'clean'.

Now that you understand the importance of the client's contribution to a successful project, you'll appreciate why we don't want to leave this contribution to the discretion of the client themselves.

Defining client obligations

Having explored the ways in which your client can contribute to a successful outcome, you should be in a reasonable position to define their obligations in a measurable way. Remember in chapter 4, when we looked at defining your obligations clearly? Now we need to go through the same process for the client.

It might be that you don't need much from your clients, or it could be that significant involvement from them is essential. Think about the following as potential candidates for inclusion (tweaked to reflect the specifics of your industry and the project):

- Access to premises/sites at agreed times and dates

- Access to certain computer systems or infrastructure

- Provision of information about client systems, operations, or other matters

- Access and interfaces to third party systems, with approval from the relevant third party if necessary

- Timely reviews and approval of documents produced, or work done by you

- Access to key staff

- Provision of administrative resources

- Provision of testing resources

- Supply of any client deliverables (whether free-issued products or materials, reports, information, etc.) in accordance with the agreed timetable or project plan

- A safe working environment for your staff while they're on site

- An escalation path in the event of disagreements about any part of the project or contract

This list is just a starting point but it gives you an idea of the sort of things you should be considering. Once you and the delivery team have agreed what they need from the client in order to deliver a successful project, your legal or contractual support can put this into nice clear drafting for inclusion in your contract.

Assessing the impact of the client's failure to perform

It may be possible to generalise about the impact of the client's failure to meet any of the obligations you've specified for them. You could decide that any failure or delay on their part will automatically lead to an equivalent delay on your part.

Alternatively, you might well be able to work around some delays to a certain extent, to give the client some leeway.

For each of the client obligations you've specified, think about what would happen if the client failed to perform as described. So if you were unable to speak to a key member of the client team for a week after the planned meeting date, how would that affect your own delivery team?

Determining fair and appropriate remedies

When you have an idea of the consequences of failure to perform on the client's part, you can think about sensible ways to deal with them.

Failures that mean your staff are sitting around for a period of time, unable to continue with their work on the project but also unable to be allocated anywhere else, might give rise to a claim for your costs for their wasted time. If this is the case, you could consider making those staff available to the client during the wasted time; if they're paying for the time anyway, they might have a way to use it that you hadn't spotted. Offering this can take the edge off an otherwise potentially confrontational request for payment for 'waiting time'.

Failures that result in delays to your programme could be addressed by extending your own deadlines accordingly. This is particularly important if the client has imposed any liquidated damages or penalties on your late delivery (see chapter 8 for details of how these work).

If the client fails to supply resources that they were supposed to, do you want to be able to procure these yourself and add the cost to your bill? Is that reasonable?

When you consider the remedies you'd like to impose on the client, remember that anything you ask of them is likely to be asked of you in return. While reciprocity is not always appropriate in a contract, as each party has different risks and obligations, it can be difficult to argue why a particular remedy is suitable if they are late, but not if you are late. So bear this in mind if you're ever tempted to request particularly severe remedies.

This is something I have to remind our customers of on a regular basis. They often begin with no contractual obligations for their own clients, but once they 'get' the value of specifying these they get quite carried away. This is fine, but can spill over into a desire to impose draconian penalties on the client for any slip or delay. I have to remind them that they shouldn't ask for anything they wouldn't be prepared to accept themselves, as you can guarantee that, if you do, you'll have some uncomfortable conversations to look forward to!

Chapter 5: Quick Summary

- A successful project needs the client to contribute too

- Before you start, be clear about which entity is your legal 'client'

- Group company framework agreements can be a great way to extend your sales reach, but you need to be careful that each buying entity is bound by your terms

- If you don't mention the client's obligations until the last minute, you can't blame them for failing to perform

- Client delays regularly contribute to projects being late and over budget

- By setting out the client's obligations in the contract, you can manage their performance and increase the chances of success

- Clients like to see that you know what's involved in delivering your project, and what you will need from them

- While you might be happy to trust the client to do what's required without getting it in writing, this isn't always effective

- As well as defining their obligations, you need to think about fair remedies if they don't perform

- Make sure these are reasonable, as the client may ask for the same to apply to you if you're late in delivering

6

If you want your commission, help your company get paid!

I am assuming here that you're on a salary package that contains some level of performance-related bonus payment. This might be in the form of a sales commission, or it could be some level of business unit or whole company profit share, or any other sort of performance metric dreamed up by your employer to motivate you to deliver the results it wants.

You might even have a clawback provision in your compensation plan, enabling your employer to recoup commission it has already paid you if the deal goes sour and the client cancels early or fails to pay.

Even if that's not the case, securing payment for the business is still an important part of your job. Yes, you'll have accounts receivable staff to generate invoices and chase payment. But in the same way that you need to make sure your company's deliverables are clearly defined even though you won't be personally responsible for delivering them, you have a great opportunity during the sales and negotiation process to establish a framework that will help your business get paid.

Linking your personal success to the company's

Most reasonably mature businesses understand that if they want to increase orders across the board, they should reward their sales staff for generating any orders. And if they want to promote a particular product over all others, rewarding you more for a sale of that product than for another one with a comparable sales cycle will help achieve that objective.

Unfortunately, even in this age of multiple sales methodologies and complex, spread sheet-driven compensation plans, many companies still get this wrong. They reward the wrong things and accidentally de-motivate staff who want to work hard and be successful. We're going to assume that you work for one of the smarter organisations that understands how to do this well. If you don't, perhaps now's a good time to be practising your influencing skills internally to bring about change – or alternatively, polishing up your CV!

Commission on order

If you're fortunate enough to be paid your commission when your company receives an order, make sure you're clear about exactly what constitutes an order. Is it a signed contract? A client purchase order referencing your terms and conditions? Any purchase order? A purchase order that's been accepted by your company?

Refer back to chapter 2 for a refresher on how a contract is made, and the 'Battle of the Forms' challenges of purchase orders. Are you comfortable that you have all the tools you need to meet whatever criteria 'an order' has to meet before you get paid your commission?

Commission on invoice raised

Raising invoices is usually associated with the achievement of some form of milestone. It may be simply time-related ('Invoices will be issued monthly in arrears') or it may be associated with having delivered something, or achieved particular outcomes.

Check back to chapter 4 to remind yourself about how acceptance works, as this can often be a trigger for invoicing. Are you happy that you've put everything in place to help acceptance happen on time?

Commission on invoice paid

While raising an invoice is more or less in your company's control (as it could raise an invoice even if the relevant milestone hadn't been met), paying it is in the hands of the client.

To increase chances of getting paid, it is obviously a good idea not to raise an invoice until you've met the agreed criteria for doing so. Otherwise it will simply annoy your client and sit on the back of the desk until the relevant criteria are met.

We'll look at other ways you can improve your chances of getting paid on time later in this chapter.

Commission on revenue recognised

This is a tough one, and we're not going to go into revenue recognition rules in detail here. They tend to vary across countries and accounting practices, and may be stricter if you work for a US-owned entity than for a UK-owned one. The dreaded Sarbanes Oxley (Google it!) has a lot to answer for, with the result that revenue recognition rules have become significantly more labyrinthine in the last decade.

In case you're not familiar with the phrase, 'revenue recognition' is what happens when a company records cash received as 'revenue' in its accounts. This usually occurs when you've done the work, or delivered the product, in respect of which the money has been paid.

So if, for example, you ordered 50 widgets from me and I asked you to pay for them all up-front at £10 each but only delivered 10 a month, I would start the contract with £500 of your cash in my bank account. But I'd only be able to 'recognise' £100 a month of that as revenue in my accounts, when I'd delivered the corresponding 10 widgets. On this basis, it would take me five months to recognise all of the £500 I'd received from you as 'revenue'.

As a very rough generalisation, revenue from sales of products or services tends to be recognised when the products or services concerned have been delivered. If the client is entitled to accept or reject the products or services based on some agreed criteria, the revenue recognition would be delayed until there was no longer any possibility of the products or services being rejected.

In many companies, services such as support and maintenance will be invoiced and payable annually in advance, but the revenue from them will only be recognised in $1/12^{th}$ portions, each month.

If your company uses revenue recognised as the criterion for determining payment of commission, it is essential that you understand the revenue recognition rules as they relate to the products or services you sell. And if you're ever considering a fancy deal structure involving unusual payment mechanisms, or strange conditions, make sure you run it past finance to understand properly the impact of the structure on your ability to recognise the revenue.

Commission on profit delivered

This is the most sophisticated and mature mechanism for calculating commission, as it's based on the successful delivery of the deal within budget rather than just its signature. It can dissuade sales people, very effectively, from pushing the product specialists or the delivery team to sign up for something they can't deliver.

However, many sales people are understandably reluctant to have more than a small portion of their income based on bottom-line profit delivered as so much of it is outside their control. If you've followed the steps set out in this book, and engaged effectively with your product marketing or project delivery teams and with your client, you will have done everything you can to facilitate a successful and profitable outcome.

EXERCISE 14:

Consider each of the following outline compensation plans. For each one, how can you use the contract to help you receive your commission as soon as possible? Download the e-workbook from www.dealmakersbook.com to help you complete this exercise.

1. Commission = 5% of order value excluding VAT, payable on order acceptance.

2. Commission = 10% of revenue recognised, payable at the end of the quarter in which revenue recognition occurs.

3. Commission = 12% of gross profit on the project, payable within 30 days of the final project milestone being met and paid for.

Define clear invoicing milestones

Considering how important invoicing is to a business, it's astonishing how many companies fail to define clear invoicing milestones in their contracts. The last thing you want, having merrily raised an invoice, is for the client to dispute it because they simply disagree that the relevant milestone has been achieved.

Linking invoices to achievements

If your invoicing milestones are simply time-related (for example, '50% of the price will be invoiced on receipt of order, with the remaining 50% being invoiced 30 days later'), they carry no obligation on your company to perform.

So you could be issuing invoices without ever having delivered anything at all. While this might be perfectly reasonable in the context of the particular deal you're doing, in many cases it makes sense, and inspires client confidence, if you link them to your achievements.

Examples of milestone achievements to which invoices can be linked include:

- Delivery of specific products/services

- Acceptance of such products/services

- Acceptance of the whole project

- Delivery of a specification or other 'milestone' deliverable

- Achieving an agreed objective

It is important that any drafting in your contract, statement of work, order or other contract document (see chapter 2) relating to invoicing milestones should be clear and unambiguous. If in doubt, ask your legal or contracts person to read it through and make sure there is only one possible way to interpret it!

Milestones must be objectively measurable

Any milestones you set out in your invoicing schedule must be objectively measurable. That is, there must be no element of subjective assessment in determining whether or not the milestone has been met.

What do I mean by this? Consider the following:

'Invoice 2 may be issued when the Services have been delivered to the Client's reasonable satisfaction.'

Is that objectively measurable? How do we know what level of service delivery is likely to make the client 'satisfied'? How do we decide whether the client is being 'reasonable' if they say they are not satisfied?

This largely comes back to the same considerations we examined in chapter 4 when we looked at the concept of 'acceptance'. The only difference is that, in this case, they may not be spelt out as 'acceptance criteria' and so may not attract the same level of attention during reviews and negotiations. You need to review all of your invoicing milestones and make sure that they meet the same high standards of objectivity and measurability that we've set for acceptance criteria, to increase your chances of getting paid on time.

Backstop dates

In the same way that we looked at 'deemed acceptance' in chapter 4, to cover us for situations where the client's failure to accept our products or services was not due to any fault of ours, so we can use backstop dates for the same purpose in our invoicing milestones.

So we might say, for example:

'Invoice 2 may be issued on the earlier of:

(a) the release by the Client of a signed Acceptance Certificate; or

(b) 30 days from the date of delivery of the Goods if no Rejection Notice has been received.'

EXERCISE 15:

Re-write each of these invoicing milestones to make them clear and objectively measurable:

1. Supplier may invoice 10% of the services fee at the start of the contract.

2. Invoicing milestone 1 shall occur on acceptance of the Goods.

3. We may invoice You for the services monthly in arrears.

4. Vendor shall issue its invoice for the Products when the Client is reasonably satisfied that the Products meet its requirements.

(Clue: for some of these, giving a clear definition of some of the words used will do the trick!) Download the e-workbook from www.dealmakersbook.com to help you complete this exercise.

Define clear payment terms

Invoicing and payment are not synonymous.

I just thought I'd put that out there in case you're wondering why, having gone through the detail of invoicing terms, there's now another section all about payment.

Your invoicing milestones, or invoicing schedule, state when you may raise an invoice for a certain sum. The payment terms, by contrast, state when the client actually has to pay each invoice. The two things rarely happen at the same time.

It takes time

Why is it so unusual to be paid immediately upon receipt of an invoice? Simply because in most organisations, particularly big ones, it takes time to navigate their payment processes.

Invoices may have to be approved, entered into various systems, scheduled for payment, and then paid.

There is also a less practical, but more common, reason for long payment terms. This is simply that the client wants to hold on to their cash for as long as possible before paying you.

Some clients, particularly very large and powerful ones, will try to persuade you that they 'are not able' to agree payment terms shorter than, say, 120 days or 90 days because 'that's how long it takes our accounts system'.

While a little bit of time is understandable to allow the practicalities of approval and payment to be dealt with, no organisation should need 90 days to pay an invoice. If you encounter this sort of argument from your client, ask them how long they get to pay their electricity supplier. Or their telephony supplier. Or their business rates. I suspect it's rather less than 90 days – in which case, they've shown that it is *possible* for them to pay quicker, even if they don't particularly want to!

Say exactly what you mean

When defining payment terms, it is tempting to use phrases that sound impressive that we might have encountered on other companies' invoices in the past, even if we're not entirely sure what they mean.

A good example of this is the phrase '30 days net'. At a contract drafting workshop recently, I asked a room full of commercial managers when they would expect to get paid if their payment terms stated:

'Our payment terms are strictly 30 days net'.

I received the following responses:

1. *We'd get paid within 30 days of the date on the invoice.*

2. *We'd get paid within 30 days of the date the client receives the invoice.*

3. *We'd get paid 30 days from the end of the month in which the client receives the invoice.*

4. *We'd get paid 30 days from the end of the month in which the invoice is issued.*

5. *We'd get paid at the end of the month following the month in which the client receives the invoice.*

6. *We'd get paid at the end of the month following the month in which the invoice is issued.*

If you issued your invoice on the first day of the month, these different interpretations could variously mean that you'll be paid within 30 days, 60 days or even up to 65 days.

Which is correct?

The answer to the question is that any of them could be reasonably justified – so they are all equally correct, and equally wrong. There is no standard legal interpretation of the phrase '30 days net'.

Hopefully that will be enough to deter you from trying to use shorthand on this most important of topics. Instead, say exactly what you mean. If you expect to be paid within 30 days of the date of your invoice, say so. If you're happy to be paid at the end of the month following the month in which your client receives your invoice, then say that. But don't use cryptic phrases in the hope that your client will have the same understanding of them that you do.

Think about the best place to specify payment terms

Where do you put your payment terms?

They could go in your main contract, signed by the client. They could appear in your proposal. They may be in your schedule, statement of work, or other scoping document. Any of these can work, according to the particular contracting structure you've chosen, provided you've followed the rules for contract formation set out in chapter 2.

The one place you shouldn't put payment terms you intend to rely on is on your invoice.

That's not to say you shouldn't refer to, or even duplicate, your payment terms on the invoice itself. It can be a useful reminder to your client's accounts payable team (who may never have seen the contract) that you expect to be paid within 30 days of the date on the invoice. But you should not leave payment terms out of your contract/statement of work/etc. on the basis that you always state them on your invoice.

Why not? What's wrong with defining payment terms on an invoice?

If you go back to the discussion of the 'battle of the forms' in chapter 2, you'll remember that anything that 'crosses the line' after the contract is officially formed is not binding on the other party, and does not make up part of the contract. By the time you send your invoice, you have usually already delivered something to the client or formed the contract in some other way. If this is the case, the payment terms on your invoice will have no legal effect whatsoever and the client will be entitled to ignore them.

So if you've stated your payment terms in your main contract, you can repeat them on the invoice for convenience. Of course, it's important to make sure that the two are consistent if you want to avoid creating confusion that can be exploited by the client to delay payment. But ultimately, the contract should contain the main statement of payment terms.

What about situations where you have different payment terms for different invoices?

It's possible, particularly in a big deal, that you might have some invoices that must be paid sooner than others. For example, there might be an initial invoice that is due to be paid upon signature of the contract before you'll start work.

The best way to deal with this is to state the default payment terms in the main contract, with a caveat allowing any different payment terms expressly set out in the schedule or statement of work to take precedence. This protects you in the event that you forget to specify payment terms in the schedule, but gives you the flexibility to define different terms for different projects and/or different invoicing milestones.

You do need to be really careful about having different payment terms stated in different places, though, and to ensure this only happens by design and not by accident. When you review multi-part contracts (containing schedules or statements of work) it's very common to encounter different payment terms in the main agreement and the schedules. While this is fine if the contract clearly states which takes precedence, it can create significant potential for disputes if no order of precedence is stated. Or, worse still, if the contract states that it 'trumps' any terms in the schedule/SoW.

This is a particular problem because it'll be the schedule that your operational client will be interested in, and will expect to take precedence. If you've negotiated (and documented in the schedule) 60-day payment terms for a particular piece of work, but your contract states that payment terms are 30 days, you will find yourself in between your client and your organisation and trying to mediate between the two.

Make sure your company gets paid!

So now you've agreed some clear, unambiguous payment milestones and set out the invoicing and payment terms that will relate to them. That means you'll issue your invoices at the right time and your client (being a decent sort) will pay promptly in accordance with the agreed terms, and everything will tick along nicely.

OK, when you've stopped rolling around laughing at my breathtaking naivety, we can get back to reality.

Make friends with 'Mavis'

What actually happens, of course, is that your invoice disappears into a corporate 'black hole', never to be seen again. When the fortunate individual assigned the task of credit control calls up to find out when it will be paid, the first response is generally, "Invoice? What invoice?"

When you've emailed/faxed/hand-delivered it for the third time and the nice accounts payable person finally has no option but to admit they have received it, the game gets more interesting.

At this point I shall pause to introduce you to 'Mavis'. Mavis represents the world of accounts payable. She's a lovely person who's very good at her job – which is holding on to the company's cash as long as possible, and using every available opportunity to delay parting with it.

It's important that you remember what a lovely person Mavis is, because she is going to be your friend. If you have any opportunity during the sales process to ask, "Who arranges payment of our invoices? Who should we talk to if there are any issues?" – please do. And if you can manage a personal introduction, that would be even better.

With very large corporate clients, Mavis may become a gestalt entity made up of many individual accounts payable people. If you can befriend one or more to the extent that they know you by name, you're increasing your chances of timely payment significantly.

Why? Because it's much more difficult to lie to someone if you've actually met them, or have some sort of relationship with them. Not that Mavis would ever *lie* exactly... but telling you that "You're on the next payment run" is all part of the tools of her trade which, as you'll remember, is keeping hold of the company's money for as long as possible.

Understand their payment process

You might find when you're discussing invoicing and payment terms with your client that they specify a long list of criteria that must be met by each invoice in order for it to be paid.

There are two ways of looking at this: (i) it's dreadful – they're creating opportunities to avoid paying you, or (ii) at least they're *telling* you about all the opportunities they'll have to avoid paying you.

In many cases, the client doesn't volunteer this information but leaves you to discover it through a long and painful game of '20 questions'. This is what happens when you ask Mavis why your invoice is not paid. She explains that you had not included the order number so it could not be processed. You fix this, reissue, and wait. Still no payment. Mavis? Kindly, she explains that now she has the order number she can see that although your invoice was sent directly to her office in London, it should have been sent to the Birmingham office first for approval and then forwarded to London for payment.

And so on. If you've been able to identify and make friends with Mavis before invoicing, you will be able to ask her *exactly* how their payment process works. You can clarify the precise form of paperwork required, to whom copies should be sent for approval, which particular reference numbers must be included – all of those little details that will help you to get paid on time. In many cases, this won't have come up during your negotiations because the person you're negotiating with simply has no idea how this stuff works. Your client relies on Mavis to sort this out, and doesn't bother him or herself with the details. So you need to bypass the client and make direct contact with Mavis to ensure you have all the information you need, to get it right first time.

EXERCISE 16:

For your most recently won client, write out their approval and payment process, specifying all the information you are supposed to put on an invoice and the various steps required for payment. Check what was on your last invoice to them – do the two match? Download the e-workbook from www.dealmakersbook.com to help you complete this exercise.

Invoice accurately

Of course, all this information has to be shared with whoever raises invoices in your organisation. They need to know all of the details that must be set out on the invoice in order for Mavis to pay you.

Depending on the size and sophistication of your organisation, this may be automated in some way; your invoicing person may be intimately familiar with your contract and its terms, or they may simply put whatever information you give them into the accounting system so that it is included verbatim on the invoice.

If you want to make sure your company is paid on time, invest a little effort in finding out how this works at your place. Ensure that you provide all of the information in a timely manner, that all details are accurate, and that you are certain the relevant invoicing milestones have been met (and can be objectively proven to be met).

Give yourself tools to address late payments

There will be times when, despite your best efforts, the client simply does not pay. If you've done everything in this chapter, the reasons for non-payment will be nothing to do with you. They could be down to cash flow issues, or simply a very highly motivated Mavis who does not see any benefit to her organisation in paying you.

For this reason, we need to ensure your contract contains some remedies to give you leverage in the event of late payment.

Charging interest

Including a contractual right to charge interest on late-paid sums is reasonable and sensible. In the UK and many other jurisdictions, you even have a statutory right to do so.

There are two issues with charging interest, however. The first is 'how much?' Particularly when bank interest rates are low, it seems rude to specify the 8% above base rate permitted by the UK's Late Payment of Commercial Debts (Interest) Act 1998. The second is 'why bother, when I know we'll never charge it anyway?'

Let's address the rate first. If the money doesn't arrive on time, your company may need to borrow cash to cover your payroll for the staff working on that client project (or your suppliers for the parts and materials used in manufacturing those products, or rent and rates...).

Depending on the amount of the loan required, the size and credit rating of your business, and the willingness of its directors and/or shareholders to provide personal guarantees, you may or may not find that you are able to borrow this amount on a short-term basis. The cost of setting up such borrowing, in terms of the time spent by your business researching, applying for and securing such a loan, may be significant. And the interest rate secured will depend on all of those factors and is likely to be significantly higher than 8% above base rate.

So next time your client says that 8% above base rate is ridiculous, and the most they'll agree to as interest for late payments is 2% above base, you have a straightforward response. "If you'd be prepared to lend to me at 2% above base rate, that would be wonderful. No? Well why should I lend to you at such a rate when the cost of short-term credit to me is much higher?"

Now what about the fact that your company has never, as long as you can remember, charged interest to anybody? It makes all this arguing about rates seem rather a waste of time and goodwill. And let's face it, goodwill is important – the last thing we want to do is to upset our hard-won client.

At this stage, I want you to think back to Mavis. How often does Mavis speak with your client (i.e. the individual who chose to buy from you) in person? Probably never. Maybe occasionally if you haven't followed the process and she needs to check you've met the relevant invoicing criteria before putting your invoice in the queue for payment. It is very unlikely that she chats with your client on a day-to-day basis, complaining about your persistent efforts to be paid.

Does Mavis believe that your legitimate quest for payment, in accordance with the terms of your contract and her detailed specifications for invoicing, is unreasonable? If she's a professional, Mavis knows full well that her company should pay your invoice. She doesn't hold this against you personally – it's a sad fact of business life that occasionally she has to part with the company's cash in order to stay in business.

No, Mavis knows she should pay your invoice. But she also knows that she's rewarded by her company for paying at the last possible minute, ensuring that the money stays in her account for as long as possible. Until the discomfort of not paying outweighs the discomfort of paying, she will continue with delaying tactics.

The easiest and least adversarial way of imposing discomfort on Mavis directly is to threaten to issue an invoice for interest if payment is not received in full within five business days. Receiving an invoice that is not covered by an existing purchase order really upsets Mavis's day, and often just the threat of it will motivate her to pay up. If not, get your business to issue that invoice – promptly, exactly when you said you would.

If calculation of the interest is an issue, check out the www.payontime. co.uk website, which contains a nifty interest calculator.

This does the trick so often, and with so little dent in relationships between the parties, that it really is worth trying the very first time a new client is late. Think of it as a training exercise – you've put lots of effort into being the best supplier you can be. Now you're going to help them be a good client.

Suspending delivery

Many companies think they have an automatic right to suspend delivery under a contract if the client owes them money. Their (entirely logical) view is that if they haven't been paid for the services or products they've delivered already, why should they deliver any more and increase their exposure?

While this makes perfect sense from a business perspective, it is not automatically the case under your contract.

If you have an obligation under your contract to deliver products or services on an ongoing basis, and you stop doing this because your client is in breach of its payment obligations, you may find that you then become in breach of the contract by your failure to deliver. Worse still, the damage that your client will suffer because you cut off their supply of your products or services may be far greater than the damage you suffer as a result of their late payment. So you could be in big trouble even though it was the client's failure to pay that triggered your action.

So contractually speaking, as in the playground, two wrongs don't make a right.

To ensure that you're entitled to suspend delivery in response to late payments, you need to add an express clause to this effect in your contract. Your lawyer or contracts specialist will be able to draft something appropriate, but it is essential that it's spelt out clearly in the contract as a remedy for late payment. Otherwise, by putting a client account 'on stop' or 'on hold', you could expose your own company to claims for damages.

On the plus side, suspending delivery when you have the contractual right to do so can be a very effective (although rather adversarial) way of motivating a client to pay up.

Retention of title

If you deliver physical products, you might want to consider retaining title in those products until the client has paid for them in full. 'Title' is the legal word for 'ownership', so this means that even though the goods might have been delivered to the client, and be on their site, they still belong to you until they've been paid for.

A properly drafted 'retention of title' clause will enable you to enter the client's premises and take back unpaid-for items if payment is delayed. While this is a rather aggressive approach and not to be undertaken lightly, it can be useful if your client becomes insolvent before they've paid you. Rather than becoming one of a number of unsecured creditors, you can reclaim your goods and potentially resell or re-work them, thus regaining some of your lost revenue.

I have a client that sells electronic equipment to restaurants, retailers and other businesses, for use at the point of sale. One of their customers, a national retailer, recently went into administration having taken delivery of over £90,000 worth of equipment that had not been paid for.

The retention of title provision in their contract helped my client to secure the co-operation of the administrator and reach a deal regarding payment and return of the units. Without this, my client would have been an unsecured creditor and would have been lucky to receive £5,000 of the £90,000 it was owed.

Chapter 6: Quick Summary

- If you want to receive your commission, you have to help the business to get paid first

- Different commission structures might encourage different invoicing and payment profiles

- Setting out a clear invoicing structure, with invoices linked to objectively measurable milestone achievements, works well

- If client action is required to achieve a milestone (such as taking a system 'live'), use a backstop date to ensure you get paid even if they're delayed

- Invoicing and payment are not synonymous – you should define each one separately

- While it does take time to process invoices and arrange payment, nobody should need 90 days to do this

- Don't use 'short cut' language to define payment terms – 'net 30 days' has no agreed legal meaning

- If you don't mention your payment terms until you issue your invoice, they won't be binding on the client as the contract is already formed

- Your buyer may not be familiar with the details of their own payment processes, so make friends with 'Mavis'

- Be really clear about what Mavis needs to pay you on time, and make sure your invoices contain everything she needs

- If the client is late in paying, you should have clear late payment remedies specified, and be prepared to use them

7

The way you deal with problems shows your true mettle

There is a saying that your clients' opinion of you is not governed by whether or not you ever make mistakes but by how you deal with mistakes when they arise.

While most clients would prefer you never to get anything wrong, it's accepted that, as human beings, we are bound to get it wrong occasionally. So let's make sure we've thought through the different areas where errors might arise, and how we are going to deal with them.

Warranties – addressing delivery problems

Most contracts will have a section about warranties in them somewhere. If they are client-originated, this is likely to be a long section! But what exactly is a warranty?

Warranties are special

In the consumer world, we tend to think of a warranty as a form of guarantee that the product we've purchased will perform as intended for a certain amount of time. The vendor or manufacturer might offer us the right to repair or replacement of the product at no cost if it fails within the warranty period. We see the guarantee as being a benefit to us as consumers.

In business-to-business contracts, there is no standard meaning of 'guarantee' that matches this expectation. A warranty, rather than meaning, by default, a 'guarantee' of product quality, is simply another category of contract term with its own special characteristics. To explain this properly, we need to delve into some contract law terminology, so this might be a good time to stock up on tea and biscuits.

Contract terms fall into one of a number of categories:

- Term

- Condition

- Warranty

A 'term' of a contract can refer to any provision of the contract. Over the years, the law has evolved to categorise different terms according to the effect that their breach would have, and the rights it would grant to the non-breaching party.

There are some terms that are so fundamental to the purpose of the agreement that if they are breached, the contract can't continue. These are described as 'conditions', because the performance of the contract is *conditional* upon those terms being fulfilled. Breach of a condition would entitle the non-breaching party to terminate the contract.

'Warranties' relate to terms that, if breached, could possibly be remedied, allowing you and the client to continue with the contract as before. The remedy might involve a practical resolution for the breach (such as a repair or replacement of the product, or re-performance of the services), and may also involve the payment of some form of compensation to the client.

From a legal perspective, the key distinction between warranties and conditions is that while a breach of condition enables the client to terminate your contract and to claim damages, a breach of warranty entitles them to damages only.

Excluding statutory warranties

In English law there are a number of statutory warranties that automatically apply to the sale of goods and services. These include a warranty that goods will be of 'satisfactory quality' and that they will be 'fit for purpose'.

If you're selling to consumers, you can't do anything about these statutory warranties. They form part of the consumer's statutory rights, and nothing you attempt to do in your contract to override or remove them will have any legal effect.

In business-to-business contracts, though, you are allowed to exclude these statutory warranties.

Why would you want to exclude statutory warranties?

The main reason for excluding them is so as to replace them with express (i.e. explicitly set out in the contract) warranties that are clear and unambiguous.

Consider the first of the statutory warranties identified above – that the goods are of 'satisfactory quality'. What does 'satisfactory' mean? Would you be 'satisfied' with the quality of the chair you're sitting on right now if you'd paid £10 for it? Probably. What if you'd paid £1,000 for it? Would you still think its quality was 'satisfactory'?

Instead of leaving the client's 'satisfaction' to chance, it's much better to specify exactly what they'll get for their money. This takes us back to the specification again (good old chapter 4); if we warrant that the products or services will comply with their specification, then both we and the client know exactly what that means. And equally, it'll be clear when we've failed to meet it.

On the services side, we might also agree to warrant that not only will we deliver in accordance with the specification or statement of work, but that we'll use staff with qualifications and experience that are appropriate for the work they'll be doing, and that those staff will perform their tasks with care.

Provide meaningful remedies

What happens if you provide a warranty but don't say what you'll do if you breach it?

The default position would be that the client would be entitled to claim damages from you. These would be assessed as being the difference in value between the product or service they should have received if the warranty had been true, and the one they actually received in practice. There might be an extra element of damages if the client has suffered tangible negative consequences of your breach of warranty.

The problem with this is that they'd have to bring a claim against you in order to benefit from this remedy. You might agree to settle out of court, but this is generally a messy and expensive way to deal with your problems.

Instead, talk to your delivery and support team about what would be a sensible way to put things right if you'd breached a particular warranty. Would it make sense to replace the product with a new one? Or repair it? If so, how will that work in practice?

In chapter 1 we looked at an example where you installed your products at the client's offshore oil platform. We considered whether, under the warranty, it should be your responsibility to go to site and fix problems/replace units, or the client's responsibility to ship faulty units back to you for repair.

In the context of your product or service, define what you're willing to offer your client as a fair and sensible remedy for a warranty breach. Remember that they'll only be claiming on this if you've failed to hold up your end of the bargain. So don't be too aggressive in limiting the scope of available remedies, or you might make a court decide that you've not actually given the client any real remedy at all. If this is the case, they may reject your warranty limits and exclusions as being unreasonable, leaving you at the mercy of the statutory warranties after all.

It is also worth considering what would happen if you were not able to fix the warranty breach, or if fixing it would cost so much money that it's not economical to do so.

In ongoing services contracts and outsourcing agreements, clients frequently request 'step in rights'. This entitles them, if you're not able to fix a warranty breach in a specified period of time, to step in and either perform the services themselves or (more frequently) to get another supplier to do so and send you the bill. From a vendor perspective this is obviously very undesirable, as you could find yourself paying your competitor to do your job. From a client's view, though, it gives them a way forward rather than just spending more time and money working with you when it appears to them that you'll never be able to deliver what you promised.

On the plus side, it's very unusual for a client to exercise its 'step in rights'. But this is a hefty remedy to make available, and should really only be offered as a last resort.

When we talk about the cost of warranty remedies to us as a provider, we also need to consider how likely it is that we'll be called upon to spend this money and deliver the remedy.

One of my clients, a supplier of high-end office furniture, told me a tale about a deal they'd lost to a competitor because of the competitor's wily use of warranties.

The furniture our client makes is of fantastic quality, and uses the very best timber, fabric and other materials. It lasts for years (I know, because I have some in my company's office that I bought when we were in Devant's first ever business premises, and it still looks great!). This means that it's very rare for a client ever to bring a claim under warranty.

Because it's very smart (and quite expensive) furniture, the majority of their customers are large prestigious companies who generally re-style and re-decorate their corporate premises every five years or so. This means that the furniture is rarely in use for longer than five to seven years before it's sold on the second-hand market. All of these things are also true of their main competitor.

When my client tendered for a large contract, they offered an excellent 10-year warranty on manufacture and materials, with a shorter warranty on moving parts (chair castors, etc.). They were confident that they stood a good chance of success as their products, while equivalent in quality to their nearest rival's, were less expensive. Imagine how devastated they were to learn that they'd lost to the competitor – on price!

When asked, the customer explained that the other company's products had a lower 'total cost of ownership' which resulted in them winning the business. It transpired that the other company, realising that their clients never actually used their products for more than five to seven years anyway, decided that there was no appreciable cost or risk to them of extending their warranty period to 15 years.

As a result, the customer was able to take the competitor's (higher) total cost figure and rather than dividing it by the 10-year period offered by our client for their warranty to get the 'cost per year' figure, they could divide it by 15. So simply by extending the warranty from 10 years to 15 years, the competitor had reduced the 'cost per year' of their products by about 17%.

Addressing problems with scope

As we saw in chapter 4, disputes around the scope of work are the most common category of all. While all the effort you've put into making sure your scope is clearly documented will undoubtedly reduce the chances of these disputes arising, we have to accept that even in the best-managed projects, differences of opinion still arise from time to time.

You are also likely to receive requests from the client for changes to that original scope, particularly if your contract is to be delivered over a long time. Business needs change, available materials and tools change, and it is inevitable that this will impact you if you have a long-term relationship with a client.

In this case, you can choose to see changes in scope as a 'problem' or as an 'opportunity'. Some organisations make most of their profit through dealing with changes, while others lose most of theirs in the same way.

Having a clear process for dealing with change is essential to maintaining good relations with your client and to keeping hold of your margin.

Change or clarification?

The first issue to determine is whether something the client is requesting is a change (i.e. billable) or a clarification (i.e. included within your price). Your work in chapter 4 will pay dividends here.

If your original scope of work or specification was very high level, and what the client is requesting relates to the precise way in which a requirement in the original spec is going to be implemented, the client could feel that their request is simply clarifying what was in the spec. For example, if the spec states 'this machine will make a variety of hot drinks', and the client then asks for these hot drinks to include coffee, tea and hot chocolate, they could (not unreasonably) claim that this was just a clarification of the original requirement.

From your perspective, you may have a machine that makes coffee and tea, but not hot chocolate. You felt that the provision of coffee and tea adequately met the 'variety of hot drinks' requirement and were therefore confident in marking your solution as being 'compliant' with this requirement. In this situation, the discussion could go either way; if you had only ever shown the client a tea- and coffee-making machine, and they had indicated that this was perfectly acceptable, you could use this to substantiate your position. Similarly, if the client had made a point about telling you how much their staff love hot chocolate, and how much they're looking forward to having it at the touch of a button, this would substantiate theirs.

So as you can see, much of the key to avoiding conflict here is to get the outputs from chapter 4 right before you start.

Control or flexibility?

Different companies have different approaches to managing change. When I ran a workshop for IACCM with around 50 commercial managers from blue-chip organisations, the group discussed the approaches to change management employed by their various companies. I was amazed at the range of approaches used.

At one end were the control-oriented companies. In these organisations, before any change was implemented the following process would occur:

- Register the change request

- Conduct change analysis, examining the risk, cost, impact on timelines and on other areas of the project of the change

- Confirm that the change is actually a change to the specification, rather than a clarification

- Prepare a proposal for the client, setting out the price of the change and relevant information from the change analysis

- The client seeks increased budget to cover the change, and raises a PO

- When a purchase order for the change has been received, schedule and carry out the change

The advantage of this approach is that both parties always know exactly where they stand. Changes are fed into the project in a well-managed and monitored way, the vendor is paid appropriately, and the client can keep track of what's going on.

The main disadvantage of this approach is that it can slow things down. If you have a fast-moving project with relatively short timescales, working through all this paperwork can have a big impact on progress. It also adds cost, since someone has to complete the analysis, create the proposal and review and approve both documents.

At the opposite end of the spectrum were the 'just get on with it and worry about who pays later' companies. Their approach to managing change in high-pressure, time-limited projects was that the parties should just focus on getting the job done rather than worrying about approvals, specifications for changes, etc. They would then do a review at the end of the project and see who owed what to whom.

The advantages of this approach are clear: it's quick, it's non-contentious (at least during the project itself!) and no time is wasted creating proposals.

The disadvantages, however, are equally obvious. If the parties are not well-aligned in their understanding of what's in and out of scope, there's the potential for the vendor to come off very badly indeed. By the time the 'totting up' takes place, the client will already have received the benefit of all the changes, but the vendor won't have been paid for them. While the vendor will have some concrete figures for the actual cost of delivering the change, as opposed to forecast costs, if the client decides that the change should have been within the original scope, and its omission was the fault of the vendor, you can see how disputes could arise.

If there is still an ongoing relationship between the vendor and the client (for example, for support and maintenance), this could temper any inclination of the client to reject claims for changes that have been performed. Otherwise, it's hard to imagine that the client would be very highly motivated to volunteer to pay for a great deal of these changes at the end of the project, given that they have little to gain by doing so.

The right approach may well lie somewhere in between. One company used a 'change bucket'. They agreed the fixed fee for the work both parties knew for sure was required at the start of the project, and then agreed a 'bucket' of money to cover changes that they both knew were likely to arise in the course of the project. As each of these changes was discussed and agreed, the funds could be drawn down from the 'bucket' without the client needing to apply for an increased budget. Any unspent 'bucket' funds at the end of the project were retained by the client.

Addressing this in the contract

The key to getting this right is discussing how you and the client want to manage changes before you sign the contract. If you discover that their organisation is at the 'control' end of the spectrum, whereas your own approach is more relaxed, you may want to include more budget for reviewing and managing changes in your pricing.

Alternatively, you and the client may be able to align your respective processes, with each of you moving some way towards the other.

When you've both agreed how changes will be managed, get your legal or contract support to help you document this clearly in the contract. If it is something that is likely to evolve, you might want to refer out to a separate change-management process, which can then be under its own independent change control. Taking this approach, rather than specifying the detailed process in the body of the contract, enables you to update the change control process without the overheads involved in major contract amendments.

Make customer support a key selling point

So far, we've talked about 'problems' in the context of warranty breaches and scope changes. The other category of 'problem' we're going to look at relates to everyday challenges and issues experienced by the user when they use your product or service.

This includes everything from "I can't work out how to merge my contacts list with my marketing email" to "Every time I press the PTT button on my radio, the tank's gun changes direction."

That last one was a genuine issue, by the way! Racal was developing and trialling some new military radio kit many years ago when I was a young engineer. It transpired that there were EMC (Electro Magnetic Compatibility) issues with the radio unit. The soldiers helping us road-test the kit in their Chieftain tanks were rather perturbed to discover that every time they pressed the 'Press to Talk' button on the radio, this accidentally sent an EMC pulse to the control system for the tank's gun, causing it to rotate.

A good thing to discover at the trial phase, it was all sorted very quickly but caused some issues at the time!

Most companies selling high-value equipment, systems or services will offer some form of ongoing support to their customers. Indeed, many mass-market products have free support helplines available to assist customers in using the product.

From your perspective, if you offer support to your clients, it's important to be clear about exactly what it means so that their expectations are properly set and managed.

Support, maintenance and user assistance

First of all, let's get some terminology straight, as these concepts are used interchangeably in some organisations.

For our purposes, 'support' relates to the fixing of defects in the product or service. So fixing the PTT/gun issue described above would definitely be considered to be a support issue. A defect, in this context, means something that stops your product or service complying with its agreed specification (again, you can see how important that spec is! Back to chapter 4 again...). Support tends to be reactive, and generally involves responding to defects that have been brought to your attention by a client.

'Maintenance', on the other hand, is a proactive effort to improve the product or service. It might involve fixing defects that your own staff has identified, or making minor enhancements to the way the product or service works. If the service involves looking after computer systems or data, you might include keeping operating systems and hardware management systems up to date as part of 'maintenance'.

Finally, there's 'user assistance'. The "I can't work out how to merge my contacts list with my marketing email" issue described above would fall into this category. Some clients will use your support helpdesk to provide user assistance to such an extent that it becomes clear they really need some proper user training. Others will hardly ever use it for this purpose, and are more comfortable using manuals and online help to assist them in their use of the product.

If you're offering one or all of these, make sure you define exactly what's covered and what's not. And if there are exclusions from the cover (for example, if the system crashes in a heap because the client deleted the root directory from the server, is that a defect covered by support? Or a request for paid consultancy services?), make them clear. It might be useful to have a 'consultancy' pot to describe the issues that fall into none of the above categories but might still be required by the client. You can then decide how much of this to offer for free (if any), and how much any chargeable consultancy should cost.

Measure things that matter

As soon as the words 'support' and 'contract' appear in the same sentence, the phrase 'Service Level Agreement' (SLA) follows soon after.

An SLA is a document setting out the various levels of service the vendor is to provide to the client. It is usually intended to form the basis for a contractual commitment so that it becomes, in effect, the 'specification' for support and maintenance.

The sort of things commonly covered in an SLA include:

- Response times (how long after an issue is reported does someone contact the client to begin resolution)

- Workaround times (how long after the issue is reported do you make some form of workaround available – a workaround can be either a temporary fix, or a way of achieving your objective without using the faulty part of the system)

- Fix times (how long it takes you to provide a permanent resolution to the problem)

- Lead times for sending replacement stock items

- Mean Time Between Failures (on average, how long is it between failures of any individual bit of kit)

- System availability (out of a total number of possible hours that the system should be available for use, how many is it actually available)

- Customer satisfaction (scores from periodic customer satisfaction surveys to see how happy users are with your service)

The interesting thing about service levels is that they focus the mind of the support team on the things that they measure. Each of these things is also referred to as a Key Performance Indicator, or KPI. From a client perspective, KPIs are intended to provide a yardstick against which to measure performance in a quantitative way. From a vendor perspective, it is easy to find oneself focusing on delivering the best service levels as measured in the SLA, rather than necessarily meeting the client's burning business need at any particular time.

So when you talk about service levels with your client, help them to focus on measuring the things that really matter to them and that are likely to result in the best user experience for them.

It is also important to make sure that you're actually capable of measuring the things defined in your SLA. It sounds silly, but you'd be amazed at the number of SLAs specifying things like 'How many rings of the telephone are permitted before a call is answered', when there is no technology in place to measure this objectively. So the measurement of success is down to people's ability to count and note down the number each time there's a call!

Service credits

Since the growth of the outsourcing market began, creation of SLAs has pushed organisations to find ways of encouraging compliance and punishing failure. Unfortunately for vendors, punishing failure seems to be considered an easier mechanism than encouraging compliance, resulting in the proliferation of 'service credits'.

A service credit is essentially a financial penalty for poor performance, as indicated by a failure to comply with an SLA. However, under the laws of England, financial penalties are not enforceable, which means that companies use the language of 'liquidated damages' to describe their service credits, rather than 'penalties'. We'll look at liquidated damages in more detail in chapter 8, but for now the important thing to remember is that service credits, properly drafted, can eat into your margin on an ongoing basis.

If possible, service credits should be avoided in your contract. If the client insists on including them, ask these key questions:

- Is the KPI that the service credit relates to objectively and easily measureable?

- Is the client able to measure and report on it too?

- Does it relate to something that has a genuine impact on the client's ability to benefit from your service?

- Is the meeting of, or failure to meet, this KPI solely within your control? (answer 'no' to this one if the acts or omissions of the client or one of their other suppliers could impact on your ability to meet it)

Only agree to a service credit if you're able to answer 'yes' to all of the questions above.

Having agreed to service credits in principle in respect of one of your KPIs, you then need to decide on an appropriate level to set it and a way of calculating it. This is a big topic and beyond the scope of this book, but it's important to consider the probability of your failing to meet the KPI and calculate a corresponding amount of likely service credit spend as part of the 'costs' of your project. This will give you a more accurate view of the genuine impact of service credits on the profitability of the deal.

If all else fails, escalate – practical dispute resolution

Ideally, we should aim to allow those on the ground to resolve any disputes. The people from your side and the client's who are involved in the day-to-day running of the contract are generally best placed to identify solutions, supported by the provisions of the contract itself.

But sometimes personalities can obscure the true nature of the issues in question. Especially where there is an element of fault on both sides, the parties can become entrenched with neither side willing to be seen to give way.

Define a clear escalation mechanism

Having a clearly defined and agreed escalation mechanism set out in your agreement can take the 'heat' out of dispute situations. If the day-to-day operational teams are clearly not making progress, passing the issue up the chain of command enables the next tier to take an objective view and work to reach agreement.

As a manager to whom a dispute is being escalated, the first thing you will ask for is a summary of the facts. This allows the emotion to be set to one side. By looking at exactly what each party should have done as set out in the contract, and what they have done in practice, the manager can assess the extent to which each party is responsible for the current situation. They should also be able to explore the risks and benefits of alternative outcomes, and to use these to seek solutions with the client.

If these discussions are unsuccessful, a further level of escalation may be required but, where possible, you should seek to resolve all issues as early in the process as you can.

Although it may seem counterproductive, this means that raising problems early is often much better for the client relationship than ignoring them and hoping they solve themselves. Catching issues when they're small makes them easier to resolve – and having agreed mechanisms in place for finding solutions will guide you through the process. It's useful to 'test drive' your dispute resolution process from time to time in the same way you might do fire alarm testing in the business; having worked through it together when stress levels are low will make it easier when the stakes are higher!

The purpose of dispute resolution is to have both parties satisfied with the outcome.

It's unusual for the fault to be all on one side in any dispute, and it's equally unusual for the resolution to be entirely in one party's hands. But the very fact that we have a dispute means that the parties are not agreed about where the balance of blame sits. If your relationship is to continue to a successful project outcome, it is essential that you're both satisfied that the resolution is fair.

One way to help your own organisation through a dispute is to focus attention on the desired outcome. As you'll recall from chapter 4, sometimes there's a difference between 'being right' and 'getting what you want'. In a dispute this is particularly true, and you often need to put your desire to be seen to be in the right to one side in order to achieve what you want to get out of it.

The knowledge that the outcome is one that works for your business can also help your team to 'bite the bullet' and smile while apologising, if an apology is what's required to move things forward!

Applicable laws, courts and mediation

Your agreements should always state the law that applies to your contract, and also the courts that have jurisdiction to resolve any disputes that you've not managed to resolve between you.

Stating the applicable law and jurisdiction is a good move because it means that you know exactly where you are in the (hopefully) unlikely event that things get bad enough for lawyers to get involved. If law and jurisdiction are not stated in the contract, they will be determined according to the nature of the agreement, the location of each of the parties and the place where the products or services are delivered, under the various international conventions that apply to international contracts. If both your company and your client are located in the same country, and all deliveries took place there, the chances are that its law will apply – but it's better to be safe than sorry.

Why does this matter? Strange though it might seem, different legal systems will interpret the same contract in different ways and will calculate damages differently. This means that a claim which would result in an award of perhaps £100k under one set of laws could give rise to damages of £1 million under another. So your choice of law could make rather a significant difference to the outcome of any dispute!

Going to court is an outrageously expensive exercise and much of this book so far has been geared towards keeping you out of court and away from disputes in general. There are now more options available for alternative dispute resolution (ADR) before you get to litigation, and if internal escalation hasn't done the trick, I'd strongly recommend you explore these before recourse to the courts. Not only do they tend to be less expensive than litigation, they may be quicker and less adversarial, and have the great benefit that they are held in private rather than in an open court.

Mediation is increasing in popularity. You and the other party jointly agree on your choice of mediator, usually selecting someone with experience in your particular business sector. There are many professional mediators available, but I'd recommend that you choose one accredited by a body such as the Centre for Effective Dispute Resolution (CEDR). Conducting a successful mediation is a great skill, and it's worth investing in an experienced mediator in whom both you and your client have confidence.

So how does mediation work? Both parties are brought together to start the day, and each states its position. The mediator then splits you into separate rooms and spends the rest of the day shuttling back and forth between you trying to move you towards a resolution. A good mediator will explore your options, and may be able to give you an unbiased view of the chances of success of your case if you were to get to court. This can be very helpful in focusing each party's mind on reaching agreement through mediation!

It is not necessary to have legal representation for a mediation, although many parties do. The difficulty with having your lawyers present, however, is that unless they are fully committed to the mediation process you may find they obstruct you on your path to agreement. Sometimes you're better off taking a pragmatic view and settling the dispute, even if your lawyer is advising you that you could 'win' if you went to court. After all, even the winners lose in litigation – cost, time and stress are all high prices to pay for the 'glory' of being told by a judge that you are in the right. It is a good idea, however, to have a solicitor or other contracts professional on hand at the end of the day. Their role will be to document the agreement you've reached during your mediation so that both parties can sign up to the agreed resolution and be bound by it. The mediation itself is a non-binding process, so if you don't complete this final step you might find that a party changes its mind after the day is over and you lose any agreement you might have reached.

Arbitration and adjudication are two other ADR mechanisms available under certain circumstances. Adjudication is widely used in construction disputes, and is a formal and well-documented process. There are many experienced and well-qualified professionals that can support you through an adjudication, and it's worth seeking advice from someone who's been through the process several times before.

Arbitration can be similar to litigation in terms of the cost and time involved in the process, with its main benefit being the privacy afforded.

Chapter 7: Quick Summary

- Dealing with problems well may have a more positive impact on your client relationships than never having any problems at all

- Warranties are contractual terms that protect the client against poor delivery on your part

- If you breach a warranty, the client may be entitled to compensation but is not automatically entitled to terminate the contract

- Specifying practical, meaningful remedies for breach of warranty is good practice, and enables you to exclude statutory warranties (which are often too vague)

- While you might see a client requirement as a contractual change request, your client might consider it to be just a clarification of what they want

- There are different ways to manage changes, from the very tightly controlled and documented, through the very flexible where you settle up at the end, to the 'bucket' approach

- Customer support can be used to address everyday problems and issues

- Service level agreements should only measure things that make a real difference to the client experience

- Service credits are a form of liquidated damages to compensate the client if you fail to meet your agreed service levels

- If you can't resolve a disagreement between you, have a clear escalation policy to enable people not directly involved in the project to try to find a solution

- Specify the applicable law and jurisdiction in the contract, so you know how it would be interpreted in a legal dispute

- Consider whether mediation might be a useful step before court action

8

Why limits and exclusions of liability are important

You will have noticed that most of this book is focused on the practical things you can do to ensure that you and the client have the same understanding of what's being delivered, and when you'll get paid. We've also looked at how you can address the inevitable problems and issues to stop them getting out of control.

There may be occasions when, despite your best efforts, a dispute arises that severely challenges your problem-solving abilities. This chapter describes some of the contractual provisions that can help manage your risk and commercial exposure if you find yourself and the business in a legal dispute.

You might feel that this chapter is serious 'lawyer territory', as it goes into considerable detail about how limits and exclusions of liability – and their evil twin, the indemnity – work. To some extent, you'd be right, but please don't skip over it for that reason. As you get more involved in deal making, you'll find these topics crop up more and more frequently. If you understand not only the legal meaning but the commercial significance of these terms, you'll be much better equipped to use them effectively in your deal structuring and negotiation.

Litigation is a losing game

First, I want to re-state the obvious fact that the best way to avoid litigation is following the steps set out in chapters 4 to 6 to deliver a successful project and get paid, and addressing any problems in line with chapter 7.

Two large commercial cases that have hit the courts in recent years both arose initially from the failure of the parties to follow these steps.

In de Beers v Atos Origin, finally concluded in 2011, Atos Origin was required to pay damages of £1.4 million to de Beers after a project to develop software for diamond aggregation failed to deliver. The fact that the judge awarded only £1.4 million in damages reflects his assessment that de Beers had in its turn caused approximately £3 million of damage to Atos Origin – the £1.4 million was the balance remaining after this £3 million was deducted from the total £4.4 million of losses suffered by de Beers.

The second high-profile case concerned BSkyB and EDS. The award of damages to BSkyB was £318 million, against an initial estimated contract value of £47.6 million. The feature of the case that made the headlines when it was announced in 2010 was the misrepresentation of EDS in respect of its ability to deliver the solution within BSkyB's required timescales, despite being aware that it would not be able to do so. The luckless EDS salesman who made this claim had his credibility demolished in court by the counsel for BSkyB in a particularly memorable fashion:

> *"Mr Galloway claimed that he had obtained an MBA from a college in the British Virgin Islands in 1996 but it emerged during the trial that it had been obtained from the Internet", the judge said.*

> *Mark Howard, QC, BSkyB's barrister, illustrated the point by presenting the court with an MBA from the same college awarded to his dog, Lulu. "Without any difficulty the dog was able to obtain a degree certificate and transcripts which were in identical form to those later produced by Joe Galloway," the judge noted, "but with marks which, in fact, were better than those given to him." (The Times, 27th January 2010)*

Although the size of the award of damages owed much to EDS's misrepresentation about its ability to deliver, the parties only found themselves in court in the first place because they had not followed the steps set out in chapters 4 to 7.

Having made the case for 'doing things properly' to avoid litigation in the first place, we do need to recognise the potential deterrent effect of having some limits and exclusions of liability in place. It should be noted, however, that in both of these cases the limits of liability in the contract failed to reduce the amount of damages eventually paid by the vendors to their clients.

It may be because of an irrational faith in the power of these clauses to dissuade parties from litigation that lawyers spend a disproportionate amount of their time negotiating them.

The IACCM conducts a survey each year, asking its members which clauses are given the most 'airtime' during their negotiations. For many years, limit of liability clauses have occupied the number 1 or 2 slot in this survey. When asked which clauses they think the time would be better spent negotiating, IACCM members overwhelmingly vote in favour of the definition of scope and change control (chapters 4 and 7 again…).

A limit of liability 'caps' your exposure if you breach the contract

So what exactly do we mean by a limit of liability? Although it's often referred to as LoL by contractual folk, it certainly shouldn't be confused with 'laugh out loud' or 'lots of love'…

If things have gone wrong because of one party's breach of the contract, the other party might be entitled to seek damages to compensate them for any losses they've incurred.

Conversely, the other party (usually the supplier) will be keen to limit the extent of their liability to pay such compensation. They might do this in one of two ways:

(i)   excluding certain categories of losses in their entirety

(ii)   putting a financial cap on their liability, either for particular categories of loss, or for all losses claimed under the contract.

A limit of liability clause aims to put a maximum level on the amount of damages that your company could be asked to pay if it breached a contract. A breach of contract occurs whenever one or other of the parties fails to comply with its terms, but not all breaches give rise to a claim for damages.

In order for a party to have a claim for damages, they must prove:

- That you breached a provision of the contract between you

- That they suffered damages as a direct result of that breach of contract

- That they used their reasonable efforts to keep the amount of damages to a minimum (referred to as 'mitigating their losses')

Only when all of these have been proven will the courts begin to assess the actual amount of damages to be paid by the breaching party to compensate the other party.

If the breaching party has a valid limit of liability provision in the contract, it will cap the amount of damages to be paid. So if, for example, the client suffered £1 million of losses, but the contractual limit of liability was £500,000, the maximum amount of damages that would be awarded under the contract would be £500,000. If the client had suffered only £300,000 of losses, the court could award all of this in damages as it falls below the vendor's limit of liability.

So the limit of liability is not a commitment to pay that sum. If we cap our liability at £500,000, but the actual losses are less than that, we'd only pay the actual losses.

You will notice that I said, "If the breaching party has a *valid* limit of liability provision", in the paragraph above.

The word 'valid' is a very important qualifier. Under English law, the Unfair Contract Terms Act 1977 (UCTA) states that any attempt in a contract to limit or exclude a party's liability is only enforceable to the extent that it is 'reasonable'. This 'reasonableness' test applies either if the breaching party is dealing with a consumer or, if with a business, it is trading on its standard terms. It does not apply if the limit of liability has been individually negotiated to the satisfaction of both parties.

What does 'reasonable' mean?

UCTA contains a schedule setting out the various criteria for determining reasonableness in limits of liability. These include identifying which party will find it easiest to insure against the particular liability concerned and the relative negotiating positions of the parties. While it doesn't specify any rules for the amount of any financial cap, over the years the courts appear to have concluded that a supplier wishing to limit its liability to the total value of the contract will not always be successful.

This means that, in many cases, you'd be better advised to have a slightly higher limit of liability than you felt you might be able to get away with in your contract (say 125% of contract value, rather than 100%), in order to increase the chances of being able to enforce it if you ended up in court. If you set the level too low and a court decided it was unenforceable, then rather than just revising your limit upwards the court would reject the entire clause. This means that you'd end up with unlimited liability, defeating the whole point of the clause.

It is worth noting that many US contracts will specify a limit of liability equal to 100% of contract value or less (I've seen 25% of contract value as a limit in the past). While such low limits may be enforceable under the laws of the state specified in those contracts, they are very unlikely to be so in the UK. I mention this only because US contracts tend to be used as templates for business agreements in the UK, and this is an area where such plagiarism really does not work!

Within this context, this is definitely an area where it's best to seek specialist legal advice if you are in any doubt about what is enforceable. But generally speaking, err on the side of a higher, rather than a lower, limit if you want to be able to rely on it.

Liquidated damages aren't always as bad as they sound

'Liquidated damages' is the name given to a pre-agreed amount of damages payable in the event of a particular contract breach.

You'll often hear them referred to as 'LDs', and most vendors negotiate hard to avoid having LDs in their contracts. In this section, we'll look at exactly what liquidated damages are, and the pros and cons of having them in your agreement.

What do we mean by 'liquidated damages'?

In this context, the word 'liquidated' essentially means 'reduced to a cash sum'. It's a way of avoiding the whole issue of proving loss and assessing damages that's described above, by deciding in advance what the damages will be.

So how does that work?

In some situations, it's quite easy to work out what losses would be likely to flow from a particular contract breach. Let's say, for example, that I operate a toll bridge which needs resurfacing. You've quoted me seven days for carrying out the work, and we've agreed that you will pay a sum of liquidated damages for each day of delay in your completion of the work.

On an average day, I see 100 cars crossing my bridge, each of which pays me a toll of 50 pence. So that's an average revenue of £50 per day, which would be a reasonable level at which to set the liquidated damages.

If your resurfacing work overran by three days, you'd owe me £150 in liquidated damages. From my perspective, the great thing about this is that I don't need to prove to you that I actually lost £150. I don't have to show that 100 cars tried to cross my bridge each day, and had to follow the diversion. All I have to do is prove that you breached the contract (i.e. were late) and that the liquidated damages clause is valid (see below). Once I've done that, you will be obliged to pay the relevant sum.

From your perspective, the good thing is that you know exactly how much a day of delay will cost you. If one of these three days was gloriously sunny, and several hundred cars wanted to cross my bridge to picnic by the river, my actual loss on that day would be considerably higher than the £50 we've agreed for liquidated damages. But because we've pre-agreed the amount of damages payable, I would not be able to claim the additional loss incurred, as I would have effectively given up my right to potentially greater compensation in exchange for the certainty of knowing I would be paid £50 for each day of delay.

But what if I decided that £50 was not sufficient compensation for a day of overrun? Let's say I asked you for £500 of liquidated damages in compensation for each day of delay.

Unless I was able to come up with a very good justification for this high sum, it could be considered to be a contractual penalty, rather than compensation for actual losses incurred. That is, rather than being intended to compensate me for my loss, it is acting to punish you for your lateness.

Under many legal systems, penalties are entirely acceptable. But under English law they are unenforceable. So if a party sets the level of liquidated damages too high in an English law contract, it runs the risk that the other party will claim that it is actually a penalty and overturn it in court. This would be a situation in which the liquidated damages clause would not be valid, and would be rejected by the court.

The phrase commonly used by lawyers drafting liquidated damages provisions is that the liquidated damages amount is 'a genuine pre-estimate of the loss' that would be caused by the breach.

This is important and will help you to ensure any liquidated damages provision can be relied upon.

It is also worth remembering that in order for the amount to be a genuine pre-estimate of the loss flowing from a breach, it must be determined in respect of a specific class of contractual breach. Defining an amount of liquidated damages to be paid in the event of 'any contract breach' would not work, as it's likely that different sorts of breach would give rise to different levels of loss or damage.

What about breaches where it would be very difficult to assess loss? Breaches of confidentiality, for example?

In these cases, you need to choose a number that you can reasonably defend and that's not so out of kilter with the potential damages you could incur that it would be considered a penalty. Liquidated damages can be very useful in such cases, as proving actual loss from something like a breach of confidentiality can be difficult; having an agreed sum may be much easier to deal with for both parties.

Why use liquidated damages?

Liquidated damages have advantages and disadvantages for both parties.

From the client's perspective, the great thing about LDs is that there's no need to go through the whole rigmarole of proving the amount of their loss, and demonstrating the various ways they've tried to mitigate it. All they need to prove is that you've breached the contract in the way specified by the liquidated damages clause, and you'll be liable to pay out the agreed sum.

So what's in it for you?

While the big disadvantage from the vendor perspective is the same as the main advantage for the customer – i.e. you have no opportunity to haggle about the amount, you just have to pay – there are times when LDs will be beneficial for you too. Unless the contract expressly says otherwise, if you've agreed an amount of LDs to be paid in the event of a particular contract breach, that will be the client's **only** remedy for that breach.

In other words, by pre-agreeing the amount of the loss, the client is giving up their right to claim any higher amount of damages that they might in fact incur.

Why would they do that? Simple – they're trading the opportunity for a higher damages pay-out in exchange for certainty, simplicity and avoidance of the costs associated with fighting a legal battle.

This can mean that agreeing to liquidated damages for a breach that could potentially cause huge losses to the client acts to cap your liability at a far more reasonable level.

If you include LDs in the contract, budget for them in the financials

So while having liquidated damages might reduce the total amount of money you'd have to pay out in the event of a particular breach, it also increases the likelihood that you'd have to pay out **something** if that breach occurred.

This means that when putting together the financials for approval in deals that include liquidated damages, you need to take advice about how to reflect these in your deal summary. Generally I would recommend that you include a certain amount of liquidated damages in your project 'costs', according to the likelihood that you will have to pay some. This will vary according to (a) the probability of you breaching the contract in the specified manner, and (b) the probability of the client enforcing the liquidated damages provision against you.

Obviously, the better a job you've done in the other contract stages, the lower the chances of your company ever having to pay out its liquidated damages. If you're very confident about your ability to perform, you may even find that agreeing to liquidated damages will enhance your company's standing in the eyes of the client, and may enable you to secure other significant contract concessions in exchange.

It is important to make sure when drafting your liquidated damages provision that it only applies to breaches that are solely your fault.

If the client has contributed to the occurrence of the breach in some way, the liquidated damages should not be payable. Your legal advisor will be able to help you cover this properly.

Exclusions of liability prevent the client claiming certain sorts of losses

While your limit of liability seeks to put a cap on the total sum you might pay out in damages, exclusions of liability seek to prevent you having to pay out any damages at all in respect of certain classes of loss.

It's worth understanding how this works, and what you're able to do within the law, if only so that you don't waste valuable time, energy and client goodwill arguing about points you're never going to win – or ones that don't deliver you any real benefit. Appreciating how these provisions work in practice will help you engage your legal counsel in a sensible and pragmatic discussion about where to draw the line in your contract negotiations. Given the amount of time usually dedicated to these issues, it might also help to shorten your sales cycle!

There are some liabilities you can't exclude or limit

Under English law (and many other legal systems), it is not permissible to exclude or limit your liability for death or personal injury caused by the negligence of your staff, or by defects in your product. Similarly, you are not permitted to exclude liability for fraud, including fraudulent misrepresentation (making statements you know to be untrue, to deliberately mislead the other party), or any other criminal acts.

Because of this, you will often see wording along the following lines:

Nothing in this Agreement shall limit or exclude Our liability for (i) personal injury or death caused by the negligence of Our employees or subcontractors in connection with their duties under this Agreement, or by defects in any Product supplied under this Agreement, or (ii) fraud or any criminal act, or (iii) any other liability that cannot be excluded by law.

While this might seem to be stating the obvious, since such exclusions are not permitted, it acts to ensure that your other exclusions and limits of liability will actually be enforceable. Without a statement of this kind, it's possible that the other party could argue your exclusion or limit of liability is not enforceable because it is an attempt to exclude liability for things that are not permitted.

Direct and indirect losses

Losses can be categorised in many different ways, and one that you may have come across is the distinction between 'direct' and 'indirect' losses. According to contract law as taught for decades, this distinction was applied according to the level of 'remoteness' of the loss in question from the breach that caused it.

There are some legal principles set out in a case from 1854 (yes, we're still working from precedents established over 160 years ago!) called Hadley v Baxendale. These have been interpreted over the years so that 'direct losses' are generally accepted to be ones that would 'fairly and reasonably' be considered to arise naturally from the breach of contract.

Under these principles, 'indirect losses' would be those that would not have been 'in the contemplation of the parties' at the time the contract was entered into.

In recent years, the courts have been more liberal in their interpretation of what is a direct and what is an indirect loss. Financial losses (loss of profits, for example) used to be considered to be always in the 'indirect' pot. But that's no longer the case – if you want to be sure that loss of profits is excluded, you have to list it out expressly as being excluded, regardless of whether it arises directly or indirectly from the breach of contract.

British Gas v Accenture

This project, to deliver a billing system for all of British Gas's 18 million gas and electricity customers, started in 2002. Things started going wrong when the two parties disputed the functionality and performance of the first two releases of the software. In 2004, they settled their initial dispute, with British Gas paying an extra £10m, and Accenture supplying an extra 18,000 man-days of effort.

In 2006, British Gas took the billing system in-house, but experienced significant problems. In 2007, they notified Accenture of these problems in writing, but Accenture deemed that, under the contract, it was not liable for the cost of fixing these problems. It asserted that British Gas had both signed off the design and tested the system extensively before accepting and using it.

British Gas (Centrica) issued a writ for £183,000,000 against Accenture in April 2008.

Its claims included:

1. *£18.7 million for distribution charges (on the basis it was charged for gas on an estimated consumption rather than actual consumption because the distributors were not provided with meter data for about 15% of its customers)*

2. *£8 million in compensation it paid to its customers to reflect the billing difficulties and poor customer service*

3. *£2 million in additional borrowing charges due to the late billing or non-billing of customers*

4. *Other sums incurred in chasing debts, additional stationery and correspondence costs*

The court was asked to determine a number of preliminary issues, including interpreting what breaches could amount to a 'Fundamental Defect' (as defined in the contract), what was the correct basis for calculating damages for a Fundamental Defect and whether any of the classes of loss claimed were excluded. Despite a valiant attempt by Accenture to argue that the claims listed above were excluded by its exclusion clauses (as loss of profits, or indirect costs), both the court of first instance and the court of appeal found in favour of Centrica/ British Gas.

The British Gas v Accenture case illustrated that even when a very competent vendor such as Accenture sets out clearly what sort of liabilities are excluded under the contract, there is still no guarantee that the exclusion will be enforceable. The more specific you can be about precisely which categories of loss are excluded, the better a chance you will stand of enforcing the exclusion. However, this case does underpin the importance of getting things right in the first place so as to avoid litigation, as it shows that even well-drafted limit and exclusion of liability clauses are not 100% reliable.

You must leave the other party with some remedy

This chapter has been all about trying to exclude your liability for damages in the event of a breach of contract.

To put this another way, these clauses are aimed at making sure that if your company messes up, it won't be liable for the full costs of the damage it causes. In some cases, it won't be liable for *any* of the costs of the damage.

As a responsible adult, I'm assuming here that you have some sense of right and wrong. If you had personally made an error that caused harm to someone else, you would expect to have to make some form of restitution. And yet lawyers spend great amounts of time (and therefore money) trying to ensure that your company doesn't suffer the consequences of its actions.

Is that fair?

The courts think not. There have been a number of cases where the vendor has so thoroughly limited its liability that the client is prevented from claiming for any loss that could conceivably result from its breach of the contract. The result? The court rejected the entire limits and exclusions of liability clause and awarded the damages it felt were appropriate.

Their view was that it was not reasonable for a vendor to enter into a contract in which it committed to deliver certain products and services to a certain standard, and for which it was well paid, if the client had no remedy for any failure to deliver.

So what does that mean for your contracts?

Firstly, it means you should consider what sort of things could possibly go wrong in your delivery, and identify appropriate ways of dealing with them. This might take you back to your warranty provisions (chapter 7). It might also make you consider the categories of losses your client could incur if you breached the contract in different ways.

For some losses, you might decide that it's fair and reasonable for you to accept responsibility for a certain cash amount if they're caused by your breach. For others, you may determine that it's much easier for the client to insure against them, or seek other ways of mitigating them, so you're comfortable excluding your own liability for them.

The key thing is to think about this, rather than defaulting to the most stringent limits and exclusions of liability that the client will let you get away with. After all, if you get it wrong they could well have the last laugh.

Indemnities don't help anybody

Indemnities vie with limits and exclusions of liability for the number 1 slot in the IACCM's 'Top 10 Negotiated Terms' survey. This means that they are consistently identified by commercial contract specialists as taking up a significant proportion of negotiation time.

Why should you care?

There are several reasons why indemnities matter to you in trying to close workable deals.

The first is that clients love indemnities. They'll ask you to indemnify them against just about anything, for just about any reason. If you don't understand what indemnities are and how they work, you could be fooled into thinking that this is just fine and dandy – after all, you have professional indemnity insurance, so what's the problem?

The second reason is that they really matter to your lawyers. Your lawyers will battle to avoid giving indemnities – and if you don't understand why, you'll be as much use to them as the proverbial chocolate teapot. By getting your head around how indemnities work, you'll be better equipped to support your legal counsel in persuading your client to drop their request for indemnities, or at least to agree to some reasonable boundaries for them.

The third is that they can become real stumbling blocks in negotiations, dragging out an otherwise amicable process. The more you understand how they work and what they achieve, the better your chances of being able to propose alternatives and shortcut this negotiation nightmare.

What is an indemnity, and why are they such a big deal?

An indemnity is a commitment by one party to meet the liabilities of another party arising from a particular event.

Let's say we had a contract under which I was to transport you to and from the airport at dates and times specified by you for a fixed annual fee. In this contract, I agree to indemnify you against all of your costs, losses and damages (fairly typical wording) arising from my failure to collect you from the airport and get you to your meeting on time.

Unfortunately, on one occasion my car broke down on the way to collect you from the airport and take you to an important meeting, so you had to jump in a taxi and pay its rates to get you there. As a result, you arrived late and lost the business you were bidding for because you missed your slot to present to the client.

Under my indemnity, I could be liable for:

- Your taxi fare

- The value of the lost business to your company

- Any other costs and expenses you incurred as a result

So for the sake of a cab fare, I could incur potentially huge liabilities.

The scope of costs and damages that you're on the line for under an indemnity will depend on the exact wording of the clause. I've seen many indemnity clauses in contracts drafted by a buyer that are, effectively, a blank cheque from the seller. They are uncapped and unlimited in every way, covering all losses linked to, or resulting (however remotely) from the breach.

Worse still, the biggest culprits when it comes to asking for indemnities are huge organisations – government departments, local authorities, global companies, banks... the very organisations whose capacity for spending money is limitless!

So not only have you written a blank cheque, but you've written it to an entity that is quite capable of bleeding your business dry and not even slaking its thirst.

(If you work for such an organisation, it's well worth having some discussions with your own legal counsel about the real wisdom of requesting indemnities from your suppliers, given the way they work in practice – see below for more on this.)

Indemnities are supposed to take away risk from one party

Organisations ask for indemnities as they believe them to take risk away. Unless otherwise stated in the contract, there is a general assumption that the party claiming under the indemnity has no obligation to mitigate its losses, and that the indemnity amount is unlimited.

The indemnified party might also expect to be protected against both its direct and its indirect losses.

Because it is not expected that there will be any limit to the amount or scope of the indemnity, the indemnified party generally expects to be able to make its claim from the indemnifying one and simply be paid. So one of the justifications that clients give for requesting an indemnity is that they want to avoid the cost and hassle of taking you to court to recover their losses.

In truth, this rarely happens. If the amount claimed is significant, your company will almost certainly contest it. This means that the usual debates about the precise scope of the indemnity, mitigation, size of losses, etc. will all occur despite the fact that the indemnity was supposed to prevent them.

Also, a number of cases have demonstrated that, depending on the precise wording of the indemnity, the courts may not allow the party relying on the indemnity to be relieved of their obligation to mitigate their losses. There have also been instances where even an indemnified claim has been limited by the courts to direct costs only, so the indemnity is not exactly the 'magic wand' that the client's lawyers might consider it to be.

Some clients expect to be indemnified against ALL risks

When you set out an indemnity provision, it is usual to specify which particular risk the client is being indemnified against.

A common candidate is your breach of any third party's intellectual property rights. We discuss intellectual property in more detail in chapter 10. For now it's enough to say that if anything you've created and sold to the client could be considered to be copying an invention, design or copyright created by a third party, it could give rise to a claim against the client. The client, not unreasonably, wants to be protected against such claims – after all, they will not be of the client's making.

Another risk that clients might ask to be indemnified against is your breach of any laws. This might include breaches of data protection legislation (more on that in chapter 9), product safety regulations, anti-bribery legislation or any other law or regulation.

This isn't all one-way, and we do sometimes encounter requests from a vendor to be indemnified by its client. These indemnities might be in respect of breaches of the vendor's intellectual property rights (particularly common if you're licensing software), or against the breach of third party rights by any materials supplied by the client for use by the vendor.

In local and national government contracts, it is common to see provisions requiring the vendor to indemnify the client against losses arising from *'any breach of this Agreement'* or, even worse, *'any loss or damage arising from or in connection with its performance of this Agreement'*.

Why is that so bad?

The indemnity regarding any breach of the agreement is pretty steep – it could require you to pay out for wasted management time if the client needed to participate in discussions with you about resolving a service level problem, for example. It is, effectively, a blank cheque from you to your client allowing them to claim for any loss whatsoever arising from even the most trivial breach of the agreement by you. While one would hope the client wouldn't abuse it in this way, and would only seek to rely on this clause in the event of a pretty serious breach, you have no guarantee that this would be the case.

What about *'arising from or in connection with its performance of this Agreement'*? Taken at face value, this would mean that you would be liable for any losses of the client resulting from your perfect performance of your obligations under the agreement, in precise accordance with the terms of the contract.

So let's say the client hired your company to install lighting outside their building, and specified that it would be of a particular brightness. Unknown to you, the client's office is in a district with very strict light pollution regulations – a fact they failed to share with you. Once you had installed the lighting (on time, within budget and looking wonderful), they received a notice from their local authority instructing them to remove it or pay a fine for light pollution.

Theoretically, the costs of removing the lighting or paying the fine will have arisen from your performance of the agreement, and so could be considered within the scope of the indemnity.

Would the client attempt to enforce the indemnity in this fashion? Again, you'd hope not. And if you did go to court, your barrister would doubtless argue that it is not reasonable for your client to seek compensation from a loss of its own making. But it's generally a good idea not to include any clause in a contract that you don't believe to be fair and reasonable, and that you would not expect to have enforced.

There are workable alternatives to indemnities

Your first response to a request for an indemnity should be a simple 'no', together with an explanation of your reasoning. If you reject the indemnity request, a client would simply make a normal claim for damages as described in chapter 8. This means that they would have the usual obligations to mitigate their losses and prove them to the court, but if you have genuinely caused the losses they will have a valid claim.

If a flat 'no' is rejected by your client, and your business decides that it is willing to take on the liabilities imposed by an indemnity, the next step is to reduce the scope of losses that are covered. You might do this, for example, by limiting them to any costs and damages awarded by a court – the following 'pseudo indemnity' uses this technique:

Indemnity: *Company, at its own expense, shall defend all claims, actions and demands ('Claims'), and shall pay any resulting damages, judgments, settlements, costs and expenses (including reasonable attorneys' fees) awarded by a court of competent jurisdiction or agreed to be paid in compensation (collectively, 'Losses') insofar as such Claims are related to a Claim that the Products infringe any patent, copyright, trade secret, database right, or other intellectual property or proprietary right of any third party.*

So while this clause is presented as an indemnity, it is limited to the cost incurred in defending and settling the third party claim. It does not indemnify the client against its own losses arising from the claim.

Check this wording with your underwriters (see below to find out why this matters), and make sure you push hard to have the clause reviewed by them – don't settle for a 'noted, subject to policy conditions' response from your broker!

Other ways of mitigating the potential risk of an indemnity include:

- Limiting very tightly the nature of the breaches that would give rise to a claim

- Expressly requiring the other party to use its reasonable efforts to mitigate its losses

- Limiting the classes of loss to specific losses only (like third party costs, for example)

- Putting a financial cap on the amount of losses that will be covered

Check your insurance before making concessions

It won't surprise you to hear that your corporate insurance (whether it's professional indemnity insurance or product liability, depending on your line of business) is full of pitfalls. Like most insurance, it goes to great lengths to identify situations where you will not be insured. But have you ever looked at the policy? Have your legal advisors?

Many people in business act according to their assumptions of what their insurance *should* cover, rather than what it actually *does* cover. This exposes them to significant risks when they negotiate contracts that mean any resulting claims would be excluded from cover.

What does it mean if a claim falls outside your cover?

It means that if a third party sues your company for its breach of a particular area of the contract, your insurers are able to shrug their shoulders and say "Over to you…" It means that your company will have to pay the costs of defending and/or settling the claim out of its own bank balance. And if there is an award of damages that's significantly larger than the current account balance of the business, it could lead to liquidation of the company to pay the damages.

So quite a big deal, then.

Obligation to enter into deliverable deals

If you look back at chapter 4, you'll remember that we've put a great deal of emphasis on making sure that you and the client have a common understanding of what you're delivering, and that the deal hangs together. Apart from being good business practice, you might find that this is actually an obligation on you if you want to be protected by your insurance.

Hiscox, an insurance firm with a reputation for plain speaking, sets this out beautifully in this excerpt from a professional indemnity policy for a software company:

'**We** *will not make any payment under this section if:*

1. **you** *failed to take reasonable steps before entering into a contract with a client, or extending the scope of an existing contract, to ensure that either* **you** *could provide the required level and quality of* **deliverables** *or services for the quoted price using the resources available to* **you** *or the contract was capable of being performed in accordance with all its terms and any representations made by* **you** *or on* **your** *behalf; or*

2. **you** *agreed in* **your** *contract with a client either to use more than reasonable care and skill or to provide something more than reasonably fit for its intended purpose or to have a greater financial responsibility for any claim covered by this insurance than would otherwise be the case at law.'*

– Hiscox, Professional Indemnity policy document
(Policy Ref: Direct – PI IT1 (2) 5972 01/08)

They also go further, obliging you to take steps to remedy problems as described in chapter 7:

'**We** *will not make any payment under this section if* **you** *failed to take reasonable steps to remedy or rectify, at* **your** *expense, any defect or failure in the* **deliverables** *or services* **you** *have supplied to a client arising either prior to* **your** *client's acceptance of the* **deliverables** *or within 180 days of acceptance or any longer period specified in* *any contract with **your** client, including a maintenance contract. This extends to **your** ensuring that **you** could correct any such defect by having the relevant versions of the source code, if available to **you**, or by keeping back-up copies of relevant software or data.'*

– Hiscox, Professional Indemnity policy document
(Policy Ref: Direct – PI IT1 (2) 5972 01/08)

Obligation to notify

One of the likely requirements of your insurance is that you will be required to notify your insurers if you enter into a particularly risky contract, or intend to take on any risks that are unusual for your business. This is particularly true if the risk could lead to a big liability.

Failure to notify your insurers could result in your insurance being invalidated – either in respect of a particular claim or altogether.

'We *will not make any payment under this section unless* **you** *notify* **us** *promptly of the following within the* **period of insurance** *or at the latest within 14 days after it expires for any problem* **you** *first become aware of in the seven days before expiry:*

    a.   **your** *first awareness of a shortcoming in* **your** *work for a client which is likely to lead to a claim against* **you.** *This includes:*

- *a shortcoming known to* **you,** *but not to* **your** *client, which* **you** *cannot reasonably put right;*

- *a complaint from* **your** *client about* **your** *work or anything* **you** *have supplied which cannot be immediately resolved;*

- *an escalating level of complaint from* **your** *client on a particular project;*

- *a client withholding payment due to* **you** *after any complaint.*

If **we** *accept* **your** *notification, this does not alter* **your** *obligation to take reasonable steps to correct any problem as provided below but* **we** *will regard any subsequent claim as notified to this insurance.*

> **b.** *any claim or threatened claim against* **you.**

> **c.** **your** *discovery, or the existence of reasonable grounds for* **your** *suspicion, that any partner, director, employee or self-employed freelancer has acted dishonestly.*

> **d.** **your** *discovery that any document, information or data of* **yours** *has been lost, damaged or destroyed.'*

– Hiscox, Professional Indemnity policy document
(Policy Ref: Direct – PI IT1 (2) 5972 01/08)

You will see that you shouldn't wait until a claim is actually filed before notifying; knowledge that you've done something that could potentially result in a claim is sufficient to trigger a notification request. While other insurers may stipulate different conditions, they frequently cover similar ground. I've chosen to use this particular policy for these examples because it is very clearly drafted, and spells out in great detail exactly what the insurers expect.

Having looked through this particular policy document in some detail, I think businesses could do worse than to use it as part of their corporate training – complying with these provisions would certainly help you to deliver better deals!

Required contractual provisions

Some policies require you to exclude indirect and consequential losses to the greatest extent that it's reasonable to do so. An example of some policy wording along these lines is shown below.

'Consequential losses

We will not make any payment under this section if you failed to limit in a contract with your client any liability for loss of turnover, sales, revenue or profits, or for loss of software or data, or for indirect, consequential or special loss, where it was reasonable for you to have done so.'

– Hiscox Professional Indemnity policy document
(Policy Ref: Direct – PI IT1 (2) 5972 01/08)

Likely exclusions

It is standard practice for insurers to exclude 'contractual liability'. This may be defined as:

'We will not make any payment for any claim or part of a claim or loss directly or indirectly due to any liability under any contract which is greater than the liability you would have at law without the contract.'

– Hiscox Professional Indemnity policy document
(Policy Ref: Direct – PI IT1 (2) 5972 01/08)

In practice, this means that you are unlikely to be insured for any liquidated damages payments, even if the total amount of the liquidated damages is less than the possible damages you could have been asked to pay by a court. Why? Because by agreeing to pay liquidated damages, you are preventing the insurers from seeking to avoid or reduce their liability. You are effectively voluntarily assuming this risk, and agreeing in advance to pay out.

This is one of the reasons why I mention above that liquidated damages should be 'costed into' the project. It might also be wise to notify your insurers that you have agreed to pay liquidated damages, even though you know you will not be able to claim for them under your policy.

Contractual indemnities will not be covered by standard insurance

An indemnity would usually fall into the category of 'voluntarily assumed losses that are greater than your liability at law', and is therefore excluded by most standard professional indemnity policies.

So what does that mean in practice?

Effectively, by insisting on being indemnified, your client is removing your ability to rely on the extensive funds that your insurers would otherwise place at your disposal, forcing you to self-insure.

So if your client brings a claim under the indemnity, and your insurers walk away from the claim, you'll have to pay up for any damages out of the funds in the company coffers. And if they're not deep enough to meet the bills, liquidation is the next step available – something that doesn't really work, either for you or the client seeking to enforce the indemnity.

This means that while the client might have thought they were getting the ultimate protection by asking for an indemnity, in reality they are limiting their cover to the cash you have in the bank and the value of your assets.

While you might think this is an unreasonable exclusion on the part of the insurer, when you consider it further it makes perfect sense. After all, why should an insurer sign up to underwriting any blank cheque you volunteer to hand over to your client? How would they stay in business if they did?

What if you've been very responsible and, prior to agreeing to an indemnity in your contract, sought advice from your insurance broker?

The typical pattern of exchanges goes something like this:

You: 'Dear Broker,

We are currently negotiating a contract with a new client. The client is requesting that we indemnify them against any and all costs, losses and damages arising from our breach of the contract. I've attached the relevant contract clauses for your review.

Please will you advise as to whether this is covered under our insurance?'

Broker: 'Dear Insured,

Thank you for your enquiry, which has been noted subject to policy conditions.'

So that means they've agreed to cover you for the indemnity, right?

No, what it means is that they've recorded your correspondence in the file. They are acknowledging the fact that you've told them about the indemnity, but your position in regard to your cover is *as set out in the policy conditions*. So if the policy includes exclusion wording like that above, you still won't be covered for the indemnity.

It is possible to buy insurance cover that will pay out under an indemnity granted by you to a client. It tends to be very expensive and often specific to a particular deal.

If you deal regularly with American clients, you could be forgiven for thinking that insurance works differently there, and that US companies are automatically insured against indemnity claims. This perception arises from the absolute disbelief you'll encounter when you tell your US client that you cannot agree to grant them the indemnity they're asking for. Many US lawyers will tell you that it's normal business practice for a vendor to grant various indemnities to their clients.

From my limited research, this simply reflects a broad level of ignorance as to the contents of their insurance policies. When investigating further, I found that standard professional indemnity insurance in the US acts in exactly the same way as it does in the UK. However, there does appear to be a stronger expectation that you will have taken out specific insurance cover that will pay out under client indemnities.

This situation is driven largely by the tendency of the US courts not to award the winning party with an amount to cover some or all of its legal costs, unlike the courts in the UK. As a result, if the US lawyers want to be sure their client will pay their bills, it is in their interests to secure a contractual indemnity that expressly makes the supplier liable for their client's legal costs in the event of a successful claim.

So as you can see, the exact wording in your insurance policies can have a big impact on what you should consider agreeing to in your contract negotiations. And even if you know that a particular liability is not covered by your insurers, and the company is prepared to take that risk, you almost certainly need to notify the insurers that you're taking it on.

EXERCISE 17:

Obtain copies of your company's main business insurance policy. This could be professional indemnity insurance, product liability insurance, intellectual property insurance or any of a number of others – your company secretary or CFO should be able to direct you to someone who can provide this.

Make a summary of points in the policy that impact on what you should and should not be doing in your contracts and share it with others in the business who structure, draft and negotiate deals. If all this seems too detailed for you, you might want to ask your legal advisor if they are familiar with the terms of your insurance policy instead – it could be a good exercise for them to perform! Download the e-workbook from www.dealmakersbook.com to help you complete this exercise.

Chapter 8: Quick Summary

- Limits and exclusions of liability are designed to reduce your commercial exposure if a dispute goes to court

- Legal action is generally lose-lose, even if you 'win'

- Following the steps described in this book can help keep you out of court – many high-profile cases arose because of a failure to do so

- A limit of liability is intended to cap your financial liability if you breach the contract, but may not always succeed

- Sometimes you're better off agreeing a higher limit of liability than a very low one, as the low one might not be enforceable under UCTA

- There are some losses that you're not allowed to limit or exclude liability for by law (such as death and personal injury caused by your negligence)

- Liquidated damages are a way of working out in advance the amount of loss a particular breach would cause

- Losses are split into 'direct' and 'indirect' by reference to a case decided over 160 years ago

- The old rules are becoming fuzzier though, and Accenture lost massive sums in a contractual dispute with British Gas when it had to pay out for classes of loss that it thought it had excluded in its contract

- You can't exclude all liabilities – it's essential to leave the other party with some form of remedy if you breach the contract

- Most insurance policies exclude liability for 'voluntarily assumed losses' such as liquidated damages

- Your insurance might also stipulate other requirements you have to comply with if you're going to rely on the policy in the event that someone takes your company to court, so it's vital that someone on the negotiating team (you or your legal advisor) is familiar with its contents and conditions

- An indemnity is supposed to protect one party against any and all risk associated with a particular event (generally some form of contract breach)

- Indemnities and limits of liability regularly top the IACCM's 'Top 10 Negotiated Terms' poll, taking up a lot of negotiation time

- The scope of an indemnity is often unlimited

- Many clients expect to be indemnified against any breach of contract, or any loss related to the contract

- Most commercial insurance policies will not cover you for any claims made under a contractual indemnity

- This means that a client claiming under an indemnity will be relying on the cash in your company's bank and its assets in order to settle the indemnity, which will almost certainly put them in a worse position than claiming for damages under your insurance

- You can negotiate alternatives to indemnities

9

Confidentiality and Data Protection protect business and personal data respectively

While data protection is a topic that has only appeared on the contractual landscape relatively recently, concerns about confidentiality have been a feature of commercial discussions for many, many years. Of all the contracts signed between businesses, the Confidentiality Agreement or Non-Disclosure Agreement ('NDA') must surely be the most frequently used.

Perhaps because of its very ubiquity, the confidentiality agreement tends not to be taken very seriously by those signing it. There seems to be something in human nature that makes us think confidentiality is something that applies only to other people.

You disagree?

Consider the number of times you've been told something secret or confidential by a friend, relative or colleague. The confidential disclosure is invariably prefaced by the words, "This is really confidential, so you mustn't tell anyone, but..." And have you, then, shared the interesting nugget with someone else – again, under the cover of "This is really confidential..."?

Never? Honestly?

It is for this reason that I advise businesses that the best way to protect their confidential information is simply not to share it!

You have an automatic right to confidentiality but the contract can make it stronger and easier to enforce

There is a common law right under English law (with many other legal systems having similar provisions) to confidentiality. Common law rights are those that are not set out in written laws (which are referred to as 'statutory rights' as your rights are granted through written statutes and regulations) but have evolved over the years through case law and custom and practice.

Your common law right to confidentiality means that if you disclose information that you have identified to the recipient as being confidential, and that is not known to the general public, the recipient is obliged to maintain your confidentiality. Much like a verbal contract, though, it can be a challenge proving that this actually occurred, and that the information was deserving of the protection granted by the common law relating to confidentiality.

By putting an express obligation of confidentiality into your contract, or creating a dedicated confidentiality agreement, you make your rights to confidentiality clear and unambiguous.

So what should you include in your confidentiality provisions?

Define your 'confidential information'

First, you need to specify exactly what constitutes 'confidential information'. Some companies like to have a very detailed list of the categories of information that will be confidential. Some limit it to material that is identified in writing or verbally as being 'confidential'. Others use a wider and somewhat looser definition that refers to 'anything that should reasonably be considered to be confidential'.

Remember also to state the exclusions from confidentiality – you will have seen these in many agreements before. They are the provisions which state that confidential information does not include information that is already in the public domain, or is in the possession of the other party without any obligations of confidentiality. Much like the section in your 'limit of liability' clause that states you're not trying to exclude liability for death or personal injury, while it appears unnecessary this will serve to help you enforce the restrictions you place on use of your confidential information.

When considering this for your business, you should think about the nature of the information that you consider to be confidential. Also consider the way that your company conducts itself and the practicality of different ways of identifying things as confidential.

You might find that the contract states that any confidential information disclosed verbally must be confirmed in writing within a fixed time period if it is to be protected under the contract. Are you and your colleagues disciplined enough to follow up meetings and presentations with written confirmations? If not, don't specify it in the contract! While we should use the contract to document our best practice, there's no point in making it represent a fictional ideal world that doesn't really exist, putting ourselves under unrealistic pressures.

Define the way it should be treated

Once you're clear on exactly what your confidential information is, set out the way it should be treated. Is it sufficient for the other party to treat your confidential information in the same way they treat their own? Do you want all copies to be numbered and registered with you? May the client share it with permitted third parties? If so, who are they? And will you be holding the client responsible if any of those third parties breach your confidentiality?

Why are you sharing this information with the client? One trap we fall into is over-sharing. If something really is confidential, consider carefully whether it needs to be shared with the client.

When you've identified why you're sharing, state it in the agreement. It's important that the agreement is clear about the purposes to which the receiving party may put the confidential information. This helps to manage and control their use of your information.

Define how long it should be kept confidential

A topic of much debate among lawyers is how long a party should be obliged to keep information confidential. My personal preference is for this period to be limited to five years from the date of disclosure (not five years from the date of the contract – otherwise you could disclose something secret four years and 364 days into the agreement, only for it to be made public a day later).

Why five years? Because most business information is more or less worthless after five years. If it hasn't found its way into the public domain by then, it's probably because nobody was interested in it!

Some lawyers prefer all confidentiality obligations to last for ever (be perpetual). They argue that information will automatically cease to be confidential when it enters the public domain, but if it has been kept secret for five years there's no justification for disclosing it publicly just because the time has expired. While this makes sense in the case of specific trade secrets (the recipe for Coca Cola, for example), I don't think it's justifiable for most of the information shared under commercial contracts. Why not?

Let's assume you're going to comply fully with all your obligations under the confidentiality provisions of your agreement. You're going to record copies taken of confidential information; you're going to archive any emails containing confidential information to a secure location; you're going to make sure that, in the event the disclosing party ever asks you to, you will be able to put your hands on every single item of confidential information they've ever disclosed to you, and return it, deleting it from your own computer systems when you've done so.

Intimidated?

Now consider having to maintain those records and archives *for
ever*. Keeping track of hard drives on laptops and desktops, phones
and iPads, so that the confidential information is carefully managed
and controlled.

And if, at some point maybe ten years down the line, the client accuses
you of unauthorised disclosure of their confidential information,
you will have to demonstrate that you've complied fully with your
obligations.

So now you can see why a shorter period makes sense. You might
still agree to an indefinite period of confidentiality protection, but
hopefully you'll make sure you have the processes in place to comply
rather than just signing and crossing your fingers!

EXERCISE 18:

Find out your company's process for recording, tracking and
destroying confidential information? Does it have one? How well
do you think it is followed? Download the e-workbook from www.
dealmakersbook.com to help you complete this exercise.

Confidentiality should be mutual

If you're signing the client's agreement, you'll probably find that it
protects their confidentiality but not yours. Of course, you may not be
disclosing anything confidential so this may not matter. Otherwise,
consider making the provisions mutual, to protect your data as well
as theirs.

In particular, if your client is likely to be buying services or products
from your competitors, or to outsource the function using your
product or service to a third party, are you comfortable with that
competitor or third party having access to your information?

This is something to be considered carefully and pragmatically.
While you don't want your competitors crawling all over your
product, think about whether it's practical to prevent your client

from outsourcing or using other contractors in the part of the business that uses it. If you decide you are willing to allow this, you might want to ensure that your client takes full responsibility for any breach of your confidentiality by such outsourcing partner or other third party contractor.

The EU Data Protection Directive has changed the global data protection landscape

Data protection applies to personal data. The EU Data Protection Directive (Directive 95/46/EC) came into force in 1995 and was given effect in English law in 1998.

It is intended to keep personally identifiable data safe, and to ensure that it is only processed for the purpose known to the data subject at the time they disclosed their data.

There are a few key definitions you'll need to be familiar with in the context of data protection:

- A *data subject* is someone about whom *personal data* is held

- *Personal data* is data personally identifiable with a particular individual, whether on its own or in conjunction with other information that is readily available to the party receiving the data

- *Sensitive personal data* is personal data that includes information about an individual's race, sexuality, criminal record, health, political or religious beliefs or trade union membership

- The *data controller* is the party who is responsible for deciding what happens to the data, and how it is stored, processed and shared

- A *data processor* is a party who processes the personal data on behalf of, and under the instructions of, the data controller

There are eight Data Protection Principles set out in both the Directive and the Act, and described by the Information Commissioner's Office (the data protection enforcement office in the UK, referred to as 'ICO') as:

Information must be:

1. *Fairly and lawfully processed*

2. *Processed for specified purposes*

3. *Adequate, relevant and not excessive*

4. *Accurate and up-to-date*

5. *Not kept for longer than is necessary*

6. *Processed in line with individuals' rights*

7. *Secure*

8. *Not transferred outside the European Economic Area ('EEA') without adequate protection*

If you are processing data using your product or service on behalf of your client, you will probably be acting as a data processor. This means that your obligations are mainly limited to only using and processing the data in accordance with your instructions from the client, and keeping it secure (the seventh data protection principle).

It is the responsibility of the data controller (usually your client) to make sure that personal data is processed in accordance with these principles. Having said that, they will usually simply pass on all of their obligations directly to you!

Some interesting case law has cropped up in the UK, as the Information Commissioner's Office has begun spreading its wings and testing its powers. This has demonstrated the importance the ICO places on a data controller carefully assessing the data security measures taken by its data processors before agreeing to transfer personal data.

Two UK cases brought this issue sharply into focus, when the ICO announced fines for serious breaches of the Data Protection Act by Ealing Council and Hounslow Council following the loss of two unencrypted laptops containing sensitive personal information. The laptops contained the details of around 1,700 individuals, and were stolen from the home of an employee; although they were password protected, the personal data was not encrypted.

Interestingly (and most frightening for businesses), the fines were issued even though there is no evidence that the data had been accessed, and no loss or damage has been reported by any of the data subjects concerned.

A further complication illustrated by this case is that if you outsource any part of the processing of personal data, you are responsible for making sure that the party to whom you outsource it has appropriate data security measures in place. In this case, Hounslow Council was using Ealing Council to process data on its behalf, and should have:

- *Put into place a contract with Ealing Council obliging it to maintain appropriate data security measures*

- *Carried out its own due diligence checks to make sure that the measures in place were adequate, and were being properly applied.*

This demonstrates that, for a data controller, it is not sufficient to simply make the data processor sign an agreement stating that it has appropriate security measures in place to comply with the seventh data protection principle; it must satisfy itself that this is true.

This obligation with regard to data processors applies also to any sub-processors that might be involved in processing the personal data.

A sub-processor would be any subcontractor to you, if you're processing data on behalf of a client. This would include, for example, a provider of hosting services that hosts, supports and backs up the servers running your software application.

International data transfers are complex (and getting more so...)

In an age where borders cease to have meaning in technological terms, and where your servers might reside in the UK or the US and be accessed by support teams in Australia or India, this issue is becoming ever more complex.

The Eighth Data Protection Principle, that information should not be transferred outside the EEA without adequate protection, causes particular challenges here.

First, let's consider what we mean by 'transferred'. At first glance, you might think this refers only to situations where the data is transferred on a wholesale basis to parties overseas. So, for example, posting a CD containing personal data to a third party in India would obviously be a transfer outside the EEA. The same would apply to a bulk-upload to a server hosted overseas.

But what if your servers are in the UK, but you have out-of-hours support staff located in Australia? When these support staff take a call, they log in to your (UK) servers to access details of the customer making the call. When they call up those customer details on to their computer screen, even if the details are not saved or downloaded anywhere on to their computer, those support staff are performing a data transfer.

This means that if you're using subcontractors outside the EEA who will be able to access computer systems holding personal data, you need to pay attention!

So how can you make international data transfers without falling foul of the law?

There are three main ways::

- Using 'model clauses'

- Relying on 'Safe Harbor' for transfers to the USA

- Binding corporate rules

Taking the last mechanism first, binding corporate rules relate to transfers of data between different country entities within a group of companies. They comprise a binding agreement between those separate legal entities (which, even if they have common ownership, are independent from a legal perspective), governing data transfers between them. Binding corporate rules are still relatively uncommon at the time of writing, although ICO is trying to encourage their use more widely.

If you are transferring data between companies that are not 'related', you may wish to use the model clauses. These can be downloaded from the ICO website, and comprise a set of provisions governing data security and data processing. They are intended to be used between a data controller and a data processor, although they are also commonly used in processor to sub-processor relationships. If you execute the model clauses, you are not permitted to change any of their terms but must sign them as they are. You will be required to complete the specific details of the transfers, the processing and the security measures in place in the schedules to the model clauses.

Finally, if you're transferring data to the USA you may wish to rely on the Safe Harbor provisions.

What's Safe Harbor?

When the EU considers countries outside the EEA for their suitability to receive data transfers, considerations include (a) whether they have comprehensive data protection laws similar to those of the EU, and (b) whether they have a governmental body capable of enforcing them.

In the USA, while there are various sector-specific privacy laws, there is no all-encompassing data protection regime comparable to that in the EEA. Similarly, there is no governmental body capable of enforcing compliance and imposing sanctions on those who fail to protect personal data.

Recognising the importance of data transfers between the US and EU, the US government created the Safe Harbor program as a means of offering protection to EEA entities wishing to transfer their data to the US. The program requires the US entity to sign up to a code of practice, agreeing to comply with the EU Data Protection Principles.

To participate in the Safe Harbor scheme, an organisation must be subject to the jurisdiction of the Federal Trade Commission (FTC) or the Department of Transportation (DoT). Organisations that are likely to be excluded from the scheme include certain financial institutions, (such as banks, investment houses, credit unions, savings and loan institutions), telecommunication common carriers, labour associations, non-profit organisations, agricultural co-operatives and meat processing facilities.

The process of signing up is relatively simple, and is purely self-certified. This means that your US subcontractor should, provided it falls under the jurisdiction of the FTC or DoT, be able to sign up for the scheme quickly and easily.

However, while it's definitely a step in the right direction, Safe Harbor is not a 'magic bullet' allowing you to relax completely when transferring data to US subcontractors or partners. It is still down to you to make sure the necessary processes and technological protections are in place, to keep personal data safe.

A group of EU data protection representatives known as the Article 29 Working Party has been researching the issues related to cloud computing, and the data protection issues it raises. In July 2012, the Working Party issued a formal 'opinion' setting out what it expects of customers and service providers using cloud services.

As well as highlighting general concerns about the potential lack of control and transparency in cloud computing scenarios, the Working Party raised concerns that the US Safe Harbor regime does not always provide adequate protection for customers' data. Rather than relying on Safe Harbor alone, it recommended that organisations seeking to export personal data to the USA should conduct their own due diligence in relation to Safe Harbor companies and consider whether additional data protection measures are necessary.

Freedom of Information or breach of confidence?

As if confidentiality and data protection were not complex enough, the UK confidentiality landscape has been further upset by the bringing into force of the Freedom of Information Act 2000 (the 'FOIA').

The FOIA was brought about in an attempt to encourage transparency in government and to enable citizens to hold their public servants to account. It relates to the right of any citizen to put questions to public bodies and public authorities, and to be entitled to receive an answer in the form of information held by that body within 20 working days.

It is possible for the public body to refuse to provide information (such as the amount they paid for your products or services) on the grounds that to do so would 'prejudice the commercial interests of any person'. However, most public bodies are very reluctant to use this mechanism to protect your commercially confidential information and are likely to have express terms in your contract stating that they can decide, at their sole discretion, whether or not to apply this measure in the event of an information request under the FOIA.

So be warned that if your client is a public body in the UK, your commercial confidentiality may be prejudiced. The flip side of this is that you may be able to find out lots of useful information about the pricing and deliverables of your competitors by making an FOIA request yourself, if they are successful in winning business that you lost.

Chapter 9: Quick Summary

- There is a common law of confidentiality that protects confidential disclosures, but having a written agreement provides more protection and is easier to enforce

- You should define what counts as 'confidential', how it should be treated, and for how long

- Overly long confidentiality periods, together with very stringent confidentiality requirements (like recording all copies made), can make it very onerous to comply

- Data protection law is intended to protect individuals' personal data, and flows from an EU Directive

- The data controller is the party determining what happens to the data, and is often your client

- Your role is likely to be that of data processor, which means your two main obligations are to only use the data for the purposes the data controller tells you to, and to use good security measures to keep the data safe

- Subcontracting data processing requires you to check that the subcontractor genuinely has the required security measures in place, and is not just 'box ticking'

- You can be fined by the Information Commissioner's Office for breaches by your subcontractor if you failed to ensure your subcontractors had adequate security procedures in place

- To transfer data outside the EEA, you need to have extra provisions in place to protect the data

- Even viewing personal data on a computer screen via a browser counts as 'transferring' it for data protection purposes

- The USA has special 'Safe Harbor' measures in place to protect data, but these cannot automatically be relied on to keep your clients' data safe

- In the UK, even confidential information may not be safe if it is disclosed to a public body, as they may disclose it in response to a request under the Freedom of Information Act 2000

10

Intellectual property rights are rights in our intellectual creations

Intellectual property rights, or IPRs, are a class of assets being built, developed and protected by companies in industries as diverse as photography, publishing, software development, domestic cleaning products, materials science and pharmaceuticals.

What is intellectual property?

Intellectual property is something that, while it may result in a tangible, physical form (such as a drawing), is the product of intellectual activity (such as an idea or invention) rather than physical. This somewhat unsatisfactory definition can be built upon by considering how such property is protected, and the body of law and commercial activity that has sprung up around the concept of 'intellectual property rights'.

Why do we care? It's possible that you, in the context of your current role, might not. But if your company spends lots of money developing and fine-tuning its products, you can see that it would probably quite like to have some sort of long-term benefit from that expenditure. If anyone could just copy their developments and reproduce them at will, there would be little incentive for anyone to invest in inventing new stuff.

This means that companies are starting to focus more and more on protecting their intellectual property – the US case of Apple v Samsung (which was decided in Apple's favour at the time of writing this book, but is likely to go to appeal) shows just how seriously innovative businesses take the subject of IPR, and the lengths they'll go to protect it.

Different classes of IPRs are 'protectable' by law

Originally conceived to encourage people and companies to invest time and money in creating new and innovative things, intellectual property rights are ones that can be protected by the law. There are different categories of rights in intellectual property that can be protected by law, each of which is designed to protect different rights and works in a different way.

You might find that more than one of these will apply to the same item, or element, of intellectual property.

Patents

Patents are probably the most well-known intellectual property right.

A patent is a formally registered means of protecting an invention that meets some strictly assessed criteria. These vary slightly according to the country in which you wish to file your patent, but generally include:

- Novelty – the invention has to be genuinely new and novel, and not have been disclosed into the public domain prior to its registration for a patent

- Inventive step – the invention has to be truly inventive, and not simply the next logical progression from the current state-of-the-art

- Capable of commercial application – the invention cannot simply be a clever gimmick. It must have some sort of commercial application

Under English law, a number of categories of invention or intellectual creation are specifically excluded from patentability:

- Scientific or mathematical discoveries, theories and methods

- Literary, dramatic, musical or artistic works

- Particular ways of performing a mental act, playing a game or doing business – so a clever business model could not be protected by a patent

- The presentation of information, or some computer programs – this is different in the USA, where patents are regularly awarded for computer programs. In the UK it is very difficult to patent computer software, although there are signs that this may be changing

- An animal or plant variety

- A method of medical treatment or diagnosis

- Against public policy or morality

New inventors are often encouraged to seek a patent for their invention, particularly if there is an obvious commercial application for it that could potentially be very lucrative.

Unfortunately, they may find to their cost that a patent application is a double-edged sword. In applying for a patent, you must describe your invention in sufficient detail for the patent office to assess whether it meets the criteria for patentability. This usually means disclosing precisely the 'clever bit' that makes it so useful and valuable. Once a patent has been granted, it is unlawful for any third party to use the patented invention without the consent of the patent owner. However, unless the patent owner has the resources to defend any potential infringements of the patent, filing for a patent is similar to taking a precious item and placing it on a velvet cushion in your hallway, with the door left open to the street.

Whilst theft of the precious item is against the law, if there is no obvious barrier preventing a potential thief from helping himself or herself, it would be no surprise if it found its way into a stranger's pocket. If, however, you had a couple of very large friends who stood either side of your precious item and glared menacingly at anyone contemplating theft, chances are it would still be safe at the end of the day.

The same applies to your patent – unless you have the resources to defend it against potential thieves, anyone can help themselves to your technology without fear of sanction. And one way of finding these resources is to partner with a much bigger company and oblige them to support you, or take the lead themselves, in defending it against potential infringers.

There are some cases when patenting is essential if you are to commercialise an invention. These occur when the design and workings of your invention would be immediately obvious to anyone who studied it in detail. If this is the case, patenting is the only protection available to you. Otherwise, you might prefer to rely on confidentiality, only sharing the secrets of your invention with third parties who have entered into a contract that protects you.

Design rights

Design rights apply to the physical design of something and can be either registered or unregistered. An unregistered design is still protected by the law, but the burden of proof on the owner of the design becomes higher. Rather than simply proving that the infringer has created a design that is similar to yours (which is the case with a registered design), if it is an unregistered design you must also prove that they saw yours and actively copied it.

The duration of protection is also longer for registered designs than for unregistered designs.

Copyright

This is the most common form of intellectual property right, and applies to the right to copy an 'artistic or literary work'. Confusingly, computer software source code is considered to be a literary work, protected by the law of copyright.

In England, copyright exists automatically, as soon as the creator has created their work. In other countries, such as the USA, copyrights must be registered before they are enforceable.

Copyright automatically belongs to its creator or their employer (if it was created in the course of their employment). This means that if you use a subcontract software programmer or designer, you should ensure your agreement with them includes the transfer to your company of copyright in the work they create for you.

Trade marks

Most companies with a name and logo will associate a certain amount of value with their name and logo. Clients, partners and suppliers will recognise them and will automatically assume that the particular logo, or name and font style, relate to your company. When a name and/or logo have been used for a long time by a business, they become trademarks of that business without requiring registration.

Much like with design rights, registering a trade mark makes it easier to defend and extends the duration of its protection.

The value of a trade mark is in the 'goodwill' associated with it. So if your company has a reputation for providing excellent quality products, someone else could copy your trade mark on their own products to encourage buyers to mistake their products for your high-quality ones, and to gain sales as a result.

Some infringers go further still, copying other aspects of your website or packaging to lead buyers to believe they are buying from you. This creates an offence called 'passing off', as they are trying to 'pass off' their business as being yours. Many trade mark infringement cases are closely linked to passing off cases, as the two tend to go together.

Business models and ideas

These present a challenge in terms of intellectual property protection, as there is not currently a mechanism for registering and protecting them by law in the UK. If you have a clever business model, then unless you are able to support it with other things that are protectable (such as your own software product, trade mark or patented technology), you are likely to find others copying you once you have demonstrated its success.

As far as ideas go, we regularly encounter inventors who have had wonderful ideas for new ways of doing things that are not protectable by any of the standard IPR registration routes. These inventors have usually not made much progress in commercialising their idea; they are sure they're on to a good thing, but acknowledge that making a prototype to prove it works will require lots of investment.

While it is often possible to find investors who are happy to put funds into such exciting and potentially lucrative ideas, the inventor should be very careful to secure protection for the idea through confidentiality agreements and other contracts. Otherwise, there is nothing to prevent the potential investor simply stealing the idea and exploiting it without the need to recognise the contribution of the original inventor.

I have a client that has developed a very distinctive business model for providing web-based recruitment services. The model is based around a success-only fixed fee, where the amount of the fee varies according to the level of exclusivity the recruiter is given to promote the opportunity, and the amount of time their customer is able to put into reviewing and responding to candidates.

Because the model is (or was, at the time of its creation) very novel, the company asked me to create some bespoke terms and conditions describing how it worked. I did, and over the years these have been refined and tweaked to address changes in the market, and respond to issues that have arisen in the business. As a result, the terms are very specific to this particular business and don't look much like those that appear on other recruitment websites.

Unfortunately, my client has suffered from its success, with many imitators emulating its business model. Over the years, these have included those who have effectively stolen their whole website, including elements of the graphic design and the web copy. They have also, on many occasions, included companies who have stolen my client's terms of business and simply 'lifted' them on to their own site.

So what means has my client been able to use to defend its business?

When the infringer stole the 'look and feel' and web copy, I wrote to them asking them to cease and desist on two counts:

- *They were committing the offence of 'passing off', trying to mislead anyone arriving on their website to believe they were buying from our client*

- *They had infringed our client's copyright in their web text*

Interestingly, because of my company's terms of business with the client, when the infringer stole the recruiter's terms and conditions it was my company's copyright that they'd infringed. This was because when I draft agreements for a client, I grant the client an irrevocable, perpetual licence to use, edit and amend the agreement within their own business, but my company retains ownership of the copyright.

So the part of the letter regarding the breach of copyright of the terms and conditions came directly from my company, Devant, rather than from Devant on behalf of the client.

To date, I've had a 100% success rate with these 'cease and desist' letters, with the infringers immediately taking down the infringing content in most cases, and within a few days for the others. One bemused recruiter explained that he had outsourced the development of his new website to an offshore web development company, and was not aware that he even had any terms and conditions on the site. The developers had obviously found our terms and adopted them lock, stock and barrel – including my client's company registration details!

If you own an IPR, you control the right of others to use it

When you own an intellectual property right, you can use it as you choose. When it comes to commercialising it, that might mean that you choose to exclude anyone else in the world (or a particular country) from using it, so that you benefit exclusively from its wonderfulness.

Alternatively, you might realise that others have more resources to exploit and generate business from your IP than you do. Or you might want to work with others to help you exploit it yourself.

What are the mechanisms for granting rights to others without giving your IPR away?

The most obvious mechanism, used by software vendors the world over, is to grant a client a limited licence to use your IP. So in the case of software, this means granting your client a licence to use the copyrighted computer source code (probably) as compiled into some form of executable.

(By the way – in English, we use 'licence' with a 'c' for the noun – "we grant you a licence to use…"and 'license' with an 's' for the verb – "we license you to use…" In America, they use an 's' for both flavours.)

If you have a patented invention, you might want to license a manufacturer to use your patent for the purpose of manufacturing goods for supply to you. Or you could grant a reseller licence, enabling them to manufacture the goods and sell them directly to end users, paying you some form of royalty for each unit made and/or sold.

These days, most commercial manufacturing seems to be done in China or other eastern countries. There are still significant concerns, however, about how safe your IPR is in the hands of a Chinese manufacturer – with some justification, given the prevalence of 'knock off' brand-name goods in Chinese markets.

The Chinese government has taken some steps to enforce the intellectual property rights of western companies outsourcing manufacture to China, clamping down hard when it discovers factories making branded goods without a licence. However, the sheer scale of the challenge means that this remains a problem for companies, and is likely to continue to do so for many years.

One of my clients whose products were being manufactured in China was concerned about potential over-production being sold through grey import channels. Attitudes to contracts are somewhat different in China from the UK. This meant that, as well as putting a sensible contract in place, my client worked very hard to develop its relationship with the manufacturer and to ensure that the manufacturer understood what was, and was not, acceptable use of the IP.

Leaving nothing to chance, the client also appointed a local agent who was educated in the UK, and who would make regular visits to the manufacturer to check that the agreement was being adhered to.

For software, you can also license a reseller to sub-license the software to their own clients. This means that the licensing relationship is between you and the reseller, and then between the reseller and the end-user. In this scenario, there would be no direct contractual relationship between you and the end-user.

As the owner of the IPR, it is for you to determine (and set out clearly in your contract) precisely what the licensee may and may not do with it. So you might allow them to make only a limited number of copies of it, for example. You might restrict the countries in which they can use your IP. You might require them to pay you some form of royalty each time they use it. You may wish to specify that they have to include your company name on each product they make with your IP, or conversely that they are prohibited from putting your company name on their products.

The key thing is to think carefully about what rights you need in order to pursue your own business objectives, what rights an end-user needs in order to benefit from the licence, and what rights a reseller needs in order to resell it. You can then work with your legal advisor to structure your licence terms so that they reflect exactly how things need to work in practice.

You may, of course, decide that continuing to own the IPR is not important to you, and choose to sell it rather than license it. There are specific procedures to be followed when transferring IPRs, particularly formally granted ones like patents, so take advice and work together with your legal advisor to make sure this is done properly. You might also find that the company's articles of association and/or shareholder agreement requires the sale or transfer of valuable intellectual property rights to be approved by a vote of directors and/or shareholders. So check where you stand before you start doing deals to sell IPR!

Enhancing your product for a client creates a complex IP landscape

If you have created a 'product' based upon your IP, and sell it to businesses, it's likely that from time to time a client has asked you to 'tweak' your product to better fit their specific requirements.

As soon as you start to venture 'off piste', enhancing your IP to meet a particular client need, you are entering dangerous ground from an intellectual property perspective.

Why's that?

EXERCISE 19:

Download the e-workbook from www.dealmakersbook.com and complete the case study exercise to see how intellectual property ownership can impact on everyday business activity, whatever your business sector.

When you begin to develop tailored functionality that closely reflects the requirements of a particular client, the design of that tailored functionality may flow directly from the requirement. If it was documented by the client, and given to you to implement, you may find that the intellectual property rights in that design belong to the client. You will almost certainly find yourself including elements of client IPR into your work as you progress. So the IP ownership of the actual enhancement is open to question, and may comprise a mixture of your IP and client IP.

If the development work for the enhancement is paid for directly by the client, things get even muddier. Even though they may have no contractual basis for believing this, clients tend to have a firmly held belief that if they paid for some research and development work, they own the results of it.

But isn't that entirely reasonable? After all, they paid for it, they should own it - shouldn't they?

While this arrangement can work if the development was very much out of line with the requirements of your other clients, it can put significant strain on your business from both a commercial and an operational perspective. Most product development companies, and even 'solutions' development companies, regularly re-use work done on one project when working on another.

Why?

Because it saves time, saves money, and avoids 'reinventing the wheel'. Effectively, it enables the business to move forward, building on what it has learned in the past. And when future clients ask you if you can develop something new for them, you are often able to take something you did before as a starting point, saving them money and reducing the risk of the project failing.

If you had handed over the ownership of the IP of each new development to the client that requested it, you would have no choice but to start again from scratch each time you needed to develop something similar. To do otherwise would infringe the IPR of the earlier client. So you can see this makes each subsequent development more expensive and higher risk, making your company less attractive as a supplier.

It also causes problems from an operational perspective. Imagine you were the development manager responsible for tracking re-use of existing materials. Each time your team wanted to build on existing work, you would have to check its ownership and make sure you're permitted to use it.

There might be particular commercial arrangements in place, requiring you to pay royalties to the 'owning' client. So you would have to work out the cost to you of incorporating such components for your anticipated number of sales vs. the cost of developing them again from scratch.

Rather than venturing down this route, you're better off insisting from the start that all IPR generated in the course of any customisations or tailoring should belong to you. The client will be granted a licence to use it, along with your other IPR.

Are there disadvantages for the client?

Several, but none that should be fatal to the deal in most cases. The first is that the client may want to sell-on the newly developed IP (sometimes referred to as 'foreground IPR') to third parties. Your ownership of it, and their licence to use it, will almost certainly preclude that. However, given that the new IP will only represent a portion of the overall solution, it's doubtful that they could usefully sell it without your pre-existing IP ('background IPR'). So any loss of opportunity for the client is likely to be theoretical rather than actual.

The second, more common issue raised by clients funding new development is that they don't want their competitors to have access to it. They feel it would be unfair for their competitors to benefit from their investment in new functionality, without the competitors having to pay for its development. While this is understandable, the funding client will have a number of benefits arising directly from its funding. It will receive the new functionality first, stealing a march on the competition. It will also have input into the content and implementation of the new functionality, so that it meets the funder's needs better than those of the competition.

If you really must, you can agree that nobody else will receive the new functionality for a certain amount of time after the funder – say six months. But even this can cause administrative hassles for the development team and other sales people, so avoid such commitments if you can.

SOFTWARE ALERT!

The rest of this chapter has a strong software focus. Those of you with no professional interest in ones and noughts and the magic they can perform should skip to the end of the chapter – you can pick up the essential nuggets in the summary, so that you know where to find them if you happen to need them in the future.

Software licensing models are evolving all the time

While IPR licensing is something that occurs with all sorts of different types of intellectual property, the software industry is the 'petri-dish' in which new models are tested, experimented with and developed most frequently.

The technological advances that have seen the birth of 'cloud computing' have also stimulated the development of a number of new cloud-based licensing models. In this section we're going to look closer at some of the key issues associated with the software licensing models that are common at the time of writing.

Perpetual vs. term licensing

The most common form of licensing for large, enterprise-wide software applications is the perpetual licence or the multi-year term licence.

This is particularly true of the sort of software that becomes an integral part of a business's operations – its Enterprise Resource Planning (ERP) system, for example. An ERP system can manage your company's payroll, HR, stock control, order processing, invoicing, job tracking and many other key business functions.

These systems are often tailored to a greater or lesser degree to the business using them. The tailoring may take the form of configuration (also referred to as data-driven tailoring) or software modifications (customisation or bespoke development). There is also a significant cost associated with the implementation and roll-out of such systems, as company data and business rules are loaded in and developed and the staff is trained on how to use them.

For all of these reasons, a business will be keen to ensure that it has a continued right to use the software for a reasonable period of time – at least the anticipated life of the software. This might vary from three years to twenty, depending on the nature of the software and the business concerned. But it is unlikely that a company will be willing to make a sizeable investment in implementing such a significant software solution without a long-term commitment from the software owner.

When software is licensed on a 'perpetual' basis, this means that the licensee (or client) can continue to use it forever, without paying any more licence fees to the vendor.

It doesn't mean that they will never pay anything to the vendor at all. As we discussed in chapter 7, support and maintenance is an important part of the ongoing vendor-client relationship. Offering a good support and maintenance package will ensure that the client's software stays up to date, and that you retain a client relationship that is positive, both in terms of revenue and client satisfaction. You might also offer upgrades and enhancements to the software over time – some of these might be included within the support fee, while others may be optional extras.

With support and maintenance, upgrades and enhancements, and additional licences to cover growth in the business, a perpetual licence arrangement still offers plenty of opportunities for recurring revenue.

There is, however, a potential fly in the ointment for the perpetual licence model. The Courts of Justice of the European Union (CJEU) have, at the time of writing, issued a judgment in the case of UsedSoft GmbH v Oracle International that is likely to act as a significant disincentive to software companies wanting to grant perpetual licences.

While the details of the case are somewhat technical (and leave plenty of other questions to be answered), the key point is that the

CJEU decided that it was perfectly legitimate for UsedSoft to sell 'second-hand' Oracle licences, even though Oracle's licence terms stated that the licence was non-transferrable. This means that if you sell a perpetual licence to a client for your software, and they subsequently decide they no longer need it, they are free to sell it on to somebody else, regardless of what it says in the contract that you used to sell them the licence!

So you can see that perpetual licences have some special risks which are not applicable to licences for a fixed term.

The key feature of a term licence is that it will, by default, come to an end at the end of its defined term. So if you've signed a three-year deal, on the first day of year four the client will no longer be entitled to use the software. This is rather a clunky way to end such a relationship, and most term licences contain an automatic rollover provision that makes them auto-renew for successive periods unless otherwise requested by the client or the vendor.

The auto-renew period could be the same duration as the original licence. This is better for you, but means that the client has to take great care to check they really want to renew, prior to the last date for notifying you whether they want to quit the licence. In practice, most organisations are very weak at this which means that auto-renew contracts can almost end up looking and feeling like perpetual ones.

From a sales perspective, it's important to be clear about which revenue counts towards your own sales targets and commission calculations. Some organisations only count the original sale. Others include renewals that you have had an active role in facilitating. Others will reward you for all renewals on deals you sold originally, even if they occur by default. The same is true of support and maintenance revenue – make sure you know whether you'll be rewarded for all support revenue from your clients or only for the initial term of support.

If the latter, that's a good motivator to encourage the client to sign up for the longest possible minimum term for their support agreement!

Software As A Service (SAAS) licensing

First, we need to differentiate between the software delivery model and the software licensing model, as they are two distinct things.

Generally speaking, software that is licensed on a perpetual or fixed-term basis will be installed on the client's own computer hardware, in their own data centre. This is not always the case, however. It is entirely possible for a client to buy a perpetual licence for the software from you and then have it hosted on computers owned and/or managed and maintained by a third party. That third party could be you, it could be a hosting provider, or it could be an outsourcing partner.

In this particular scenario, the software licensing model is 'perpetual or fixed-term licence'. The client could, if they chose, migrate 'their' licensed software on to computers owned and managed by a different party if they were unhappy with the current hosting or outsourcing partner. But this would have no impact on their right to use the software itself.

The SAAS licensing model differs significantly from this in that both the hosting of the software AND the right to use it are bundled together in one deal.

So if you are buying software as a service from me and decide you don't like my hosting, you will not automatically be free to move the software on to the server and hosting provider of your choice. I will be the one able to decide where it is hosted – and I may decide that it will only be hosted on my servers, or those of my preferred hosting partner.

SAAS tends to be used for software that is not tailored or customised from one client to the next. It may involve each client using essentially the same installation of the software, albeit with login and security provisions that prevent them from seeing one another's data.

From a vendor perspective, this makes it easier to maintain as all clients will always be on the latest version of the software. It also means that your business model is based on regular (often monthly) recurring payments. These might go up and down according to the actual usage of the software by the client during that month, or they might be fixed for a particular term.

The SAAS model works for clients where they have a need that varies over time and only want to pay for what they use. If the software is interchangeable with other packages delivering similar functionality, so much the better; if I don't like the changes you're implementing in your pricing, I can migrate my data off your software and move it elsewhere. In practice, this is rarely as easy as it sounds, with the result that clients believing they are buying flexibility and low commitment actually end up tied to a particular vendor more tightly than they anticipated.

As client companies are becoming more savvy in this respect, you may be asked to make commitments regarding pricing and availability of your software for an extended period. These may be rather unbalanced, since the client will be free to withdraw from use of your software on very short notice. From a negotiation perspective you can trade commitments both sides, so that your commitment to fixed pricing and availability of the software is mirrored by a longer term subscription from the client.

While the SAAS model provides for regular income, it generally rolls the support and maintenance and hosting fees into the main SAAS fee rather than billing these separately. So bear this in mind when looking at potential revenues and make sure that your monthly fees include a licence component rather than just covering the support and hosting costs.

It is also difficult to charge for upgrades and updates under an SAAS model, as the client expects these to be introduced 'for free'. If you introduce additional modules of new functionality, these can be priced separately as 'extras', but enhancements to existing modules will almost certainly have to be given away.

The Microsoft Question. *When drafting reseller agreements for software, my colleagues and I regularly encounter what has come to be known in our business as 'the Microsoft Question'.*

This crops up so often that I feel it is worth me taking some time to set it out in full here. It arises when we talk about the way the software is going to be licensed and paid for.

If you recall from chapter 2, in order to make a binding contract there needs to be an offer, acceptance and consideration between the parties. So if I am licensing my software to you, I offer you the use of my software, subject to certain limitations and restrictions, in consideration of the licence fee that you will pay to me. There is some give and take on both sides, creating the binding contract that allows me to enforce my licence restrictions and you to enforce your licence rights.

Now let's put a reseller into the picture. I license my software to the reseller, for resale. I've offered the reseller the right to sublicense my software in exchange for a fee to be paid to me by the reseller. This fee could either be related to the number of end-user licences the reseller sells, or it could be a flat one-off fee, an annual fee, or anything else he and I agree.

The reseller then licenses the software to you, granting you certain rights to use it in exchange for the licence fee that you pay to him.

In this picture, there are two distinct but related contractual relationships. Between me and the reseller, there is an agreement allowing me to control the basis on which he sublicenses my software, and allowing him the right to enforce warranties and other contract terms against me.

Between you and the reseller, there is an agreement allowing the reseller to control the basis on which you use my software, and allowing you the right to enforce warranties and other contract terms against the reseller.

There is a legal principle that states that one cannot sell what one does not have, and that applies equally to reselling of software as to reselling of goods. That means that the reseller cannot grant you any rights in my software that I have not expressly allowed him to. He can offer you his own services, or other products, in connection with the software. So, for example, he could sell you an enhanced support package, or some installation services, without any reference to me. But if I had specified, for example, that the software could only be licensed for use in companies in the pharmaceutical industry, he could not license it to you for use in the construction industry.

So now you can see the relationship between the three of us – me, the reseller and you – and how the money flows. In this picture, there is no direct contractual relationship between me and you – the reseller sits in the middle.

This means that, under your licence agreement, you would not be entitled to bring any legal actions for breach of warranty against me; you would have to bring them against the reseller, and he in turn could bring a similar action against me.

Similarly, if you were to breach your licence agreement and use my software in the construction industry, I would not have any contractual recourse against you; I would have to take my action against the reseller, and get him to enforce the terms of his licence agreement with you.

Now we go to the Microsoft model. If you go to your local computer vendor and purchase a copy of Microsoft Office, you will pay your money (the 'consideration') to the vendor. When you open your Microsoft package, you will see that there is a licence agreement associated with the software, and that in order to install the software, you have to 'click to accept' the licence terms. These terms state very clearly that this licence to use the software is being granted by Microsoft itself, not by the vendor from whom you purchased the licence.

So where does that fit in our contractual chain? There is no direct contractual link, using the offer-acceptance-consideration model, between you and Microsoft. So if you wanted to enforce the terms of your licence agreement against Microsoft, or (more likely) if Microsoft wanted to enforce the terms of the agreement against you, what would be the contractual basis for doing so?

There are two answers to this question. The first, following the strict legal rules for construction of a contract, is that there is no direct contractual relationship between you and Microsoft. The second answer is that in a dispute between you and Microsoft, this would be irrelevant. Their financial and legal 'firepower' is such that the dispute would be most unlikely to ever get to court, and so the mechanics of this licence agreement would not be tested.

So this brings me back the 'the Microsoft question'. This is the question asked by software vendors wanting to use resellers to take the end-user's money, but wishing to enter into a direct licence agreement themselves with each end-user licensee. The question goes, "But why can't I do this and still be able to enforce the terms of my licence agreement directly against the licensee? It works for Microsoft."

The answer is, "Because you're not Microsoft."

For a business with less firepower than this global giant, particularly if that business wants to put itself in the strongest possible position to enforce its intellectual property rights against its licensees, it's safest to stick to the rules. By having a direct contractual relationship with your licensees (i.e. they pay the licence fee to you, or a sales agent takes the money on your behalf and you grant the licence to the licensee directly) you maximise your chances of being able to enforce your terms.

Many thousands of software vendors, selling shrink-wrapped software through retailers, use this same Microsoft model, largely without problems. In each case, the licence fee is relatively low and the risk to the business of a licence breach by an individual licensee is similarly low. If you fit this description, the Microsoft model may also work for you.

But if you sell large, expensive software solutions on a business-to-business basis, where the cost of breach of a single client could be huge, it's probably better to be safe than sorry. I'm not saying you would never succeed in enforcing your terms if you followed the Microsoft model. But if you don't have their legal and financial power, why put yourself in a position where your ability to do so might be in question?

'Click to Accept'

Under the perpetual and term licence category above, we looked at major enterprise-wide software packages. For these, you will almost certainly be entering into a signed agreement with the client that may have undergone some negotiation and amendments from your standard terms. And even in the SAAS section, if the software concerned is going to be used by a large number of users in the same organisation, you may well sign a contract with the company itself that sets out the terms on which all of their staff may use your software.

If your software is aimed at individual PC users, you are more likely to use 'shrink-wrap' or 'click-wrap' software licensing mechanisms.

These are effectively just a different way of establishing a contract between your company and the user of the software, and letting them know about the licence terms and conditions that apply to their usage. In the 'shrink-wrap' model, you may print the licence conditions on the product's packaging and assert that by unwrapping the cellophane from the package, the customer has accepted the terms.

In the 'click-wrap' or 'click to accept' model, when the user comes to install the software on his or her machine it will ask the user to 'accept' the licence terms by clicking on a box. The same route can be used to establish a contract in the SAAS world, when individual users sign up for the service.

There are a couple of challenges with this model that have not been properly tested in the courts and so remain unclear.

Why don't these licences appear in court cases?

This may be because it is a method of licensing that tends to be preferred for lower value software, and therefore users are not inclined to spend lots of money litigating their disputes. Or it may be that for the money spent, customers are happy to accept any modest shortfalls in the product or service. Or perhaps all such software packages perform beautifully, and no contract breaches by the vendor have ever occurred.

The potential issues with 'click to accept' licences are:

- The disconnect between payment and acceptance of the terms (see 'The Microsoft Question' above)

- Proving that the licensee has seen and knowingly accepted the terms

With respect to the first of these, as well as the software author – reseller – licensee issues there are also challenges about the authority of the user to accept the terms at all. If the user is an individual within a business, they may or may not be authorised to enter into contracts on behalf of that business.

Many companies selling software will use this licensing approach precisely because there is little chance that the software licence will ever be reviewed by the client's legal representatives.

EXERCISE 20:

Download the e-workbook from www.dealmakersbook.com and complete the case study exercise to see how your contract terms can significantly impact the potential outcome of a problem with a software package.

While the 'click to accept' model might be very quick and easy, avoiding the need for time-consuming and expensive contract negotiations, if it is important that your business is able to rely on your terms you might want to consider more express mechanisms for agreeing terms.

The issue of customers not having seen the terms arises from the fact that in many software packages, both online and installed, the user is not required to read or even scroll through the licence terms before they are permitted to click the 'Accept terms' button.

This can be addressed by the vendor by the simple act of putting the 'Accept terms' button at the bottom of the scroll box displaying the terms themselves, or de-activating it until the user has scrolled through the terms.

It is also advisable to provide an option enabling the user to download and/or print the terms prior to accepting them.

While neither of these guarantees that the user will have read and understood the terms, they demonstrate that you've used your reasonable efforts to encourage them to do so. Consequently they will support you in enforcing these terms against the user if you ever need to.

If you don't make any effort to ensure the user has seen and understood your terms, you make them more or less pointless.

As we discussed in chapter 2, if we want the contract to do a good job as the 'User Guide for the Commercial Relationship', it's important that the client is able to understand what's expected of them so that they can comply. Similarly, it's important for them to understand what they can expect of you! If you make sure your 'click to accept' terms are drafted in as clear and friendly language as possible, and are laid out to make them easy to review online, you will go a long way towards meeting these objectives.

Escrow

No discussion of software licensing is complete without a quick look at the topic of escrow.

Escrow is an arrangement in which a trusted third party (the 'escrow provider') looks after an asset on behalf of its owner. If certain events occur (known as 'release conditions'), the escrow provider releases the asset to one or more third parties identified in the original escrow agreement.

This mechanism can be used in house purchases, where the escrow provider holds the cash for the purchase while contracts are exchanged. In the software context, the asset held by the escrow provider is the source code of the software.

The idea is that if a release condition occurs, the escrow provider will release the source code to the licensees who are signed up to the service (and will usually pay the annual fees required to benefit from it).

Typical release conditions for software source code escrow include the software owner being unable or unwilling to continue supporting the software, or the software owner becoming insolvent. So by releasing the source code, the licensee is (theoretically, at least) able to support the software by itself.

The software owner is generally in control of the drafting of the escrow agreement, which will be based on the standard terms of the escrow provider. In some circumstances, the licensee(s) will have some say in what goes into that agreement. Things of interest to them will include the release conditions, the number of updates to the source code that will be made each year, and whether the escrow provider carries out any verification services on the source code.

Verification services are time-consuming and therefore expensive, but greatly increase the value of the escrow to the licensees. To 'verify' the source code deposited by the owner, the escrow provider uses the instructions provided by the owner, together with any third party compilers, operating systems and other software specified by the owner (more cost!), to 'build' a working set of object code from the deposited source code. It then installs this object code and verifies that it is a fully working copy.

Without verification services, there is no guarantee that all the components necessary to recreate the working software have been deposited, and are up to date. So a licensee may simply be left with a mess of uncompilable source code.

Even with the verification services, there is no guarantee that the licensee will be able to use the source code to support its own software, for a reasonable cost. Anyone who has ever tried to understand how someone else's code works, without the benefit of having the author there to explain it, will know just how big a challenge this is, particularly if the software is 'big' and complex.

Escrow remains, however, something that many licensees see as a valuable 'insurance policy' against the vendor's insolvency or intransigence.

Chapter 10: Quick Summary

- Intellectual property rights are the legally protectable rights in our inventions, documents, designs, trademarks and software

- They can be protected by patents, by copyright law, and by either registered or unregistered design rights and trademarks

- It is not possible to protect ideas and business models under English intellectual property law, other than by keeping them confidential

- The owner of an intellectual property right can either exploit it by using it themselves, or by charging others a licence fee to use it

- You can also permit resellers to sub-licence your intellectual property

- The software retail model in which the licence is sold by the retailer, but entered into directly between the user and the licensor, causes some contract construction challenges but generally seems to work (and is not often challenged in court)

- When selling complex, expensive, business-to-business software, it's better to use a model in which there's no room for dispute about the enforceability of the licence terms

- Making client-specified changes to your intellectual property causes complexity in terms of ownership

- Ownership of changes and new developments should be agreed at the start

- New software licensing models are evolving all the time, but currently the most common are either a long-term/perpetual licence or some form of hosted 'software as a service' model

- Escrow can give the licensee comfort that they'll have access to your source code if you become insolvent, but in reality this may be of little use to them

11

A whistle-stop guide to the 'legalese' at the back!

We've looked at the main functional areas of the contract in some detail. In chapters 4 and 5 we considered 'Who does what, when' to make sure each party's obligations and expectations were clearly addressed. In chapter 6 we made sure that we knew when payment could be expected, and how to make sure it occurred when due. And in chapters 7 and 8 we looked at practical ways to address problems that might occur and legal ways to limit their impact.

Along the way, in chapters 9 and 10, we've considered data protection, confidentiality, and intellectual property issues.

If you've ever scanned through or reviewed contracts for your business, you'll know that there is a whole stack of contract provisions that don't appear to contribute much to the 'meat' of the contract, but appear somewhere at the back. These terms are commonly referred to as 'boilerplate' and are often simply copied from one contract to another without any particular consideration of whether or not they work in this context.

In this chapter we'll take a quick gallop through the most common boilerplate clauses. We'll look at why they matter and what to watch out for. I've arranged them in alphabetical order, to help you find the one you're looking for if you're using this as a reference section, but this isn't necessarily the order in which they'll appear in your contracts.

Applicable Law

In chapter 7 we looked at dispute resolution, and I explained the importance of **Applicable laws, courts and mediation**.

The law applicable to the contract is usually stated somewhere near the back. It's important to state it explicitly in the contract, and to set out clearly the courts that have jurisdiction to decide any disputes arising from the contract. Bear in mind, if you're going for English law, that there is no such thing as 'UK law' or 'British law'. England and Wales share a common legal system, but while there are a number of statutes (that is, written laws) that apply in the same way in England and Wales and in Scotland and Northern Ireland, there are also some legal principles and statutes that differ. Any English person who's ever tried to buy a house north of the border will be able to attest to this!

In this section, you'll also specify whether mediation, arbitration or adjudication will be used to remedy such disputes. There's more discussion on this topic in chapter 7.

From a sales perspective, the applicable law might seem like an easy thing to concede if your client is in another country to you and has asked to change it to their law, or to the laws of a 'neutral' third country. Unfortunately, the applicable law effectively provides the 'lens' through which the rest of the contract is read, and determines how its legal provisions will be interpreted. It can also cause other statutes and legal principles to be implied into your contract – laws and principles of which you might be totally oblivious.

If you're considering agreeing to a different legal system from your own, check that you have access to local legal counsel who can advise you about this stuff. It may be an expensive exercise, so ensure you've budgeted for it. In case you're contemplating going ahead without this review, though, the costs of getting it wrong could be significantly higher than the legal fees associated with making sure you have it right!

Assignment

In chapter 5 we considered exactly who we were contracting with. Sadly, having the right company sign up to your agreement in the first place is not the end of the story when it comes to contracting parties. Many contracts have a provision regarding 'assignment or transfer of any of the parties' rights or obligations under this agreement'.

This is also a clause often seen as one that's easy to grant concessions on; these concessions might relate to allowing the client to assign the agreement, or removing your own right to do so. But what does assignment mean?

The client's right to assign or novate the agreement

The terms 'assign' and 'novate' are frequently confused (even, occasionally, by lawyers!). To be able to 'assign' your rights under an agreement allows you to permit a third party to benefit from the rights the agreement grants to you.

A common example of this is when a company uses invoice discounting (also known as 'factoring') to improve its cash flow. Effectively, the company assigns the **right** *it has to be paid under a contract to the factoring provider.*

So when its customer pays an invoice, rather than paying the company it contracted with, it will pay the cash to the factor.

The factor does not become responsible for delivering the company's products or services under the contract – that obligation remains with the company itself. It simply acquires the right to receive payment of sums that the customers owe the company.

So you can 'assign' rights and benefits under a contract (unless it expressly says you can't). But the important thing to remember about assignment is that you cannot assign *obligations*. This means that while you can allow a third party to get paid for the work you've done under a contract, you can't hand over your responsibilities for delivering under the contract to another third party.

Why not? It makes sense, really. If you were the client and you'd chosen a company to be your supplier, on the basis of whatever long and complex list of selection criteria you had devised, you wouldn't take kindly to that company just handing over its responsibilities to someone else that you hadn't vetted.

But what about subcontracting? Isn't that handing over your responsibilities?

No. The difference is that when you subcontract certain obligations, you *still remain responsible to the client for the performance of those obligations*. So if your subcontractor messes up, it's your responsibility to put it right as far as the client is concerned. Of course, you'll then try to get the subcontractor to compensate you for any resulting losses, but the key thing is that, as far as the customer is concerned, it's *you* who's responsible. And you're the one carrying the legal liability. It's this legal liability that you can't assign.

What about novation?

Novation is different. It's a mechanism allowing you to hand over both your rights *and* your responsibilities under a contract to a third party. But because this is a pretty big deal (see above!), it requires the client's express consent. Generally, this will be given via a three-way agreement signed by you, the client, and the party taking over the contract from you.

Now that you understand what novation and assignment mean, we need to see why your client might want to be able to do them, and what impact that has on you.

Why would anyone want to novate or assign?

There are a number of reasons why a company might want to assign or novate a contract. Maybe the contract no longer performs the function for which it was entered into, and the company wants to transfer it to another in its group. Perhaps the company has

224

been acquired, and the acquirer wants to transfer all of its assets (including its contracts) to itself and wind up the original entity. Or maybe the contract itself is seen as a lucrative and valuable asset which the company wants to sell.

From your point of view, one reason you might object to the client assigning the benefit of your contract is if it were to assign it to a competitor of yours. If this happened, you might find yourself disclosing the secrets of your success to your arch rival – not ideal. Another reason would be if the entity to whom the contract was assigned was not a trustworthy custodian of your intellectual property (more on intellectual property in chapter 10).

In theory, even if the client assigned the benefit of the contract to a third party, the client itself would remain responsible for ensuring all of their obligations (such as the obligation to pay, and the obligation to respect your intellectual property) under the contract were met. So if the third party (called the 'assignee') failed to pay you, you could take action against your client (the 'assignor') and make them pay up. Similarly, if the assignee breached your intellectual property rights, you could sue the assignor for damages.

However, this adds another layer of complexity and expense to what would already be a complex and expensive process of trying to seek a remedy through the courts. You might well prefer to avoid it altogether by simply stating that the client is NOT permitted to assign or transfer any of its rights or obligations under the contract!

When it comes to novation, the client would have to seek your consent anyway – so don't worry too much about expressly prohibiting this in the contract.

Be aware that asking for rights for yourself, or expressly prohibiting the other party from exercising certain rights, is likely to trigger a request for reciprocity from the client – so think carefully before specifying that you may assign and/or novate the contract. Consider whether or not you'd be happy allowing the client to do the same. If not, can you and your legal advisor come up with some justifiable reasons why not? Otherwise, you're likely to find this creates negotiation challenges that could damage your relationship.

Contracts (Rights of Third Parties) Act 1999

This bit of legislation may not be listed as a heading in your contract, but is highly likely to be referenced at odd points throughout it. If you're selling overseas, it's one that will be picked up by the other side's legal counsel and you'll probably be asked what it is, and what it does. So here you go...

For many hundreds of years, English law worked on the basis of a concept called 'privity of contract'. This meant that only the parties to a contract were entitled to enforce its terms.

So if you and I had signed a contract that stated you would mow my mother's lawn once a month and you failed to do so, I would be the only party entitled to claim damages for your failure to perform. My mother would have no rights, as she was not a party to the original contract.

The Contracts (Rights of Third Parties) Act 1999 (the '3rd Parties Act') changed this, enabling named third parties (or categories of third party) to enforce their rights under a contract to which they were not an original signatory. In the example above, if I stated in our contract that my mother was a third party beneficiary under the Contracts (Rights of Third Parties) Act 1999, my mum would be able to pursue you herself if you failed to mow her lawn.

This brought about a fundamental shift in the way contracts could be used. It also created a new boilerplate clause that has since appeared in the great majority of English commercial contracts! While the 3rd Parties Act requires any third party beneficiary to be expressly identified in the contract, most businesses don't want to take the chance that some third party mentioned in the course of a contract might be construed as being a beneficiary.

As a result, you will frequently see a clause stating that '*A person who is not a party to this Agreement has no rights under the Contracts (Rights of Third Parties) Act 1999 to enforce any term of this Agreement*'.

There might be situations where you do want a third party to be able to benefit from the agreement. If you are acting as a reseller, it might be a condition of your reseller agreement that you enable the original vendor to benefit from your limits and exclusions of liability, or other rights, under the contract with your client.

This means that if the client was unable to obtain a satisfactory remedy from you, and decided to 'leapfrog' you and go straight to the original vendor, that vendor would be able to benefit from the contractual limits you had put on your liability, even though it had no direct contract in place with the client.

If this is the case, your exclusion clause above will expressly reference whatever provision permits the reseller to benefit as a third party:

'A person who is not a party to this Agreement has no rights under the Contracts (Rights of Third Parties) Act 1999 to enforce any term of this Agreement except as explicitly provided by Clause XX of this Agreement.'

Endeavours – Best and Reasonable

There is much discussion in legal and business circles about the correct use of the terms 'best endeavours' and 'reasonable endeavours'. Generally, your clients will expect you to make your 'best endeavours' to deliver everything you said you would, when you said you'd deliver it, and to comply with any other obligations you might have in your agreement.

On face value, this seems entirely reasonable. After all, why wouldn't you try your best? It can be difficult to argue with a client who is saying, "So you're telling me you're not going to do your best to deliver these products in line with the target quality standards?"

If you've ever had this conversation with your legal advisor, though, you'll be aware that the very thought of agreeing to 'best endeavours' sends them all hot and cold, requiring a long sit-down in a darkened room...

Why refer to 'endeavours' at all?

You might (with some justification) ask why we can't just say that we shall do a particular thing – why would we want to 'endeavour' to do it? Is this just legalese getting carried away with itself?

Endeavours are useful where it is simply not possible to make a concrete commitment to achieving a particular objective –for example, where your success in accomplishing a specific outcome depends on things outside your control.

A common example would be where a software vendor agrees to use its **reasonable endeavours** to fix bugs in the software within a particular number of hours or days. Anyone who has experience of trying to fix software bugs will know that it is not possible to make a concrete commitment to have a bug resolved in a particular length of time – some apparently simple bugs can take a very long time to nail down, and even longer to resolve!

Using **endeavours** enables you and your client to agree that you will do your best, but won't be punished if you're not able to meet the commitment despite trying your hardest.

Determining exactly how hard 'your hardest' should be is the job of the qualifier – **best** or **reasonable**.

Reasonable endeavours

In most normal business contexts, **reasonable endeavours** is perfectly good enough. It applies whenever the party making the endeavours is expected to do everything that a good provider, or rational client, would do in such circumstances. It wouldn't generally be expected to take measures that would be against its own commercial interests, though – this is where the 'reasonable' bit comes in.

Best endeavours

Best endeavours applies whenever the party making the endeavours is expected to do everything within its power. If you commit to use your **best endeavours** to meet a particular obligation, you could be expected to take measures that would be against your own commercial interests if that was necessary to enable you to meet the obligation.

The bar for using your **best endeavours** is set rather higher than it is for **reasonable endeavours**. Does that mean that nothing is off limits? No effort too great?

While a company that is committed to using its **best endeavours** to meet a particular obligation might not be expected to run its own business into the ground, or bankrupt itself in its efforts to deliver, it should expect to go above and beyond the level of 'reasonable' and potentially to endure some level of hardship, if necessary, to enable it to meet the **best endeavours** obligations.

All reasonable, best commercial

Rather worryingly, when the courts were asked to take a look at the issue of deciding how far a party should go having given its **best endeavours** commitment (in the case of *Jet2.com Limited v Blackpool Airport [2012] EWHA Civ* 417), they decided that **all reasonable endeavours** and **best endeavours** meant the same thing.

Confused? Me too. To make sure you don't find yourself having accidentally given your 'best endeavours' when you were just trying to make your customer happy by going a bit further than 'reasonable', don't go anywhere near such fudges as 'best commercial', 'all reasonable', 'all reasonable commercial'.

Stick to either **best** or **reasonable**, and steer clear of any other variations on the theme.

Entire Agreement

In chapter 4 we looked at which documents were appropriate to include as descriptions of what we were delivering to the client. We considered the relative merits of purchase orders, proposals, specifications of work and schedules.

The truth is that in the course of a sale, particularly if it's a high value sale of something big and complicated, we are likely to share all sorts of information with our client. We'll be delivering presentations, demonstrations, proposals, tender responses, quotations, white papers and many other documents. In addition to the material we supply on paper, we'll be providing information electronically. And we'll also be making verbal statements, answering questions and having informal chats.

So when it comes to figuring out exactly what is, and what is not, part of your contractual commitment to the client, you can see there's a bit of an editing job to be done.

While I'm not saying for one moment that you would ever have said, written, demonstrated, hinted or implied anything about your product or service that is not absolutely, 100%, indisputably true, you might not necessarily want to be held contractually to all of it.

A typical sales brochure, for example, might assert that 'this state-of-the-art product is guaranteed to improve productivity!' Really? Under any circumstances? What will you do if a client buys the product and experiences no productivity improvements? Or if they identify that there are other products far more technologically advanced than yours, refuting your claim to be 'state of the art', and therefore want their money back?

You can see how easy it is to say wonderful things in a marketing document that, while generally true, are not expressed in a manner that makes them appropriate for inclusion in your contract.

The job of the 'entire agreement' clause is to spell out precisely which commitments you intend to be bound by. It will usually do that by limiting the 'agreement' to the contract document itself and any schedules and appendices that are physically attached to it. It may extend to certain other documents that are expressly referenced in it by name (and date and version number, ideally!). But it should certainly not include any 'marketing fluff' that you might have showered upon the client in the course of the sales process.

The client, not unreasonably, may well push back on the exclusion of marketing documents, proposals and RFP responses from the contract. Their argument is that all of these contributed to their decision to buy from you, and they expect you to stand by what you've said.

Faced with this response, you should ask the client exactly which other statements that you made during the sales process have formed an essential part of their decision to buy from you. If they identify key points that are not included within the suite of contractual documents you've listed, you need to consider each of them and decide whether:

- You are happy to stand by that obligation contractually, and can draft an appropriate clause for inclusion in your specification/statement of work/contract, etc. that is sufficiently clear and unambiguous to work contractually; or

- You cannot turn that particular point into a clear contractual obligation, or it was actually an inaccurate or incorrect assertion that you are not able to commit to

In the second case, you need to be really clear about this with the client – if this issue is so important to them that they based their buying decision on it, but you're not able to commit to it contractually, do they really want to go ahead?

You might be wondering why on earth I'm advocating that you flag this up to the client, risking the failure of the deal before it has started.

The reason is that if you just quietly go ahead, knowing you can't meet the client's expectations but relying on the contract to protect you, the deal is doomed. I know that's rather strong language, but this is an important point!

The case of BSkyB v EDS, described in chapter 8, is an excellent example of where things can go horribly wrong if the parties proceed with the client being misled. *Please* don't do it. It's better to lose the deal than to continue under false pretences and end up losing your corporate shirt.

Force Majeure

You may have heard the phrase 'force majeure' in conversation (depending on what sort of people you chat to, of course!), used as a general purpose 'get out' for not having done something. As in "I know I was going to hang out the washing, but it rained/my mother called/I had a sudden need for beer – force majeure!" As you'd expect, in a legal context there are some things that are considered acceptable force majeure events (rain would work in this situation), and others that aren't (need for beer). Others (mum giving you a call) could be borderline – possibly acceptable as a mitigating circumstance, but possibly not...

The force majeure clause in the contract sets out the conditions under which either you or your customer will be relieved from your obligations under the contract for any period that you're unable to perform due to circumstances beyond your control.

There are two ways to tackle this clause: the short way or the long way!

Some lawyers like long, comprehensive force majeure clauses that list all the things they can think of that they consider will 'let you off the hook', and also the things that they consider should, actually, be within your control.

Force majeure conditions typically include incidents like fire, flood, war, civil unrest and terrorist activity. Excluded conditions might include labour disputes (which you could resolve by paying your staff more!) or failures on the part of your subcontractors (as you should have appropriate terms and management processes in place to avoid this).

The 'short way' doesn't list individual conditions but simply refers to events 'beyond a party's reasonable control'.

This is much vaguer and may lead to disputes about what you should and should not have been able to control, if you ever need to call upon this particular clause. On the other hand, given that whatever actually happens is unlikely to be on your long list anyway, you might decide to go for the short list and save time.

In an ideal world, you would consider the particular sale you're contracting for, the locations involved and the possible risk events, and identify those that are specifically applicable to your situation.

Independent Contractor

This provision generally contains a list of possible relationships between you and the other party that do NOT apply! It is common in subcontracting relationships and in agreements for the supply of services. This is because the client wants to be sure that your staff members are not considered to be their own staff or agents, and that the two of you are not in partnership.

There are plenty of good reasons for wanting to make this clear. If your staff were able to claim they are employees of the client, they might be able to ask for TUPE rights, redundancy, holiday pay or other claims. Understandably, the client isn't so keen on this prospect!

Equally, if you were an agent of the client, you would be able to make commitments that bind the client contractually.

This provision might go even further, and expressly state that you are responsible for the payment of employment taxes and national insurance contributions (or similar in other jurisdictions) of your employees. Client companies are understandably sensitive about this issue, since a tax regulation referred to as IR35 (together with subsequent case law) has resulted in many companies that use contractors being considered as the employer of the contractor and liable to HMRC for their PAYE.

Some clients will ask to be indemnified against any such costs. To address this, you might say that you will pay any such sums due in respect of your employees, and will pay fines awarded against your client in respect of your employees in the event that they're considered to be employees of the client. While not ideal, this definitely beats the indemnity option.

Notices

Now we really are in dullsville, contractually speaking. Or dull-but-importantsville, I should say. This provision states how each of you must notify the other of anything contractually significant, like an alleged breach of contract or a desire to terminate at the end of a particular period.

It should specify the address and (if the parties still have one!) fax number, and potentially the email address to which notices should be sent, and the person for whose attention they should be marked. Ideally, this should refer to a job title rather than a name, to allow for turnover of staff.

Why is this so important?

There have been cases where a party has written to the other to give notice to terminate (either because they are entitled to under a particular contract provision, or because the other party has breached the agreement) but has not followed the specified process. Because of this, their request to terminate has itself been considered a breach of the agreement, allowing the other party to bring a claim against them!

The email question has become particularly important in recent years, as many companies will receive email communications more reliably (and certainly more quickly) than written, posted ones. You might want to consider stating in your agreement that normal operational contractual communications may occur by email, but that delivery by hand, post or fax must be used for formal notices of default or of termination.

Whatever method of delivering notices you agree on, make sure that if you wish to notify the other party of something contractual, you follow the process set out in the contract precisely.

Severability

A severability clause simply states that if a particular clause is not enforceable by the courts (or is deemed unlawful), it can be 'severed' or struck out without impacting the remainder of the document. There may be more detailed drafting explaining that this only applies where the agreement still works without the clause to be severed; obviously, if it was the main clause describing the key object of the contract, this wouldn't work at all.

While the severability clause is useful, in order to make it truly effective you should make sure your lawyer splits any contentious drafting into as many small clauses as possible. This means that if any point is considered unlawful, it can be removed with the minimum impact on the remainder. If all clauses are long, you may lose more than you absolutely had to.

Survival

When your contract comes to an end, you will generally expect to be relieved of your obligation to deliver products or services to the client. If they owed you money immediately prior to termination, though, and hadn't paid up by the time the contract came to an end, you would still expect to get paid. So while there are some provisions that you would want to finish with the agreement, there are others that you'd want to hang on to.

The 'survival' clause is supposed to tell you which clauses carry on and which finish when the contract does.

Typical wording in a survival clause might state:

'Any provision of this Agreement that should, by its nature, survive termination of the Agreement shall so survive.'

That clause seems as helpful as a chocolate teapot – 'by its nature'? Huh?

The alternative way of drafting this clause without leaving so much to the imagination is to list all of the clauses that you want to continue in effect after the contract itself has finished. So:

'The following clauses shall continue to be in effect after the termination or expiration of this Agreement: Clause 1 (Definitions), Clause 4 (Payment), Clause 5 (Limits and exclusions of liability), Clause 6 (Confidentiality)...'

To work out which clauses should survive and which shouldn't, read through the final contract and consider each clause in turn. Does it make sense for this clause to continue after the contract is done? Make your list and check it against the list in the 'survival' clause. If there's a difference, go through it with your legal advisor and see if the difference is for a good reason or simply because there has been an error. It's a good idea to do this check when the rest of the contract is agreed.

Term and termination

This clause sets out how long the parties expect the agreement to last, and under what circumstances either of them can bring it to an end. It may also suggest specific consequences of termination. It can have a big impact on revenue recognition, and certainly on total forecast revenue. You can imagine that there is a big difference between a rolling one-month contract and a twelve-month contract with a right to renew on one month's notice.

In the first case, you're only ever certain of one month's revenue at a time. Essentially, the plug could be pulled at any moment, and your relationship could end rather abruptly. If you have this sort of agreement, you'd expect to take very few commercial risks, ensuring that all of your implementation costs, cost of sale, etc., were covered in the first month of the deal. If you had a longer term agreement (say, a three-year contract), you might be prepared to amortise some of those expenses over the term of the contract, making it cheaper for the client in the early months.

When it comes to ending the contract before the end of its defined term, there are two common termination conditions: for a material breach that is not remedied within a specified time (or is not capable of being remedied at all), and for the insolvency of the other party.

Working out which provisions are 'material' to the contract, and if breached will always give rise to a 'material breach', is an imprecise art. It will vary from contract to contract and from individual situation to individual situation. A complete failure to deliver would generally be considered 'material', but a recent case showed that, in some circumstances, even a significant delay in delivery could be considered to be a material breach.

Breach of provisions relating to confidentiality and intellectual property rights could be considered material breaches if they are particularly important to the contract at hand. Check back to chapter 7 where we looked at terms, conditions and warranties; breach of a condition will certainly count as a 'material breach'.

Breach of warranties is generally not considered to be a material breach giving rise to the right to terminate, but would entitle the client to make a claim for damages.

Sometimes clients may request the right to terminate **'for convenience'**. This means there is no cause for termination – they simply don't want your services or products any longer. This is a big concession in an agreement and you probably won't want to agree to it unless there is also some appropriate compensation built in for early termination.

Some clauses will survive termination, e.g. fees and payment, and these should be expressly stated in the survival clause (see above).

You should consider what the consequences of termination might be under the different potential circumstances. So there might be different consequences if you terminate for the client's breach from those that apply if they terminate for yours. Consider what should happen to any intellectual property that has been exchanged, to any work in progress, and to any confidential information.

Time is of the Essence

This is one of those clauses that crops up from time to time in conversation, and which most business people feel they understand instinctively. Sadly, though, it doesn't simply mean that timescales are tight so get a move on! Saying in the contract that time is of the essence makes timely delivery a condition of the contract. That means that if you're late (even by an hour), you've committed a material breach of the contract, and the other party can terminate (see above).

Stating that 'time is of the essence' may occur towards the end of the agreement, or may appear close to the description of the particular task in respect of which timing is particularly important.

This provision is often included where it's not really needed, out of habit as much as anything else. Unless it's clear to you that time genuinely is of the essence, and late delivery will render your performance of the contract useless to the client, push back on its use in your contract.

Ideally your contract should state that, while you will use your reasonable endeavours to meet the timescales set out in any agreed plans, 'time shall not be of the essence of the Agreement'. This will protect your business against the client claiming that "It was obvious that time was of the essence, because of the nature of the deal – we didn't need to say so explicitly in the contract!"

Variations

The contract should include some sort of provision describing how contract variations may occur. It might simply say that no variation is valid unless made in writing and signed by authorised representatives of both parties. Or it might describe a rather more detailed process. If you want to be sure that casual discussions between yourself and the client, or between your respective project managers, cannot be interpreted as contract variations, having a clear provision to cover this is essential.

Chapter 11: Quick Summary

- Most contracts contain a number of clauses that are rarely reviewed and adapted to reflect the detailed circumstances of the contract and deal concerned

- These are commonly referred to as 'boilerplate' provisions and the most common are described in detail in this chapter

- Some of these can have significant impacts on how the deal is managed, so you should always read and review them with care

- Check with your legal counsel if you're not sure how a particular boilerplate clause will work in the context of your deal

- Make sure you comply with the specific requirements of boilerplate clauses, particularly the 'notices' clause if you need to give legally significant notices to your client

12

Manage the contracting process to improve forecasting

Before we get stuck in to this chapter, I want you to give yourself a big pat on the back. You are now better informed about how to use contracts to help you deliver successful deals, and great client relationships, than pretty much anyone else you know.

Even if you've skipped some of the more technical legal bits (you can always go back and look at them when you need to), you should have a pretty good idea about:

- How contracts can help you sell

- The positive contribution your contracts can make to great client relationships

- How matching what you're selling with what the client is buying will improve client satisfaction and your margins

- Some great tricks for getting paid on time

- Why the legal stuff matters, and how the Sales Prevention Squad genuinely has your best interests at heart!

In this chapter we're going to pull all this together and look at the process of getting from a hot sales prospect that really likes your offering through to a signed deal.

After all, this is what it's all about – it's all very well 'selling' but as the old Blues saying goes, "It ain't over 'til the fat lady signs…"

Now you understand the nuts and bolts, you can take control

Before you grab the bull by the horns and start leading your organisation through the contracting process, check and see if there is already a documented process in place. Some very mature organisations have comprehensive processes for taking a deal from the 'agreement to buy' stage through to a signed contract. Many, many more have nothing in place whatsoever, leaving the individuals involved to make it up as they go along.

So find out if your business has a process, and if so, how it works. If not, don't panic – this chapter will help you work with your colleagues to develop one that works for you.

Components of the contracting process

The components common to most contracting processes include:

- **Authority Levels** – These determine who is authorised to sign off on deals of different values. More mature businesses will break this down and assign authority levels to different members of the legal, product, delivery, finance and sales team. The levels may relate to cash sums – e.g. the deal price – or to specific risk areas. Or they might pull both of these together to create some more sophisticated risk assessments.

  For example, you might be authorised to sign off a deal for your standard products, on your standard trading terms, up to a value of £250,000, but you might require a higher level signatory if the same deal is on non-standard contract terms. It's important to be clear about your own authority, and who to go to for approvals if you want to move beyond your own level in terms of granting concessions or agreeing different deal structures.

- **Approval Process** – Whereas authority levels identify who must approve concessions and deal elements during negotiations, the approval process sets out how you seek approval for the finally negotiated deal. As part of this process you might be required to complete some form of 'deal summary' setting out the key deal points (see the example below). This will serve to brief each of the parties in the approval chain so that they can make an informed decision about whether to approve the deal, without having to go into all the details.

  It can be tempting to gloss over any deal points that you suspect the approvers won't like – particularly if they don't fall under any of the standard headings in your deal summary, and it would be easy to 'forget' to mention them. You know what I'm going to say here: in matters contractual, seeking forgiveness after the fact rather than approval before the deal's done is a very risky strategy, and not to be recommended.

  If you 'bend' the process to get something through that probably shouldn't be approved, you might find that the protection your company will offer you under normal circumstances evaporates, leaving you with personal liability for the consequences. Even if you don't end up personally liable, it's certainly not going to help your career prospects!

- **Contract Negotiation Process** – Although contract negotiation is obviously an essential part of getting to contract signature, very few organisations have a formal negotiating process as part of their contracting process. The negotiating process should include a description of:

o **Who does what** – Within your business, which departments/job titles participate in negotiations? What role does each of them perform in the negotiation? We'll look at team negotiations and the roles of individuals in more detail below.

o **How contract issues will be dealt with** – Will you exchange contract mark-ups with the client using Word 'track changes'? Do you only ever send PDF versions of contracts out of the business? Should contract risks and issues be identified and tracked using a risk register? (See the example below.)

o **Which communication mechanisms you will use** – Will all negotiations take place face-to-face? Over the telephone? By email? Using Skype or other web-conferencing facilities? Do you have particular rules about how each of these tools may be used in the business? Must contract documents be encrypted before sharing over email or other electronic tools?

o **How you plan and manage progress** – Many negotiations are relatively uncontrolled. The argument is that since you are not able to control the actions of the client, there's no point trying to manage the process. You might as well just go with the flow, as it will take as long as it takes. Having a structure for negotiation planning, monitoring and control will help you bring deals in on time and flag up potential issues early.

Example Deal Summary Template

<table>
<tr><td>DEAL SUMMARY</td><td colspan="2">Client Name:</td><td colspan="2">Client Location:</td></tr>
<tr><td>Sales person</td><td>Name:</td><td>Telephone:</td><td>Mobile:</td><td>Email:</td></tr>
<tr><td>Contract</td><td>Signed [Date]</td><td>Location:</td><td colspan="2">Approvers:</td></tr>
<tr><td>Deal value</td><td>Licences:

G. Margin %:</td><td>Services:

G. Margin %:</td><td>Hardware:

G. Margin %:</td><td>Recurring:

G. Margin %:</td></tr>
<tr><td>Deliverable summary</td><td>Licences:

Risk:
Low/med/high</td><td>Services:

Risk:
Low/med/high</td><td>Hardware:

Risk:
Low/med/high</td><td>Recurring:

Risk:
Low/med/high</td></tr>
<tr><td rowspan="3">Relationship summary</td><td colspan="2">Deal Sponsor:
Job title:
Email:
Phone:</td><td colspan="2">Main operational contact:
Job title:
Email:
Phone:</td></tr>
<tr><td colspan="2">Main commercial contact:
Job title:
Email:
Phone:</td><td colspan="2">Main technical contact:
Job title:
Email:
Phone:</td></tr>
<tr><td colspan="2">Client commitment to success:
Low/med/high</td><td colspan="2">Client competence:
Low/med/high</td></tr>
<tr><td rowspan="2">Invoicing and payment</td><td colspan="3">Invoicing Milestones:
M1 [Description][target date] £[x]
M2 [Description][target date] £[x]
M3 [Description][target date] £[x]</td><td>Payment terms:
[x] days from date of invoice</td></tr>
<tr><td colspan="2">Accounts payable contact:
Job title:
Email:
Phone:</td><td colspan="2">Special invoicing conditions:</td></tr>
<tr><td>Service levels</td><td colspan="2">Service level definitions:</td><td colspan="2">Consequences of missing SLAs:</td></tr>
<tr><td>Contractual risks</td><td>e.g. LoL = 250% of contract value</td><td>e.g. Indemnity for 3rd party IP breach</td><td colspan="2">e.g. Client can terminate for convenience on 90 day's notice</td></tr>
</table>

Example Risk Register

Risk Register: [contract name]

Risk Summary

[Outline the key risks and issues with the contract and, where appropriate, proposals for avoidance or mitigation.]

Risk Priorities:

1 = High
2 = Medium
3 = Low
Q = Question
A = Advisory note

Risk No.	Clause	Risk Description	Action to mitigate or avoid the risk	Status	Priority	Date
1.						
2.						
3.						
4.						

Assemble your team

If your process specifies a particular team structure for negotiations, that's great. Provided it's a structure that works well for your organisation, you should follow that and can skip this section. If you think it could possibly be improved upon, read on and see whether the ideas here might make your contract negotiations more effective.

In any negotiation team there can only be one 'negotiator'.

What do I mean by that?

The 'negotiator' is the only person on the team who is empowered to make concessions, and to authorise the sharing of information.

That doesn't mean to say that only the negotiator speaks (or emails) during the process of negotiations. It just means that they are the one in control, who manages what their fellow team members concede or share.

Why does that matter?

Many years ago, my firm undertook a project for a major telecommunications and broadband provider, re-negotiating their IT support and maintenance contracts. This provider spent millions of pounds a year keeping their IT infrastructure in good condition, including significant amounts on support for software they had not implemented since they originally bought it, several years earlier.

In the course of our review we identified many areas where cost savings could be made, and engaged with the various suppliers to talk through the options available to our client. Our objective was to retain a high level of support, but to trim out unnecessary expenditure by using alternative providers where possible.

It transpired that the ERP solution used by the organisation was likely to be replaced in the next year or two, so there was no point in the company continuing to put money into the vendor's 'upgrade pot' since they were unlikely to implement any further upgrades. There was also a possibility to move the day-to-day support to a third party provider, delivering considerable cost savings.

The ERP provider was distinctly unimpressed by this approach. Rather than coming to the table to discuss how it could support our client in a more cost-effective manner over the next couple of years, and facilitate a smooth migration, it made a call to the CTO of the client company. In this call the account director raged at the client CTO at the indignity of having our firm approach him about potential savings. Taken unprepared, the CTO did his best to calm his supplier, assuring him that he would "sort this out".

So the next call I made to the ERP account director was met with a smug, "We've spoken to the CTO, and you're to leave our contract alone!"

You can imagine how frustrating this was, having put considerable effort into investigating alternatives for the client. After discussing the matter with the CTO (who was very apologetic), we agreed that this contract would be dealt with according to our advice. And the CTO agreed that he would deflect any further calls from the account director (and similar people at his other suppliers) back to us.

The strategy worked, and we succeeded in making a significant dent in the client's ongoing costs while delivering similar levels of service.

This was a good lesson in the importance of having an agreed negotiator in any deal, and properly briefing all other team members (and any others who might be approached by someone trying to circumvent the process), to avoid the other party trying to 'divide and conquer'.

In addition to the negotiator, there are two other key roles in the negotiating team. The first of these is the 'summariser'. Their job is to keep track of concessions made and deal-points agreed by the parties in the course of negotiations, and to summarise these from time to time when requested to do so by the negotiator.

The summariser is essential, and even if you're personally a very strong negotiator I would always advocate taking a summariser along with you to big negotiations. This is especially true if you know the other party will be assembling a big team.

Why?

Because being in the front-line negotiation role is a very tiring position, and from time to time you just need some breathing space! Having someone to run through where you've got to so far can give you the time you need to gather your thoughts, re-evaluate your position against the plan, and prepare for the next tranche.

Having an experienced negotiator in the summariser role can be great, providing they're able to stop themselves jumping in if they think the negotiator is struggling!

In a recent negotiation workshop I was running, we had two teams negotiating in a role-play. On each team was one of the company's most experienced negotiators – the Managing Director on one, and the Finance Director on the other. Each team had nominated its least experienced negotiator to be the negotiator in the role-play, on the (very sensible) basis that the experience would benefit them the most.

Within about a minute of the negotiation beginning, the MD and FD were negotiating furiously with each other, while their nominated negotiators watched in amusement.

After some constructive feedback, the second session went much better. The MD and FD fully appreciated that their direct intervention seriously undermined the credibility of their chosen negotiator, but the strain of not diving in was visible!

The best summarisers will be able to pull together a list of concessions and agreed points in such a way as to emphasise the concessions you've made to meet the requirements of the client. They will be careful to acknowledge any significant client concessions, and thank the client, but a skilled summariser will make it clear that the client is really getting a very good deal in this negotiation!

Even a summariser with absolutely no negotiation experience can be invaluable. For one project, I was required to travel to Istanbul to negotiate with a large company there on behalf of my client. It was a client that I knew very well, and for whom I acted as 'virtual commercial director', so I was entirely comfortable with my negotiating boundaries.

However, nobody from the client Board was available to join me for the negotiation, and I knew that the Turkish company would assemble a large team from its side. I asked the Board if I could take one of their pre-sales engineers with me, in the role of summariser.

I chose a chap who'd been on my negotiation training several months earlier, although he had not yet been in a position to use his new skills.

Jez and I spent several hours planning our negotiation, and agreeing how he would support me. As expected, there were six Turkish negotiators waiting for us when we arrived. The negotiations were tense and arduous, with regular intense discussions in Turkish on the other side of the table. Having Jez to give me a 'breather', by periodically summarising our progress, enabled me to stay focused and conclude the negotiations in line with our plan.

The third role in your negotiation team is that of 'observer'. This is something of a luxury, but if you're able to have a three-person negotiating team it's well worthwhile. As it sounds, this role involves watching the other side during negotiations, looking for clues about their respective authority levels and their position on different points.

The observer will be able to share their observations on body language and physical clues given by the client when your team has an opportunity to 'take 5' and speak privately. These clues can be extremely useful in informing how best to take your negotiations forward. For example, they might suggest you should direct particular arguments at a different member of the client's team to whom others appear to be deferring.

You'll notice that this discussion of roles has focused purely on each individual's role *in the negotiating team*. Their roles in the business do not have to dictate their role in the team; while you might think your lawyer should lead negotiations, it may be that their skill lies in observing body language rather than problem solving. The person responsible for delivery of the project may be an excellent summariser, capable of cutting through hours of waffle and obfuscation to nail the key points of the negotiation.

As the sales lead, you might find that your relationship with the client enables you to propose solutions to contractual impasses, and encourage the client to consider alternatives to their stated position. This could equip you perfectly for the 'negotiator' role. One thing you will find is that having a good understanding of the potential business issues associated with the various contract terms will stand you in good stead here. Knowing that you are not likely to make risk-laden contractual commitments will encourage the lawyers to allow you to take the lead and drive the negotiations forward.

Alternatively, you might feel that you'd prefer to have the legal representative lead negotiations. If there are a number of contentious issues, it can be useful to be able to retain your 'good cop' role, letting other members of the team play 'bad cop'. Be careful about this approach, though; I have been called in to rescue negotiations in the past, where the lawyer was so aggressive that the client was on the point of calling off the whole deal!

Why plan your negotiations?

Negotiation planning is like exercise – we all know we should do more of it as it's good for us, but somehow other things always manage to get in the way!

Good preparation makes a huge difference to the successful outcome of negotiations. So why is it that the great majority of face-to-face negotiations are preceded by nothing more than "Let's meet in the coffee shop round the corner, half an hour before we're due to meet with the client. We can plan our negotiation and discuss our tactics."

The rest of this chapter sets out some specific activities that you should plan for and schedule, together with the other members of your negotiating team. Trust me – the more of this you do, the better prepared you'll be, and the more creative and flexible you'll be able to be in your negotiations. More importantly, the creative and flexible suggestions you propose will all move you closer to your objectives rather than further away, because you'll be clear about what those objectives are.

Prepare your plan

Your negotiation plan should have a number of steps that we will examine in more detail later in this chapter. In brief, they are:

- Agree on your objectives for the deal

- Identify what you think the client's objectives are

- Examine potential routes to close the gap between their and your objectives, including points that can be traded and alternative approaches

- Negotiate the deal, with regular reference back to your objectives

- Manage the approval process through to signature

While it is difficult to know exactly how long these steps will take (particularly the 'negotiate the deal' step), you should be able to put a rough time plan in place. It may be that you're not able to do this until you've carried out the first three items in the planning process, and can see how far apart the parties are and how big a challenge you have ahead of you. Whatever the situation, you should aim to have some target timelines against which you can measure your progress.

This won't necessarily match up to your forecasting with regard to when a deal will close, but it shouldn't be too far away. In particular, if you know you have at least a month of contract negotiations ahead of you, don't tell your boss the deal will close this month! Putting time pressures on yourself makes you vulnerable to manipulation by the client. If you've ever bought a car, you'll know that the best time to get a great deal is close to the sales person's year end, when they're desperate for that last sale to help them meet their target.

Don't unwittingly put yourself in that position with your own clients. You may, of course, choose to use the 'year end approaches – sign up now to benefit from this time-limited offer' approach as part of your negotiation strategy. We all know that sometimes it's necessary to create a 'compelling event' to encourage the client to take action. But if you do choose this approach, make it a considered part of your negotiation plan and make sure you are clear in making the promised concession conditional on the contract being signed by the specified deadline. And be firm if they miss the date, removing the concession from the contract before it's signed!

Share some of the plan with the client

There are some elements of your own negotiation planning and process that you should share with the client in order to make effective progress.

In terms of team structure, it is helpful for you and the client to know who will be involved in negotiations from each side. You don't have to disclose each team member's role, but simply exchanging contact details can facilitate progress in line with the plan.

Bearing in mind that you may not want to disclose any internal time pressures to the client, as discussed above, it can still be useful to agree the general timeframes in which each of you expects to complete negotiations. This can help both of you ensure appropriate resources are available to support the process. For example, if you're expecting to be reaching the 'approvals' stage during the last week of September, ask the client if their approvers will be available during that period.

It is often useful to schedule some periodic face-to-face or telephone sessions if the majority of your negotiations are taking place by email. These help to realign your positions, and are often much more effective in enabling you to tackle contentious issues than email communications.

By getting some calls and meetings in the diaries of all team members well in advance, you avoid the 'deal standoffs' that can result when nobody can move forward in the absence of a key decision maker.

Agreeing the mechanism by which drafts will be exchanged and updated will also smooth the process. If you use a document comparison tool, rather than Word 'track changes', make sure the client is comfortable with this means of monitoring edits. It's essential that each of you is able to trust the other not to use the various word processing tools to slip changes into the agreement without bringing them to the other party's attention.

While very few businesses would do this deliberately, misuse of the tools can give the impression that this is exactly what you've done. So discuss this issue up front and agree how changes to the contract will be tracked, agreed and accepted.

Now let's look at the detailed planning activities.

Be clear about your objectives

This might sound obvious, but it's surprising how many companies go into a negotiation without ever having an internal discussion to agree exactly what it is they want out of it.

What do we want from this deal?

It may be that everyone just assumes the answer to this question is 'the best deal we can get'.

While that may be true, it's not very helpful when you're involved in a negotiation, as it requires you to make value judgments about what's 'best', what's 'acceptable' and what's 'not acceptable'.

Aim to start your negotiation with the longest possible list of 'wants'.

Why?

Think of your negotiation like a game of chess: the more pieces you have on the board, the better your chances of winning. If you start the game with only your king and queen, you'll have nothing to give away, and little room to manoeuvre; but if you have lots of 'wants', you can do some trading and still come out well. Remember the distinction between 'wants' and 'needs' that we discussed in chapter 4? Apply the same distinction when considering your own wants, and make sure you don't confuse the two. The more of your 'needs' that you can re-frame as 'wants', the better for your negotiating position!

Within your organisation, the list of 'things we want' might well be different depending on who you're asking at the time, so looking at the question from a number of perspectives can help.

From your personal perspective, you might be looking to meet a sales target, establish yourself in a new sector/a new account, earn some quick commission to meet a particular financial need, or demonstrate your readiness for promotion or a pay rise.

As a business unit, you might be hoping to win the first sale of a new product, or the first implementation in a new sector. You may have under-used manufacturing capacity, and be willing to take on sub-optimal deals simply to keep the factory busy during a quiet time. Or you might be under threat from a competitor trying to steal your existing client, and be willing to go above and beyond your usual excellence simply to retain your customer.

From a corporate perspective, you may want a high profile 'win' before reporting to shareholders at year-end or quarter-end. A press release about your success with a new brand-name client could be highly desirable, even if the profit margin is less than ideal. Alternatively, you might have had a year with excellent turnover but lower than expected margins, and be keen for a highly profitable deal to redress the balance.

Cash flow might be the number one issue on the Board's mind right now, so that they'd be willing to sacrifice overall margin in exchange for some early payment milestones.

By exploring all of these within the organisation, and with other members of the negotiating team, you should be able to build up a good picture of what really matters to your organisation.

Explore alternative 'acceptable' outcomes

When you understand what's important to the business, you can start to look in more detail at the potential alternative outcomes. This game can quickly get very complicated – imagine having to plot numerous alternative realities, based on a number of possible decision points, and you can see why.

Consider the 'moving parts' in your negotiation. These are usually made up of:

- Deliverables

- Price

- Contract terms (risk)

For each of these, you should have a range of possible outcomes. This enables you to seek alternative combinations to deliver the balance that the company desires. Of course, there will be breakdowns within each of these sections: deliverables could be split into products and services, price could be split into the cash sums and the payment terms, and the contract terms have many components, each with different impacts.

In respect of each point, consider your ideal outcome, the point at which you'd be satisfied (if not exactly thrilled) and your 'walk away point'. This latter is essential to keep you on track during your negotiations. It's amazing how easy it is to find yourself the wrong side of your walk away point, having got carried away in negotiations...

Document your goals and build support for them

Once you and your team are clear about what you want from the deal, document it. Share your objectives with all stakeholders in the business (these should be identified in your process, as described above), and secure their buy-in.

If you uncover disconnects during this process it's important to address them now, before you start negotiating with the other party.

So if, for example, the business unit manager wants the deal signed before quarter-end, so as to hit his or her financial targets for the quarter, while the CFO is more concerned about making sure you get a significant chunk of the revenue this financial year, you need to resolve this fast. Generally, while the CFO may have the higher position, the business unit manager will be closer to the deal and may be able to drive the negotiation more directly. Whatever the case, be sure that all stakeholders have bought into your proposed objectives.

As you move through the negotiation process, keep these stakeholders in the loop. They may be very useful to you as you progress, if it's necessary to seek escalation in order to close the deal. They'll appreciate having been kept up to speed with the state of play, rather than having to get to grips with the deal from scratch minutes before you want them to participate in a negotiation.

Make sure everyone in the team is on the same page

As you work through the process of establishing your negotiation objectives, be sure to involve all members of your negotiation team. They should all agree the common objective to be sure that they will approach each challenge from aligned perspectives.

As we discussed earlier, each team member should know their role. If a non-negotiator is approached by a member of the client's team, asking for information or concessions, they should know to pass the enquiry to the negotiator. This may be done in a more subtle way, but it's essential that the team does not allow their negotiator to be undermined by behind-the-scenes deals.

Understand the client's objectives

If it's sometimes difficult getting to the bottom of your own company's objectives, understanding what the client wants from the deal is even more of a challenge.

Check back to chapter 4, where you should have done some work to find out exactly what your client thinks they're buying. Of course, you may not be able to believe everything they tell you – they'll be keen to get the best possible deal, and not to expose the strength of their need or desire for your product or service. They may want to make you believe there are still other competitors in the game, to encourage you to make concessions. And they may be comfortable playing games to secure better commercial terms.

All of this means that the most obvious way to find out what matters to the client – simply asking them – might not be terribly reliable.

What does the buyer want from this deal?

To make the task easier, follow the same process you did for your own company. Start by looking at the individual within the client's business with whom you're negotiating.

What is likely to be important to them personally? A successful implementation? The lowest price? Finishing the project on time? Doing business with individuals they trust? Working with a partner whose expertise nicely complements their own, without overshadowing it?

And as a department, what are their goals likely to be? How are they measured and rewarded? What would happen to them if this deal fell through?

Then step back and consider the macro-level. This could require you to read things like the Chairman's Statement to the Shareholders, to see how the business is being positioned. Does your company help the client to move in this direction?

We looked at these issues in detail in chapter 4, so hopefully you will have already made some progress here.

As you've looked at the different combinations of possible outcomes that will be acceptable in varying degrees to your organisation, try to conduct the same exercise for your client.

And then, of course, use every opportunity available to you to test your assumptions. You would hope that by the end of this process you'll have a pretty good idea of what matters to your client – but planning your own negotiation strategy on this basis, without testing and checking as you proceed, is very rash. For example, if you assumed that price was most important to the client, you might find yourself discounting more than you need to. If the actual issue is reliability, you could make more progress by demonstrating your excellent track record, without needing to make price concessions.

Use the negotiator's toolkit to become a more effective negotiator

While this isn't a negotiation book, we do by necessity have to look at the key elements of contract negotiation in order to traverse the gap between an agreed sale and a signed deal. So let's look at some of the specific skills and attitudes that will help you become a more effective negotiator.

It's the deal, stupid

The first thing to remember is that this negotiation is not about you. Making yourself look clever/hard-nosed/powerful/generally lovely (whilst possibly very gratifying) is not the objective. The objective is to secure a deal that meets the goals you and your team have agreed.

So leave your ego outside, and focus on the deal. It helps to think of the deal as a concrete 'thing' on the table. You and the client both want these negotiations to be successful, so that you can deliver a great product or service. Your challenge is to find a solution to the problems and issues that crop up as you move through the negotiation – preferably one that meets both your objectives and theirs.

This means that your problem-solving skills will be invaluable in helping you through the negotiation process. If this isn't your strength, make sure there's someone on your negotiation team who is good at looking at things from all angles to see how else you could achieve the same objective. Engineers tend to be pretty good at this, as do many sales people. You might find your sales director has some good creative ideas too.

With your knowledge and understanding of how contracts work, you should be in a very good position to do this effectively. Think about how you can move the various component parts of the deal around, to address the client's concerns without exposing your organisation to too much risk. And always run your potential solutions past your legal counsel and the rest of your team before suggesting them to the client.

In the course of a face-to-face negotiation, you might have a brilliant idea as to how to address a particularly thorny problem. It is always good to establish the concept of 'time out' before you begin a negotiation meeting. This means that you can request some time out to try out your brilliant idea on your colleagues in private, rather than either (a) floating it to the client first, and earning yourself a kick under the table, or (b) delaying progress on the negotiations by postponing that point until 'next time'.

Ask questions – and listen to the answers!

A key problem-solving skill, which is also vital for a successful sales career (so hopefully you've got this covered!), is asking questions. Make your questions relevant, non-threatening and useful. Use questioning to test your assumptions and to explore potential alternatives.

The bit that many negotiators fall down on, amazingly, is actually listening to the answers. I've been in negotiations and seen a negotiator ask the other party a really great question. While the other person is considering their response, the negotiator jumps in with more questions or – even worse – answering the question for them!

If you've asked a good question, where the answer matters to you, just shut up. Keep quiet. Schtum!

The answer will come, and you'll be glad you waited. When it does, please, please listen carefully. Don't filter what the other person's saying through your own opinions and expectations. Genuinely listen, trying to hear carefully everything that they are saying – and the things they're softly stepping around and avoiding.

How do you know if you've listened well?

Reflect back on what you think you've just heard. Use phrases like, "So, if I've understood you correctly..." to paraphrase your understanding of what they've said. Check that you've got it right and be prepared to be corrected. Your mission here is to understand the other party's point of view – not to judge it, or to try to change it, just to understand where they're coming from.

Sometimes the answer you receive won't shed the light you'd anticipated. If that's the case, ask more questions, better targeted, to provide the needed information. Remember, this isn't an inquisition – be gentle and interested, and you will be able to uncover the information you require.

Think before answering

What about when the client is asking you questions?

First, remember that you don't have to answer everything instantly. Pause, consider the question and think about your answer before responding. What do you think the client really wants to know? Is this information you're prepared to share? Is it information your negotiator (if that's not your role) will *allow* you to share?

While you might not always want to give a full and unedited response to questions, you should be honest. There are many reasons why honesty is a good policy. One of the biggest and most selfish is that it keeps life simple. The truth is the truth, and you don't have to work hard to remember which version of the truth you've shared with which person.

Remember that trust, once lost, is incredibly hard to recoup. So stick to the truth and you won't have to worry about damaging trust.

Suggest alternatives – but trade, don't give away

Earlier in this chapter we talked about exploring alternative 'acceptable' outcomes. The more of these you've identified and agreed with your team in advance, the more flexibility you will have in the negotiation itself. If it becomes clear to you that you're not going to be able to swing your ideal outcome in a particular area for which you have an approved fallback position, think about the best way to present that fallback option.

Generally, your alternative position will involve certain commitments from the client in order for them to secure a concession from you.

Why not just offer the concession and be done with it?

In an ideal world, a party receiving a concession with no strings attached would be deeply grateful, and would love you forever. In the commercial world, though, they're more likely to say, "Fine, now let's talk about..." and start softening you up for the next one!

By asking for something in return when you are preparing to give a concession, you set the expectation that you never give something for nothing. The size of the concession you request in return will either indicate the 'cost' to you of the one you're giving (where the 'cost' may be determined in terms of money, risk or simply inconvenience) or the stage of the negotiations that you've reached.

Generally, as you start to close your deal you should increase the size of concessions you request in return, to indicate to the other party that there's not much left where that one came from! This discourages them from asking for more and more from you as they realise each request will cost them something significant.

So how do you actually ask?

A useful phrase to use is, "If you could do [X] for me, I'd be prepared to do [Y] for you," or, "If you... then I..."

By putting what you want from the other party first, you avoid the uncomfortable situation where you make your offer, "I could do [Y] for you..." and they dive in quickly to accept before you've had a chance to say what you want in return!

This is where it's useful not only to have rehearsed some alternative acceptable outcomes with your team, but also to have created a long list of things that you might possibly ask the other side for. Even if some of the things you ask for in your "If you... then I..." statements are not particularly important to you, or especially expensive or difficult for the other party to agree to, they still perform their job of balancing the negotiations and discouraging further requests for concession.

Getting your deal to signature is cause for celebration!

So you've finally worked your way through the process, brought your team, your stakeholders and your client with you, and reached the stage where the contract is signed.

Congratulations! That's fantastic. And if you've followed the guidance I've shared with you, the contract should be a great basis for building your relationship with the client, and delivering excellent value to them and superb returns to your business.

There will be some administrative issues that need to be sorted out before you can pop the champagne, and it's your job to make sure these are done properly (after all, your commission depends on it!).

Secure hard-copy signatures and file them safely

These days, many contracts are signed, scanned and emailed, or signed and faxed. There are also electronic e-signature services that allow a party to give their approval to a contract without a physical copy of the document being produced.

Once 'signature' has occurred, make sure that you have a signed copy of the document (signed using whatever valid signature method you've agreed with the other party) filed safely in a location where you and other members of the business will be able to find it in the future.

If you have a contracting process in your business, it will doubtless include instructions for filing signed contracts so that they can be retrieved quickly and easily when needed. If not, here's your chance to invent one.

Given the huge sums of money involved, I am regularly amazed when clients experiencing contractual issues tell me they "can't find a signed copy of the contract." They'll have lots of versions of the electronic document, including the one that they *think* was signed in the end, but they won't be able to lay their hands on a copy that actually includes the relevant signatures.

I've been asked, "Shall I call the client and see if they could send me the signed copy from their records?"

Of course, if that's the only way you have to secure a copy, that's what you have to do. But if you do find yourself in a dispute, it doesn't do much for your negotiating position!

So make sure your hard-won contract is kept somewhere safe and secure where others in the business can access it when required.

Hand over effectively

If you've been able to have a member of the product or delivery team involved in your negotiations (which I acknowledge is a luxury not available to everyone), the handover requirements will be greatly reduced. However, for most businesses it's necessary to put some effort into making sure that they:

- Understand all of their obligations

- Know what they can expect from the client

- Appreciate the consequences of failure (with each key obligation)

- Know what they should do in the event of problems

- Have a clear escalation path if this doesn't work

It is also important to do a handover to the finance team so that they know:

- The final deal value

- The invoicing schedule

- The delivery milestones associated with each invoicing milestone (if any)

- The payment terms agreed

- The contact details for the client's accounts payable team (Mavis!)

- Any specific invoicing requirements (addresses to be sent to, copies to, etc.)

- The appropriate escalation path within the client organisation in the event of late payment

- What their remedies are in the event of late payment

If you're purely a new business salesperson, and will not have personal responsibility for managing the account on an ongoing basis, you will also want to give a thorough debrief to your successor in the account. This will be even more detailed than the others, covering the legal, financial, technical, operational and political/ personal elements of the sale.

Now celebrate!

If you think back to where we started, we were talking about legal, delivery and finance as the Sales Prevention Squad. Hopefully, your experiences will have shown you now that they can perform a really useful role in helping you to close your deal and secure your commission.

The chances are that the product, development and pre-sales teams will have spent many long hours working on proposal documents, demos, white papers, answers to questions. And your legal support will have been burning the midnight oil turning around contract updates quickly so as not to hold up the negotiations.

These guys (and I include the female members of the team in this collective noun!) have all contributed enormously to your success.

So the final step in closing this deal should be to celebrate as a team. The drinks should be on you at this stage, as you show the team how much you appreciate their help and support. It might cost you a few quid now, but trust me, next time you need support at short notice, it will stand you in very good stead!

Chapter 12: Quick Summary

- Until the deal is signed, it's not won

- Taking control of the contracting and negotiation process will help you forecast wins more accurately

- A good contracting process should specify authority levels, approval processes, and the mechanics of how the negotiations should be conducted

- Consider who will be part of the contract negotiation team and whether their role should be that of negotiator, summariser or observer

- You can only have one negotiator, so make sure nobody in your business accidentally undermines them by making concessions without their knowledge or consent

- Agree how you will conduct the negotiations and exchange draft documents

- Plan and manage your progress through the negotiation, agreeing timelines with the client if possible so as to ensure the right people are available at the right times

- Planning the negotiation strategy with the team greatly increases your chances of coming out with what you want

- Be clear about your objectives, and solicit input from different levels of your organisation

- Work out what the client's objectives are and validate these through good questioning and listening

- Leave your ego outside the room when you negotiate – the outcome is more important than looking good

- Listening carefully will give you the information you need to close your deal

- When you get to signature, make sure you have securely filed signature copies

- Celebrate and involve all who contributed to your success!

Onwards and upwards

Of course, getting to a signed contract is just the beginning of the commercial relationship you want to have with your clients. Let's wrap up with a look at what you can do to support your company post-signature. If your role is new business sales, you might be expected to cut and run as soon as the ink is dry. But if you have any interest in ongoing sales to this client account, or in the recognition of revenue under the contract, it's as well to take a wider view of your responsibilities once the deal is done.

Encourage bad news management

Have you ever wondered why a company's share price on the stock market will go down instead of up if it reports results much better than anticipated? It is an example of the City's distaste for surprises – analysts like to see evidence that you're in control of your business, and will deliver the results you forecast, good or bad.

The same is true of client projects. Delivering massively ahead of schedule can be as unsettling for a client as being wildly late.

Fortunately, you will have done an excellent job in chapter 4 to make sure that what you're selling and what the client thinks it's buying are one and the same. This means that they are unlikely to have unpleasant surprises of the "But I thought it would also make hot chocolate..." variety.

It is not your role to manage the product or delivery team too, but you can be very influential in terms of how they interact with your client. Encourage them to identify problems and issues early, and produce plans to mitigate. You can be a great help to them in sharing details of problems or issues with the client without causing stress and worry. And thanks to the hard work you've put into developing trust with the client, you are in the perfect position to convey the way forward and obtain client buy-in.

There is a common complaint among clients that the sales person was "All over us like a rash" during the sales process, but once the contract was signed, "We didn't see them for dust!"

This is a dreadful waste of the great relationship you've developed – one that, if nurtured, can generate future business and put you in the perfect position to help your own team manage issues with the client.

There will be times when the client is late delivering on its obligations, when its staff delivers work that's not of the quality or completeness you need, or when other contractors to the client fail to share information or equipment as required. You might be able to help soften any approach from the company when it comes to gently reminding the client of its contractual obligations.

Proactively checking in with your client from time to time enables you to collect feedback, correct any misconceptions and effectively manage your own PR. It is also the best way to spot new opportunities early! This is, of course, part of your account management role and I'm sure I'm preaching to the converted here.

Encourage regular use of the contract

In chapter 2 we discussed the use of the contract as doorstop, weapon or User Guide. You will encounter plenty of people in your business and others who still believe that the contract should be put in the cupboard, or a special box, with 'In case of emergency, break glass' written on the front.

Encourage your team and the client to use it for reference, ensuring you all benefit from the hard work that went into creating it. Touch base regularly with the client to ensure they're still able to meet their obligations, and with the team to make sure everything's on track. Make sure warranty and support issues are being managed as they should, and that your delivery team has a clear understanding of its responsibilities.

Encourage the finance team to refer to the contract to ensure billing is performed correctly.

In short, sow the seeds that the contract really can add value as the User Guide for your commercial relationship. As everyone becomes more comfortable referring to it, you'll find that their contractual literacy grows and subsequent contract negotiations become less lawyer-focused and more delivery-focused.

EXERCISE 21:

Before you start to wind down, here is one final exercise to pull all of this together. Take your completed table from exercise 1, and your 'vision statement' from exercise 3. In the light of everything you've learned, are there any things you'd like to change? Now consider how well your legal or commercial team does in meeting the needs you've expressed. Do you think they appreciate what it is you need from them? Download the e-workbook from www.dealmakersbook.com to help you complete this exercise.

Conduct project reviews and share learning

At the end of the project, set aside time with your own team and with the client to review how things went.

With your sales director, review the sales cycle to see how well you did in terms of forecasting the various pipeline stages. Could the sales cycle have been shorter, taking into account the nature of the project and the client? Did your investment in getting the contract right deliver an improved client relationship and better prospects for future sales? Was the cost of sale acceptable given the returns?

With your lawyers, discuss how effectively the negotiation process was managed. Consider the concessions that were made during the process, and identify any that caused you problems further down the line. Similarly, see if there were particular contractual points that made your life easier and kept you out of trouble.

With the delivery team, ask them if issues arose over scope of work, specification and change control. Sometimes even the best specified projects will encounter challenges in this area, as the client 'tries their luck'. But it's useful to see if and where such problems arose, and what worked well in dealing with them. Use this information to feed back into your next deal, to reduce the room for misunderstandings and disagreements.

Talk to finance to see how this project did against its forecast margin. This is often the best indicator of successful project management, since poorly managed projects end up delivering extra work for no revenue to keep the client on side. Find out how well your support with 'Mavis' worked in getting invoices paid on time. Identify ways you can clarify the invoicing and payment process even further to improve future cash flow.

And of course, have a wrap-up meeting with the client to see how well the project worked from their perspective. Did you meet their initial expectations? Were their expectations well managed in the course of the project? Did they feel changes were managed fairly and efficiently? How well did the contract negotiation phase work for them? What could you do better next time?

By going through this process you'll collect enormous amounts of valuable information. Your final task is to share this information with others – in your sales team and elsewhere in the organisation. Use what you've learned to feed back into your sales, contracting, negotiation and delivery process.

In some organisations there can be a clear silo mentality, where 'stepping outside of your box' is unwelcome. Be a trailblazer for cross-functional communication by sharing your thoughts, ideas and suggestions and actively promoting participation in the contracting process across the business.

A little help from your friends…

You might feel that you could do with a helping hand in spreading the word within your company, and that an independent third party would be useful in facilitating these discussions. If so, drop me a line and my team and I would be happy to support your business in its contractual evolution.

And if, as you start using what you've learned from this book, you have feedback and suggestions for me that could contribute to improving future editions of this book and help other readers, please do share them.

You can do this directly, by emailing me at tiffany@dealmakersbook.com

Or you can join in the discussion on Twitter: @tiffanycontract #SellMoreDeliverBetter.

Or you can contribute to the LinkedIn discussions, under the group: 'Deal Makers – sell more & deliver better'.

And remember, if you'd like to download the free e-workbook that accompanies this book to help you get more out of the exercises, go to the book website www.dealmakersbook.com and follow the links.

I look forward to hearing from you!

About the author

Tiffany Kemp lives in Berkshire with her husband, two children and dog.

She discovered contract law in 1998, when she realised that the contract negotiations she was conducting in her sales role might be a bit more successful if she had a clue what she was doing. After trying without success to find a 'contract law for non-lawyers' class at her local college, she bit the bullet and completed a Masters Degree in Business Law at De Montfort University.

In 2003 she created Devant, a company dedicated to helping small and medium sized companies punch above their weight in their contractual relationships. Her engineering background (she started her career as an RF engineer, developing military radio for Racal) stood her in good stead, enabling her to overcome the 'lawyer phobia' of her early clients by talking about what they did, and how they did it.

Devant has grown since the early days but remains focused on seeking out new ways to help companies structure, contract for and deliver better deals.

Today, Tiffany is a speaker, trainer and mentor, encouraging business leaders to engage with the contracting process as a positive contributor to their selling and delivery success.

Author photo by hyde-end.net

275

Notes:

Notes: